Y0-BUW-381

Dimensions
of the Future
Alternatives for Tomorrow

Dimensions of the Future
Alternatives for Tomorrow

MAXWELL H. NORMAN

Phoenix College

Holt, Rinehart and Winston, Inc.

NEW YORK, CHICAGO, SAN FRANCISCO, ATLANTA, DALLAS, MONTREAL, TORONTO

Library of Congress Cataloging in Publication Data

Norman, Maxwell H   comp.
Dimensions of the future.

1. College readers. I. Title.
PE1122.N66   808'.04275   73–15733

ISBN: 0–03–001006–3

Printed in the United States of America

5 6 7   059   9 8 7 6 5 4 3

HERE ARE SOME PREDICTED EVENTS WITH A LOW PROBABILITY OF OCCURRING IN **THIS** CENTURY, ACCORDING TO A RAND CORPORATION STUDY. THE YEAR LISTED WITH EACH IS THE MEDIAN DATE FOR ITS OCCURRENCE, AVERAGED FROM THE PREDICTIONS OF 82 EXPERTS FROM VARIOUS FIELDS.

Genetic manipulation	2000
Large-scale ocean farming and mining	2000
Household robots for routine chores	2000
Automated highways	2004
Man-machine combinations	2010
Intelligence-raising drugs	2012
Chemical control of aging	2020
International guaranteed income	2022
Antigravity	2024
Reliable mind reading	2025
Communication with extra-terrestrials	2026
Direct mind-to-mind communication	2030
Immunization against radiation	2030

From research done by The RAND Corporation for Don Fabun and Kaiser Aluminum and Chemical Corporation.

I do not believe the greatest threat to our future is from bombs or guided missiles. I don't think our civilization will die that way. I think it will die when we no longer care. Arnold Toynbee has pointed out that nineteen of twenty-one civilizations have died from within and not by conquest from without. There were no bands playing and flags waving when these civilizations decayed. It happened slowly, in the quiet and the dark when no one was aware.

LAURENCE M. GOULD
President Emeritus,
Carleton College

If you do not think about the future, you cannot have one.

JOHN GALSWORTHY

Preface

A few years ago, philosopher-educator Mortimer Adler pointed out to a college audience that, anthropologically speaking, *Homo sapiens* dates back about 33,000 years. For the first 24,000 or so of these years, primitive man's muscle and brain were totally devoted to the struggle for existence.

Perhaps 9,000 years ago, a superior brain discovered how to domesticate grain and animals—and the first revolution, the immensely important Agricultural Revolution, was born. Gradually, over a period of hundreds or perhaps thousands of years, families and tribal groups were no longer forced to wander from one hunting ground to another in search of food and shelter. At long last, man became able to devote some time to activities that differed from those of other animals: he had the opportunity to think, to dream, to wonder.

Aside from the utilization of wind and water power, more than 8,000 years passed before the next great sociological upheaval—the Industrial Revolution—began to have an impact on the continuum of history. This was the fundamental change that brought the replacement of man's muscle by the might of machine power. Though two centuries have passed, less than half of the world's population has actually participated in the Industrial Revolution. For those affected, however, the "thrust" of man, his fundamental life-style, has changed radically.

There is a third revolution, equal in importance to the first two, though it has been in the making for only 25 years. Despite its enormous impact on the industrialized nations of the world, its name is barely recognized. Revolution three, the Cybernetic Revolution, however, has not waited for recognition. It is the root cause of the knowledge explosion; it is the basis for what writer Don Fabun calls *the dynamics of change.*

"Cybernetics" is one of the thousands of new words introduced into our language because of expanding technology. For our purposes, cybernetics is defined as the combination of automated machinery and the electronic computer. It is this combination that has fueled the knowledge explosions in almost every field. Economist Kenneth Boulding described the era succinctly when he wrote, "The world of today is as different from the world I was born into as that world was from Julius Caesar's. . . . Almost as much has happened since I was born as happened before. . . ."

This book does not attempt to deal with several vital problems of the present. That is, if there is to be a future at all, we must make three immensely important assumptions:

Mankind will not destroy itself by nuclear war.

Mankind will not allow humanity to perish in the stink of its own pollutants.

Mankind will recognize the fact that our spaceship earth has the capacity for a limited number of passengers and that steps must be taken *now* to limit population growth.

These are not casual assumptions. They are crucial responsibilities, the responsibilities of every human being—and we have perhaps one decade to deal with them. They are not discussed here because they are so vital that they deserve thorough investigation and action in and of themselves. They are the vital problems of the present; our thrust is aimed at the vital problems of the future.

Accordingly, this volume is devoted to the discussion of thirteen aspects of the future, aspects that are critical to an understanding of the Cybernetic Revolution.

First, four contemporary writers, deeply involved in their concerns for mankind, describe futures ranging from a world on the brink of self-destruction to a world that promises universal growth. Obviously, their forecasts differ radically.

The next topic is *the basic nature of man,* which is subject to question by anthropologists, psychologists, philosophers. Chapter 3 discusses the geneticists who are rapidly approaching the perfecting of techniques which may lead to the improvement of both the physical and mental characteristics of the individual—and, in the process, may provide the few with techniques which could control the many.

We consider also the alternatives in the future of marriage and the family. There are the accepted dangers inherent in the overpopulation of a finite planet. The genetic engineers are on the verge of making normal childbirth unnecessary. Women are taking positive action in the relation to their function in society.

We then discuss the ramifications of the enormous expansion of knowledge and technology and the application of the computer to automated machinery. New sources of energy for our power-hungry world are described, as is the speed-up in communications in a world shrinking, metaphorically, almost daily.

New chemical and electrical techniques can expand the mind or—as some fear—lead to mind-control. Here, again, we must examine the choices.

Inherent in the interlocking of technological and social developments are crystallized questions of distribution, economics, and government. Can abundance become a hazard? And if the expectations of many futurists come to pass, will the resulting "leisure" become a problem or a delight?

Some clues to where we might be going are provided in Chapter 12 on Utopias-Dystopias. Then there is the all-important question of how we are to be prepared for the future. The future of society can be magnificent or disastrous, but there is no question that education will play an important role in fashioning the future. Chapter 13 is devoted to discussions of this role.

Futurists, people concerned with the directions our civilization may take, vary in their views, just as their philosophies differ. In anticipating the future, it becomes apparent that there are no absolutes; the results of tomorrow's research could upset a carefully planned course toward a preconceived end.

There are no easy answers; there are opposing points of view. Whenever possible, these differences of opinion have been presented.

Dimensions of the Future is designed to help you explore the effects of change, now and in the future, to bring into focus the various aspects of the adjustments you may have to make, and to help you reach conclusions about what you can do to improve the quality of life.

But knowledge of future potentials is not enough. We *must* evolve a set of goals and priorities based on that knowledge. Oversimplifying, I would say that we must attempt to answer two basic questions:

1. Given a choice, what kind of person would I want to be?
2. What kind of world would I want to live in?

The questions may seem simple; answering them, however, will take considerable thought.

In the society of the future, obviously there is no set course. What we do have is a series of possibilities, alternatives, if you like, prescribed by concerned individuals who firmly believe that the future must not simply "happen"; it must be extrapolated, imagined, planned for. To allow man to drift into tomorrow is to court disaster.

And our goals and priorities must be flexible. As new information is discovered, new technologies are developed, and new philosophies are expounded, we must accept the fact that our goals and priorities must be subject to "change." There has never been a period in history so challenging, so dynamic.

Yours is the generation that must make the decisions. To do this, we must be informed. *Dimensions of the Future* aims to make you aware of the questions and of some alternative answers. But it cannot choose for you.

• • •

To assist in considering the alternatives for tomorrow and the major points in each selection and their ramifications, an Appendix prepared by Dr. Laurie Zwicky of the University of Houston is included. This Appendix consists of questions for discussion and writing relating to each selection. In addition, there is biographical information about each author.

An Instructor's Manual, also prepared by Dr. Zwicky, is available from the publisher. The manual emphasizes rhetorical principles and strategies that are used in the selections.

• • •

It is almost impossible to thank the many people who have contributed to this volume. Interested students, colleagues, friends—all helped to bring into focus the issues discussed, and even to attempt to name the individuals would consume pages. It would be unthinkable, however, not to make special mention of Jane Ross, Editor, English Language and Literature, at Holt, Rinehart and Winston, whose concern about the direction humankind will take in the years ahead encouraged me to undertake the assembly of the articles that follow; Pamela Forcey, Senior Project Editor at Holt, whose endless patience and help brought the book into its final form; my wife, Enid Norman, who not only ministered to a preoccupied husband for almost two years but also helped in every phase of the work from the selection of the articles used to the proofreading of the final book. Without these three, *Dimensions of the Future* would never have appeared.

M.H.N.

November, 1973

Contents

Contents: Highlights Quotations

ideas. In an open society, it is none of the government's business what ideas a man puts into his mind; likewise it should be none of the government's business what drugs he puts into his body."

DRUGS AND THE FUTURE Frank J. Ayd, Jr., M.D. "We are synthesizing compounds which, if they ever were controlled by fanatical leaders, could be used to subjugate and dehumanize men in ways heretofore impossible."

THE SEARCH FOR THE MEMORY MOLECULE David Perlman "The day is very near when the intellectual capacity of human beings will be affected by products of the chemical as well as the teaching laboratory."

10 CAN WE SURVIVE LEISURE? 201

From *OF TIME, WORK AND LEISURE* Sebastian de Grazia "The machine, the hero of a dream, the bestower of free time to men, brings a neutralized idea of time that makes it seem free, and then chains it to another machine. . . ."

IS MAN A WORKING ANIMAL? Stuart Chase "We are reasonably safe in concluding that man is a working animal, in the sense of requiring some activity to interest and involve him, if not in the sense of the Puritan ethic. Without such involvement he is at a loss—if not, indeed, a mental case."

CAREER PROGRAM IS STEP FORWARD Robert S. Rosefsky "When did we, as children, acquire a meaningful understanding of the real world of work—in terms that we could relate to?"

THE DECLINE OF SPORT E. B. White "In the third decade of the supersonic age, sport gripped the nation in an ever-tightening grip. The horse tracks, the ballparks, the fight rings, the gridirons, all drew crowds in steadily increasing numbers. . . ."

11 ECONOMICS AND GOVERNMENT IN A DYNAMIC SOCIETY 225

CONSUMERS OF ABUNDANCE Gerard Piel "The evidence that full employment is no longer an attainable objective seems to be growing. . . . At that point the nation will have come really close to being a workless society."

From *THE TWO CULTURES: AND A SECOND LOOK* C. P. Snow "It is technically possible to carry out the scientific revolution in India, Africa, Latin America, the Middle East, within fifty years. . . . We have very little time. So little that I dare not guess at it."

NULL-P William Tenn "Now, at last, America has turned. . . . The young democracy of the west, which introduced the concepts of the Rights of Man to jurisprudence, now gives a feverish world the Doctrine of the Lowest Common Denominator in Government."

DISTRIBUTION OF ABUNDANCE: EQUAL INCOMES FOR ALL Technocracy, Inc.   "North Americans must install a new social system which can distribute 'abundance' to all our citizens now, and guarantee a high standard of living for the future citizens of this Continent."

12 UTOPIA-DYSTOPIA: HAVE WE A CHOICE?   251

From *WALDEN TWO* B. F. Skinner   " 'Then you don't offer complete personal freedom, do you?' said Castle, with ill-concealed excitement. 'You haven't really resolved the conflict between a laissez-faire and a planned society.' 'I think we have. Yes. But you must know more about our educational sysem.' . . ."

HARRISON BERGERON Kurt Vonnegut, Jr.   "The year was 2081, and everybody was finally equal. They weren't only equal before God and the law. They were equal every which way."

From Epilogue to *UTOPIA OR OBLIVION* R. Buckminster Fuller   "My task as an inventor is to employ the earth's resources and energy in such a way as to support all humanity while also enabling all people to enjoy the whole earth. . . ."

From *ISLAND* Aldous Huxley   " 'But cure,' said Will, 'is so much more dramatic than prevention. And for doctors, it's also a lot more profitable.' 'Maybe for your doctors,' said the little nurse. 'Not for ours. Ours get paid for keeping people well.' "

13 EDUCATION—FOR POWER AND PLEASURE   283

VISITING DAY 2001 A.D. George Leonard   "When a child takes the chair to begin learning, another radio receiver senses his presence through his EID [Electronic Identification Device] and signals the central learning computer to plug in that particular child's learning history."

THE COMPUTER IN EDUCATION Anthony G. Oettinger with Sema Marks "Computers, serving as expensive page turners, have therefore been used to mimic programmed instruction texts."

MAN MUST LEARN HOW TO LEARN Sydney J. Harris   "This 'obsolescence of knowledge,' especially in scientific fields, is changing the whole idea of what constitutes a 'good' college education. And it reaffirms those of us who have been saying for a long time that learning how to learn is the most important part of education."

THE FUTURE OF LEARNING: INTO THE 21ST CENTURY John I. Goodlad "The right to learn is the goal we seek for the twenty-first century. We want for our children a range of learning opportunities as broad as the unknown range of those talents. We want a learning environment that nurtures those talents. . . ."

1
THE FUTURISTS
VIEW HEAVEN—OR HELL

Yet it is part of the glory of being man that we can plan our futures so that our dreams approach reality. There is nothing in the universe that we can rely on to consider our welfare except our own reason.—*Gerald Feinberg, 1968*[1]

The future of the future is determined not only by what may be possible or probable in economic, technical, or sociopolitical terms, but also by what man himself deems necessary, allowable, and ultimately desirable, in human terms.

—John McHale, 1969[2]

Finding out what we want should become a major object of attention. . . . There is a vast difference between letting changes occur under the impact of technological advances and choosing the changes we want to bring about by our technological means.—*Bertrand de Jouvenal, 1965*[3]

The best that can be said for the futurists, and for prophets of all kinds, is that their predictions force men to examine the likely outcome of what they are doing, and then add a little to the limited choice and control men have over events.—Time, 1971[4]

Reference numbers refer to source notes on page 311.

"futurist" might be defined as anyone whose major concern is the direction—or directions—that society may take in the years ahead. Actually, the broad field of study concerned with the forces that have—or may have—a powerful effect on the whole of society is so new that not even those involved in this field have agreed on a name for it. "Futurism" has been suggested; "futuristics" and "futurology" are other terms that have been used.

The important idea is that more and more thoughtful individuals from every level of society have become increasingly aware of the accelerated pace of societal change and the knowledge-technology explosion that has caused it.

Certainly we are not dealing with a new phenomenon. The Old Testament has its prophets. Centuries later, Jules Verne and H. G. Wells fascinated readers with their predictions of the future. In still more recent times, we have had Aldous Huxley and George Orwell, to say nothing of the myriads of science-fiction writers who for almost five decades have challenged, excited, and frightened us. What *is* unique to our own time is the fact that the literary creations of fertile minds have, through technology, become realities—that man has the ability to make any "wall come tumbling down"; that sleek submersibles can remain under the surface of our oceans for weeks, even months, carrying in their bellies the potential death of millions; that beak-nosed aircraft are capable of making London-New York flights in less than three hours; that earthmen have walked on the moon.

What need, then, for futurists? And why the rapid increase in their number? And why, so abruptly, has it become more and more apparent that mankind must become future-aware? The answer is simple. We have just begun to taste the fruits of an expanding technology. And though some of the products of our new knowledge are gratifying, even heady, others leave us with a sour taste and grinding fears. From 250,-000 miles away, we see how small our "global village" is. From face-to-face contact, we see how ugly our inner cities have become. From high-speed computer printouts, we have suddenly grasped the dimensions of our exponential population growth; at the same time we realize that this mediocre planet circling an unimportant star in one of millions of galaxies is, in fact, finite. We now know that our generously endowed natural gifts cannot last forever. We contrast "standard of living" with "quality of life"; we even begin to question the time-honored correlation of *Gross National Product* and *progress.*

These are some of the issues with which futurists are concerned:

Will man-made machines become our masters? Or will they provide us with the leisure and affluence that will allow the individual to develop his talents to their utmost? Can the human nervous system withstand the shock of tumultuous change, or should we at least try to slow the research and development that is aimed at evolving new techniques, new products, new patterns of living?

There are no easy answers. And even among the newly emerging futurists themselves, there are strong differences of opinion. Broadly, futurists fall into two categories, the exrapolationists (sometimes called extrapolists) and the Utopians (occasionally, Utopists).

"Extrapolation" means projecting on the basis of values that are already known. For example, demographers have used the figures of the world's population increase over the past two millennia to project world population for 1980, the year 2000, and so on. Essentially, extrapolationist futurists use the trends of the past and the present to predict objectively what kind of future will result from the operation of these trends. Their ability to anticipate has been enormously advanced by the instrument fundamentally responsible for our accelerating rate of change, the computer.

Utopians, on the other hand, maintain that the momentum of the forces of technology can be controlled; in fact, they feel strongly that for the first time in history, the affluence made possible by cybernation and automation *enables mankind to determine its own goals and the priorities needed to reach those goals.* Their thinking centers on the two questions mentioned in the Preface: What kind of people do we want to be? And what kind of world do we want to have? Utopians are fully aware that all such goals and priorities must be flexible and that there must be a constant re-thinking of them.

In general, two principles are held strongly by both groups of futurists: First, we must recognize that the questions demanding solutions are *international* in scope. Second, natural resources are limited; an uncontrolled population growth cannot result in anything but disaster— and disaster *in the foreseeable future.*

Alvin Toffler's *Future Shock* questions our ability to withstand the increasing rate of change. We are being flooded with "newness": new technologies, new customs, new knowledge. For the unaware, the momentous changes in society may be beyond their human capacity for adjustment.

"The Predicament of Mankind" by Dennis L. Meadows is a superb example of the utilization of extrapolation in predicting "what is to come." It will shock you. On the other hand, Robert Theobald's article from *An Alternative Future for America II* should give you a concrete idea of what our future could be as viewed by one of our most prominent Utopians.

An excerpt from F. M. Esfandiary's *Optimism One* is a strong claim for the betterment of mankind. You will see that he does feel that ours can be a better world.

Knowledge of change, planning, predicting, and forecasting—this is the role of today's futurist. We must all become conscious of the alternatives open to us if humankind is to survive.

INTRODUCTION TO
FUTURE SHOCK
Alvin Toffler

[1] This is a book about what happens to people when they are overwhelmed by change. It is about the ways in which we adapt—or fail to adapt—to the future.

[2] Much has been written about the future. Yet, for the most part, books about the world to come sound a harsh metallic note. These pages, by contrast, concern themselves with the "soft" or human side of tomorrow. Moreover, they concern themselves with the steps by which we are likely to reach tomorrow. They deal with common, everyday matters—the products we buy and discard, the places we leave behind, the corporations we inhabit, the people who pass at an ever faster clip through our lives. The future of friendship and family life is probed. Strange new subcultures and life styles are investigated, along with an array of other subjects from politics and playgrounds to skydiving and sex.

[3] What joins all these—in the book as in life—is the roaring current of change, a current so powerful today that it overturns institutions, shifts our values and shrivels our roots. Change is the process by which the future invades our lives, and it is important to look at it closely, not merely from the grand perspectives of history, but also from the vantage point of the living, breathing individuals who experience it.

[4] The acceleration of change in our time is, itself, an elemental force. This accelerative thrust has personal and psychological, as well as sociological, consequences. In the pages ahead, these effects of acceleration are, for the first time, systematically explored. The book argues force-

fully, I hope, that, unless man quickly learns to control the rate of change in his personal affairs as well as in society at large, we are doomed to a massive adaptational breakdown.

[5] In 1965, in an article in *Horizon,* I coined the term "future shock" to describe the shattering stress and disorientation that we induce in individuals by subjecting them to too much change in too short a time. Fascinated by this concept, I spent the next five years visiting scores of universities, research centers, laboratories, and government agencies, reading countless articles and scientific papers and interviewing literally hundreds of experts on different aspects of change, coping behavior, and the future. Nobel prizewinners, hippies, psychiatrists, physicians, businessmen, professional futurists, philosophers, and educators gave voice to their concern over change, their anxieties about adaptation, their fears about the future. I came away from this experience with two disturbing convictions.

[6] First, it became clear that future shock is no longer a distantly potential danger, but a real sickness from which increasingly large numbers already suffer. This psycho-biological condition can be described in medical and psychiatric terms. It is the disease of change.

[7] Second, I gradually came to be appalled by how little is actually known about adaptivity, either by those who call for and create vast changes in our society, or by those who supposedly prepare us to cope with those changes. Earnest intellectuals talk bravely about "educating for change" or "preparing people for the future." But we know virtually nothing about how to do it. In the most rapidly changing environment to which man has ever been exposed, we remain pitifully ignorant of how the human animal copes.

[8] Our psychologists and politicians alike are puzzled by the seemingly irrational resistance to change exhibited by certain individuals and groups. The corporation head who wants to reorganize a department, the educator who wants to introduce a new teaching method, the mayor who wants to achieve peaceful integration of the races in his city—all, at one time or another, face this blind resistance. Yet we know little about its sources. By the same token, why do some men hunger, even rage for change, doing all in their power to create it, while others flee from it? I not only found no ready answers to such questions, but discovered that we lack even an adequate theory of adaptation, without which it is extremely unlikely that we will ever find the answers.

[9] The purpose of this book, therefore, is to help us come to terms with the future—to help us cope more effectively with both personal and social change by deepening our understanding of how men respond to it. Toward this end, it puts forward a broad new theory of adaptation.

[10] It also calls attention to an important, though often overlooked, distinction. Almost invariably, research into the effects of change con-

centrate on the destinations toward which change carries us, rather than the speed of the journey. In this book, I try to show that the *rate* of change has implications quite apart from, and sometimes more important than, the *directions* of change. No attempt to understand adaptivity can succeed until this fact is grasped. Any attempt to define the "content" of change must include the consequences of pace itself as part of that content.

[11] William Ogburn, with his celebrated theory of cultural lag, pointed out how social stresses arise out of the uneven rates of change in different sectors of society. The concept of future shock—and the theory of adaptation that derives from it—strongly suggests that there must be balance, not merely between rates of change in different sectors, but between the pace of environmental change and the limited pace of human response. For future shock grows out of the increasing lag between the two.

[12] The book is intended to do more than present a theory, however. It is also intended to demonstrate a method. Previously, men studied the past to shed light on the present. I have turned the time-mirror around, convinced that a coherent image of the future can also shower us with valuable insights into today. We shall find it increasingly difficult to understand our personal and public problems without making use of the future as an intellectual tool. In the pages ahead, I deliberately exploit this tool to show what it can do.

[13] Finally, and by no means least important, the book sets out to change the reader in a subtle yet significant sense. For reasons that will become clear in the pages that follow, successful coping with rapid change will require most of us to adopt a new stance toward the future, a new sensitive awareness of the role it plays in the present. This book is designed to increase the future-consciousness of its reader. The degree to which the reader, after finishing the book, finds himself thinking about, speculating about, or trying to anticipate future events, will provide one measure of its effectiveness.

[14] With these ends stated, several reservations are in order. One has to do with the perishability of fact. Every seasoned reporter has had the experience of working on a fast-breaking story that changes its shape and meaning even before his words are put down on paper. Today the whole world is a fast-breaking story. It is inevitable, therefore, in a book written over the course of several years, that some of its facts will have been superseded between the time of research and writing and the time of publication. Professors identified with University A move, in the interim, to University B. Politicians identified with Position X shift, in the meantime, to Position Y.

[15] While a conscientious effort has been made during writing to update *Future Shock*, some of the facts presented are no doubt already

obsolete. (This, of course, is true of many books, although authors don't like to talk about it.) The obsolescence of data has a special significance here, however, serving as it does to verify the book's own thesis about the rapidity of change. Writers have a harder and harder time keeping up with reality. We have not yet learned to conceive, research, write and publish in "real time." Readers, therefore, must concern themselves more and more with general theme, rather than detail.

[16] Another reservation has to do with the verb "will." No serious futurist deals in "predictions." These are left for television oracles and newspaper astrologers. No one even faintly familiar with the complexities of forecasting lays claim to absolute knowledge of tomorrow. In those deliciously ironic words purported to be a Chinese proverb: "To prophesy is extremely difficult—especially with respect to the future."

[17] This means that every statement about the future ought, by rights, to be accompanied by a string of qualifiers—ifs, ands, buts, and on the other hands. Yet to enter every appropriate qualification in a book of this kind would be to bury the reader under an avalanche of maybes. Rather than do this, I have taken the liberty of speaking firmly, without hesitation, trusting that the intelligent reader will understand the stylistic problem. The word "will" should always be read as though it were preceded by "probably" or "in my opinion." Similarly, all dates applied to future events need to be taken with a grain of judgment.

[18] The inability to speak with precision and certainty about the future, however, is no excuse for silence. Where "hard data" are available, of course, they ought to be taken into account. But where they are lacking, the responsible writer—even the scientist—has both a right and an obligation to rely on other kinds of evidence, including impressionistic or anecdotal data and the opinions of well-informed people. I have done so throughout and offer no apology for it.

[19] In dealing with the future, at least for the purposes at hand, it is more important to be imaginative and insightful than to be one hundred percent "right." Theories do not have to be "right" to be enormously useful. Even error has its uses. The maps of the world drawn by the medieval cartographers were so hopelessly inaccurate, so filled with factual error, that they elicit condescending smiles today when almost the entire surface of the earth has been charted. Yet the great explorers could never have discovered the New World without them. Nor could the better, more accurate maps of today have been drawn until men, working with the limited evidence available to them, set down on paper their bold conceptions of worlds they had never seen.

[20] We who explore the future are like those ancient mapmakers, and it is in this spirit that the concept of future shock and the theory of the adaptive range are presented here—not as final word, but as a first approximation of the new realities, filled with danger and promise, created by the accelerative thrust.

THE PREDICAMENT OF MANKIND

Dennis L. Meadows

Man appears to be heading toward a calamitous Day of Reckoning. Unless his rapidly growing population and expanding industrial capacity is somehow brought under control, the earth's natural resources will be exhausted and the environment so polluted that the world no longer will be livable.

Every year the earth gains about 70 million people. By the year 2000—now less than 29 years away—the world could have seven billion people (twice as many as now), and possibly even more.

Overpopulation is an old story to biologists, who have studied the phenomenon in animals ranging from deer to fruit-flies. When food is abundant, an animal population increases until the food supply no longer suffices; then many of the animals starve to death or, malnourished, fall easy victims to disease and predators. The die-off reduces the population until the food supply is again adequate, whereupon the process may begin again—provided that no non-renewable essential resources have been destroyed or consumed in the process. Unless man finds some way to limit his population growth, he appears to be headed for such a die-off.

The rise in population is accompanied by vigorous efforts to build more power plants and factories and produce more goods so that people can enjoy a higher standard of material wealth. This growing industrialization intensifies the pollution caused by mushrooming population—and it uses up the earth's natural resources at an ever more rapid pace. Many of these—coal, oil, natural gas, and high quality mineral ores—are impossible to replace.

Some scientists suggest that, before the human race is checked by starvation, it may be suppressed when the air becomes unbreathable and the water undrinkable. Even if a few human beings survived, they could not recreate civilization because the essential mineral resources would then have been used up.

Concerned about the approaching crisis, Italian industrialist Aurelio Peccei formed a group of scientists, economists, educators, and businessmen known as the Club of Rome. The Club located financial support for a team at the Massachusetts Institute of Technology to apply the systems dynamics method developed by Professor Jay Forrester, in a computer simulation model of global interactions of population, natural resources, pollution, capital, and food production.

—Editors, *The Futurist*

[1] Three convictions unite the members of the Club of Rome:

[2] *1.* The long term prospects of our global society are poor at the moment, and the situation appears to be deteriorating.

Reprinted by permission of *The Futurist,* published by the World Futurist Society, P.O. Box 30369, Bethesda Branch, Washington, D.C. 20014.

[3] 2. The only viable solutions to global problems will be those with a transnational perspective and a planning time horizon much greater than those currently exhibited by any state.

[4] 3. Scientific attempts to identify the fundamental interactions which determine the rate and direction of global evolution, realistic assessments of our feasible options, and concerted efforts to achieve a more satisfactory global situation can lead to a substantial improvement over our current situation.

[5] Within the context of those convictions, an MIT team under my direction has been engaged in a set of empirical research and simulation modeling studies to identify the long-term global prospects and to evaluate alternative policies in terms of their impact during the next 50 to 200 years.

· · ·

[6] This past year the group under my direction has been involved in extending that model and converting it to a research instrument which is accessible to demographers and other professionals. As revised, the main model uses the terminology of various professionals in the appropriate sectors, and draws on their theories and their data. We have disaggregated the model, that is, separated out its various parts so that each

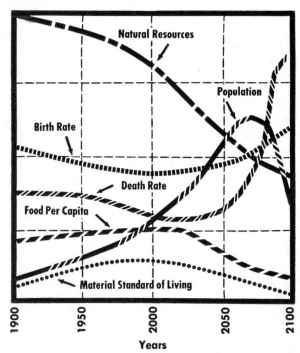

This sample simulation of the global model used by the MIT researchers shows how the depletion of natural resources could halt population growth. This projection shows a rapidly rising death rate in the latter half of the 21st century.

could be studied individually. We have also tested the whole model and have generated a series of initial conclusions. I would like to focus on them and be a little more specific about our main model.

Population Growth Rate Must Soon Slow

[7] The world population now stands at 3.6 billion people and its doubling time is 32 years and decreasing. Many other aspects of global growth have doubling times of 7 to 10 years. This population growth is the end result of a sequence of industrial, medical, and agricultural innovations which began about 200 years ago in England. The growth rate is absolutely unprecedented in history. Until about 200 years ago the doubling time for population was about 1500 years. It had been close to that throughout all recorded history. Today's growth rate is a very transient phenomenon, and one whose end most of us will witness.

[8] We see absolutely no possibility on the basis of the work we have done over the last year of supporting 14 billion people on the globe, even momentarily. If you will accept that conclusion for purposes of discussion, it means that we will witness, some time in the next 50 years, a very, very strong transition to a much slower population growth, and with that, a much slower rate of capital accumulation.

[9] Simulation is, I believe, the only analytical approach capable of understanding the determinants and implications of that transition, its different possible configurations, and the way in which we can impact on it with our current policies. Simulation is the only tool available to provide the foundation that we need in order to begin to look at the problem. Most analytical tools developed by the social scientists will ultimately be used to get data for the models used in simulations. And simulation also is needed to identify the critical data and to provide a conceptual framework through which they may be related.

[10] Our group at MIT has developed a model of the interactions among population, pollution, natural resources, food production, and economic development. The model permits a variety of useful policy analyses, but we do not conceive of it as the end result of our work. Implementing policy in the real world requires a time horizon and degree of detail inappropriate in the global model. Thus more detailed simulation models must be undertaken to bridge the gap between long-term global behavior and short-term regional policy making. A global model is useful only if it gives you an overall context for the detailed models.

[11] Let me give you just a simple example: If one focuses on starvation as a global problem, it is very easy to decide that the main objective of the agricultural sector is to provide food. If you attack the problem in that context you come up with the Green Revolution, a brilliant success in terms of producing food. But from the global model we see that an equally important function of the agricultural sector is to provide

employment. In most areas of the world there are no effective funds transfer mechanisms which can ensure at least a minimum purchasing power for the unemployed. Only employment can serve as a means of obtaining income. For most of the world's people, employment comes only through agricultural work. The Green Revolution may very well create massive unemployment in the agricultural sector. By looking at the interaction among the various sectors with a global model, you are more likely to avoid a dangerous, suboptimal solution.

World 3: The Global Model

[12] Let us now look a little more closely at the interactions of population and capital, which strongly influence all global problems—unemployment, starvation, disease, pollution, the threat of warfare, and resource shortages.

[13] No attempt to understand our long-term options can succeed unless it is firmly based on an understanding of the relationships between population and capital and of the ultimate limits to their growth. World 3—our current world model—explicitly represents the growth forces as a function of the biological, political, economic, physical, and social factors which influence them.

[14] Population and birth constitute a positive feedback loop. More people produce more births and more births result in more people. Wherever there is a dominant positive feedback loop of this form, exponential growth will be observed. Wherever exponential growth is observed there must be a positive feedback loop of this type. For example: Capital produces industrial output; greater output, all else equal, results in a larger investment and thus in more capital. The interactions among population and capital determine the rate at which each of them grows. The interaction takes many forms. . . .

[15] If a greater fraction of output is diverted from investment, the growth rate of capital decreases. Output may be diverted to consumption and services, to agriculture, and to military expenditures. As consumption and services increase, health and education improve, average lifetime becomes greater, deaths decrease, and population grows. Similarly, output may be diverted into agricultural capital which results ultimately in greater food and food per capita as well as a higher average lifetime. The primary determinant of the fraction of output reinvested is the output per capita. Where production per capita is low, most of the output must be diverted to consumption, services, and food. Those investments interfere with the accumulation of a large capital base and, at the same time, stimulate the growth of population. Population can increase much more easily than capital in traditional societies. Thus a population with a low output per capita finds it very difficult to achieve economic growth.

[16] Output diverted into military expenditures substracts capital from the system and does not generate future growth directly. Industrial output also leads to the depletion of natural resources. As natural resources decline, the efficiency of capital decreases and the output/capital ratio goes down.

[17] *Output per capita is the single positive force acting to slow the population explosion.* As output per capita increases, the desired family size declines, the birth rate goes down, and population growth typically decreases. Additionally, as death rates decline there is a further decrease in desired family size. A large portion of the world's parents bear children primarily as a source of support in their old age. If there is a high mortality rate, one must bear three or four sons to insure that one will live. Thus as the perceived death rate decreases, birth rates also decline. Output has one additional impact. Output leads to the generation of pollution. Pollution decreases food, and also decreases the average lifetime. Most global problems have important roots in this simple set of interactions.

[18] For example, behind the program to implement the Green Revolution has been the assumption that an exogenous increase in food production capabilities of the less developed countries would permit less output to be invested in agriculture and more to be reinvested in capital, moving the process of capital investment into the phase of self-sustaining growth. A secondary argument has been that the increased food per capita would decrease deaths somewhat and thereby depress the birth rate.

[19] In fact an alternative conclusion might be justified. The increased food from the Green Revolution might as easily increase the food per capita, decrease the death rate, and leave population to grow very rapidly. Should this happen, the increase in population might be very much greater than the increase in capital. Output per capita could remain the same or even decline, thereby drawing a larger percentage of output into consumption and services and maintaining the stagnant economy.

[20] The Green Revolution has been implemented only for three years. Thus the resolution of this issue is still a few years off. However, it is ironic that while billions of dollars were spent in massive modeling efforts to think through every step of a program to land three men on the moon, no similar effort was made to understand beforehand the possible implications of the Green Revolution for our ability to maintain three and one half billion people on the globe. The global model is a first tentative step in the development of tools necessary for such analyses.

· · ·

Preliminary Conclusions from the World Simulation

[21] The World 3 model is based on the best available data found and summarized through our six months of effort. It has been evaluated by

experts in universities, in national governments, and in various United Nations agencies in the U.S. and abroad. There is little disagreement with the preliminary conclusions:

[22] *1.* There is no possibility of sufficient technological and cultural progress occuring in the next 100 years to sustain as many as 14 billion people on our globe. Since the doubling time of population is currently 32 years and decreasing, this means that sometime within the next 60 years population growth will undergo a profound deceleration.

[23] *2.* There is no possibility of bringing the vast majority of those living in the developing countries up to the material standard of living enjoyed by the developed nations.

[24] *3.* There is a strong probability that the western nations will witness a marked decline in their own material standard of living within the next three or four decades.

[25] *4.* There is no unique, optimal long-term population level. Rather there is an entire set of trade-offs between personal freedom, material and social standard of living, and the population level. Given the finite and diminishing stock of resources on this globe, we are inevitably faced with the necessity to recognize that more people implies a lower standard of living.

[26] *5.* There is, in theory, no fundamental human value which could not be better achieved through a substantial lowering of the global population base.

[27] *6.* There is a very strong probability that the transition to global equilibrium will involve a traumatic decline in population. It is our conclusion that the overwhelming task for the Club of Rome is to identify and implement that set of policies which will permit us to negotiate an orderly transition to equilibrium. We must bring a transition which, though it will cause drastic changes, will leave us with most of the attributes which we value in our society and which will preserve options for those who must live on this globe a century and more from now.

[28] No one we have talked with has offered any scientifically-based disagreement with the above conclusions. To the contrary, many at high levels of the United Nations, the World Bank and similar organizations hold personal opinions much more pessimistic than those of our project staff.

[29] Now there are other problems concerning values, such as achieving an equitable distribution of income, but each of them is tempered by the characteristics of the impending transition to equilibrium.

[30] We have thus far not found the availability of data to be a constraint on our research. We already know enough about the major processes which govern global interaction to construct more useful models than are currently available. The real constraint on global simulation is that we lack the unifying theories of global evolution which indicate to

us how it is that technology, population, and values interact. Where models are not available today, it is because we lack those underlying theories. However, as we begin to develop those theories, their confirmation, extension, and testing will lead us into very serious data problems. We can foresee in our work with some of the more advanced models (the models on pollution, for example) that we will reach a point where we will lack necessary data.

Our experience suggests it is not useful to conceive of a single, monolithic, all-purpose world model. Good models bear a one-to-one relationship with specific phenomena. Many of the phenomena that interest us have global relevance. When you identify such a phenomenon and build a model to explain it, then you have one member of a whole family of global models. That imples, incidentally, that you do not get a useful global model by taking many submodels, a model of a city, a model of a river basin, a model of the seas, etc. and linking them all together. That would be very difficult technically and it certainly would not be useful.

· · ·

We have taken the first halting steps towards the use of simulation to understand and control global problems. There are large research problems, to be sure, both in the theory of model building and in the availability of data. However, the real world problems are enormous—and there is not much time left to find and implement solutions.

THE NEW REALITY
Robert Theobald

[1] The new reality of today is a very simple one: man now has the power to do what he wants to do. This development is revolutionary because until just this moment of history man has been constrained by his environment. As a result of this novel power, man's present cultural system has become irrelevant, in the same way as man's cultural system became irrelevant when he moved from his hunting and gathering stage to his agricultural stage.

[2] The reasons man has this power can be very briefly set out. First,

Robert Theobald. Excerpt from "The New Reality," reprinted from *An Alternative Future for America II;* © 1968, 1970 Robert Theobald; by permission of The Swallow Press, Chicago.

he has power because he has energy, energy being derived today primarily from fossil fuels, but coming tomorrow from nuclear energy. Nuclear energy has the peculiar characteristic that it not only produces energy but in the very process of producing energy it can create more fuel to produce more energy. We are very rapidly getting to the energy potential for a perpetual motion machine. Energy can be used for anything that man wishes—to produce metals from low grade ores, to turn the desert into a garden or whatever it strikes his fancy to do.

[3] The second reason for our power I like to call "alchemy." By that I mean the ability to manipulate the basic building blocks of nature to create materials with the types of properties that one desires. The word alchemy is appropriate for two reasons. It reminds us that some of the materials we have created are already considerably more valuable than gold, and it reminds us of what would happen to the economic system if we simply developed the ability to produce gold. In other words, the economic system is running on a mythology; and the mythology is extraordinarily vulnerable.

[4] The third factor which gives us power is the educational possibilities of our culture. For the first time it is possible for a very substantial proportion of the population to learn for twenty-two years of their lives or more. The fact that we are still running colleges which are largely producing surrogate computers is not the fault of the situation but only the fault of the people within the system. By "producing surrogate computers" I mean that we are educating people who can give answers to questions which have already been posed, which is what a computer can do, rather than teaching them how to pose questions. This is disastrous because the computer will certainly learn to answer structured questions better than we can.

[5] The fourth factor that we have going for us is the computer. The computer is a wonderful instrument.

[6] A computer is a wonderful way of solving problems. But you had better be careful because the computer will give you the "right" answer. This is illustrated in the story about a war planner of a friendly power who asked its computer "What steps should I take to do the most harm to Russia?" The computer, after whirring a few times, came back with an answer, "Bomb the United States." The computer was strictly logical because if this friendly power bombed the United States "intelligently," the U.S. would assume that it had been bombed by Russia. It would then bomb Russia and it could certainly do much more harm to Russia than the friendly power could, because America had more bombs. Theoretically, the great advantage about human beings is that when they see that sort of chasm they stop and say "No, that wasn't what I meant." But computers aren't that sensible.

[7] Using a computer is a good way of getting away from responsi-

bility. We use it in California as a justification for logging redwood groves. The way that this gets done is to instruct the computer to build the best road, and then to inform the computer that the best road is the cheapest road. Next one feeds into the computer the values for the various strips of land, and of course you put in a very low value for the redwoods because, after all, they are not doing any good, are they? The computer then designs a road which goes through the redwood system. Then one says "It wasn't our fault. You know, logic compels us to build the road through the redwood groves. We regret this as much as anybody else."

[8] The computer is a very good servant and a very bad master. There is rather distressing evidence that the computer is becoming a new god. When the computer has spoken, who shall question it? There is no doubt in my mind that the computer has been one of the factors that has led us into the present disastrous situation in Vietnam. I think that everybody now agrees that Vietnam is a disastrous mess. People may disagree about what should have been done or what ought to be done now, but the assumption that errors have been made is common to all of us. One of the factors that got fed into the computer is that the willingness of societies to surrender is a function of the number of bombs dropped on it. Being British I have some grave doubts about this!

[9] Man's new power is not, despite the apparent realities, simply an American or a Western phenomenon. That it can be so limited is one of the great comforting myths. I am asked why I talk about the whole world in these terms. I am told to look at Asia, at Latin America, at Africa, all of whom do not have power. But everybody knows that *mankind* has power. We live, as McLuhan has put it, in a global village. And the fact that some continents do not yet have the power does not prevent them from knowing that they ought to have the power and that they can have the power if the rich are willing to develop it and share it with them.

[10] It would appear at first sight as though a society in which man had power over the conditions of his life would be extremely desirable: indeed, at some level, it is. But this power doesn't mesh with our present social system, and as a result we fall into five very serious traps. The first of these traps is what I call the war trap, the fact that in our international system the ultimate sanction in international dispute is war. Each country must therefore be able to defend itself against any potential attacker, which means that it must install and indeed invent any weapon or defense system that it can. This results in a profoundly unstable world. We have to take the same leap in international affairs as we took in personal affairs some time ago when we abolished dueling. I was taught when I was young that we abolished dueling because people became humane. I have reached the conclusion that this is not true,

but that basically people discovered that dueling with modern weapons was too dangerous. Let me point out that we now have available approximately thirty tons of TNT per person, plus enormous destructive potential through biological and chemical weapons. The statement that "war will wipe us out or we will wipe out war" remains as true as it was when it was first stated, but we have numbed ourselves to its reality.

[11] The second trap is the efficiency trap. We run a society in which if something can be done more efficiently, immensely strong forces come into action to ensure change. But the very fact that man has such power over his environment means that he may wish to preserve certain possibilities of human activity which are not efficient. He must therefore change the socioeconomic rules governing international trade and the relationship between income and work.

[12] This can be seen most clearly in relationship to job patterns. In our society everybody must hold a job, unless he is independently wealthy or in a certain very limited group. Computers and machinery are becoming more efficient but men are not becoming more efficient nearly as fast. The efficiency of computers doubles at the present time about every three years, and the cost of computer work probably goes down to one-tenth of its previous cost. At the same time the cost of hiring a worker continues to rise. It is therefore not surprising that a very severe problem of unemployability is emerging. The data are now quite clear: there are more and more people at the bottom of the society who do not have jobs and who are not about to get jobs.

[13] There are only two ways out of this trap. One of them is the idea that the government should become the employer of last resort. That sounds good until you analyze it. What happens when the government becomes the employer of last resort? Some 1,000,000 or more unemployables are placed under the control of federal bureaucrats. These people are unskilled, uneducated, untrained and uninterested in work. The program runs for six months and then Congress wants to know what's going on. It levels charges of inefficiency and lack of control, so the bureaucrats start to tighten up. They pass rules such as: anybody who is fifteen minutes late for work loses a day's pay. Another rule might be: in order to ensure efficient operation of the system, nobody may change his government-supported job more than once in six months. I would suggest a short word for the result of such rules—an old-fashioned word—slavery. If you think it is an unfair word, I would suggest that you look at some existing national and state welfare policies. The only other alternative is the guaranteed income which says that people are entitled to income as a right and that society has a responsibility to find meaningful work for people to do.

[14] The next trap is the consumption trap, which is related to our productive capacity. If everybody has to have a job we must be willing

to consume everything we can produce. We must therefore convince people they should buy. This is particularly visible in our patterns of advertising for children from ages one to five, in an era where television is the prime parent. Television encourages frenetic consumership and permanent debt. "Daddy, Daddy, please buy me . . ."

[15] I said this on TV recently, and somebody said to me, "Well it is really quite all right because children have understood by the age of ten that all advertising is false, anyway." And I said, "You know, if you are right—and you may be right—you have probably explained to me why it is that young people are thoroughly discontented with the society in which they find themselves."

[16] The fifth trap is the education trap. If you have to bring up people so that they will accept the present traps—the war trap, the efficiency trap, the job trap, and the consumption trap—you dare not set people free to think and study. The educational system ceases to be an opportunity for people to find out for themselves what they believe and becomes a method of manipulating people into accepting what the society currently accepts. It serves as a method for inculcating a set of beliefs from the past which are not relevant to today's world.

[17] We have to understand what has happened to us. We are living in a new generation. This new generation has been brought up within new realities. The people now in college were usually born after the end of the Second World War. Their key realities are basically alien to older people. One of those realities is the fact that the atomic bomb has made international violence impossible in the long run. This rejection of international violence is now causing an understanding that even internal violence must be abolished if we are to survive. The other reality can be best set out in the words of a young colleague of mine: "abundance is a free gift." It is awfully difficult to believe, if one has never done real work as defined by society, that one is personally responsible for and entitled to that which one has inherited, and to claim that one has produced the food, clothing and shelter needed for his upbringing.

UNIVERSALIZING TECHNOLOGY
F. M. Esfandiary

[1] Modern technology cannot wait for the human psyche and for class struggles to go through their relatively slower evolution. This new technology is impatient. It is dissolving barriers which otherwise would have taken decades, even centuries, to erode.

[2] You need not be literate to watch films, television, or listen to transistors. Illiteracy is losing its meaning. The illiterate is no longer the uninformed or the uninvolved.

[3] The ten-year-old New York child may not read or write well, but he is the most knowledgeable child in history.

[4] Illiterate peasants around the world do not need more schools. They need more communication satellites.

[5] In the Old World lack of information and lack of contact made for self-centeredness, self-righteousness, self-interest. Illiteracy too created its own insularity and self-centeredness. Everything was generalized from one's own experiences. Patriotism, orthodoxy, nationalism were inevitable.

[6] Today entire generations are growing up with a perspective of the whole planet from outer space. For the very first time in our history we are being conditioned to view our world as a unit—one single sphere.

[7] Then too global technology is making it increasingly easier to view the world in its totality. In our era of communication satellites and supersonics there can be no insularity, no fragmented view of the world. The young fellah in North Africa is now able to watch an Idaho farmer at work, enjoy live sports events in Mexico City, follow a conference of scientists in Moscow. Over half a billion people around the planet almost simultaneously watch a live entertainment program or listen to a United Nations conference. On July 20, 1969, nearly *one billion people* simultaneously watched mankind's first landing on the moon. One billion people. That is nearly one out of every three persons on earth.

[8] Negotiations are now under way to work out permanent arrangements for a single satellite communications network to cover the entire planet. Within a few years we will be able to establish instant communication—by radio, television, telephone, computer, laser—with any town or city in the world.

[9] "The Russians destroyed the concept of nationality," Arthur C. Clarke writes, "when they sent Sputnik splashing across a hundred frontiers.

But because this is perfectly obvious, it will be some time before every-one sees it and governments realize that the only runner in the space race is—man."

[10] Modern technology is revolutionizing and denationalizing *all* aspects of life. Nearly every large city in the world is now international. A mounting avalanche of travelers, information, and goods sweeps through, universalizing everyone and everything. The national city hardly exists. Soon every town and every village will also be universal.

[11] It is entirely fitting that the United Nations headquarters is in New York City, World Health Organization in Geneva, U.N. Industrial Development Organization in Vienna, UNESCO in Paris, International Planned Parenthood in London, U.N. specialized agencies in Belgrade, Cairo, New Delhi, Tokyo, etc. These are all international cities. New York, the most international metropolis of our times, belongs as much to its huge international community as it does to the Americans. Without its millions of first-generation foreign residents, its overseas and out-of-state visitors, students, businessmen, United Nations personnel, and others, New York City would be a prosaic small town.

[12] Large hospitals around the world are also going universal. They not only have multinational medical staffs and patients but medical treatment itself is being internationalized. Today medical students in Europe watch open-heart surgery performed thousands of miles away in Texas. Specialists in Washington, D.C., examine the heartbeat of a patient in Tours, France, diagnose another patient in Tokyo, then within *minutes* provide analyses of their conditions via global telephone and satellite.

[13] Thanks to modern communication and transportation facilities, most major publications are also international. For instance the *London Times, Daily Telegraph, Economist. Paris Match, Elle, L'Express, Le Monde. Epoca, Il Tempo, Oggi. Time, Newsweek, Life, Look, International Herald Tribune, New York Times, Playboy. Stern, Der Spiegel, Constanze, Quick. Pravda, Soviet Life, Soviet Woman, China Today, Peking Review, China Pictorial, Jeune Afrique, La Prensa* . . .

[14] Most of these publications address the world, compete for world markets, report on world conditions. Many of them can be obtained on news racks in Kuwait and Kansas City and Caracas. Regardless of their bias, these and other world publications are helping create universal co-involvement.

[15] Modern technology is helping convert our planet into a family courtyard. Our very psyches are enmeshing. An American senator is assassinated. Within seconds news flashes around the globe. The world is stunned and mourns. Merchants in Nairobi and Tokyo close down their shops, women weep in the streets of Moscow, a man dies of a heart attack in Greece.

[16] The Russian or Indian is surprised that he can be driven to tears

at the death of an American president or senator. The American or Spaniard is astonished that he can feel deeply saddened by the death of a Russian cosmonaut.

[17] Can there be any doubt that a universal conscience is rapidly developing? We are all growing more and more involved in one another's lives, more and more sensitive to one another's sufferings, more and more enhanced by one another's triumphs.

[18] The nationalist who wants modern technology but does not want intrusions into his country's internal affairs is also being absurd. He is contradicting himself.

[19] Radio, television, telephone, tape-recorder, teletype, computer— they are all intrusions into domestic affairs of nations. No conquering army can intrude as deeply and as totally as modern technology. The concept of the *nation* is steadily becoming obsolete.

2

ARGUMENTS ON THE NATURE OF MAN

Many of the forms of human behavior are not inborn but rather are learned. Specific behavior patterns can be changed by psychological, chemical and physical methods. Human nature is therefore not something unalterable but can be changed.—*Gerald Feinberg,* 1968[1]

[In *On Aggression*] Lorenz argues that all behavior, animal and human, is the product of evolution. We, and the animals, are prisoners of ritual, of behavior patterns that may be eons old.
                                                  —*Franklin Russel,* 1966[2]

Man is not the end product of evolution. In fact, according to a University of California at Los Angeles social theorist, man is already obsolescent.

He said the next phase of evolution will be that of superintelligence and superconsciousness, in which man will have faded into the background.

"Man will be part of the backdrop, much as lower animals and plants are part of the backdrop now," said Robert McCracken, assistant professor of anthropology, in an interview.
                                        —*Los Angeles Times Service,* 1971[3]

The man or woman who contemplates draws back from the course of actions to ask about their total meaning, to ask who he is in relation to the course of action, and to rechart his course. He is like a driver who stops long enough to consult the map and check his location and direction.—*Wayne Oates,* 1971[4]

Reference numbers refer to source notes on page 311.

s the Utopians would put it, given a choice, what kind of human beings can we become? The question is simple, but the answers can be most complex. Almost all of the possible futures discussed in these readings depend on your own evaluation of this basic point. If we assume that man was made in the image of God, we certainly have a lot of explaining to do, particularly after reading newspaper headlines. And how are we to decide whose concept of God is the "right" one?

If we set aside the religious point of view, we meet headlong the theories of the anthropologists—man is the product of evolution and is subject to the natural laws that created twentieth century *Homo sapiens*. But even here we face opposing theses. Konrad Lorenz, Desmond Morris, and Robert Ardrey would have us believe that hostility, aggression, and competitiveness are inherent in the animal kingdom. Since a human is but a further step in the continuum of evolution, he or she is instinctively, despite thin veneers of civilization, hostile, aggressive, and competitive. If these traits are inherent, then regardless of technological progress —perhaps even as one result of it—war will be with us forever, hostility will always be a sublimated instinct, and each of us will covet his neighbor's possessions. Desmond Morris holds this position in the selection from *The Naked Ape.*

Not so, say equally famed anthropologists Ashley Montagu, Margaret Mead, and Robert Alland. The evolutionary continuum is not that perfect; the qualities of aggression so astutely observed in animals by Lorenz do not carry over into the far more complex mind of a human being. As evidence of the lack of continuity in the evolutionary process, Montagu points out that man is the only animal which kills its own kind, individually and in mass action. His thesis is stated in an excerpt from *Man in Process.*

Moreover, we cannot leave this question to the anthropologists alone. For almost three quarters of a century, psychologists have been wrestling with the issues. And here, too, we have a wide divergence of opinion. Sigmund Freud was greatly influenced by the researches of Darwin. Man is not a being different from animals or superior to them," he said. "He himself originates in the animal race and is related more closely to some of its members and more distantly to others." Freud's concept of *id* held that it is powerful, anti-social, and irrational. Man was in constant conflict with himself and society. Thus Freud and Morris agree on man's fundamental hostility. "Culture has to call up every possible reinforcement to erect barriers against the aggressive instincts of men. . . ."

John B. Watson and others about the turn of the century opposed this viewpoint. Man's behavior was said to be based on external, environmental influences. Control the environment, especially in the important years of infancy and early childhood, says B. F. Skinner, today's most outstanding behaviorist, and you will find that neurotic conflict is not only learned by the child but it is learned primarily as a result of conditions created by the parent. Behaviorists, too, believe that man is an animal, differing only in the type of behavior practiced. Hence aggression is only a possible type of behavior, and there is a twist: A controlled environment can diffuse if not totally eliminate the "natural" instinct for aggression.

Frank Goble's *The Third Force* offers a new approach to the psychology of human beings which has been most powerfully promulgated by Abraham Maslow. Maslow's ideas were strongly influenced by Margaret Mead, Carl Rogers, Rollo May, and others. Seeking a "psychology for the peace table," he sought a rationale that aimed "to prove that human beings are capable of something grander than war and prejudice and hatred." While not totally either Freud or Skinner, Maslow believed that the rules for psychological study should be based on the analysis of the healthy, satisfied, "self-actualized" person rather than on the mentally ill. Maslow found a significant difference between the behavior of human beings and that of animals and felt that those instincts which we may have inherited are not necessarily bad. His approach was subjective, as evident in his statement that "human beings seem to be far more autonomous and self-governed than modern psychological theory allows for." Maslow's "humanistic" approach is epitomized in the article by Carl R. Rogers in this chapter.

The question of the nature of man is basic to the future of man. If aggression is instinctive and can be controlled only by the veneer of civilization, is not man doomed to eventual self-destruction? But if hostility is fundamentally "culture-created," and if humankind is truly capable of logic and reason, has not the time come when we can conclude that war solves nothing?

FIGHTING
Desmond Morris

[1] If we are to understand the nature of our aggressive urges, we must see them against the background of our animal origins. As a species we are so preoccupied with mass-produced and mass-destroying violence at the present time, that we are apt to lose our objectivity when discussing this subject. It is a fact that the most level-headed intellectuals frequently become violently aggressive when discussing the urgent need to suppress aggression. This is not surprising. We are, to put it mildly, in a mess, and there is a strong chance that we shall have exterminated ourselves by the end of the century. Our only consolation will have to be that, as a species, we have had an exciting term of office. Not a long term, as species go, but an amazingly eventful one.

• • •

[2] How does the aggression work? What are the patterns of behaviour involved? How do we intimidate one another? We must look again at the other animals. When a mammal becomes aggressively aroused a number of basic physiological changes occur within its body. The whole machine has to gear itself up for action, by means of the autonomic nervous system. This system consists of two opposing and counter-balancing sub-systems—the sympathetic and the parasympathetic. The former is the one that is concerned with preparing the body for violent activity. The latter has the task of preserving and restoring bodily reserves. The former says, "You are stripped for action, get moving"; the latter says, "Take it easy, relax and conserve your strength." Under normal circumstances the body listens to both these voices and maintains a happy balance between them, but when strong aggression is aroused it listens only to the sympathetic system. When this is activated, adrenalin pours into the blood and the whole circulatory system is profoundly affected. The heart beats faster and blood is transferred from the skin and viscera to the muscles and brain. There is an increase in blood pressure. The rate of production of red blood corpuscles is rapidly stepped up. There is a reduction of the time taken for blood to coagulate. In addition there is a cessation in the processes of digesting and storing food. Salivation is restrained. Movements of the stomach, the secretion of gastric juices, and the peristaltic movements of the intestines are all inhibited. Also, the rectum and bladder do not empty as easily as under normal conditions. Stored carbohydrate is rushed out of the liver and floods the blood with

sugar. There is a massive increase in respiratory activity. Breathing becomes quicker and deeper. The temperature-regulating mechanisms are activated. The hair stands on end and there is profuse sweating.

· · ·

[3] The simplest form of artificial weapon is a hard, solid, but unmodified, natural object of wood or stone. By simple improvements in the shapes of these objects, the crude actions of throwing and hitting became augmented with the addition of spearing, slashing, cutting and stabbing movements.

[4] The next great behavioural trend in attacking methods was the extension of the distance between the attacker and his enemy, and it is this step that has nearly been our undoing. Spears can work at a distance, but their range is too limited. Arrows are better, but they lack accuracy. Guns widen the gap dramatically, but bombs dropped from the sky can be delivered at an even greater range, and ground-to-ground rockets can carry the attacker's "blow" further still. The outcome of this is that the rivals, instead of being defeated, are indiscriminately destroyed. As I explained earlier, the proper business of intra-specific aggression at a biological level is the subduing and not the killing of the enemy. The final stages of destruction of life are avoided because the enemy either flees or submits. In both cases the aggressive encounter is then over: the dispute is settled. But the moment that attacking is done from such a distance that the appeasement signals of the losers cannot be read by the winners, then violent aggression is going to go raging on. It can only be consummated by a direct confrontation with abject submission, or the enemy's headlong flight. Neither of these can be witnessed in the remoteness of modern aggression, and the result is wholesale slaughter on a scale unheard of in any other species.

[5] Aiding and abetting this mayhem is our specially evolved co-operativeness. When we improved this important trait in connection with hunting prey, it served us well, but it has now recoiled upon us. The strong urge towards mutual assistance to which it gave rise has become susceptible to powerful arousal in intra-specific aggressive contexts. Loyalty on the hunt has become loyalty in fighting, and war is born. Ironically, it is the evolution of a deep-seated urge to help our fellows that has been the main cause of all the major horrors of war. It is this that has driven us on and given us our lethal gangs, mobs, hordes and armies. Without it they would lack cohesion and aggression would once again become "personalized."

[6] It has been suggested that because we evolved as specialized prey-killers, we automatically became rival-killers, and that there is an inborn urge within us to murder our opponents. The evidence, as I have already explained, is against this. Defeat is what an animal wants, not murder; domination is the goal of aggression, not destruction, and basically we do

not seem to differ from other species in this respect. There is no good reason why we should. What has happened, however, is that because of the vicious combination of attack remoteness and group co-operativeness, the original goal has become blurred for the individuals involved in the fighting. They attack now more to support their comrades than to dominate their enemies, and their inherent susceptibility to direct appeasement is given little or no chance to express itself. This unfortunate development may yet prove to be our undoing and lead to the rapid extinction of the species.

[7] Not unnaturally, this dilemma has given rise to a great deal of displacement head-scratching. A favourite solution is massive mutual disarmament; but to be effective this would have to be carried to an almost impossible extreme, one that would ensure that all future fighting was carried out as close-contact combat where the automatic, direct appeasement signals could come into operation again. Another solution is to de-patriotize the members of the different social groups; but this would be working against a fundamental biological feature of our species. As fast as alliances could be forged in one direction, they would be broken in another. The natural tendency to form social in-groups could never be eradicated without a major genetical change in our make-up, and one which would automatically cause our complex social structure to disintegrate.

[8] A third solution is to provide and promote harmless, symbolic substitutes for war; but if these really are harmless they will inevitably 'only go a very small way towards resolving the real problem. It is worth remembering here that this problem, at a biological level, is one of group territorial defence and, in view of the gross overcrowding of our species, also one of group territorial expansion. No amount of boisterous international football is going to solve this.

[9] A fourth solution is the improvement of intellectual control over aggression. It is argued that, since our intelligence has got us into this mess, it is our intelligence that must get us out. Unhappily, where matters as basic as territorial defence are concerned, our higher brain centres are all too susceptible to the urgings of our lower ones. Intellectual control can help us just so far, but no further. In the last resort it is unreliable, and a single, unreasoned, emotional act can undo all the good it has achieved.

NATURE AND THE
MYTH OF WAR
Ashley Montagu

[1] Fundamentally, man is quite an intelligent animal, but he is a victim, alas, of the two-handed engine of his culture which distorts his mind and renders him unintelligent. Outworn traditional teachings have made of Western man a shockingly unintelligent creature who lives under the continuous and unrelieved domination of a chaos of ideas more degrading, more stupid, more idiotic, and more saddening than it may ever be possible to describe. This confused morality has, without question, been substantially responsible for his present deplorable state. For the processes and patterns of thought of every child born into the Western world today have been conditioned according to the prescriptions of these teachings, so that culturally Western man has come to be a function almost entirely of the reigning spirit of confusion and prejudice. And since in his conduct he functions without effort as a victim of confusion and prejudice, he arrives at the belief that it is thus "natural" to act and to think. In this way is produced the mentally and spiritually bludgeoned individual who gropes his way confusedly through life—and whose number is legion. It is in his world alone that today war still remains a legitimate and defensible means of settling a dispute or forcing an issue.

• • •

[2] So-called race prejudice among lower animals, like their so-called natural fears and terrors, are acquired, not inborn. Experiments on young animals first carried out by Benjamin Kidd many years ago, and by numerous investigators since, have conclusively proved that the "instinctive" fear and terror of their allegedly natural enemies exhibited by the adult members of the species are emotions which are generally completely absent in the young, and are acquired only by learning from other members of the species or by individual experience. A lamb or any other animal, for example, which has had no long association with members of its own species from whom it could have acquired fear—or past experience with lions—will exhibit not the slightest fear of a lion when confronted with one.

[3] No animal or human is born with any fear or prejudice whatsoever, of snakes, mice, or the dark, to cite but a few of the most familiar

common fears usually considered of "instinctive" origin. All such fears or prejudices are acquired by learning and may, and usually do, act as conditioned reflexes, simulating physical reflexes which are innate but which in the former cases are conditioned to reach culturally—not biologically or instinctively.

. . .

[4] In America, where white and black populations frequently live side by side, it is an indisputable fact that white children do not learn to consider themselves superior to Negro children until they are told that they are so, a fact which is saddeningly illustrated by the words of a white American farmer from the South who, in answer to the query as to what he thought of the Negro, replied, "I ain't got anything against niggers; I was fourteen years old before I know'd I was better than a nigger."

[5] Numerous other examples could be cited of the cultural acquisition of prejudices, but to enter into a fully satisfactory discussion of the mechanism of race prejudice here would be quite impossible. It need only be said that it has been abundantly proven that race prejudices, or ideas of any kind, are inherited in just the same way as our clothes are, not innately but culturally. The statement so often made that "war is a universal and everlasting law of Nature" is at best a shallow judgment, for it seems never to occur to those who make it that the "conflicts" which they are pleased to term "war" and which are alleged to take place between animals in the wild state are pertinent only when they refer to the conflicts between animals of widely separated species, orders, and, almost universally, classes. Thus, mammals prey upon reptiles, reptiles upon birds, and birds upon insects. Lions will attack almost anything that moves, so will, to a lesser extent, wolves and hyenas. Domestic cats will kill small rodents and birds; monkeys will kill and eat birds and insects. But in all these examples chosen at random not a single animal will "fight" with a member of its own species in the sense that it will fight with members of other species, orders, or classes of animals. In the wild state it is not the practice of animals to prey upon or fight with each other but rather with animals of widely separated kinds. When they do fight with each other the results are rarely fatal and approximate more often than not to play. Of course, very hungry animals will devour, upon occasion, members of their own species, but this is a form of conduct which is normally resorted to only in extreme necessity. In serious conflicts between wild or domesticated animals of the same species the fight is rarely between more than two individuals, and is usually provoked by the same causes and is fought from motives similar to those which cause men to fight with one another; namely, the possession of a sexually desirable mate or an object of physical value such as food. But this sort of fighting is a very different thing from the fighting which we

know as war. War is an organized attack of one community upon another community, and as such is never fought by animals other than those of the "human" variety. It is impossible to produce a single instance from the animal kingdom, outside of man, in which it is shown that within a definite species a form of behavior resembling warfare is waged by one group upon another, or for that matter upon any other order or class of animals—as a means of improving the species or what not. If one thing is certain it is that it is *not* natural for members either of the same species or of any other to wage war upon one another. War, let it be said at once, is the most unnatural, the most artificial, of all animal activities, for it originates in artificial causes, is waged by highly artificial entities called states, is fought from artificial motives, with artificial weapons, for artificial ends. Like our civilization war is an artificial product of that civilization itself, the civilization that has been achieved by the repeal and the repudiation of those very processes of so-called "Nature" which the Bernhardis are pleased to regard as an everlasting universal law.

[6] We have already seen that there is good reason to believe that aggressive race sentiment and prejudice are comparatively recent acquisitions of man. So, too, there is very good reason to believe that warfare is but a recent development resulting from the artificial and perverted activities of men living in highly civilized groups. Among the extinct races of men of whom we have any knowledge no evidence of anything remotely resembling warfare has ever been found. Plenty of weapons of a rather simple nature have been discovered in association with the remains of ancient man but these were clearly for use against animals and not against his fellow men. Adam Smith long ago pointed out that a hunting population is always thinly spread over a large area and possesses but little accumulated property. Primitive man was, and in many cases still is, a hunter and no doubt, as is the case among most existing nonliterate peoples, his hunting grounds were marked off by definite boundaries—boundaries separating different communities—"but these boundaries were sacred and, as no one would think of violating them, they could not form a cause of war." Wars for conquest among nonliterate peoples are completely unknown.

• • •

[7] In the modern world undoubtedly the most potent cause of war is economic rivalry—a purely cultural phenomenon having no biological basis whatsoever. The desire for foreign concessions and foreign markets, the increase in population, *lebensraum*—such things will upon little provocation set nations in opposition and at each other's throats. It is from such economic causes that patriotism, chauvinism, and the widespread fear of aggression—which more than anything else serves to consolidate the group and is responsible for the generation of race sentiment and prejudice—are born.

[8] If all this is true, then it is apparent that war arises not as the result of natural or biological conditions but from purely artificial social conditions created by highly "civilized" modes of living.

. . .

[9] Man has reached his present supremacy of reason through the inhibitive and integrative powers of his mind, the ability to reject and suppress what he considers to be undesirable, the ability to *control*. Human society depends upon the maintenance of that ability of the mind to control, not so much the brute in man, for there is really little that is brutal in him that is not forced upon him, but those elements which under miseducation are capable of making a brute of him. All that is fine, noble, beautiful, and desirable in our civilization has been achieved by the supersession of mind over Nature, and much of this has been achieved through the resolute determination of individual minds not so much to conquer and to vanquish what is customarily called "Nature," red in tooth and claw, but to enlist the aid of "Nature" in the service of man and to control it effectively. All that is so ugly and inhuman and so destructive in our civilization is due to the activities of those who are anxious to exploit their fellow men to their own advantage and who use measures of control only toward this end. To them war is a profitable activity, for it increases their fortunes and thus their power. It is individuals of this order, in all countries, and from the earliest historical times, who make wars, not "Nature." "The fault, dear Brutus, lies not in our stars, but in ourselves."

. . .

[10] The tradition of thought which renders possible such glib talk of war and its supposed natural causes as I have here surveyed represents the bequest to us from the remote past of obsolete modes of thought which are conspicuous for their profound irrationality. So powerful is this traditional detritus that it has not failed to influence many of the most respected minds of our day to the extent of making mathemagicians of our mathematicians, casuists of our philosophers, and an apologist for war of the gentlest and kindest of anthropologists. This tradition constitutes a Gordian knot that one must sever completely, since it resists being untied. At present this tradition of thought constitutes the sole constrictive force operating upon the mind of man as well as being the main impediment in the way of its rational functioning, coercing the good in him toward evil and, in short, representing a tyranny of the strongest and subtlest power. If man is to be saved from himself before it is too late this tyranny must be broken. This can be achieved only by the unequivocal action that must follow the reasoned dissolution of such errors of belief and thought that form so great a part of our traditional social heritage today.

THE PERSON OF TOMORROW
Carl R. Rogers

[1] I am fascinated these days by what I am convinced is a most significant phenomenon. I am seeing a New Man emerging. I believe this New Man is the person of tomorrow. I want to talk about him.

[2] Though I am excited and full of anticipation about this person of tomorrow, there are aspects of the situation which are very sobering. I believe the New Man has characteristics which run strongly counter to the orthodoxies, dogmas, forms, and creeds of the major western religions—Catholicism, Protestantism, Judaism. He does not fit at all into traditional industrial management and organization. He contradicts, in his person, almost every element of traditional schools, colleges, universities. He doesn't fit well into the military. Since our culture has developed all these orthodoxies and forms of present-day life, we have to ask ourselves seriously if this New Man is simply a deviant misfit, or whether he is something more hopeful.

[3] This is another reason for thinking deeply and soberly about him. He is almost the antithesis of the Puritan culture, with its strict beliefs and controls which founded our country. He is very different from the person admired by the industrial revolution, with that person's ambition and productivity. He is deeply opposite to the Communist culture, with its controls on thought and behavior in the interest of the State. He in no way resembles the medieval man—the man of faith and force, of monasteries and Crusades. He would not be congenial with the man produced by the Roman Empire—the practical, disciplined man. He is also very alien to today's culture in the United States, which emphasizes computerized technology, and the man in uniform—whether military, police, or government inspector.

[4] If, then, he is new in so many ways, if he deviates so deeply from almost all of the gradually developed norms of the past and even the present, is he just a sport in the evolutionary line, soon to die out or be discarded? Personally I do not believe so. I believe he is a viable creature. I have the conviction that he is the person of tomorrow, and that perhaps he has a better chance of survival than we do. But this is only my own opinion.

[5] I have talked about him at some length, but I have made no attempt to describe his attitudes, his characteristics, his convictions. I should like to do this very briefly. I would like to say that I know of no

Commencement Address, Sonoma State College, California, 1969. Reprinted by permission of the author.

one individual to whom all of the following statements would apply. I am also keenly aware that I am describing a minority, probably a small minority, of our present-day population, but I am convinced that it is a growing minority. What follows is a groping, uncertain characterization of what I see as the New Man. Some of his qualities are probably temporary ones, as he struggles to break free from the cocoon of his culture. I shall try to indicate these. Some, I believe, represent the process person he is becoming. Here then are some of his characteristics as I see them.

[6] He has no use for sham, façade, or pretense, whether in interpersonal relationships, in education, in politics, in religion. He values authenticity. He will not put up with double talk. He hates statements such as these: "Cigarette smoking is a romantic, exciting, pleasurable, satisfying thing—(and of course it kills many through lung cancer)." Or, "We are following a noble pathway in protecting South Viet Nam and living up to our commitments and treaties—(but in doing so we kill thousands of men, women and children, many of them completely innocent, others whose only crime is that they have a goal for their country different than ours)." He hates this kind of thing with a passion. He regards the current culture as almost completely hypocritical. I believe that this hatred for phoniness is perhaps the deepest mark of the New Man.

[7] He is opposed to all highly structured, inflexible institutions. He wants organizations to be fluid, changing, adaptive, and *human*. It will be clear from what follows deep is his dislike for bureaucracy, rigidity, form for form's sake. He simply will not buy these qualities.

[8] He finds educational institutions mostly irrelevant and futile so far as he is concerned. His unrest—in college and high school—arises out of a hundred specific issues, but none of these issues would be important if his school were truly meaningful for him. He sees traditional education as it is—the most rigid, outdated, incompetent institution in our culture.

[9] He wants *his* learning to involve feelings, to involve the *living* of learnings, the *application* of relevant knowledge, a *meaning* in the here and now. Out of these elements he sometimes likes to become involved in a searching for new approximations to the truth, but the pursuit of knowledge purely for its own sake is not characteristic.

[10] Religious institutions are perceived as definitely irrelevant and frequently damaging to human progress. This attitude toward religious institutions does not mean at all that he has no concern for life's mysteries or for the search for ethical and moral values. It seems, in fact, that this person of tomorrow is deeply concerned with living in a moral and ethical way, but the morals are new and shifting, the ethics are relative to the situation, and the one thing that is not tolerated is a discrepancy between verbal standards and the actual living of values.

[11] He is seeking new forms of community, of closeness, of intimacy,

of shared purpose. He is seeking new forms of communication in such a community—verbal and non-verbal, feelingful as well as intellectual. He recognizes that he will be living his transient life mostly in temporary relationships and that he must be able to establish closeness quickly. He must also be able to leave these close relationships behind, without excessive conflict or mourning.

[12] He has a distrust of marriage as an institution. A man-woman relationship has deep value for him only when it is a mutually enhancing, growing, flowing relationship. He has little regard for marriage as a ceremony, or for vows of permanence, which prove to be highly impermanent.

[13] He is a searching person, without any neat answers. The only thing he is certain of is that he is uncertain. Sometimes he feels a nostalgic sadness in his uncertain world. He is sharply aware of the fact that he is only a speck of life on a small blue and white planet in an enormous universe. Is there a purpose in this universe? Or only the purpose he creates? He does not know the answer but he is willing to live with this anxious uncertainty.

[14] There is a rhythm in his life between flow and stability, between changingness and structure, between anxiety and temporary security. Stability is only a brief period for the consolidation of learning before moving on to more change. He always exists in this rhythm of process.

[15] He is an open person, open to himself, close to his own feelings. He is also open to and sensitive to the thoughts and feelings of others and to the objective realities of his world. He is a highly aware person.

[16] He is able to communicate with himself much more freely than any previous man. The barriers of repression which shut off so much of man from himself are definitely lower than in preceding generations. Not only is he able to communicate with himself, he is also often able to express his feelings and thoughts to others, whether they are negative and confronting in nature, or positive and loving.

[17] His likes and dislikes, his joys and sorrows are passionate and are passionately expressed. He is vitally alive.

[18] He is a spontaneous person, willing to risk newness, often willing to risk saying or doing the wild, the far-out thing. His adventuresomeness has an almost Elizabethan quality—*everything* is possible, anything can be tried.

[19] Currently he likes to be "turned on" by many kinds of experiences and by drugs. This dependence on drugs for a consciousness-expanding experience is often being left behind as he discovers that he prefers to be "turned on" by deep and fresh and vital interpersonal experience, or by meditation.

[20] Currently he often decides to obey those laws which he regards as just and to disobey those which he regards as unjust, taking the con-

sequences of his actions. This is a new phenomenon. We have had a few Thoreaus but we have never had hundreds of people, young and old alike, willing to obey some laws and disobey others on the basis of their own personal moral judgment.

[21] He is active—sometimes violently, intolerantly, and self-righteously active—in the causes in which he believes. Hence he arouses the most extreme and repressive antipathies in those who are frightened by change.

[22] He can see no reason why educational organizations, urban areas, ghetto conditions, racial discrimination, unjust wars, should be allowed to remain unchanged. He has a sustained idealism which is linked to his activism. He does not hope that things will be changed in fifty years; he intends to change them *now*.

[23] He has a trust in his own experience and a profound *distrust* of all external authority. Neither pope nor judge nor scholar can convince him of anything which is not borne out by his own experience.

[24] He has a belief in his own potential and in his own direction. This belief extends to his own dreams of the future and his intuitions of the present.

[25] He can cooperate with others with great effectiveness in the pursuit of a goal which he is convinced is valid and meaningful. He never cooperates simply in order to conform or to be a "good fellow."

[26] He has a disregard for material things and material rewards. While he has been accustomed to an affluent life and readily uses all kinds of material things, taking them for granted, he is quite unwilling to accept material rewards or material things if they mean that he must compromise his integrity in order to do so.

[27] He likes to be close to elemental nature; to the sea, the sun, the snow; flowers, animals, and birds; to life and growth, and death. He rides the waves on his surfboard; he sails the sea in a small craft; he lives with gorillas or lions; he soars down the mountain on his skis.

[28] These are some of the qualities which I see in the New Man, in the man who is emerging as the person of tomorrow. He does not fit at all well into the world of the present. He will have a rough time trying to live in his own way. Yet, if he can retain the qualities I have listed so briefly, if he can create a culture which would nourish and nurture those qualities, then it may be that he holds a great deal of promise for all of us and for our future. In a world marked by incredibly rapid technological change, and by overwhelming psychological sham and pretense, we desperately need both his ability to live as a fluid process, and his uncompromising integrity.

3

GENETICS: CAN WE PERFECT US?

It may soon be possible to propagate people in much the same way as we now propagate roses—by taking the equivalent of cuttings. According to the Nobel Prize-winning geneticist Joshua Lederberg, writing in *The Bulletin of the Atomic Scientists,* we should consider the implications of this now; since it would offer the possibility of genetically identical individuals like multiplied identical twins. . . .—*John Davy, 1966*[1]

A Belgian research team has for the first time completely analyzed the chemical makeup of a gene that dictates the production of a protein, an achievement that appears to bring closer the day when genes can be made to order and turned on and off at will.
—*New York Times Service, 1972*[2]

The problem is that we will trust just about any scientist to build a spaceship. We aren't even too fussy about who builds the super-bombs, who makes the deadly gases. . . .

But who trusts which scientists to supervise gene selection by controlled mating? What scientist do we trust enough to have him proportion out genes and chromosomes or alter the acids that transmit hereditary characteristics?—*Carl T. Rowan, 1973*[3]

Under attack are many of the traditional assumptions that underline not only biology and medicine but all science and technology. Among them are the beliefs that scientific progress is automatically good, that what is medically beneficial to the individual is necessarily good for society, and that scientists are the best judges of the direction in which their research should go. . . .
—*Jane E. Brody and Edward B. Fiske, 1971*[4]

Reference numbers refer to source notes on page 311.

The most explosive technological issue—of the moment, at least—is that of genetic control, a possibility almost beyond our imagination until the last few decades. That we might order perfect children to our own specifications was undreamed of. Few could have conceived that the test-tube babies of Huxley's *Brave New World* might become a real alternative. That was not for us! Yet today Huxley's ideas are being perfected.

Don Fabun, a most imaginative and creative editor of The Kaiser Aluminum and Chemical Corporation *News*, queried eighty-two experts at the world-famous RAND Corporation early in 1966 (see table on page v). He asked them to estimate a date at which man would be able to control his own heredity. Their guesses averaged out about the year 2000. They were wrong. It will be far sooner than that!

In 1970, less than five years later, four bio-engineers (a term that didn't even exist a decade ago) pleaded with an audience at a conference called by the World Futurist Society to realize that their research was moving ahead so rapidly that they were close to mastering at least two techniques for controlling the quality of the physical and mental characteristics of our progeny. Their position was that all of their training, efforts, and labors were about to bear fruit as practical, effective procedures. What frightened them was the fact that while they were equipped by training and experience to perfect these new methods, they felt totally inadequate to decide whether or not the techniques should be made available to humankind. Scientists they were; theologians, moralists, lawyers, politicians they were not.

An even more portentous illustration of the direction taken by current research is found in a film titled *Genetics: Man the Creator*, produced by Hobel-Leiterman of Toronto under the direction of molecular biologists Kurt Hirschorn and Robert Francoeur. These University of Toronto experts report that two earth-shaking procedures will be ready for use with human beings *by the end of this decade*. In essence, we are being told simply that within the next few years, men and women will have the capability of producing children *without any reproductive act whatsoever on the part of the parents.*

Let us briefly consider the three major approaches that the laboratories are using today.

The Nobel Prize-winning research of Watson and Crick determined that the enormously complex shape of the DNA molecule is a spherical helix. It was in 1953 that these two young scientists discovered the shape of deoxyribonucleic acid to be a double spiral staircase in which are hidden the mysteries of heredity—and, in higher creatures like man, perhaps intelligence and memory. Since this all-important molecule is the basis for the human gene, geneticists have devoted themselves to learning more about how to eliminate undesirable characteristics of genes—tendencies toward heart disabilities, hemophilia, and so on.

Let us assume that a couple planning to have a child discovers that because of a hereditary defect, the chances are great that the child might be deformed at birth. If medical science were able to provide a pill, a shot, a treatment that would eliminate this possibility, there is little doubt that the couple would gladly take advantage of the new technique.

Now let us take the situation a step further. Let us assume that both parents are of somewhat small stature. A second treatment could assure them of a child of average height—or two inches above average. Should we? Possibly, yes. Now how about a guarantee of the sex of the child, or the color of hair or eyes or size of bone structure? We'll have to think about those. Now how about an intelligence level superior to that of the parents—why not close to genius level? Now, wait just a minute . . .

Gene control is in the works. It is by far the most complex of the techniques this chapter deals with, and undoubtedly the farthest away from perfection. But it is feasible, and if not you, then your children may be able to specify the characteristics of their child-to-be.

A second technique is called "cloning," a newly-created term for the duplication of living things from single cells of a "parent." It was perfected almost a decade ago with carrots. A few years later, using a variation of the original procedure, cloning became a comparatively simple process with frogs. The nucleus of a frog ovum is removed and replaced with a cell from the liver of a bullfrog. And with the proper environment, the end result will be a bullfrog identical to the male parent. Or we can produce 20 identical frogs. Or 200 or *2000*. Cloning for humans, say the Toronto scientists, will be ready for use by 1980. How about 100 Einsteins? Ten thousand Albert Schweitzers? How about a million Hitlers . . . ?

And finally, the *Time* excerpt in this chapter discusses *in vitro* reproduction. Any genetically perfect sperm is joined with any genetically perfect ovum in a perfected synthetic uterus filled with synthetic amniotic fluid with an artificial umbilical tube, and presto! Perfect children, a true master race. Disturbing? Exciting? Degrading? Enthralling? Undemocratic? Both cloning and asexual, *in vitro* reproduction will be ready by 1980, say the molecular biologists. *And who is to say whether or not they should be used?* The vast majority of the so-called educated people of our world are not even aware of these potentials. Should the question be decided democratically? How can this be done if the huge majority of those concerned have not even informed themselves about the possibilities, to say nothing of having given them serious, considered thought? Or should we leave the decision to "them"—those mysterious powers in high places or secret hideouts?

The *Time* piece, "Man into Superman: The Promise and Peril of the New Genetics," describes the research of today's molecular biologists. Lord Ritchie-Calder in "The Doctor's Dilemma" argues strongly against any effort to change our heredity. "Invit: The View from the Glass Oviduct" from *Saturday Review/Science* tells us what is happening *now*, and Rita Kramer may raise your eyebrows with "The No-Child Family: Going Against 100,000 Years of Biology."

It is your children we are talking about, or, at best, your children's children. This is truly a dimension of the future . . . your future.

MAN INTO SUPERMAN: THE PROMISE AND PERIL OF THE NEW GENETICS
Time

Reshaping life! People who can say that have never understood a thing about life—they have never felt its breath, its heartbeat—however much they have seen or done. They look on it as a lump of raw material that needs to be processed by them, to be ennobled by their touch. But life is never a material, a substance to be molded. If you want to know, life is the principle of self-renewal, it is constantly renewing and remaking and changing and transfiguring itself.

—*Doctor Zhivago* by Boris Pasternak

[1] Perhaps it was simply a matter of chance, a random throw of the molecular dice. Perhaps some greater, transcendent force was at work in the earth's primeval seas. Yet from the moment of its miraculous genesis three billion years ago, life has been continually renewing and remaking itself, an evolutionary process that has led to the appearance of a unique creature quite unlike any of those before him. Thinking, feeling, striving, man is what Pierre Teilhard de Chardin called "the ascending arrow of the great biological synthesis."

[2] Now, only some 35,000 years after the birth of modern man—a brief interval on the evolutionary time scale—the arrow is pointing in a dramatic new direction. Not only has man begun to unlock the most fundamental life processes, but he may soon be able to manipulate and alter them—curing such killer diseases as cancer, correcting the genetic defects that account for perhaps 50% of all human ailments, lessening the ravages of old age, expanding the prowess of his mind and body. Says Caltech's Robert Sinsheimer, one of the architects of the biological revolution: "For the first time in all time, a living creature understands its origin and can undertake to design its future."

· · ·

[3] Artificial insemination, once the exclusive province of livestock breeders, also offers escape from some genetic mishaps. An estimated 25,000 women whose husbands are either sterile or carry genetic flaws have been artificially inseminated in the U.S. each year, many of them with sperm provided by anonymous donors whose pedigrees have been carefully checked for hereditary defects. Some 10,000 children are born annually of such conceptions.

[4] Doctors also see possibilities in artificial inovulation, a procedure in which an egg cell is taken directly from the ovaries, fertilized in a test tube and then reimplanted in the uterus. By carefully scrutinizing the developing embryo in the test tube, doctors could spot serious genetic deficiencies and decide not to reimplant it, thus avoiding an abortion later on. If the embryo is normal, it could even be reimplanted in the womb of a donor mother and carried to term there, enabling the woman either unable or unwilling to go through pregnancy to have children that were genetically her own.

[5] Even test-tube babies, once the stuff of science fiction, are now not only possible, but probable. Dr. Landrum Shettles of Columbia University and Dr. Daniele Petrucci of Bologna, Italy, have shown that considerable growth is possible in test tubes. Shettles has kept fertilized ova growing for six days, the point at which they would normally attach themselves to the lining of the uterus. Petrucci kept a fertilized egg alive and growing for nearly two months.

[6] Indeed, only development of an "artificial womb" capable of supporting life stands in the way of routine ectogenesis, or gestation outside the uterus, and now even this problem may yield to solution. Scientists at the National Heart Institute have developed a chamber containing a synthetic amniotic fluid and an oxygenator for fetal blood, and have managed to keep lamb fetuses alive in it for periods exceeding two days. Once their device is perfected, the baby hatchery of Aldous Huxley's *Brave New World* will be a reality and life without birth a problem rather than a prophecy.

[7] Man may eventually be able to abandon sexual reproduction en-

tirely. That startling and perhaps unwelcome possibility has been demonstrated by Dr. J. B. Gurdon of Britain's Oxford University. Taking an unfertilized egg cell from an African clawed frog, Gurdon destroyed its nucleus by ultraviolet radiation, replacing it with nucleus of an intestinal cell from a tadpole of the same species. The egg, discovering that it had a full set of chromosomes, instead of the half set found in unfertilized eggs, responded by beginning to divide as if it had been normally fertilized. The result was a tadpole that was the genetic twin of the tadpole that provided the nucleus. Gurdon's experiment was also proof of what geneticists have long known: that all of the genetic information necessary to produce an organism is coded into the nucleus of every cell in that organism.

[8] Man, say the scientists, could one day clone (from the Greek word for throng), or asexually reproduce himself, in the same way, creating thousands of virtually identical twins from a test tube full of cells carried through gestation by donor mothers or hatched in an artificial womb. Thus, the future could offer such phenomena as a police force cloned from the cells of J. Edgar Hoover, an invincible basketball team cloned from Lew Alcindor, or perhaps the colonization of the moon by astronauts cloned from a genetically sound specimen chosen by NASA officials. Using the same technique, a woman could even have a child cloned from one of her own cells. The child would inherit all its mother's characteristics including, of course, her sex.

[9] Dramatic as cloning may be, it is overshadowed in significance by a technique that may well be practiced before the end of this century: genetic surgery, or correction of man's inherited imperfections at the level of the genes themselves. When molecular biologists learn to map the location of specific genes in human DNA strands, determine the genetic code of each and then create synthetic genes in the test tube, they will have the ability to perform genetic surgery.

[10] Some molecular biologists envisage using laser beams to slice through DNA molecules at desired points, burning out faulty genes. These would then be replaced by segments of DNA tailored in the test tube to emulate a properly functioning gene and introduced into the body as artificial—and beneficial—viruses.

[11] The concept is not as farfetched as it sounds. Real viruses are merely segments of DNA (or RNA) surrounded by largely-protein sheaths; they penetrate the cell nucleus (leaving their sheaths behind) and take over the cellular DNA.

[12] The potential of the technique is already being tested by an international research team in the treatment of two children whose hereditary inability to produce the enzyme arginase had resulted in severe mental retardation. The team infected the youngsters with a natural virus, the Shope papilloma, which contains DNA that triggers arginase

synthesis. Although the experiment is expected to produce no improvement in the children's mental condition, it may belatedly trigger the production of the missing enzyme and prove that viruses can carry beneficial messages to the cells.

[13] There is other evidence that the beginning of genetic surgery is not far off. Dr. Sol Spiegelman of Columbia University has synthesized an artificial virus that is indistinguishable from its natural model and has used it to infect bacteria and produce new viruses. He and his colleagues have little doubt that they will also eventually create "friendly" viruses and use them to cure disease rather than cause it—by using the viruses to stimulate the production of the chemical products upon which health and life itself depend.

[14] Prophylaxis is important, but man's molecular manipulations need hardly be confined to the prevention and cure of disease. His understanding of the mechanisms of life opens the door to genetic engineering and control of the very process of evolution. DNA can now be created in the laboratory. Soon, man will be able to create man—and even superman.

[15] Researchers have found that they can increase the life span of laboratory animals by underfeeding them and thus delaying maturation. This phenomenon, they believe, occurs because a smaller intake of food results in the formation of fewer cross linkages—connecting rods that link together and partly immobilize the long protein and nucleic acid molecules essential to life. If scientists can retard cross linking in man, they may well slow his aging process. Scientists also hope that they can some day do away with disease, genetically breeding out hereditary defects while breeding in new immunities to bacterial and other externally caused ailments. Finally, they look forward—in the distant future and with techniques far beyond any now conceived—to altering the very nature of their species with novel sets of laboratory-created genetic instructions.

[16] Current predictions about the appearance of re-engineered man seem singularly uninspired. Some scientists argue that man's head should be made larger to accommodate an increased number of brain cells. They do not, however, explain what man would do with this additional gray matter; there is good reason to believe that man does not use all that he presently possesses. A few others note that the efficiency of man's hands could be increased by an extra thumb and his peripheral vision enhanced by protruding eyes—improvements that seem unnecessary in the light of man's expanding technology.

[17] Some favor less obvious alterations. They have suggested that man be given the genes to produce a two-compartment stomach (a cow has four) that could digest cellulose; that mutation could be advantageous if man fails to increase his food supplies fast enough to feed the planet's

growing population, but superfluous if he does. They also want man programmed to regenerate other organs, such as he now does with the liver, so that he can repair his damaged or diseased heart or lungs if necessary.

[18] Others call for even more specialized humans to perform functions that in reality will probably be done better by machines. British geneticist J. B. S. Haldane called for certain regressive mutations to enable man to survive in space, including legless astronauts who would take up less room in a space capsule and require less food and oxygen (larger and more powerful spacecraft would seem to be an easier and less monstrous solution). Haldane also suggested apelike men to explore the moon. "A gibbon," he said only half-jokingly, "is better preadapted than a man for life in a low gravitational field."

[19] Eventually, scientists fantasize, man will escape entirely from his inefficient, puny body, replacing most of his physical being with durable hardware. The futuristic cyborg, or combination man and machine, will consist of a stationary, computerlike human brain, served by machines to fill its limited physical needs and act upon its commands.

[20] Such evolutionary developments could well herald the birth of a new, more efficient, and perhaps even superior species. But would it be man?

THE DOCTOR'S DILEMMA
Lord Ritchie-Calder

[1] In the brief lifetime of the protesting youth of today, we have had four major epochs—the atomic age, the computer age, the space age, and the bio-engineering, or DNA, age. Each of them is as significant as the Bronze Age, the Iron Age, the Renaissance, or the Industrial Revolution, and all have been telescoped into the postwar years. The first has given Man the capacity to veto the further evolution of his own species by bringing on a nuclear holocaust. The second has given the machine the ultimate capacity to replace human labor and ape the logical faculties of the human brain. The third has broken the gravitational fences of our

Reprinted with permission from the September/October, 1971, issue of *The Center Magazine*, a publication of the Center for the Study of Democratic Institutions, Santa Barbara, California.

planet and at the cost of forty billion dollars has put man on the moon. The fourth is more portentous, for it is ignorance masquerading as knowledge.

[2] Thirty-five years ago, a wise man, Sir Frederick Gowland Hopkins, Nobel Prize-winning scientist, said to me, "A vitamin is a unit of our ignorance. Every new vitamin that is discovered is the reminder of the food factors we have not discovered." Which is another way of putting Claude Bernard's aphorism, "True science teaches us to doubt and in ignorance to refrain." He was not calling for a halt to research. He was calling for sure footing. I would call it "going into an uncharted minefield with a mine detector."

[3] We know what we did with the secret of matter; we exploded it as a cataclysmic bomb. And we have not caught up with the moral, military, or political consequences yet. In 1945, the safebreakers forced the lock of the nucleus before the locksmiths knew how it worked. Since 1945, we have spent billions of dollars providing high-voltage accelerators for nuclear physicists to find out what the fundamental particles, the wards of the lock, really are.

[4] What we are playing about with now is the secret of life. We know the DNA code and we know that the genetic specifications thus encoded for the production of a person from a fertilized ovum, if spelled out in English, would fill five hundred volumes the size of the Encyclopaedia Britannica. And any misprint—a slip in the sequence, a mutation—will repeat itself through successive generations. We certainly do not know the code for "will," "judgment," "inspiration," "morality," "evil," "kindness," "brutality."

[5] Even the crude changes which are now possible are fraught with incalculable dangers. It is possible to modify germs. A British scientist died of the germ he "invented." An eminent colleague said, "Thank God he did not sneeze. He could have started a world epidemic against which there would have been no natural immunity."

[6] This capacity to manipulate the genes of living things certainly represents an ethical crisis. It is only a matter of time (and with the intensification of research the interval gets shorter and shorter) when we shall be able to transpose or dispose the DNA groupings so that we can determine artificially how cells will behave. We shall correct the misbehavior of cells that we call cancer. We shall modify hereditary defects and then we shall provide prescriptions for better specimens. But who are "we"? The Nazis had the idea of Aryan supermen and they aimed to "purify" the genetic code by eliminating unwanted genes by means of the gas chambers and the biological experiments in the concentration camps.

[7] No doubt the computer could produce a better model. Falling in love may be a corny way to dispense random genes but somehow I feel that it is preferable to computer-selected characteristics to be chemically

converted into the DNA code and transmitted to posterity. There would be garbled versions, like a printer's cliché, repeating themselves generation after generation.

[8] The ethical crisis is felt and expressed by the scientists responsible. The Nobel Prize for the double helix of DNA was shared by Francis Crick, James Watson, and Maurice Wilkins. Crick, in expressing his concern, hopefully suggested that common sense will prevail and that the wilder genetic possibilities will not happen because "people simply will not stand for them." Watson appeared before a congressional subcommittee to urge that restrictions should be imposed on human-cell manipulation. Wilkins has become the president of the British Society for the Social Responsibility of Science.

[9] George Beadle, who received a subsequent Nobel Prize for his DNA work, urged his colleagues not to embark on genetic manipulation because the effects would be irreversible. And, anyway, he pointed out that we had not done nearly enough in the cultural improvement of the species. "Especially after birth," he said at the Guildhall in London, "the information that is fed into the nervous system in massive amounts plays a large and important role in determining what we are. It includes a large input of cultural inheritance." Salvador Luria, another Nobel Prize winner, has said, "geneticists are not yet ready to conquer the earth, either for good or for evil," and he called for some sort of body, national or preferably international, to apply ethical constraints. Short of tampering with the DNA code there is much to be done in correcting genetic aberrations. There is an obvious need for more genetic clinics where couples can have tests and advice if there is any reason to suspect that they may have genetically handicapped children, that is, with serious hereditary effects. They should be discouraged from having children or should have the condition corrected by well-confirmed methods.

[10] But we are already shuffling and redealing the cards of posterity. Artificial insemination, by which the infertile father consents to being the before-conception foster-father of his wife's child by an anonymous donor, is now regular practice. In animals, it is a practical proposition to have an ovum which has been fertilized in the womb of a mother transferred to the womb of another whose genes have no part of the offspring but who will carry it through gestation to delivery. This is one way film stars might produce children without risk to their figures or shooting schedule. It is only the obstetrical version of the lady of the manor, before the days of feeding bottles, putting her baby out to the village wetnurse. This would be the prenatal foster-mother.

[11] Artificial insemination can be carried a step further. Just as we have sperm banks with the male genes kept on ice, so there can be ova banks. This suggests fascinating possibilities of anachronous matings. H. J. Miller suggested in *Out of the Night* in 1935 that the frozen sperm

of Stalin might have been used to fertilize generations of Soviet women, but imagine Shakespeare's genes artificially mated with those of Mrs. Siddons and parturated by a Hollywood starlet. Imagine what would happen to the hereditary peerage if the freeze-packed thirteenth earl was begotten after the fifteenth.

[12] We have antisterility pills producing four, five, and six babies. Sex determination is an imminent likelihood and that will produce problems for the demographers if we have fashions in babies as we have fashions in clothes and some biological Dior decides that the vogue should be male babies.

[13] It is urgent that we should consider what is happening in that other form of bio-engineering—organ transplanting. There would not, at first sight, seem to be much ethical difference between having a nose straightened or a face lifted by plastic surgery or having an organ replacement. Indeed, one could maintain that the internal organ was more humanly necessary than superficial cosmetics. The ethical dilemma, however, is of a different order.

[14] Before kidney transplants people had an ethical unease about renal dialysis—the artificial kidney machine. Unquestionably it was a great technical advance making it possible to treat kidney dysfunctions from which thousands die. But the machine was, and is, expensive and involves intensive care of the patient by doctors and nurses. For whom the machine? In the United States the dilemma was evaded but not solved by having lay panels, like juries, making life-or-death choices. In Britain, where the National Health Service entitles everyone, rich or poor, to have access to any necessary treatment, the responsibility rests on the medical staff. It was (and still is) a difficult decision.

[15] Assume that some V.I.P., a famous man of advanced years, and a boy of fifteen both require the available machine, to whom would it be allocated? The living museum piece whose obituary would be thus postponed or the boy who might live to be a Nobel Prize winner or a criminal? Nor must we forget the doctors and nurses who have died of infectious hepatitis, the occupational hazard of renal dialysis.

[16] With the discovery of chemical means of counteracting immunological rejection it became possible to transplant actual organs. The natural defensive system by which the body can repel germs or reject alien tissue, genetically incompatible, could be repressed so that the graft would "take." Thus a stranger's kidney could be transferred to a patient (again, to whom the suitable kidney?). That led to heart transplants and heart-and-lung transplants. An essential condition is that the organ must be "fresh."

[17] To the point of scandal we have had a near Burke-and-Hare situation. (Burke and Hare were the Edinburgh grave-robbers who supplied Knox, the anatomist, with cadavers for dissection and finished up

by providing warm corpses.) Doctors, collaborating with the heart surgeons, would remove the heart at the moment of "death" and rush it to the operating theater. But what is the "moment of death"? The old method of holding a mirror to the mouth to get the mist of breathing has been long discarded. The pulse or the beating of the heart is no longer the test. The test is the encephalograph to detect brain waves. If there is no signal the patient is dead. Thus the seat of life has become the brain. If it was hopelessly damaged or ceased to function, the instant removal of the heart was considered justified.

[18] Apart from the ethic of the decision, this raises the question, what is the ultimate object of the entire exercise? Assume (and it is a safe assumption) that any and every organ is capable of being transplanted and that a human artifact could be reconstituted out of "spare parts." To what end? Presumably to service the brain, the vestigial remains of life. But the brain, however marvelous, is a biological computer. One can debate whether it is even the "mind." It is certainly not the human personality *in se*. Our personality is compounded from the chemistry and the responses of the whole body—not just the endocrines but our lymph glands and our gastric propensities as well. We are not only remaking a machine of cells and tissues, we are remaking a personality. The question arises as to the identity of the person modified by surgical plumbing. What is the legal, moral, or psychiatric identity of a human so altered by medical manipulation that he has become an artifact?

[19] There is another severely practical but profoundly important question. What is the cost in money but also in human sacrifice of the diversion of scarce facilities and scarcer medical manpower to the intensive care of those "interesting cases"? Even those who get it are a tiny fraction of those who may need it. Thousands, tens of thousands, hundreds of thousands and, in the wider world, millions of useful lives are being wasted and an immense amount of suffering is being endured because of the lack of conventional treatment.

[20] There is another dilemma. With all this "doing over," with plutonium pacemakers being implanted and attached to the heart; with the promise of miniature computers being connected to our brain to compensate our failing memories; with electronic stimulators promised to enliven our "pleasure centers"; with all the advances in biochemistry and geriatric care; and with the protection against and treatment of infectious disease, we can expand the span of life. We can keep people alive indefinitely. This is a social problem of first magnitude. It is also a personal problem for all of us: it involves a basic human right—the right to live or die with dignity.

[21] There is a need for a consensus of conscience; an international tribunal of ethics; a surveillance, which need not be suppression, of the kind of things which are happening and which, irresponsibly, can en-

danger mankind; for a new personal ethic for doctors and medical scientists. The Hippocratic Oath, noble in its intention, no longer serves. It has been overtaken by events. The "judgment" which innovation imposes on the doctor exceeds the professional common sense which the "good doctor" could apply in good conscience. In the phrase of the biophysicist, Leroy Augenstein, "he is being asked to play God."

[22] I have, as consultant to the human rights division of the United Nations concerned with the technological threat to those rights, suggested that we bring together a body of wise men from all over the world and from diverse cultures to consider the inventory of opportunities but also of mischief, actual and potential. They must give us a basis for a working philosophy. They must produce instruments and institutions, legal and professional, which can apply ethical restraints. They must, for the individual scientist and doctor, produce a new Hippocratic Oath.

[23] The poet Clough wrote, "Thou shalt not kill; but needst not strive officiously to keep alive." While I personally am grateful for the time I have borrowed through medical science, I have no desire to be a zombie, nor a vegetable, nor an interesting specimen of bio-engineering. As a parliamentarian I have been considering the possibility of a bill which is simple in intent but, in legal terms, difficult to draft. I want any individual in full possession of his faculties to say, and make binding on others, the conditions under which he would not be kept artificially alive.

[24] The operative phrase in any such bill would be "in full possession of his faculties," because when the time comes and his earnest doctors and his devoted family are, with the best intentions, conspiring to keep him alive, he will not be in any position to decide. This is not a question of birth certificates, nor senility; the circumstances can arise at any age through accident or, indeed, through delayed resuscitation on the operating table, when the higher cells of the brain are deprived of oxygen. In the compassion of true medicine respect for human dignity cannot accept the living dead, the bio-artifact, the non-person.

INVIT: THE VIEW FROM THE GLASS OVIDUCT
Saturday Review/Science

[1] The name has a vaguely Scandinavian sound with the accompanying promises of advanced sex. It is *Invit,* and it will be the result of the most advanced sex the planet has seen to date, though possibly not of the type you are thinking about.

[2] Invit has been conceived not in a woman's body but in a laboratory apparatus. When he or she is born—and elements of the scientific community feel the birth will be within the next twelve months—Invit will be recorded as history's first known "ectoconceptus" (one conceived outside the womb), the progenitor of the test-tube baby.

[3] Invit will be British. Disregard that misleading Scandinavian echo —the name is derived from the Latin *in vitro,* meaning a biological reaction taking place in an artificial apparatus, rather than within a living organism, *in vivo.*

[4] The midwives are a group of intense and tight-lipped scientists and physicians led by Robert G. Edwards of Cambridge University's physiology laboratory. The actual birthplace, however, will be the Oldham General Hospital near Manchester, and the obstetrician-in-attendance is to be the hospital's Dr. Patrick Steptoe.

[5] In the amphitheater (in thought at least) will be the world's most distinguished physiologists, including a vocal and highly critical group of Nobel laureates who believe that Edwards is committing an abominable act. James Watson of DNA fame, for example, has publicly demanded that Edwards abandon the Invit experiments. Max Perutz, also a laureate and a senior scientist for the British government's Cambridge-based Medical Research Council, has called Edwards's work a "stunt" and believes that "the whole nation should decide whether or not these experiments should continue." Common themes in both men's words are that Invit might be terribly deformed *à la thalidomide,* resulting in a massive public backlash against all science, and that the Edwards technique—if successful—might open the door to a *Brave New World* form of genetic engineering.

[6] Edwards's administrative superiors in the physiology laboratory, however, defend the work. The Edwards artificial conception approach has been tested exhaustively in mammals, they say, and occurs in a stage

of embryonic development when the danger of there being birth defects is at its lowest.

[7] Interestingly, much of the impetus behind the Invit experiments stems from an unlikely source—the prospective mother.

[8] Mother?

[9] She will be one of some fifty willing women chosen by Edwards for the creation of Invit. The women are principally in their mid-thirties. Some are doctors; others are doctors' wives or nurses. They are sterile, principally because of blockages in their oviducts. Their ova, consequently, cannot make contact with sperm cells. They and their husbands above all want to become parents, and so they turned to Edwards when his experiments became public knowledge more than a year ago.

[10] Edwards's scientific feat was to find exactly the right hormonal moment to remove eggs from a female volunteer (by laparoscopy, a technique that involves a needlelike instrument inserted through the navel into the egg sac), the right way to select sperm donated by the husband, and the correct liquid medium to encourage both sperm and egg to interact. He succeeded not only in achieving fertilization of an egg by such means but in coaxing the embryo to divide more than 100 times. This is more than enough to prepare Invit for "implantation," or attachment to the uterine wall—the moment many scientists believe to be the time when life really begins.

[11] Edwards plans to induce the creation of Invit by bringing about contact of egg and sperm in an ordinary cell-culture dish, putting the budding mixture into an ordinary laboratory incubator, and then implanting the embryo at the appropriate stage of division—into the woman's receptive uterus, again by laparoscope. The mother-to-be will then go through the usual nine months of waiting as would any pregnant woman.

[12] Invit, then, will be born. If normal, Invit will be examined, studied, interviewed, coddled, and analyzed for the rest of its life—but discreetly, in the Cambridge way. Invit will be shielded from a curious world, perhaps not even told of his (or her) origin.

[13] And nature will have been bypassed in her most intimate and awesome of acts, conception.

THE NO-CHILD FAMILY: GOING AGAINST 100,000 YEARS OF BIOLOGY

Rita Kramer

[1] Cathy and Wayne N. are in their late 20's, have been married five years, and are childless. The last time a member of Cathy's family asked, "When are you going to start a family?" her answer was, "*We're* a family!"

[2] Cathy and Wayne belong to a growing number of young married couples who are deciding not to have children. A recent survey showed that in the last five years the percentage of wives aged 25 to 29 who did not want children had almost doubled and among those 18 to 24 it had almost tripled. What lies behind this decision which seems to fly in the face of biology and society?

[3] Perhaps the most publicly outspoken childless (or "childfree" as they like to put it) couple are Ellen Peck, author of "The Baby Trap," and her husband William, an advertising executive who is president of the National Organization for Non-Parents, which the Pecks founded last year to defend the social and economic interests of what they feel is a discriminated-against minority group: couples without children. The Pecks insist neither they nor the organization are against parenthood, just against the social pressures that push people into parenthood whether it is what they really want and need or not.

[4] "It's a life-style choice," Ellen says. "We chose freedom and spontaneity, privacy and leisure. It's also a question of where you want to give your efforts—within your own family or in the larger community. This generation faces serious questions about the continuity of life on earth as well as its quality. Our grandchildren may have to buy tickets to see the last redwoods or line up to get their oxygen ration. There are men who complain about being caught in a traffic jam for hours on their way home to their five kids but can't make the association between the children and the traffic jam. In a world seriously threatened by the consequences of overpopulation we're concerned with making life without children acceptable and respectable. Too many children are born as a result of cultural coercion. And the results show up in the statistics on divorce and child-abuse."

[5] Her husband adds, "Every friend, relative and business associate is pressuring you to have kids 'and find out what you're missing.' Too

many people discover too late that what they were missing was something they were totally unsuited for."

[6] And Ellen again: "From the first doll to soap operas to cocktail parties, the pressure is always there to be parents. But let's take a look at the rate of parental failure. Perhaps parenthood should be regarded as a specialized occupation like being a doctor. Some people are good at it and they should have children; others aren't, and they should feel they have other alternatives."

[7] Less evangelical than the Pecks, who appear regularly in the media extolling the virtues of nonparenthood, but equally convinced that having children is not for them, a number of young husbands and wives who were asked about their decision not to have children made these comments:

[8] *The main reason we enjoy our lives together is because we are together. I am not in the kitchen washing baby bottles while he thinks of an excuse to get out of the house because the baby is screaming.*

[9] *The thing I find amusing is there are people our age with two or three children, struggling along, and they tell us we are missing something. Meanwhile we ride in a new car, own our own lakefront home, spend our summers on our boat, go away every weekend, and spend every Christmas holiday skiing in Europe. And they tell us we are missing something.*

[10] *I'm sure there are some very happy families with children, but the unhappy ones far outnumber the happy ones. I don't want to take that chance.*

[11] *Most married people I know had no choice. They were programed to have three children and be Cub Scout leaders. Then there are those of us who stop to think about the big fantastic world out there waiting to be explored. I feel that most people are so busy washing diapers and trying to balance the budget that they merely exist and look around them, but never see. They're too busy wiping runny noses.*

[12] *After five years, both sets of parents are putting on the pressure for us to have kids. They have taken to calling our cat and two dogs their "grandchildren."*

[13] *A man's life isn't anywhere near as greatly altered as a woman's once the baby arrives. He may need to increase his earnings, but there is still the job, a productive life outside. The woman will have to sacrifice many things. I would feel trapped in that role.*

[14] *It's depressing how crucial my sister and I are to my mother—she more or less lives for us. I will never let that happen to me.*

[15] *I want to live my life while I'm young. My parents were always telling me that after my younger brother and I were out of school they would do all the things they wanted to do. My father will be 60 by the time my brother's out of college.*

[16] *I don't think it's selfish to stay childless. Who are you hurting? It would be worse to become pregnant and not really want the baby. It might start out as a great ego trip, but all you'd wind up with would be problems.*

[17] *When we say we don't want kids, people ask us, "What if everyone felt the way you do?" What a silly question.*

[18] Are these the voices of immature, self-centered egotists or of responsible adults considering the consequences of their decisions?

[19] Professional observers agree that many people have children for the wrong reasons, sometimes for no reason at all. Men often drift into fatherhood without ever making a deliberate choice. For many women pregnancy can be a way to escape from unresolved conflicts, to achieve instant identity or strengthen a poor self image, to gratify a need for the attention and affection they feel they never had as children.

[20] I talked with a number of specialists in the field of human behavior about what these couples had said. Their reactions varied widely. A family therapist described the decision not to have children as "a basic instinctual response to the world situation today," implying that something like the herd instinct in animals was operating as a response to the dangers of overpopulation, crowding, pollution and nuclear war, causing women to feel a reluctance to reproduce and leading them to seek new ways of realizing themselves outside of family life.

[21] More than one psychiatrist suggested that those who want to remain childless are narcissistic—making a virtue out of necessity by rationalizing their inner conflicts about giving care *vs.* being taken care of. "These are people who can't tolerate the idea of caring for children, who have no margin of love to spare them," said one, adding, "You're going against something with 100,000 years of biology behind it." A colleague of his chimed in, "Well, we all rationalize our deficits, and these people probably *shouldn't* have children whatever their real motives are, for the same reason there ought to be liberal abortion laws. There should only be enthusiastic parents in this world."

[22] Some observers suggest that perhaps what we are seeing is not a real change at all, that, like the sexual revolution, it is not really a revolution in behavior but in expression. "It may be," says one Connecticut psychoanalyst, "that an identifiable group that has existed all along is simply coming out of the closet, like homosexuals or swingers. The spirit of the time is to do your own thing and not hide it, and these people

may reflect an increased frankness and openness rather than any real change."

[23] Dr. Helen Kaplan, associate professor of psychiatry at The New York Hospital–Cornell Medical Center and head of its Sexual Disorder Program, thinks there has been a kind of sexual revolution and that what it amounts to is the separation of morality and sexuality. "Sex used to be permissible only for purposes of procreation in marriage. We no longer think it is immoral to have sex without having children and that leaves couples with a choice about whether they want to have them or not. They no longer have to feel guilty about not wanting it."

[24] Dr. Kaplan believes there is a strong maternal urge in many women from early childhood on—"and it's not just culturally determined, either"—but that women vary tremendously in their degree of maternal need. And while women who experience deep maternal drives can't give up having children without feeling a real sense of deprivation, not all women feel this way.

[25] Psychologist Donald M. Kaplan (no relation to Helen) believes that while some people have always opted not to have children, the increased frequency we are seeing is in those children of the nineteen-forties and fifties who were raised by parents whose character style had shifted from what sociologist David Riesman called "inner-directed" to "other-directed," and that these other-directed parents had two relevant effects on their children. One was to give them a greater feeling of "narcissistic entitlement"—what one expects from life. The other was the loss of a sense of certainty. They are more open to self-doubt, he says, more preoccupied with their bodies, their life-styles, less able to maintain stable attachments to others. The decision to have a baby, he thinks, is the kind of decision such people might be most likely to postpone. It can't be modified, can't be undone.

[26] "Many of these young adults are ambivalent about relinquishing the role of the one who is cared for and taking on that of the one who does the caring," says Dr. Kaplan.

[27] Dr. E. James Anthony is professor of child psychiatry at Washington University School of Medicine and co-author of "Parenthood, Its Psychology and Psychopathology." In a recent conversation Dr. Anthony said, "Many people I've talked to are very concerned about their own future and the future of children in this rather troubled world. In the past there was always a feeling implicit in the culture that parenthood was something very significant, attractive, enriching, creative. Now it seems to be going by the board. There seem to be so many other opportunities for women to express themselves creatively and family life requires them to give up so many things that the emphasis on family life as a good and creative thing, a way to contribute to the future of the world, doesn't really ring a bell with many young people.

[28] "I think that part of what's happening is that the ambivalence of parents today is being passed on unconsciously to their children. Children are a great deal of trouble, and perhaps more so today than ever before. They can be a pain in the neck. Their precocious development, adolescent acting-out, drug-taking, all loom as problems. The young people feel, 'If they don't really want us, why should *we* want to have children?' Then they rationalize this feeling in terms of the external questions like what the world has to offer. They ask questions like, 'Why add to the population explosion? Why create people who will have to face all the problems that are approaching in the next century?'

[29] "Just how deeply ingrained are mothering and fathering? Does such a thing as fatherliness really activate men? Can they do without it easily? Some suggest it's just a question of having a fling and then nine months later having to think about the responsibilities of a family. Many young men say they don't feel the need to immortalize themselves in children.

[30] "With women, there's the question of what has been called 'the disappointed womb'—whether there is a real need in women to experience something in what Erikson calls that 'inner space.' Many women I talk with are conscious of this kind of enrichment, they talk about being fulfilled in pregnancy, of feeling complete and better than they have ever felt in their lives—but, later, many find handling children is a bit of a nuisance. Still, having a child has been experienced as marvelous, miraculous. What happens if a woman abrogates this experience? It's a much more serious decision for her than for a man. There is something powerful about this basic biological means of creation. To deny oneself may be a little like Beethoven having this powerful talent and being told you must never use it.

[31] "Despite their stated motives for not having children, the question arises whether young people really in fact lead richer lives today. I find that many college students today feel strangely empty. They live in a world full of stimuli of all sorts but lack a sense of inner satisfaction that may relate to these basic biologic things."

[32] Whatever else they disagree on, the experts all seem to be saying that it's not whether you have children or don't that really matters, what matters is that you are comfortable about what you do. If you don't have children and you have much inner conflict about it, you'll be miserable in your childlessness; if you have children and regret it, you'll be miserable and your children will be miserable too. The point seems to be to know yourself, to accept your deeper feelings and not make such an important life decision because it's the thing to do or to satisfy unrealistic fantasies, or to give your parents what they want or to escape from other responsibilities.

[33] Some people are afraid to admit their own feelings of the kind

many of the childless couples interviewed could accept about themselves —what they called being "selfish." They are ashamed to admit they would rather travel than bring up children. But what if that *is* what would make them happiest? Deeply held feelings are not easily changed and if you do not recognize what yours really are, you will not make the choices that are right for you.

[34] For many, if not most people, the joys of parenthood as well as its problems are what life is all about. To see one's children grow and develop into individuals, and to see oneself continue on in them, can be the richest experience between one's own birth and death. But there are also people for whom living a full life and realizing themselves take other routes. And we live in a time in which attitudes seem to be freeing up in a way which enables increasing numbers of men and women to question the way "everybody" lives if that is not the way that is right for them. The more people continue to ask themselves such questions as whether or not they really want to raise a family before they begin to do so, the fewer unhappy parents and troubled children there will be.

4

WOMAN AND MARRIAGE: NOW WHAT?

A mink coat, a job, and all those shiny electrical appliances are no longer enough, it appears, for the American Woman. She wants something bigger, shinier, and far more explosive—an even break.
—*Vera Glaser, 1969*[1]

We all live too long now for our social institutions to work right . . . . Our system of marriage and family life, for instance, was designed for a world in which most people were old at 40 and dead at 50. The average couple had eight or ten children—and by the time they had left home all their parents had strength to do was to putter around the garden and play with their grandchildren for a few last peaceful years.—*Alison Lurie, 1972*[2]

Motherhood is in trouble, and it ought to be. A rude question is long overdue: Who needs it? The answers used to be 1) society and 2) women. But now, with the impending horrors of overpopulation, society desperately *doesn't* need it. And women don't need it either. Thanks to the Motherhood Myth—the idea that having babies is something that all normal women instinctively want and need and will enjoy doing—they just *think* they do. . . .
—*Betty Rollin, 1970*[3]

Men and women progress together or not at all.—*Gloria Steinem, 1972*[4]

Reference numbers refer to source notes on page 311.

re we justified in drawing some conclusions at this point? Is it possible that a rational international policy will result in worldwide population control? Can we conclude that many women will choose *not* to bear children?

A corollary to "Invit" could be that there will be women whose main occupation would be the bearing of other couples' children *for* those couples—for a price, and for a variety of reasons. As a case in point: Mr. and Mrs. A earnestly desire a child. Mrs. A has a serious arthritis condition and needs constant cortisone treatments. The possibility that she might be able to bring a baby to term under these circumstances is close to zero at this time. Using *in vitro* techniques, doctors arrange for an ovum from Mrs. A made fertile by Mr. A's sperm to be inserted into the uterus of another woman who carries the fetus through the normal gestation period and then presents it to the biological parents. Nothing is unique about this in the animal world even now. In a similar fashion a new breed of sheep was introduced in the state of Washington several years ago. Fertilized ova were carried across seven thousand miles of land and sea in the uterus of a rabbit. The ova were inserted into the uteri of local ewes, and a few months later, baby lambs were born who had no blood relationship to their "mothers" at all.

What will be the position of those women who no longer choose to be "baby factories"? Or the increasing number of intelligent, educated women who have decided on careers other than that one which society has expected of them for generations? Are we about to unleash the enormous brain power of half of humankind into enterprises other than housekeeping and child training?

"Sexual equality is not the issue," says Gene Hoffman, mother of seven children, actress, and writer. "I want recognition of my value and uniqueness as a person—not as a woman." The dissatisfaction of woman with her role exemplifies the turbulence of a society in change. The total effect, even in a comparatively short-range view, may be one of the most significant results of all the changes now in process. Whether men like it or not, they are being forced to recognize women as *people,* individuals with needs, desires, ambitions, and above all, an urgent determination to find satisfying new roles.

If the activities of sex partner, housekeeper, child raiser, and cook become less important for millions of women, what is the future of marriage? And what kinds of marriages will there be? How long will marriage last? Do we still attach enormous significance to that official "piece of paper"? Back in the twenties, Judge Ben B. Lindsay, a high court official, suggested that couples might have a two-year trial period that he called "companionate marriage." This notion created a societal explosion which rocked the country. Given the current state of flux in sexual and social mores, a similar suggestion would not even rate a two-inch story on the obituary page. "Trial marriages" have become commonplace and the sensationalism that only a few years ago caused shock and breast beating and cries of "What did we do wrong in bringing up our children?" has all but disappeared. There have even been suits to allow legal marriages between individuals of the same sex, accompanied by a greater acceptance of homosexuality as a way of life. Morton Hunt analyzes these changes in our mores in "The Future of Marriage." He sees a more flexible marriage pattern as a part of the future, as well as a greater fulfillment for each individual in the partnership and the end of the master-servant relationship.

In *Future Shock* Alvin Toffler discusses the transience of today's society, the super-mobility of roots, values, material goods, and of the family itself. For example, in the environs of every large industrial plant there are huge trailer courts, some very elaborate and luxurious, which house many of the workers. It has become commonplace for Dad to announce to his family that at the end of the month, they are moving to northern California or to the Boston industrial area because he is changing his job. And it is almost as commonplace for eighteen-year-old son John to decide to stay on at the old plant rather than to make the move with the family. Grandmothers and grandfathers long ago were separated from the family group; they are living in retirement in sunny Arizona or staying on in Illinois or Ohio to spend their later years among old surroundings and old friends. The nuclear family is already becoming archaic, just as is that society in which sons learned their father's trade or inherited the farm from Grandpa. More often than not, the trade has disappeared and what was 160 acres of wheat is covered with housing subdivisions.

But this disruption of close, meaningful ties sometimes results in unfulfilled needs, feelings of alienation, yearnings to be part of a community larger than the immediate, somewhat tenuous family group. The excerpt from marital anarchist Robert Rimmer's *Proposition 31* describes a new kind of marriage, though it may be new only to our particular culture at this phase of history. Frederik Pohl in "Day Million" takes us far into the future with a stunning description of what marriage may someday become. Science fiction writer Pohl's story may raise your eyebrows, but we must remember that in the belief of his characters, *we* are early primitives. And remember, too, that in the belief of our eminent RAND Corporation experts (page v), household robots will be available for routine chores by the year 2000. How old will your children be then?

SEXUAL EQUALITY IS NOT THE ISSUE
Gene Knudsen Hoffman

[1] The notion of equality between the sexes is a thorny one. We've labored over it so long and suffered such unexpected, often negative, results in our efforts to achieve it. I'm beginning to think we need radical new insights, directed toward a radical new goal. We must raise the problem to a higher level.

[2] I'd like to make two proposals that feel valid to me.

[3] First: equality is not a proper goal for the sexes. If we try to equalize men and women, there will always be bitterness and inequities. There are basic differences between us. Unless there is some remarkable discovery in the biological science, men simply will not bear children, nor will they experience other phenomena related to being female (and vice-versa). And—unless we go Kibbutz—the mother is the psychologically key person in the child's infancy. She is the one who can give or withhold life. She must, therefore, care for the baby through the critical years of extreme dependence, and sometimes longer. (I'm not denying the possibility of devising more equitable arrangements for child care. I like George Owen's notion that each person work less so each can devote more time to home and children. That we can certainly do, and some are already doing it.)

[4] Second: I don't want "equality" with men, or anybody else. I want something much more. I want recognition of my value and uniqueness as a person—not as a woman. I want opportunity to perform creative work. I want to be listened to in any council *for which I have prepared myself*. I want full freedom, and cooperation to evolve as a human being, to gain wisdom and knowledge. To be sure, I want certain rights guaranteed to me, not because I am a woman, but because I am a human being. Whatever is agreed upon as proper to *people* should be mine.

[5] What's preventing me and other women from achieving this status?

[6] I think the fault is deep, but not inaccessible. I think it lies imbedded in the goals we've set for ourselves. I think most of us, men and women, whether in "the movement" or out, married or unmarried, black or white, have accepted society's goals (or some version of them) as norms for ourselves.

[7] At an earlier period, society's goals may have been valid. I don't

think they are now. Many of us can perceive that goals of fame, fortune, even goodness and Godliness, are improper goals for human beings. They strait-jacket us, prevent us from evolving organically (to use the Howard Brinton term). To this category, I'd like to add what I believe is one of the most stultifying goals of all: marriage. I think the *goal* of marriage keeps men and women in the old dominant-submissive roles. It limits growth for both of them.

[8] There is only one proper goal for a man or a woman. It is living. To live fully, we must first become people: human beings. This may or may not include marriage, parenthood, a career, or money-making.

[9] We become human beings by developing our faculties, all of them. Our intellectual, artistic, creative, intuitive faculties and many more. There's a competition or conformity inherent in such a goal. Everyone can evolve in the most unique and diversified ways imaginable.

[10] "But!" I hear protests. "If we don't prepare for marriage, we'll be miserable husbands and wives. If we don't prepare for parenthood, we'll perpetuate the monstrosities of former parent-child relationships."

[11] To which I respond: "It isn't marriage we should prepare for, it's relationship with others. It isn't parenthood we should prepare for, it's understanding of human growth needs of all people, whatever age." We all need to learn how to create and live in an environment which sustains, which nurtures, which cherishes. If we can learn this, we'll be marvellous marriage partners and parents, and we'll do marvellously if we decide marriage isn't for us. With living as the goal of life, we don't reduce our interests or awareness; we increase and expand them.

[12] In his manifesto for the "New Politics," Harvey Wheeler describes the world of tomorrow as "the world of the peoples' University" instead of "the world of the working man's factory." I find that a thrilling prospect. It feels harmonious with what I see as our delightful challenge to develop ourselves into people.

[13] If our goal is life, then caring for baby has new dimensions. The new insights it brings can be projected into other areas. A peace conference at the United Nations would be much more fruitful if it were an extension of a healthy, harmonious relationship in the home. I see men and women, parent and child, helping each other to their common fulfillment.

[14] There are two groups where I feel the experiment is already under way. One has a long history of equable relationships between the sexes. The other is practically unproven.

[15] One of the areas I see the flowering of both sexes is within The Society of Friends. I have found there, to an unusual degree, men and women exchanging responsibilities. Both are willing and able to perform the "menial tasks" formerly assigned to women. Yet in the councils, men

and women expect much of one another and listen with respect and eagerness to hear if it is forthcoming.

[16] I expect this works as well as it does because Quakers are more devoted to the recognition and cherishing of each individual than to social progress. And yet, the progress goes on, too.

[17] The other group to which I refer is a highly personal one. I am very tentative about it because it is all so incipient. I refer to a small group of young people I know who have experimented with LSD. They say, and they act as though they mean, that the "mind expanding" experience is important to everyone so we can all "get into communication on new levels." I have heard no suggestion that experimenters should be segregated.

[18] As I observe the few I know intimately, I feel their goals have changed. They're not fanatic to save the world, or society, or themselves. They're concerned, but not driven.

[19] As they phrase it, they appear to be out to understand their own and other peoples' hang-ups, to learn how to relate more fully to the world and to one another.

[20] They appear to feel each person has many unrealized potentialities which will greatly enhance the world and themselves if they develop them. There doesn't appear to be any male-female competition for these potentialities. Each seems eager to complement the other, to add his quantum to the body of the whole.

[21] I find some of these young people are developing a new regard for human beings, a new respect for the internal realities of people, a new awe and wonder about the mystery of creation.

[22] I don't know that one needs LSD to achieve this, but I do feel these young people seem to be approaching life with something like mutually valued sensitivity, and are searching for new ways to live in harmony with themselves and others.

[23] I don't know how to implement this Society Devoted To Living, on any grand scale. I'll have to leave that to the organizers amongst us. But if just one little proposal of the "Triple Revolution" were put into effect—that of the guaranteed annual income—we'd all be freed for the life of self-discovery and awareness.

[24] A friend of mine, an artist, once said: "Your talent is for your work; your genius is for your life."

[25] How exciting it would be to release our common genius to express our diversity, our variety, and, ultimately, our long-awaited humanity!

THE FUTURE OF MARRIAGE
Morton Hunt

[1] All in all, then, the evidence is overwhelming that old-fashioned marriage is not dying and that nearly all of what passes for rebellion against it is a series of patchwork modifications enabling marriage to serve the needs of modern man without being unduly costly or painful.

[2] While this is the present situation, can we extrapolate it into the future? Will marriage continue to exist in some form we can recognize?

[3] It is clear that, in the future, we are going to have an even greater need than we now do for love relationships that offer intimacy, warmth, companionship and a reasonable degree of reliability. Such relationships need not, of course, be heterosexual. With our increasing tolerance of sexual diversity, it seems likely that many homosexual men and women will find it publicly acceptable to live together in quasi-marital alliances.

[4] The great majority of men and women, however, will continue to find heterosexual love the preferred form, for biological and psychological reasons that hardly have to be spelled out here. But need heterosexual love be embodied within marriage? If the world is already badly over-populated and daily getting worse, why add to its burden—and if one does not intend to have children, why seek to enclose love within a legal cage? Formal promises to love are promises no one can keep, for love is not an act of will: and legal bonds have no power to keep love alive when it is dying.

[5] Such reasoning—more cogent today than ever, due to the climate of sexual permissiveness and to the twin technical advances of the pill and the loop—lies behind the growth of unwed unions. From all indications, however, such unions will not replace marriage as an institution but only precede it in the life of the individual.

[6] It seems probable that more and more young people will live together unwed for a time and then marry each other or break up and make another similar alliance, and another, until one of them turns into a formal, legal marriage. In 50 years, perhaps less, we may come close to the Scandinavian pattern, in which a great many couples live together prior to marriage. It may be, moreover, that the spread of this practice will decrease the divorce rate among the young, for many of the mistakes that are recognized too late and are undone in divorce court will be recog-

nized and undone outside the legal system, with less social and emotional damage than divorce involves.

[7] If, therefore, marriage continues to be important, what form will it take? The one truly revolutionary innovation is group marriage—and, as we have seen, it poses innumerable and possibly insuperable practical and emotional difficulties. A marriage of one man and one woman involves only one interrelationship, yet we all know how difficult it is to find that one right fit and to keep it in working order. But add one more person, making the smallest possible group marriage, and you have three relationships (A-B, B-C and A-C); add a fourth to make two couples and you have six relationships; add enough to make a typical group marriage of 15 persons and you have 105 relationships.

[8] This is an abstract way of saying that human beings are all very different and that finding a satisfying and workable love relationship is not easy, even for a twosome, and is impossibly difficult for aggregations of a dozen or so. It might prove less difficult, a generation hence, for children brought up in group-marriage communes. Such children would not have known the close, intense, parent-child relationships of monogamous marriage and could more easily spread their affections thinly and undemandingly among many. But this is mere conjecture, for no communal-marriage experiment in America has lasted long enough for us to see the results, except the famous Oneida Community in Upstate New York; it endured from 1848 to 1879, and then its offspring vanished back into the surrounding ocean of monogamy.

[9] Those group marriages that do endure in the future will probably be dedicated to a rural and semiprimitive agrarian life style. Urban communes may last for some years but with an ever-changing membership and a lack of inner familial identity; in the city, one's work life lies outside the group, and with only emotional ties to hold the group together, any dissension or conflict will result in a turnover of membership. But while agrarian communes may have a sounder foundation, they can never become a mass movement; there is simply no way for the land to support well over 200,000,000 people with the low-efficiency productive methods of a century or two ago.

[10] Agrarian communes not only cannot become a mass movement in the future but they will not even have much chance of surviving as islands in a sea of modern industrialism. For semiprimitive agrarianism is so marginal, so backbreaking and so tedious a way of life that it is unlikely to hold most of its converts against the competing attractions of conventional civilization. Even Dr. Downing, for all his enthusiasm about the "Society of Awakening," as he calls tribal family living, predicts that for the foreseeable future, only a small minority will be attracted to it and that most of these will return to more normal surroundings and relationships after a matter of weeks or months.

[11] Thus, monogamy will prevail; on this, nearly all experts agree. But it will almost certainly continue to change in the same general direction in which it has been changing for the past few generations; namely, toward a redefinition of the special roles played by husband and wife, so as to achieve a more equal distribution of the rights, privileges and life expectations of man and woman.

[12] This, however, will represent no sharp break with contemporary marriage, for the marriage of 1971 has come a long way from patriarchy toward the goal of equality. Our prevalent marital style has been termed companionship marriage by a generation of sociologists; in contrast to 19th Century marriage, it is relatively egalitarian and intimate, husband and wife being intellectually and emotionally close, sexually compatible and nearly equal in personal power and in the quantity and quality of labor each contributes to the marriage.

[13] From an absolute point of view, however, it still is contaminated by patriarchalism. Although each partner votes, most husbands (and wives) still think that men understand politics better; although each may have had similar schooling and believes both sexes to be intellectually equal, most husbands and wives still act as if men were innately better equipped to handle money, drive the car, fill out tax returns and replace fuses. There may be something close to equality in their homemaking, but nearly always it is his career that counts, not hers. If his company wants to move him to another city, she quits her job and looks for another in their new location; and when they want to have children, it is seldom questioned that he will continue to work while she will stay home.

[14] With this, there is a considerable shift back toward traditional role assignments: He stops waxing the floors and washing dishes, begins to speak with greater authority about how their money is to be spent, tells her (rather than consults her) when he would like to work late or take a business trip, gives (or withholds) his approval of her suggestions for parties, vacations and child discipline. The more he takes on the airs of his father, the more she learns to connive and manipulate like her mother. Feeling trapped and discriminated against, resenting the men of the world, she thinks she makes an exception of her husband, but in the hidden recesses of her mind he is one with the others. Bearing the burden of being a man in the world, and resenting the easy life of women, he thinks he makes an exception of his wife but deep-down classifies her with the rest.

[15] This is why a great many women yearn for change and what the majority of women's liberation members are actively hammering away at. A handful of radicals in the movement think that the answer is the total elimination of marriage, that real freedom for women will come about only through the abolition of legal bonds to men and the establishment of governmentally operated nurseries to rid women once and for all of

domestic entrapment. But most women in the movement, and nearly all those outside it, have no sympathy with the anti-marriage extremists; they very much want to keep marriage alive but aim to push toward completion the evolutionary trends that have been under way so long.

[16] Concretely, women want their husbands to treat them as equals; they want help and participation in domestic duties; they want help with child rearing; they want day-care centers and other agencies to free them to work at least part time, while their children are small, so that they won't have to give up their careers and slide into the imprisonment of domesticity. They want an equal voice in all the decisions made in the home—including job decisions that affect married life; they want their husbands to respect them, not indulge them; they want, in short, to be treated as if they were their husbands' best friends—which, in fact, they are, or should be.

[17] All this is only a continuation of the developments in marriage over the past century and a quarter. The key question is: How far can marriage evolve in this direction without making excessive demands upon both partners? Can most husbands and wives have full-time uninterrupted careers, share all the chores and obligations of homemaking and parenthood and still find time for the essential business of love and companionship?

[18] From the time of the early suffragettes, there have been women with the drive and talent to be full-time doctors, lawyers, retailers and the like, and at the same time to run a home and raise children with the help of housekeepers, nannies and selfless husbands. From these examples, we can judge how likely this is to become the dominant pattern of the future. Simply put, it isn't, for it would take more energy, money and good luck than the great majority of women possess and more skilled helpers than the country could possibly provide. But what if child care were more efficiently handled in state-run centers, which would make the totally egalitarian marriage much more feasible? The question then becomes: How many middle-class American women would really prefer full-time work to something less demanding that would give them more time with their children? The truth is that most of the world's work is dull and wearisome rather than exhilarating and inspiring. Women's lib leaders are largely middle-to-upper-echelon professionals, and no wonder they think every wife would be better off working full time—but we have yet to hear the same thing from saleswomen, secretaries and bookkeepers.

[19] Married women *are* working more all the time—in 1970, over half of all mothers whose children were in school held jobs—but the middle-class women among them pick and choose things they like to do rather than *have* to do for a living; moreover, many work part time until their children have grown old enough to make mothering a minor assignment. Accordingly, they make much less money than their husbands, rarely

ever rise to any high positions in their fields and, to some extent, play certain traditionally female roles within marriage. It is a compromise and, like all compromises, it delights no one—but serves nearly everyone better than more clear-cut and idealistic solutions.

[20] Though the growth of egalitarianism will not solve all the problems of marriage, it may help solve the problems of a *bad* marriage. With their increasing independence, fewer and fewer wives will feel compelled to remain confined within unhappy or unrewarding marriages. Divorce, therefore, can be expected to continue to increase, despite the offsetting effect of extramarital liaisons. Extrapolating the rising divorce rate, we can conservatively expect that within another generation, half or more of all persons who marry will be divorced at least once. But even if divorce were to become an almost universal experience, it would not be the *antithesis* of marriage but only a part of the marital experience; most people will, as always, spend their adult lives married—not continuously, in a single marriage, but segmentally, in two or more marriages. For all the dislocations and pain these divorces cause, the sum total of emotional satisfaction in the lives of the divorced and remarried may well be greater than their great-grandparents were able to achieve.

[21] Marital infidelity, since it also relieves some of the pressures and discontents of unsuccessful or boring marriages—and does so in most cases without breaking up the existing home—will remain an alternative to divorce and will probably continue to increase, all the more so as women come to share more fully the traditional male privileges. Within another generation, based on present trends, four of five husbands and two of three wives whose marriages last more than several years will have at least a few extramarital involvements.

[22] Overt permissiveness, particularly in the form of marital swinging, may be tried more often than it now is, but most of those who test it out will do so only briefly rather than adopt it as a way of life. Swinging has a number of built-in difficulties, the first and most important of which is that the avoidance of all emotional involvement—the very keystone of swinging—is exceedingly hard to achieve. Nearly all professional observers report that jealousy is a frequent and severely disruptive problem. And not only jealousy but sexual competitiveness: Men often have potency problems while being watched by other men or after seeing other men outperform them. Even a regular stud, moreover, may feel threatened when he observes his wife being more active at a swinging party than he himself could possibly be. Finally, the whole thing is truly workable only for the young and the attractive.

[23] There will be wider and freer variations in marital styles—we are a pluralistic nation, growing more tolerant of diversity all the time—but throughout all the styles of marriage in the future will run a predominant

motif that has been implicit in the evolution of marriage for a century and a quarter and that will finally come to full flowering in a generation or so. In short, the marriage of the future will be a heterosexual friendship, a free and unconstrained union of a man and a woman who are companions, partners, comrades and sexual lovers. There will still be a certain degree of specialization within marriage, but by and large, the daily business of living together—the talk, the meals, the going out to work and coming home again, the spending of money, the lovemaking, the caring for the children, even the indulgence or nonindulgence in outside affairs—will be governed by this fundamental relationship rather than by the lord-and-servant relationship of patriarchal marriage. Like all friendships, it will exist only as long as it is valid; it will rarely last a lifetime, yet each marriage, while it does last, will meet the needs of the men and women of the future as no earlier form of marriage could have. Yet we who know the marriage of today will find it relatively familiar, comprehensible—and very much alive.

from

PROPOSITION 31
Robert H. Rimmer

[1] When Jun and Sylvia arrived to drive us to Television City—once again they were acting as chauffeurs—Horace and I were still trying to convince Tanya and David to come along and join the studio audience of the Joe Kraken Show to give us moral support. As he came through the door, Jun slipped me an envelope and whispered, "You're on your own."

[2] David and Horace didn't hear him; I smiled uneasily at David. It might not be too late to read Proposition Thirty-One to them, but there would be no time for the discussion that would inevitably follow. In the bathroom, while I fiddled with my makeup, Tanya sat on the toilet and read the typewritten draft to me. When she said, "Wow, I hope this doesn't paralyze Horace's vocal cords," she didn't help to quiet my fears.

Still, a speechless Horace seemed quite unlikely. And if he didn't like the Proposition, he had only himself to blame. After all, I was his protégée.

[3] Before we left, David laughed as he hugged me. "When I married you," he said, "I suspected the worst. You're the kind of intense person who can't stop playing with matches even when you're sitting on a powder keg. If I were at the studio, I might have to restrain myself from running up and punching Kraken in the nose." Tanya was more practical. "The way things are, Shea, someone really has to stay here with the kids. I'll be praying for you both."

[4] On the way to the studio, the envelope in my pocketbook, I listened as Horace voiced his last-minute doubts and his fear that we would both make asses of ourselves. I prayed, too, that Horace, David, and Tanya would forgive me if the powder keg exploded.

[5] David tape-recorded the show, which turned out much better than the play I never got around to writing, and he played it back for Horace and me late that evening. In the version below, I've added the italicized comments:

[6] KRAKEN (*smiling unctuously at Horace and me, the Untouchables, and benevolently at John Vestal and the Reverend Strate*) Our guests tonight, Mrs. Nancy Herndon, a housewife, and Horace Shea, who I believe *was* Professor of Sociology at Cal Institute (*oily close-up*). I say *was*. Due to some rather wild happenings a few days ago at the Shea home, Professor Shea has been temporarily suspended from the faculty. The Institute is rather concerned, and maybe you are too, if you've been reading your newspapers. The Herndons and the Sheas may or may not be just one more collection of the sort of kooks who have overrun Southern California and are trying to destroy every belief that you and I hold sacred and that have made this country great. But this is a democracy, so we'll give them their chance to defend themselves.

[7] On my left is John Vestal, one of our former State Senators, and now running for reelection. John Vestal, as you know, is active in the crusade to restore moral sanity to California. Next to him is the Reverend Harvey Strate, of the Greater Los Angeles Council of Churches. Dr. Strate is a champion in the cause of strengthening the family by a return to sound religious values.

[8] In the unlikely event that you don't know all about it, Mrs. Herndon and Professor Shea and their legitimate spouses, who are not with us tonight, and four other prominent citizens of this area, were raided by the police last week at the home of Professor Shea and carried off naked to the police station. From everything I have read, it seems likely the police interrupted a wife-swapping party on the suspicion that marijuana was being used for additional titillation. Frankly, I'm somewhat amazed that Mrs. Herndon and Professor Shea dare to appear on this

program; at least, their nerve does them credit. If I were in their shoes, I'd want to slink out of town before a decency committee decided to tar and feather me and ride me out on a rail. Well, if there's one thing you have to admit about our fringe groups, it's that they've lost all their modesty. They don't seem to know what shame is, and they're nauseatingly vocal. But kooky or sane, and whether they make you hold your noses or cheer, Joe Kraken believes that every citizen of this great democracy has a right to know what's going on. To get to the heart of our subject for tonight, may I ask you, Mrs. Herndon, are you the mistress of Professor Shea? I gather there's a Mr. Herndon somewhere in the boondocks.

[9] NANCY (*jittery*) David, my other husband, and Tanya, Horace's other wife, are baby-sitting with the children. They're watching this program at home.

[10] KRAKEN (*snorting*) Your other husband! His other wife! Really, Mrs. Herndon, you're putting me on. Having two husbands or two wives is bigamy. America may have given up on some things, but bigamy is still illegal. She's kidding, isn't she, Professor Shea?

[11] HORACE Not at all. We simply believe that in our present-day society a merger of two small families will give all the members of them greater family identity and greater economic strength, and that it will also give the adults sexual variety within the family.

[12] KRAKEN Then you do in fact sleep with Mrs. Herndon, and Mrs. Shea sleeps with Mr. Herndon. It seems to me those words you just said are a high-sounding way to dignify wife-swapping.

[13] NANCY (*burning*) We're not wife-swappers. Wife-swapping is a one-night stand, usually, with numerous couples. The Herndons and the Sheas are involved in a complete commitment to each other.

[14] KRAKEN Have you ever tried wife-swapping as you define it?

[15] NANCY No! And I'm not interested; that would devalue sex.

[16] KRAKEN But what you are doing *is* adultery, isn't it, Mrs. Herndon?

[17] NANCY I read somewhere, Mr. Kraken, that you've been married several times. Isn't that a polite form of adultery as well as bigamy?

[18] KRAKEN (*sternly*) We're not here to discuss my life, Mrs. Herndon.

[19] NANCY Let's not call it your life. Let's call it Mr. X and the several Mrs. X's that Mr. X has copulated with and had children by.

[20] KRAKEN They have used the legal processes available to them to maintain one relationship at a time.

[21] NANCY For varied copulation. If one observes the legal forms, it's possible to achieve the joys of bigamy or adultery and still be considered a responsible citizen and even a good Christian.

[22] VESTAL While you and your friends are attempting to sue me, Mrs. Herndon, as a cover-up for your activities, may I point out that at

least in divorce and remarriage the rights of the children are protected. Since we are not here to discuss the other aspects of your morality, which to my mind are the *real* issue, may I at least point out that our society, quite rightly, recognizes only monogamous marriage. Your premise would destroy the family and the morals of the community. No child would know who his father and mother were, and future generations would have to be the wards of the state. The way you say you're living may not be against any California law that's enforced, but it should be. If the churches have failed, and we haven't yet heard from the Reverend Strate, then I say we need a law with teeth in it to protect us from ourselves.

[23] NANCY I agree with you, Mr. Vestal. Since you have such faith in the law, you certainly wouldn't object to group or corporate marriage if it were a legal form of marriage in California.

[24] VESTAL (*disgustedly*) I can assure you, I'm not interested in pipe dreams.

[25] NANCY (*laughing*) Perhaps not for yourself. But if a majority of the voters in this state demanded such a law, I'm sure you would uphold it.

[26] VESTAL (*coldly*) I have a feeling, Mrs. Herndon, that your brain has been damaged—I hope not by the use of drugs. Obviously, the possibility you suggest is remote.

[27] NANCY (*trying not to laugh at Horace's surprised expression*) Perhaps not so remote as you may think, Mr. Vestal. I would like to read a Proposition to you, and enlist your aid in getting a petition through the Secretary of State. Perhaps we may even succeed in getting this Proposition on the November ballot . . .

[28] KRAKEN (*interrupting*) This is not a political platform, Mrs. Herndon.

[29] NANCY (*insistent*) This happens to be quite germane to this discussion. I agree with Mr. Vestal. For the security of our children, the Herndons and the Sheas should be able to formalize our marriage in a legal civil or religious ceremony. I think many of your listeners will sympathize with our proposal.

[30] KRAKEN (*resigned*) Go ahead. Nuts and bolts cheerfully assembled on the Joe Kraken Show.

[31] NANCY (*reading*) To the Secretary of State of the State of California: We the undersigned, being duly qualified and registered voters of the State of California and constituting not less in number than eight percent of the entire vote cast for all candidates for governor in the last election, hereby petition the Secretary of State and request that the following proposed law, to be known as the California Corporate Family Law, be submitted directly to the electors of the State of California for their adoption or rejection at the next succeeding general election or as provided by law. . . . the text of said proposed law is as follows: The

people of the State of California enact an act to permit not more than three married couples, past the age of thirty, to join together under a new civil marriage provision of the present state laws in a joint form of marriage to be known as group marriage or corporate marriage, establishing a family unit that will exist independently of the individual members and have all the rights now permitted under the existing laws of corporations, such family corporations to appoint from their legal members by marriage, or from the issue of these marriages, directors to govern the affairs of these family corporations and to continue with their full human powers to carry on the purposes of such corporate living which will be construed as follows: To create a joint family environment for the financial security and independence of its members, and to provide for all members an environment that fulfills their needs, both emotional and economic, so they can live fully self-actualized lives and develop, to the full limit, their abilities as human beings. It being a further provision of the law that such Corporate Families, once established, may, on the vote of the majority of the directors past the age of twenty-one, dissolve the Family Corporation if there are no children under the age of eighteen in the unit and if there are children under the age of eighteen, that the Corporation may also be dissolved by such majority vote if any two of the original incorporators shall undertake to assume responsibility for all children under the age of eighteen and to maintain a suitable home environment for them that shall be in conformity with the original purpose of the corporation. It is further to be permitted to the incorporators to assume for legal purposes one surname for all members of the corporate family, which may be either a single agreed-upon surname or a new joint name combining the surnames of the original incorporators.

[32] NANCY (*pausing and smiling sweetly at the panel and enjoying Horace's astonishment*) There is more, but I think that makes the point, Mr. Vestal. If that Proposition became law, it would restore some of the moral sanity you're so anxious about.

[33] KRAKEN (*to Horace*) Am I mistaken, or does this idea come as a surprise to you? I know it damn well shocks the hell out of me.

[34] HORACE (*laughs*) When you're married to two women, nothing comes as a surprise. Anyway, I applaud Nancy's Proposition. It blends with an experiment now going on in several colleges where the sexes live together unmarried through the three or four years of undergraduate work. After graduation there could be eight to ten years for monogamous marriage, followed by corporate marriage. Such a way of life, if it were accepted, would not only wipe out a great deal of sexual neuroticism, but might well cut the divorce rate in half and ultimately provide all men and women with a new kind of adventure, encompassing several phases, as they grew in their abilities to handle complicated emotional relationships.

[35] STRATE (*jarred out of his ecclesiastical reverie*) Your multiplication in marriage sounds like sheer nonsense. Marriage is a pact between two persons, one male, one female. You and Mrs. Herndon and your absent spouses evidently miss the essential quality of marriage. Marriage is not a sexual playground. It is a commitment the individuals make to God. While I'm not a Catholic, I believe that, in a larger sense, marriage is a sacrament. To quote Matthew, "And a man shall be joined to his wife, and they two shall be one flesh."

[36] HORACE (*smiles broadly*) Really, Dr. Strate, we shouldn't quote the Bible at each other. Matthew also quoted Jesus as saying, "For after the resurrection there is no marrying, or being married, but they shall live as the angels do in heaven." Jesus, in the Acts of the Apostles, asserted: "All mine thine, and all thine mine." Isn't it possible Jesus meant a sharing of the sexual relationship as well as property? Remember, women were considered property in those days. Paul advised in Corinthians that "They that have wives be though they had none." Wasn't Paul's real meaning that men should cease regarding women as property? interpretation to fit modern conditions. The Bible is magnificent history. You won't mind if I say I'm wary of religionists who try to force biblical As history we should enjoy it, both for its perceptions and for its clues as to our failures as human beings. If you trace the monogamous concept of Christian marriage, won't you find it rooted in the patriarchal domination that may have been necessary to the Jews in their time? Today, survival is no longer a matter of the male's skill as hunter or husbander. We've passed beyond the problem of satisfying the needs for food, clothing, and shelter. If I were a religious man, I would think the new awareness of our necessity to satisfy the hunger of man for love and understanding might put us closer to whatever kind of God may exist in the universe or in our tiny world.

[37] STRATE (*smiling*) I admire your seeming idealism, Mr. Shea, but your actions, as reported by the newspapers, belie what you are saying. Whether you accept the Bible or not, modern psychology reinforces the Christian and Jewish laws by teaching us that neither man nor woman is emotionally equipped to share, either in the marriage or in the sexual relationship.

[38] KRAKEN I congratulate you on your tolerance, Reverend. I would put it more bluntly. No man or woman *in their right mind* is going to share their husband or wife with another male or female.

[39] NANCY It's quite apparent, Mr. Kraken, when you were a young man you believed the woman *you* married *must* be a virgin. Down to fifty years ago, more or less, the male *insisted* on the prerogative of being the first to pierce the hymen of his beloved. Now, most people believe premarital relationships are not only inevitable, but make good sense, and we even laugh about postmarital relationships beyond the family.

We laugh, but we cry when it happens to us. Isn't it conceivable to you that we're pointing the way to the possibility of a new kind of marital relationship that preserves the family and that avoids the emotional ugliness of adultery?

[40] David flipped the off-button on the tape recorder.

[41] "There's a lot more." I scowled at him. "At least another half hour, unless you and Tanya got distracted and forgot to record it."

DAY MILLION
Frederik Pohl

[1] On this day I want to tell you about, which will be about ten thousand years from now, there were a boy, a girl and a love story.

[2] Now, although I haven't said much so far, none of it is true. The boy was not what you and I would normally think of as a boy, because he was a hundred and eighty-seven years old. Nor was the girl a girl, for other reasons. And the love story did not entail that sublimation of the urge to rape, and concurrent postponement of the instinct to submit, which we at present understand in such matters. You won't care much for this story if you don't grasp these facts at once. If, however, you will make the effort you'll likely enough find it jampacked, chockful and tiptop-crammed with laughter, tears and poignant sentiment which may, or may not, be worthwhile. The reason the girl was not a girl was that she was a boy.

[3] How angrily you recoil from the page! You say, who the hell wants to read about a pair of queers? Calm yourself. Here are no hot-breathing secrets of perversion for the coterie trade. In fact, if you were to see this girl you would not guess that she was in any sense a boy. Breasts, two; reproductive organs, female. Hips, callipygean; face, hairless, supra-orbital lobes non-existent. You would term her female on sight, although it is true that you might wonder just what species she was a female of, being confused by the tail, the silky pelt and the gill slits behind each ear.

[4] Now you recoil again. Cripes, man, take my word for it. This is a sweet kid, and if you, as a normal male, spent as much as an hour in a room with her you would bend heaven and Earth to get her in the sack.

Dora—We will call her that; her "name" was omicron-Dibase seven-group-totter-oot S Doradus 5314, the last part of which is a colour specification corresponding to a shade of green—Dora, I say, was feminine, charming and cute. I admit she doesn't sound that way. She was, as you might put it, a dancer. Her art involved qualities of intellection and expertise of a very high order, requiring both tremendous natural capacities and endless practice; it was performed in null-gravity and I can best describe it by saying that it was something like the performance of a contortionist and something like classical ballet, maybe resembling Danilova's dying swan. It was also pretty damned sexy. In a symbolic way, to be sure; but face it, most of the things we call "sexy" are symbolic, you know, except perhaps an exhibitionist's open clothing. On Day Million when Dora danced, the people who saw her panted, and you would too.

[5] About this business of her being a boy. It didn't matter to her audiences that genetically she was male. It wouldn't matter to you, if you were among them, because you wouldn't know it—not unless you took a biopsy cutting of her flesh and put it under an electron-microscope to find the XY chromosome—and it didn't matter to them because they didn't care. Through techniques which are not only complex but haven't yet been discovered, these people were able to determine a great deal about the aptitudes and easements of babies quite a long time before they were born—at about the second horizon of cell-division, to be exact, when the segmenting egg is becoming a free blastocyst—and then they naturally helped those aptitudes along. Wouldn't we? If we find a child with an aptitude for music we give him a scholarship to Juilliard. If they found a child whose aptitudes were for being a woman, they made him one. As sex had long been dissociated from reproduction this was relatively easy to do and caused no trouble and no, or at least very little, comment.

[6] How much is "very little"? Oh, about as much as would be caused by our own tampering with Divine Will by filling a tooth. Less than would be caused by wearing a hearing aid. Does it still sound awful? Then look closely at the next busty babe you meet and reflect that she may be a Dora, for adults who are genetically male but somatically female are far from unknown even in our own time. An accident of environment in the womb overwhelms the blueprints of heredity. The difference is that with us it happens only by accident and we don't know about it except rarely, after close study; whereas the people of Day Million did it often, on purpose, because they wanted to.

[7] Well, that's enough to tell you about Dora. It would only confuse you to add that she was seven feet tall and smelled of peanut butter. Let us begin our story.

[8] On Day Million, Dora swam out of her house, entered a transportation tube, was sucked briskly to the surface in its flow of water and

ejected in its plume of spray to an elastic platform in front of her—ah—call it her rehearsal hall.

[9] "Oh, hell!" she cried in pretty confusion, reaching out to catch her balance and finding herself tumbled against a total stranger, whom we will call Don.

[10] They met cute. Don was on his way to have his legs renewed. Love was the farthest thing from his mind. But when, absentmindedly taking a shortcut across the landing platform for submarinites and finding himself drenched, he discovered his arms full of the loveliest girl he had ever seen, he knew at once they were meant for each other. "Will you marry me?" he asked. She said softly, "Wednesday," and the promise was like a caress.

[11] Don was tall, muscular, bronze and exciting. His name was no more Don than Dora's was Dora, but the personal part of it was Adonis in tribute to his vibrant maleness, and so we will call him Don for short. His personality colour code, in Angstrom units, was 5,290, or only a few degrees bluer than Dora's 5,314—a measure of what they had intuitively discovered at first sight: that they possessed many affinities of taste and interest.

[12] I despair of telling you exactly what it was that Don did for a living—I don't mean for the sake of making money, I mean for the sake of giving purpose and meaning to his life, to keep him from going off his nut with boredom—except to say that it involved a lot of travelling. He travelled in interstellar spaceships. In order to make a spaceship go really fast, about thirty-one male and seven genetically female human beings had to do certain things, and Don was one of the thirty-one. Actually, he contemplated options. This involved a lot of exposure to radiation flux—not so much from his own station in the propulsive system as in the spillover from the next stage, where a genetic female preferred selections, and the sub-nuclear particles making the selections she preferred demolished themselves in a shower of quanta. Well, you don't give a rat's ass for that, but it meant that Don had to be clad at all times in a skin of light, resilient, extremely strong copper-coloured metal. I have already mentioned this, but you probably thought I meant he was sunburned.

[13] More than that, he was a cybernetic man. Most of his ruder parts had been long since replaced with mechanisms of vastly more permanence and use. A cadmium centrifuge, not a heart, pumped his blood. His lungs moved only when he wanted to speak out loud, for a cascade of osmotic filters rebreathed oxygen out of his own wastes. In a way, he probably would have looked peculiar to a man from the 20th century, with his glowing eyes and seven-fingered hands. But to himself, and of course to Dora, he looked mighty manly and grand. In the course of his voyages Don had circled Proxima Centauri, Procyon and the puzzling worlds of Mira Ceti; he had carried agricultural templates to the planets

of Canopus and brought back warm, witty pets from the pale companion of Aldebaran. Blue-hot or red-cool, he had seen a thousand stars and their ten thousand planets. He had, in fact, been travelling the starlanes, with only brief leaves on Earth, for pushing two centuries. But you don't care about that, either. It is people who make stories, not the circumstances they find themselves in, and you want to hear about these two people. Well, they made it. The great thing they had for each other grew and flowered and burst into fruition on Wednesday, just as Dora had promised. They met at the encoding room, with a couple of well-wishing friends apiece to cheer them on, and while their identities were being taped and stored they smiled and whispered to each other and bore the jokes of their friends with blushing repartee. Then they exchanged their mathematical analogues and went away, Dora to her dwelling beneath the surface of the sea and Don to his ship.

[14] It was an idyll, really. They lived happily ever after—or anyway, until they decided not to bother any more and died.

[15] Of course, they never set eyes on each other again.

[16] Oh, I can see you now, you eaters of charcoal-broiled steak, scratching an incipient bunion with one hand and holding this story with the other, while the stereo plays d'Indy or Monk. You don't believe a word of it, do you? Not for one minute. People wouldn't live like that, you say with a grunt as you get up to put fresh ice in a drink.

[17] And yet there's Dora, hurrying back through the flushing commuter pipes toward her underwater home (she prefers it there; has had herself somatically altered to breathe the stuff). If I tell you with what sweet fulfilment she fits the recorded analogue of Don into the symbol manipulator, hooks herself in and turns herself on . . . if I try to tell you any of that you will simply stare. Or glare; and grumble, what the hell kind of love-making is this? And yet I assure you, friend, I really do assure you that Dora's ecstasies are as creamy and passionate as any of James Bond's lady spies', and one hell of a lot more so than anything you are going to find in "real life." Go ahead, glare and grumble. Dora doesn't care. If she thinks of you at all, her thirty-times-great-great-grandfather, she thinks you're a pretty primordial sort of brute. You are. Why, Dora is farther removed from you than you are from the australopithecines of five thousand centuries ago. You could not swim a second in the strong currents of her life. You don't think progress goes in a straight line, do you? Do you recognize that it is an ascending, accelerating, maybe even exponential curve? It takes hell's own time to get started, but when it goes it goes like a bomb. And you, you Scotch-drinking steak-eater in your relaxacizing chair, you've just barely lighted the primacord of the fuse. What is it now, the six or seven hundred thousandth day after Christ? Dora lives in Day Million, the millionth day of the Christian Era. Ten thousand years from now. Her body fats are polyunsaturated,

like Crisco. Her wastes are haemodialysed out of her bloodstream while she sleeps—that means she doesn't have to go to the bathroom. On whim, to pass a slow half-hour, she can command more energy than the entire nation of Portugal can spend today, and use it to launch a weekend satellite or remould a crater on the Moon. She loves Don very much. She keeps his every gesture, mannerism, nuance, touch of hand, thrill of intercourse, passion of kiss stored in symbolic-mathematical form. And when she wants him, all she has to do is turn the machine on and she has him.

[18] And Don, of course, has Dora. Adrift on a sponson city a few hundred yards over her head, or orbiting Arcturus fifty light-years away, Don has only to command his own symbol-manipulator to rescue Dora from the ferrite files and bring her to life for him, and there she is; and rapturously, tirelessly they love all night. Not in the flesh, of course; but then his flesh has been extensively altered and it wouldn't really be much fun. He doesn't need the flesh for pleasure. Genital organs feel nothing. Neither do hands, nor breasts, nor lips; they are only receptors, accepting and transmitting impulses. It is the brain that feels; it is the interpretation of those impulses that makes agony or orgasm, and Don's symbol manipulator gives him the analogue of cuddling, the analogue of kissing, the analogue of wild, ardent hours with the eternal, exquisite and incorruptible analogue of Dora. Or Diane. Or sweet Rose, or laughing Alicia; for to be sure, they have each of them exchanged analogues before, and will again.

Rats, you say, it looks crazy to me. And you—with your aftershave lotion and your little red car, pushing papers across a desk all day and chasing tail all night—tell me, just how the hell do you think you would look to Tiglath-Pileser, say, or Attila the Hun?

5

THE KNOWLEDGE-
TECHNOLOGY EXPLOSION

When a distinguished but elderly scientist states that something is possible, he is almost certainly right. When he states that something is impossible, he is very probably wrong.—*Arthur C. Clarke, 1963*[1]

No one can know what the outcome of the knowledge explosion will be, but as one indication of its present vitality, it has been estimated that the current worldwide production of new scientific research would fill 168 volumes of the *Britannica* every 24 hours.
—*Robert Kirsch, 1967*[2]

Physics may tell us how to build a nuclear bomb but not whether it should be built. Biology may tell us how to control birth and postpone death but not whether we ought to do so. Decisions about the uses of science seem to demand a kind of wisdom which, for some curious reason, scientists are denied. If they are to make value judgments at all, it is only with the wisdom they share with people in general.
—*B. F. Skinner, 1971*[3]

Philip W. Jackson (in *The Teacher and the Machine*) reminded us that the threat is never simply from technology; machines are neutral. The threat is people capable of treating other people as machines.
—*Joseph Featherstone, 1971*[4]

Reference numbers refer to source notes on page 312.

magine a worldwide conference, called together at the end of 1945, of thousands of scholars, scientists, linguists, historians—all the learned minds from every corner of the earth, experts in every field from anthropology to zoology. Suppose that the sum total of their knowledge was categorized and weighed and suppose that the conclusion was reached that man had amassed 1000 units of information. In the next twenty years that figure had doubled: Just ten years later it doubled again, and that 4000-unit figure is expected to double again by 1985 or sooner and every decade or less thereafter.

The conference and the figures are imaginary, but the figures do indicate the real growth of the knowledge explosion. "Explosion" is not a completely accurate term—an explosion is actually a "sudden, violent outburst," one which has a beginning and an end. Our knowledge explosion seems to have no end; rather it is self-fueling and grows greater day by day. To many individuals the constant changes that result are threatening; long-accepted "eternal verities" are shaken, and the bases of their philosophies are no longer secure. That "man must work by the sweat of his brow" is not certain any more, nor is the idea that two young people are married "till death do us part." Others see the enormous growth of information as an escape from the binding chains of economic scarcity, financial insecurity, and the many boring, dull tasks that have been a necessary part of their everyday lives.

We are accumulating new information about space and the oceans, new alloys and the molecular structure of brain cells, new drugs and the origins of *Homo sapiens.* Data is pouring out of research laboratories so fast that we have to develop new devices to disseminate it, new words to describe it, new procedures to assimilate it and new machines to use it. Perhaps most important of all, we have to make new psychological adjustments to participate in this era of change without losing our sanity. For the informed, life entails endless decision-making, and both that activity and planning have become more difficult.

For example, new communications satellites might make it possible to eliminate most local radio and television stations all over the world, which could substantially improve the quality of broadcasts through decreased costs per viewer. This sounds good, efficient, and logical. But who decides what programs are to be used? What happens to the employees of local stations and to strictly local broadcasts such as news programs and storm warnings? Total efficiency might not always be desirable, but that statement involves contradictions of many of the values on which our way of life is based. (This question is not purely hypothetical; scientist-author Arthur C. Clarke foresees international education satellites by the end of the seventies. He has been an adviser to the government of India on a program which will have such a satellite broadcasting birth-control and agricultural information to every Indian village by 1975. A battery-powered television receiver will pick up signals from a high capacity space reflector parked high above New Delhi.)

The first selection in this chapter comes from NBC's *Comment!* In the program transcribed here, four world-famous scientists, three of them Nobel Prize winners, discuss "The Frontiers of Science," with Edwin Newman as commentator. Next, Dr. Gerald Feinberg emphasizes the need for long-range planning in a chapter from his book, *The Prometheus Project*. Eugene S. Schwartz warns us of the dangers of a runaway technology in the introduction to his book, *Overskill;* and Daniel S. Greenberg, in an article titled "Don't Ask The Barber Whether You Need A Haircut," advises that we cannot allow science and technology alone to control the future of our society.

Alvin Toffler's article in Chapter 1 emphasizes the problems raised by the writers of these articles. A major question is whether human beings are capable of remaining stable in a world of accelerating change.

A most significant aspect of today's turbulence is our lack of awareness of omnipresent forces. Such ignorance is not limited to the uneducated; it is also found in the halls of learning of the sophisticated West.

Too many historians look only to the past and are unconcerned with current happenings and the potentials—for both good and evil—of tomorrow. Physicists deeply immersed in developing new uses for the laser beam give little thought to the sociological implications inherent in their research. Professors of business education ignore predictions that much of the decision-making now done by middle management may be done by computers within the next ten or twenty years.

The "man in the street" is usually so involved in his own problems that he pays little attention to the importance of the decisions that must be made within the next few years, decisions that will affect the future of humankind. Nevertheless, awareness of the problems, the need to understand the knowledge-technology explosion, is critically important *now.* Time has become more precious than ever before. If we do not know the questions, if we do not recognize the alternative answers, if we are not willing to participate in the decision-making process, then participatory democracy is doomed. Decisions cannot be made by individuals who are ignorant of the religious, moral, legal, and ecological factors involved.

The real problem, then, is ignorance, apathy, or disbelief. Knowledge limited to the few is an invitation to dictatorship. The knowledge-technology explosion must become everybody's business.

THE FRONTIERS OF SCIENCE
Comment!

[1] EDWIN NEWMAN *Hello, I'm Edwin Newman. In our program today, we're going to try to locate the frontiers of science. That is to say, the subject will be what science can do and what it cannot, and what science should do, and what it should not.*

[2] *We have four guests. They are the American physicist, Murray Gell-Mann, a Nobel Prize winner. The German physicist, Werner Heisenberg, Nobel Prize winner. The British biologist, Solly Zuckerman. And the American biologist, George Wald, a Nobel Prize winner.*

[3] *The questions to which* Comment! *is devoted today may never arise in a stark, votable way. There probably will never be a referendum on whether to stay with science, or go back to nature. But scientific developments, and their industrial and technological applications, affect our lives enormously, incalculably.*

[4] *The question of the social and political control of science is therefore increasingly urgent. And these are the things that our guests will be talking about today.*

[5] NEWMAN *It's easy to get in over one's head when discussing science at the level at which our guests today practice it. Murray Gell-Mann is responsible for a theory called the "Eight-Fold Way," which he named after Buddha's list of eight virtues for achieving harmony in life.*

[6] *This theory enables the particles in the nucleus of the atom to be grouped into a few distinctive families, and that, it is believed, will lead to greater understanding of the nucleus of the atom than ever existed before.*

[7] *Murray Gell-Mann, as what I've already said indicates, is a theoretical physicist. He's a professor at Cal. Tech., and he won the Nobel Prize for physics in 1969.*

[8] MURRAY GELL-MANN We have long been engaged in encouraging

Reprinted from *Comment!*, a publication of the National Broadcasting Company.

technology. Why are we now so concerned about limiting new technologies and the widespread deployment of existing ones? For one thing, largely as a result of the application of technology, we are at the stage in our highly developed country where we can solve some of the old problems of disease, hard labor, narrow horizons.

[9] At the same time, we're becoming capable of making really large-scale changes in our planet, the living things that share it with us, and even in the nature of human beings. We can no longer afford to make use of technological innovation in a way limited only by conventional economic costs. Our market economy operates within a system of incentives and controls and we need to design modifications of that system, to place more emphasis on protecting us from unwanted effects of technology.

[10] Unfortunately, it's a highly technical matter to design such incentives. For example, in attempts to control our photo-chemical smog here in Los Angeles, by requiring automobile manufacturers to limit emission of unburned hydro-carbons, and for health reasons, carbon monoxide, we effectively encourage them to raise the flame temperature of engines, in order to maintain high performance. As a result, the emission of oxides of nitrogen went up and smog is as bad as ever.

[11] From the economic and social point of view, I would like to see strategies evolved that would not place the burden of reforms unfairly on the poor, who are not mainly responsible, for example, for our ecological problems.

[12] All this is technical. To take account of these complexities we need something like systems analysis that tries to estimate the effect of everything on everything else. But we have to watch out for some of the evils of conventional systems analysis in which things difficult to put into numbers or put through a computer are often left out, even though these things may be enormously important to us. Including beauty, dignity, diversity, privacy, quiet, the avoidance of too much irreversible change in our natural surroundings, and the feeling on the part of the ordinary person that he has some measure of control of the rapid change taking place around him.

[13] What we need is systems analysis with heart, infused with what I would call humane rationality—avoiding the fashionable extremes of narrow rationality and of insufficient rationality.

[14] We need to develop technologies that accomplish the usual things in a less obnoxious and intrusive manner. We want new technologies to counteract some of the ill effects of older ones and we want to be able to provide new and attractive employment for people whose activities have to be phased out. Meanwhile we need to continue with the old task of overcoming poverty and disease.

[15] For all of this, we need not less scientific research and technologi-

cal development but more—in order to provide a long menu of possibilities from which society can select a few tasty and nutritious dishes that are indicated by the process of technology assessment.

[16] So far I've talked about our national situation, but many of the effects of technology are world wide, on the planet, the human race, and our institutions. What about technological limitation or renunciation as an international concern?

[17] So many areas of the world are very poor—as with our own poor, we must take care that the burden of renunciation does not fall mainly on them. As for the other rich, developed areas, they pose a major problem, since political and commercial rivalry massively impedes technological renunciation. The situation reminds us of the arms race and military affairs, and we need, in my opinion, to work towards technology control agreements, tacit or explicit, much as we work toward arms control agreements. In the long run, we must move toward building the necessary world institutions. The various types of negotiations may even help each other.

[18] Whether on a national or a worldwide scale, can we rise to the challenge? Can we learn to use our scientific knowledge responsibly? Perhaps what we need after all is to undergo a kind of spiritual revolution. To cultivate a reverence for the universe, for its beauty and diversity, as revealed by science and its wonder, as revealed by art. And to cultivate a sense of modesty about our position in the universe and a sense of responsibility for living in harmony with it.

[19] NEWMAN *In 1926, Werner Heisenberg published a mathematical theory called the quantum matrix mechanics. It is considered to be one of the two basic theories underlying all modern atomic, nuclear, and subnuclear physics. In 1932, when Heisenberg was 31 years old, he was awarded the Nobel Prize.*

[20] *Heisenberg remained in Germany during World War II, which was one reason American and British physicists thought the Nazis must be working on an atom bomb. As it happened, in 1942, Albert Speer had read a report by Heisenberg on atomic energy research, and had concluded that the possibility of making a bomb was too remote, so the German bomb project never got very far.*

[21] *From 1946 to '58, Heisenberg taught at Goettingen University. Since 1959 he has been director of the Max Planck Institute for Physics and Astrophysics.*

[22] WERNER HEISENBERG In recent years, the hope for general progress has lost the convincing strength it had fifty or a hundred years ago. It is true, the progress of science and technology has been beneficial in many respects, but at the same time, it also has had damaging effects, for instance, on our environment, on our relations to art, on our whole style of life, which cannot be ignored.

[23] In short, we have now learned the ambivalence of science. The same progress of medicine which saves the lives of innumerable sick people, may give rise to overpopulation and to starvation. By science and technology, we certainly change the conditions of life on our planet, but we seem to be less sure whether the total sum of benefit and damage will be positive or negative.

[24] This is a new situation and it reveals new and unexpected dangers, and these dangers should be considered as a challenge which requires our response.

[25] Let me first say which reactions on this new situation we should try to avoid. We should not draw the rash and radical conclusion that science and technology are unnecessary in the future, are rather harmful than useful, and should generally be replaced by interests in entirely different activities. It would be equally wrong if we would try to belittle the dangers, to forget about the damages to our environment, and would go on with scientific and industrial expansion as ever before.

[26] What is needed is, on the contrary, an attitude of caution, a careful study of the causes of danger, an application of the old principle of trial and error to the new tasks. In many cases, the dangers may be met by new inventions or discoveries, in others, it may be necessary—especially in the highly civilized countries—to reduce some of the artificial comforts of our present status, and to return to a more natural life.

[27] In any case, looking into the future, we should expect that the economic growth will become gradually slower, and will eventually come to a standstill, and that this will be an advantage and not a drawback to our living conditions. This latter point is most essential: The term, "living conditions" implies our environment, our psychological situation, our ease of life, our freedom from too many obligations, and in this respect, living conditions may well be improved by slowing down economic expansion.

[28] The guiding principle in this process of adaptation to a more stationary world will be the necessity to consider any special progress in science or technology as a part of the whole, as something that cannot be separated from the general problems of our way of life, our environment, our political behavior. This obligation—to keep in mind the unavoidable connection and interplay between all actions—will set, and should set, limits to our blind confidence in science and technology, but not necessarily to science and technology itself.

[29] The solution of these problems requires a great effort, perhaps a rather radical change in our way of thinking. But this effort will, to some extent, again involve science and technology, not as a goal, but as a tool. In this sense, we should understand the lesson we have just learned on the ambivalence of scientific progress.

[30] NEWMAN   *Solly Zuckerman is a knight, which means that he's*

referred to as "Sir" Solly, and when he retired not long ago as scientific advisor to the British government, he was made a Baron, which means that he will soon be known as "Lord" Zuckerman, if that is the title he chooses. In the way the British have, he is also entitled to have various initials after his name. OM, KCB, FRS, MA, MD, DSc, and so on.

[31] O.M. stands for Order of Merit. It is a distinction conferred on very few. Sir Solly also holds the American Medal of Freedom, by the way.

[32] Solly Zuckerman was born in Capetown, South Africa, in 1904. As a biologist, he has taught at many universities, including Yale. He also writes extensively and his last book was on today's subject. It was called, "Beyond the Ivory Tower: The Frontiers of Public and Private Science."

[33] SOLLY ZUCKERMAN The impact which new science, and for that matter, new technology is likely to have on our social institutions, on the future state of our society, is hardly ever predictable. The nature and significance of new discoveries or of discoveries not yet made cannot be defined in advance. Neither democracy nor any other form of government can prevent new knowledge from guiding our social institutions into unknown channels. It's done this in the past. It does so now. And it's likely to continue doing it in the future. That's the basis of my argument.

[34] I fully recognize that some people say that this is not so—that it is possible to see in advance what impact new technologies will have on social institutions, and to adapt them correspondingly. But I just can't accept this. The Herman Kahns and other so-called futurologists who tell us what the year 2000 is going to be like are living in worlds of their own creation. The ideas they put forward are simply projections of current trends, and depend on the logic which in effect says that because events have moved in this way up to now, they're more likely to do so in the future than to change. Another of their basic assumptions is that all one has to do in devising a picture of tomorrow, is to look at the developments—the R and D—which are in the pipeline now—faster computers than exist today, better drugs, better communications, supersonic transport, and so on. And they then tell us that these potential developments dictate the social framework of tomorrow.

[35] The ponderous utterances of these oracles are neither scientific nor intellectually very profound. Human institutions do not adapt in a predictable way to changes in the physical apparatus of life. And social habits not only change unpredictably: they also change very slowly.

[36] Did Stephenson and Watt have the slightest conception of the vast social changes which the first steam engine of the industrial revolution would bring about even if indirectly—the vast urbanization, the spreading of slums, of public education, of public sanitation, and so on? Did the first Henry Ford see what the Model T and its successors were going to do to our cities and countryside? Even those countries which operate in accordance with the most advanced planning techniques—

the USSR, for example—do not plan for more than five years ahead. And they always have to change their plans in the light of the obstinate way people often refuse to behave just how the computer says they will.

[37] Obviously there are certain things which can be vaguely seen ahead. We can discern the likely impact of some new technological development. Society, theoretically has it in its power to say, "I like this. Push on with it." Or, "I don't like this. Stop it." We are beginning to ask whether the relentless growth and application of modern technology is or is not eroding essential social values, whether the full price we shall have to pay for this growth is just, or exhorbitant, whether the new development is helping to destroy the physical environment of the future.

[38] The decision to halt the development of the SST is one example of this new mood—almost a very significant example of its kind. There are others not quite so striking. But there are signs that man is beginning to try consciously to control the applications of technology, rather than to continue to live as the impotent victim of the momentum which exists within technology.

[39] We've a long way to go yet. The impact of technology on the population of the world is always uneven, both in extent and in time. The deleterious by-products of the use of DDT may be regarded as outweighing its initial value in the United States or in some parts of the United Kingdom—but DDT is a social necessity in a country like India, where malaria has to be kept under control.

[40] The world is a very unequal place, and this in itself creates vast difficulties in controlling the applications of technology. Nonetheless, we shall have to move swiftly, if the task has not become hopeless because of expanding population. Up to now the growth of science and technology has helped to improve man's material lot enormously. This it has done without much effort on our part to steer the directions in which they develop. We shall undoubtedly have to improve our navigational ability in future if our successors are to benefit from science and technology in the way we have, and in the way our forebears did.

[41] NEWMAN *George Wald was a co-recipient of the Nobel Prize for Medicine in 1967. That was in recognition of work that began in 1932 with his discovery of Vitamin A in the retina of the human eye.*

[42] *That work has gone on. And it has been said that almost all that is known about the chemical process by which the retinal pigment in the human eye transmutes light into sight comes, directly or indirectly, from George Wald.*

[43] *Dr. Wald has taught at the University of Chicago, the University of California, and the Kaiser Wilhelm Institute in Berlin. He's now a professor of biology at Harvard.*

[44] *A few years ago he made a celebrated denunciation of the war in*

Vietnam, and he has often expressed sympathy with the student revolt, the youth culture.

[45] GEORGE WALD Science is one thing, and technology another. Science is the attempt to understand all reality. As such, it is altogether good, as our culture interprets the good. Any other view would be a plea for ignorance.

[46] Technology, however—the application of science to useful ends—is an altogether different kind of enterprise. It may be good, or bad, or much more rarely, indifferent, depending upon the circumstances. Technology is for use, and in any properly conducted society, every venture in technology, new and old, should be constantly reviewed and judged, in terms of the needs, goals, and aspirations of the society.

[47] We ask more and more nowadays the question, should one do everything one can? We used to take it for granted that the answer was, yes. I think we realize now the answer is, no. Among the many things we can do, we need to choose which to do, and which not to do.

[48] We need to do those things that are socially useful. Who is to make those choices? Part of the sickness of our present society is that those decisions are being made almost entirely by the producers of technology—by those who see in the technology opportunities to gain, or increase power, or increase status. I think that in a properly conducted society the final decision needs to be made, not by the producers of the technology, but by those who will have to live with the product.

[49] Do we have institutions for making such decisions? I think we do; but at present they are not working very well, or perhaps better said, they are not working for us.

[50] One example is the ABM, the anti-ballistic missile. Physicists have been almost unanimous in condemning it. Every presidential science adviser, up to, though not including Lee Dubridge, Mr. Nixon's former adviser, has rejected the ABM in all its forms.

[51] We're told that it won't work, that we don't need it, that it will decrease rather than increase our security. Yet we're getting the ABM. Why? Perhaps the best answer is: twelve billion dollars in contracts. In our present society twelve billion dollars speaks a lot more loudly than any number of scientists.

[52] Often where one might most hope for decency, one is offered instead, efficiency. People are proud of doing efficiently what, perhaps, shouldn't be done at all. The matter of saying, "I may be doing the wrong thing, but see how well I'm doing it." Efficiency, however, is a good only when coupled with other goods. If what's being done is wrong, doing it efficiently only makes it worse. That brings us to computers.

[53] We have, by now, to deal with the cult of the computer. Many persons are willing to surrender all judgment when told that a computer

has come out on the other side. But computers have no judgment. They're the perfect case of the idiot savant: like those almost feeble minded persons who are geniuses at mathematical computation. Computers come out on the side, not of judgment, but efficiency. If what's being done is wrong, the computer helps to do that wrong thing more quickly and efficiently.

[54]   Our trouble is altogether with those choices: what to do, and what not to do. We have no quarrel with technology as such, only with its misuse.

[55]   Man has been defined as the tool using animal. The point is now as it has always been—to make those tools serve man, not degrade him. To make them serve life, not death. We need a technology for man. One that will foster his humanity. That is, indeed, our only hope.

SOME ROADS THAT WILL BE OPENED
Gerald Feinberg

Irreversible Changes and Decisions

[1]   In the next fifty years it is possible that, for the first time, decisions will be consciously made whose consequences will radically transform human life. Radical transformations have, of course, occurred before in history, for example with the discovery of agriculture, and again with the Industrial Revolution. What is new this time is that the changes may occur as the result of decisions based on a rational analysis of what the desired goal is, together with some understanding of the probable consequences of action.

[2]   In the Agricultural and Industrial Revolutions, the transformations took place over quite long periods and involved a number of minor, more or less independent steps. There was little knowledge on the part of the innovators or the societies adopting the innovations of what the long-

From *The Prometheus Project: Mankind's Search for Long-Range Goals* by Gerald Feinberg. Copyright © 1969 by Gerald Feinberg. Reprinted by permission of Doubleday & Company, Inc.

range effects would be.[1] It is likely that a sizable fraction of the inhabitants of pre-industrial Europe or of the pre-agricultural neolithic tribes would have strenuously resisted the innovations had they known of their eventual consequences. (The Luddites, who did resist industrialization, were motivated by more personal considerations, such as the loss of their livelihoods.) We, their descendants, are usually happy that this did not occur.

[3] The present situation has several qualitatively new features that make it more desirable and probably also more feasible to calculate the effects of a decision. There is first of all the contracted time scale over which the changes could take place. While the Agricultural Revolution took several millennia and the Industrial Revolution several centuries to develop, the results of the decisions I will discuss may come about much more rapidly, because of the interdependence of different parts of the modern world and the greater magnitude of the forces controlled by contemporary technology. As a result of these factors, we should expect that the time scale for major changes in human civilization will soon be about one generation. The time people require to learn new things might limit any more rapid change, although this mental ability may be improvable artificially, and there is also, as we shall see, the possibility of intelligent nonhuman influences, which might shorten the time scale even further.

[4] If our lives may be transformed so rapidly that the world in which a man is educated to live no longer exists when he is an adult, then some analysis is called for of what changes will occur as a result of some step. The same factors that lead to a shortening of the time scale also tend to make such analysis easier. Thus the advance of technology means that more of the factors entering into any change are under human control, and hence more easily calculable, than in earlier times, when uncontrollable natural causes played a more important role. Also, the technical unity of the world that is developing implies a greater homogeneity of conditions, which should make it easier to estimate the effects of a decision.

[5] Another feature of some present and future decisions that is relevant here is their "irreversible" character. That is, as a result of some decision, the human way of life may change so drastically that there is no realistic possibility of returning to the previous way. Furthermore, this change may foreclose forever a whole range of options that men

[1] This was the case for the Industrial Revolution in England, but not necessarily in other countries such as Japan, where industrialization came later. It would be very useful to study the conscious motivations such as derivative industrialization. This could provide some insight into our own future dealings with technological advances.

might otherwise have followed. This irreversibility comes from several sources. One is the trend toward homogeneity of the human race. Because all human societies are becoming similar, it is unlikely that any islands of humanity could remain untouched by changes put into effect by the rest of the world. This trend is sure to increase as communication improves and the recognition of the unity of mankind becomes more widespread. Hence any sweeping change in man is likely to become worldwide; there will be no reservoir of unchanged men to follow alternative possibilities, unless we consciously choose to maintain such a reservoir.

[6] Another source of irreversibility is the changes in the most fundamental aspects of human existence, such as man's biology, or his psychology, that the decisions may involve. As we shall see in some specific instances, such changes necessarily intensify certain aspects of human life at the expense of others. In the new situation that will then be created, some new possibilities will exist, but some old ones will vanish. We can make an analogy with a traveler at a fork in a road where there are many routes. Although he can follow any one route, he cannot take them all, and taking one precludes following any of the others. Furthermore, if he follows one branch for very long, it may be difficult or impossible to retrace his steps later, and the different branches may lead to very different destinations. This situation is aptly described by Robert Frost in his poem, "The Road Not Taken." To be sure, all choices involve the elimination of some possibilities, but when we are considering fundamental changes in man, the possibilities that we are ruling out by the change may be very substantial ones, and we had better know the consequences of what we are doing.

[7] Somewhat paradoxically, it may be easier to determine these consequences for "world-shaking decisions" than for less important ones. In the former case some of the consequences are so important that we can concentrate on the factors determining these and neglect other incidental results. Hence it seems possible to determine in advance when some action may have irreversible effects and, at least in broad outline, what these effects would be.

[8] In such cases we can take advantage of developments in the social sciences. It is not just temporal chauvinism that makes one feel that we are better armed than any period in the past with methods for analyzing complicated intellectual problems. For one thing, there is a larger number of people working on such problems. For another, the cumulative character of human intellectual effort makes an insight that was achieved only with difficulty in one generation the working tool of the next. Finally—and this will be of more importance in the future— we have developed computers that can perform some operations not possible to humans because of the time and accuracy required. There-

fore, while it cannot yet be claimed that the social sciences can make accurate predictions in very complicated situations, we are much better off in this respect than previous cultures have been.

[9] The questions that immediately arise are, who should make these "world-shaking decisions," and on what basis should they be made? A common characteristic of all the critical decisions that may arise from the progress of science is that their consequences will last for a long time, and affect many people. Therefore, they should be made on the basis of fundamental principles, taking these long-term effects into account. Ordinarily, decisions are not made on such a basis in our society or any other, with the possible exception of some religious institutions. Political institutions, particularly in the democratic countries, have been designed so that it is difficult for one government administration to commit its successors very firmly to any course of action. This has worked as a built-in safety factor against temporary excesses of zeal and has often served a useful purpose in this way. It has also, however, tended to discourage government from thinking about problems that have a longer time scale than one or two decades. The Soviet government has a better record in this respect, probably because of its positive attitude toward social planning in general.

[10] I think it unlikely that the organs of government will have spontaneously changed enough by the time of the world-shaking decisions to be sufficiently sensitive to the long-term issues involved. Furthermore, in the process of governmental decision-making there are inescapable elements of such immediate concern as getting elected, which tends to blur matters of principle. It would therefore be unwise to leave the initiative of deciding about the technological possibilities to the workings of governments, even though these are the natural institutions through which society will react to these possibilities.

[11] I think it would also be unwise to leave such decisions to the scientists who originate the technical innovations, as has sometimes been suggested. Scientists are too selective a group to encompass the variety of interests and yearnings displayed by mankind as a whole; their decisions are unlikely to be based on all of the factors relevant to something that will affect so many people so profoundly. The other side of this coin is that scientists, particularly those engaged in a particular piece of research, are likely to put a high premium on completing that research without too much concern over whatever social consequences it may eventually produce. This is not meant as a negative moral judgment, but rather as an empirical observation.

[12] Finally, I think that the suggestion of leaving such decisions to the scientists misses the point that such decisions require a consensus on goals, which does not yet exist. Scientists are trained to discover facts, not to reach an ethical consensus. It is therefore a misconception of their

function, as well as a misunderstanding of the relation between matters of ethics and matters of fact to place on the scientists a burden that belongs to all of us.

[13] A better approach to the problem of making world-shaking decisions would be for various groups, with as wide a composition as possible, to discuss these problems. If such a discussion is carried through on a broad enough scale, it can create a climate of understanding of what we want in which government action can be relatively automatic, without requiring much of the systematic analysis for which government institutions are ill-suited. Under these circumstances, which I hope might be an outgrowth of the Prometheus Project, the government might really serve the "general will of the people" in making these decisions.

[14] If something like this does not happen, it seems probable that decisions with very great consequences will be made on grounds of simple expediency, either by whoever first becomes capable of carrying through some development, or by some government body that has neither the will nor the capability to see the long-term effects of the decision. If we wish to avoid this, an ethical framework must be provided for the analysis of long-term effects. After this is done, a "calculus" of important decisions will become as feasible as it is necessary. Let us then examine some examples of decisions that we will soon have to face, and we will see that without a new ethical basis, rational decisions will be impossible.

[15] In the last few years there has been a substantial increase of interest in the prediction of future developments in technology.[2] These predictions have ranged from individual leaps of imagination in restricted fields to systematic efforts by teams of experts in many disciplines to make general predictions of what technology will and will not have accomplished by a given time, often the year 2000. These attempts at prophecy are quite interesting, but I do not think we can rely on them even for setting the limits of what we can expect technology to accomplish.

[16] In general, past attempts to predict the future development of technology over any long period have been rather unsuccessful.[3] Most of them, even those made by scientists, have erred on the side of pessimism

---

[2] For example, there is the American Academy of Arts and Sciences Commission on the Year 2000, part of whose conclusions are published in the Summer 1967 issue of the magazine *Daedalus*. Another example is *The Year 2000* by Herman Kahn and Anthony J. Weiner, The Macmillan Company, New York, 1967.

[3] Many ludicrous examples of attempts to predict the limits of technology can be cited. Rather than doing so here, I refer the reader to the excellent book *Profiles of the Future*, by Arthur C. Clarke, Harper & Row, New York, 1962, whose first two chapters contain an analysis of some such efforts. The book then goes on to make some optimistic guesses about the future of technology. I suspect however that even Clarke's optimism will fall short of reality.

rather than optimism. One may guess that the reason for this is that the daily work of scientists requires a careful distinction between what is known and what is unknown, whereas successful conjectures about future advances often involve speculation about what may be accomplished by methods as yet unknown. For that reason, predictions by science fiction writers, who are more willing to speculate, perhaps because they have less to lose professionally by doing so, have generally been better at anticipating really spectacular advances in technology than those by scientists.

from

INTRODUCTION TO
OVERSKILL
Eugene S. Schwartz

[1] The issue is not one of technological optimism or technological pessimism. Posing the problem in this form begs the question. The problem is one of human survival. The role technology can play in the struggle to retain human life on the planet is one of the problems mankind now faces. "It seems possible that the new amount of technological power let loose in an overcrowded world may overload any system we might devise for its control; the possibility of a complete and apocalyptic end of civilization cannot be dismissed as a morbid fantasy."[1] This statement by Don K. Price, former president of the American Association for the Advancement of Science, calls for a new technological realism. The drama now being played out on planet earth does not brook any facile simplifications of a Janus-faced technology that has the potential for both good and evil. Wise men will, it is implied, accentuate the good; venal or ignorant men will choose the evil. Technology as a human-devised means to solve problems is itself in question.

[2] Belatedly, Western man is beginning to realize what he has wrought on his limited habitat. The earth is a finite territory with finite

Reprinted by permission of Quadrangle/New York Times Book Company.

[1] Don K. Price, "Purists and Politicians," *Science*, CLXIII (January 3, 1969), 25–31.

resources. In wasting and despoiling this bounty, man is faced with limits—limits in space, in food, in raw materials, in pure water, in fresh air. The ravaged earth does not fight back but presents its stricken face to a civilization that only now is dimly becoming aware of the limits on the possible and can acknowledge its hubris in nothing more than contrite despair and fear.

[3] The violence against the earth and man that has been the mainspring of the Industrial Revolution has run amok as the possibilities for future civilizations begin to be foreclosed. Technology has hastened the process of foreclosure by homogenizing the world and further reducing alternative futures before the peoples of the earth. With its shibboleth of efficiency, "progress" has jeopardized human survival, for nature through countless millennia of evolution has never been efficient. Survival has been achieved through safety, through maintenance of reserves, through following myriads of paths, through exploration of many potentials, through proliferation of species, through unpredictable divergences and mutations, both biological and social.

[4] What has gone wrong with the "progress" that has led man in but a short three hundred years to the edge of disaster? Has frail man with a propensity for both good and evil misused "reason"? Have the "relations of production" in private hands subverted the utopia that might have been? Has science for too long been influenced by a reductionist technique whereby it is assumed that breaking everything down into its smallest parts will reveal the whole, whereas a holistic science of interdisciplinary endeavors will make the necessary adjustments? Has piecemeal "progress" been too fragmented, whereas a cybernetic model of an integrated "system" will lead to more efficient planning and control? If man has unlocked the secret of the atom and trod upon the moon, cannot similar crash programs, through the mobilization of money and scientist-technicians, solve the problems that endanger man?

[5] It is the thesis of this book that the answer to the above questions is uniformly "no." Man has not misused the "reason" of science and technology to bring us to our present state. Instead, the tragedy of the present was inherent in the basic premises of science from its early formulations of the modern age, beginning with Galileo Galilei, Francis Bacon, and René Descartes, and no reformulation of the questions with which science deals will alter these philosophical defects.

[6] What then of technology? There is a school of thought that says all technology is bad. It is a destroyer of all human values; it is autonomous and has become an end in itself. Another school, the predominant one, states that technology is a great blessing, powering "progress" and advancing humanity while improving man's condition as predicted by the Enlightenment prophets. A third school maintains that technology is but the continuation of the advances that mankind has registered

throughout the ages. It is nothing new, marks no revolutionary break with former practices, and is well recognized as a factor in social change.[2]

[7] An increasing number of technicians, administrators, and scholars, however, confronted with the crises to which technology has contributed, are beginning to ask questions about the role of technology in society. Out of this questioning has come a range of suggested policies. There are those who speak of controlling science through law. The United States Constitution, for example, would add the right to a wholesome environment to the Declaration's rights "to life, liberty, and the pursuit of happiness." The futurists contend that by predicting possible futures on the basis of present and foreseen developments, the future can be controlled and policies, both private and governmental, can be undertaken to realize the most desirable futures. Technology assessment, its proponents claim, can analyze in advance the benefits and risks of exploiting new technological capabilities. Decisions would then be made by political and economic institutions to select those technologies that promise positive results, while those with deleterious results would be withheld. This latter policy is consistent with the views of those who urge technological renunciation or technological disarmament. Man's finger, in this view, is on an environmental trigger that can destroy man as surely as can nuclear weapons. The way to control is through abjuring those technological developments that may have short-range benefits but long-range defects.

[8] The most vocal and widespread policy advocated to meet the crisis engendered by the revolutionary transformation of the earth and society by technology is—more technology. Writing in *Science*, the mouthpiece of the American scientific establishment, Professor Harvey Brooks of Harvard states the case for more technology to cure the ills technology has brought in its wake:

> With respect to the great modern problems—what I call the four P's of population, pollution, peace, and poverty—it may be that articulating these is the most important part of the problem—that once these needs are formulated in the right way, the technological solutions will become obvious, or will fall into place.[3]

[9] Can the reorientation of technology solve the problems technology has created? Can an extension of the scientific genius undo what the genius has done? Can more, larger, and more efficient techniques retrieve man from the catastrophes that threaten him and that arose from fewer, smaller, less efficient techniques?

[2] Emmanuel G. Mesthene, *Technological Change: Its Impact on Man and Society* (New York: New American Library, 1970), pp. 15–19.

[3] Harvey Brooks, "Applied Science and Technological Progress," *Science*, CLVI (June 30, 1967), 1712.

[10] Again the response is negative. New and more powerful techniques cannot solve the problems that technology has engendered because technology is a dialectical process arising from the relationships of man's interaction with nature. Technology is subject to change and conflict. It has limitations and constraints. It can also be self-destructive—and destructive in a way that is not derived from unreason or inefficiency but from the process itself.

[11] The dialectical process of technology is not only self-destructive; it also undermines the science which supports it. The scientific enterprise and an expanded technology are likely to negate themselves and to extirpate mankind in the process.

[12] Ours is an exhaustible world. We have lost much of our freedom to experiment and to choose because of the pressing urgency of the converging crises brought on, in the main, through the agency of the scientific and technological revolutions. We have lost space by shrinking the earth, and we have compressed time to the extent that a child grows up in a world that changes faster than he can adapt to it. If we rush pell-mell into a troubled and dangerous future with the same slogans and practices that have brought us to this situation, can we expect other than disaster?

[13] Man's massive and total assault against nature has been characterized by abysmal ignorance and monumental stupidity. The assault has been led by a political economy that has elevated greed, selfishness, and acquisitiveness to holy virtues and has been abetted by a science and technology that excluded all morality and ethics from its practices. No individual or group bore responsibility for the uses to which knowledge and praxis were put. It is as if the "invisible hand" of political economy were to be matched with an "invisible hand" that would mesh the disparate and diverging sciences and technologies into a human enterprise that would promote human welfare.

[14] The "invisible hands" have brought unimagined wealth and comfort to a small fraction of the earth's population in the short space of three hundred years. To achieve this ephemeral end, the earth has been stripped of its resources and the human habitat has been made nearly uninhabitable. Faced with converging crises and the failure of the "invisible hands" on the economic and the ecological fronts, we are now told that the answer to our problems is "more of the same." More science, more technology, more research. The hubris that has brought man to the brink of catastrophe propels man on to accelerate that catastrophe.

[15] Man, at the peak of a nebulous "progress," is threatened on one hand by a suffocating death and on the other hand by annihilating disintegration. We must now re-examine the tenets that brought us to this state. The reason that is a faith must be re-evaluated. The science that

reached for the moon as mankind began to lose the earth must be questioned. The tools that harnessed nature but destroyed her in the process must be recast.

DON'T ASK THE BARBER WHETHER YOU NEED A HAIRCUT

(Greenberg's First Law of Expertise)

Daniel S. Greenberg

[1] It used to be called planning, but with alterations and hyperbole matching the leap from beer to malt liquor, it has been metamorphosed into "technology assessment" or "future studies," replete with an international conference circuit, a newly established congressional Office of Technology Assessment (OTA), and generous government grants, including $83,000 from the National Science Foundation for Daniel Bell of Harvard to preside over a study of past studies of the future.

[2] Recession being the current condition of grant land, the emergence of a growth industry open to all disciplines (technology assessment prides itself on what they call multidisciplinarity) has drawn favorable reviews —and why not? Technology assessment is a recondite calling, known to few but those who benefit from engaging in its practice. And newcomers to its existence generally feel that, with the sneak side effects of technology so well demonstrated—from automotive pollution to healing drugs that, incidentally, produce cancer—it cannot but be useful to have assemblies of "experts" help us all to look over the horizon. Which is what they will be seeking to do at Congress's OTA, at a new International Institute of Systems Analysis that twelve nations, east and west, have established in Vienna, at Herman Kahn's Hudson Institute and other "think tanks," as well as at scores of universities.

[3] However, we mortals may well ask, like livestock in the feed-additive controversy, "What's in it for us?"

[4] The answer is that the tag "technology assessment" extends the mantle of "science," tattered though that may be these days, to a primitive craft that does not merit—but, nevertheless, will seek to command—great public and political respect as an instrument of impartial wisdom. If past patterns of the advice business are followed—and there is no reason to expect otherwise—the assessors, though proclaiming their independence and even believing themselves, will play the tune of their paymasters or look for new work. (The financial decline of government-supported think tanks, such as Rand, is directly traceable to reprisals by congressional hawks offended by the internal opposition and, eventually, the defections of Randsmen Daniel Ellsberg and less-celebrated think-tankers. Similarly, the Institute for Defense Analyses has taken congressional lumps for a study opposing the SST.)

[5] Like household pets, most assessors, advisers, and counselors sense the virtue of harmony with their masters, a process that extends even to the prestigious National Academy of Sciences, which, though chartered as an independent adviser to government, draws some 95 per cent of its $35-million-a-year budget from the federal agencies that it advises. Not often does the academy offend its customers—which is related to the fact that, in phrasing their inquiries, not often do the customers provide opportunity for offense. What they want, and usually get, is the academy's lustrous imprint on what they want to do or say anyway.

[6] But doesn't technology assessment, assuming skillful performance, enhance the likelihood of better-informed political decisions? The answer is not necessarily yes, for one of the great put-ons of contemporary politics is that deficiencies of technical data underlie many bum decisions. As a matter of fact, few, if any, governmental decisions are ever purely technical; when referred to as such, they usually turn out, upon examination, to be political decisions with large technical components. Should the space program ride on a reusable shuttle or on expendable boosters? Technical? Hardly. The answer depends on the future scale of the space effort, which, in turn, swings on the military and electoral value of a thriving aerospace industry, the intangibles of "national prestige," and the urge to keep the Soviets running hard and expensively to keep up with us in space. NASA, which naturally favors the growth of space work, and hence the shuttle, assigned the inquiry to Lockheed and a New Jersey consulting firm, Mathematica, Inc., which emerged with findings in favor of the shuttle. NASA proclaimed the conclusions as expert and delivered them to Congress. It may be assumed that, if John Gardner's Common Cause had let the study contracts, different contractors would have been involved and different conclusions would have emerged.

[7] In an era in which kept consultants, bankrolled by major institutions, heavily influence the public process, how can the interested but

nonexpert citizen evaluate the prescriptions offered on behalf of his well-being?

[8] It isn't easy, and it is going to get harder as these institutions continue to arm themselves with new ranks of "experts." But there are some hopeful approaches beyond Greenberg's First Law of Expertise, the corollary of which is: *The creators of a technology constitute the worst possible source of advice as to whether it should be utilized.*

[9] Case in point: Secretary of War Stimson, toward the end of World War II, asked the leaders of the atom bomb project whether their creation should be used. Receiving the question at the end of a four-year around-the-clock effort to build the bomb, they naturally replied in the affirmative. From this episode we derive the further principle that not only should the technical leaders be excluded from the decision regarding use of their creation but their sponsors should also be excluded from conjuring up outside advice. In the advice business the desired answer is always obtainable.

[10] Next, since the professionals who gravitate to technology assessment generally come from advanced-degree callings that shun squabbling in public as vampires shun the cross, efforts should be made to set them on each other and promote adversary proceedings. This has been one of the healthiest developments to come out of the involvement of well-qualified scientists in the environmentalist movement. As a result, the in-house and hired experts of the Atomic Energy Commission are everywhere confronted by hostile experts, and the AEC's lullabies about nuclear safety have been exposed as self-serving nonsense.

[11] Going one step further, great effort should be expended toward encouraging and honoring inside experts who put public well-being above institutional loyalty and defect. The implied or explicit pledge of public silence that is normally extracted for the dubious honor of being allowed "inside" does not serve the public interest, and those who break ranks in response to a higher sense of responsibility merit praise rather than opprobrium. Thus, when Richard Garwin of IBM publicly spoke out against the SST while still serving as an adviser to the White House science office—for which he has studied the project—the advisory clique condemned him for breach of confidence. They, of course, were performing in the programed fashion in which they had been raised. But a suitable outcome would be for some organization or other to bestow a nice medal on Garwin. Not that he'd care about it, but the example would benefit others who have shared the impulse but lacked strength.

[12] Finally, to get to tactical specifics: In the promotion of new technologies two innocent-hand-on-the-knee gambits have often been employed—with great effect. First is the "prototype" argument, which contends that the venture is an experiment for which design and construction of a model or two are necessary for collecting the relevant information

concerning whether to proceed. Sounds sensible enough, but construction of the prototype is inevitably followed by the argument that, having gone this far and spent so much, it would be foolish to stop now. Case in point: the disastrously expensive Anglo-French Concorde sst. And then there's the one-in-a-million argument, routinely raised concerning the possible hazards of new technologies. What isn't mentioned is that one in a million can occur anywhere en route from the first to the millionth chance and, as has been the case with several "impossible" nuclear reactor accidents, the occurrence can be earlier as well as later.

[13] When doctors of technology disagree, the concerned citizen is best advised to heed the expert who has least to gain from the proposition at hand.

6

AUTOMATION-CYBERNATION: THE THIRD REVOLUTION

Even those who most vigorously deny the importance of the immediate impact of automation and cybernation accept that its long-range effect will be to replace people by machines. For example, Charles Silberman in his book, *The Myths of Automation*, which was designed to debunk the significance of the development, states: "Sooner or later, of course, we will have the technical capability to substitute machines for men in most of the functions men now perform."—*Robert Theobald, 1968*[1]

IBM's 360-196 does make an error about every 30 seconds, but that's equivalent to one human mistake every 100 years. It performs in a few hours all the arithmetic estimated ever to have been done by hand by all mankind.—*Henry J. Taylor, 1973*[2]

One of four of all the occupations that will be in existence in the U. S. in 1980 doesn't even exist today.—*Sylvia Porter, 1971*[3]

By the year 2000 . . . the average individual will have a disposable annual income of $25,000. . . . But chances are, he won't be working for it. Only one out of ten will be employed and the rest—those who, today, are blue collar, office and middle management people—will be paid to be idle. . . . In this post-industrial phase of easy-street affluence, that very idleness is going to be one of the toughest problems. Hard to fill time. Hard to take pride in make-work projects. Hard to find value and purpose in life.
      —*Nekoosa-Edwards Paper Company advertisement, 1971*[4]

Machines are going to do the jobs now. Man has got to learn to live.
                                                      —*Sir Julian Huxley, 1959*[5]

Reference numbers refer to source notes on page 312.

ore than 2,500 years ago, Hesiod of Greece said, "But before virtue the immortal gods have put the sweat of man's brow." Genesis tells us that "in the sweat of your face you shall eat bread until you return to the ground. . . ." That man must work to survive became a categorical imperative, an accepted fact of life. For many millennia, long hours of daily toil were essential to survival. The Puritan work ethic has become so firmly implanted in our culture that any variation from this accepted pattern is eyed with suspicion and disdain. "Welfare" implies laziness and sloth, despite the fact that the percentage of those receiving it who can work but won't is unbelievably small.

But the cybernetic revolution (which, in brief, entails automated machinery directed by computers) is rapidly moving towards a point in time when man's brainpower will be freed, just as the Industrial Revolution freed his muscle power. And, when this occurs, we may anticipate fewer and fewer jobs available for workers at all levels. What then will be the status of welfare? Even today, despite increases in "real" Gross National Product figures, unemployment continues high. Is the four-day week the answer? Or, as some economists have it, the three-day week? And what will we do with our free time? How will we sustain those who cannot find work of any kind?

Cybernation deserves further explanation. The control principle is based on *feedback,* a common example of which is the thermostat which regulates the temperature of your home. The house cools off; a bimetallic strip in a wall-mounted control reacts to the colder air and contracts in such a way that it closes an electrical circuit which then turns on the furnace. When the temperature returns to the desired setting, the strip bends in the opposite direction, breaks the circuit, and the furnace turns off. It is this feedback or "sensing" principle which has made possible endless worker-free, machine-controlled activities.

Automatic production devices are not new. The turret lathe, introduced well before World War II, is a fascinating tool which inhales lengths of raw metal; sequentially applies a series of cutting, threading, boring, polishing heads; and then expels comparatively finished usable parts. In use for more than thirty years are automatic woodworking machines, almost a block long and about the width of a panel truck, capable of converting raw lumber to complete chest drawers, ready for painting. In fact, Archimedes, in the third century B.C., invented a water device which automatically opened temple doors. So it is not the automatic machine itself which precipitated the cybernetic revolution. It is the combination of automated machinery with a computer that directs the machine after sensing devices, often thousands of them, feed back to the computer constant reports as to the quality and quantity of the finished product.

To the uninitiated, the results are often astounding. A modern bread plant in Phoenix, Arizona, produces 400,000 pounds of baked bread in a normal five-day week, from unloading the raw materials to the finished, sliced, wrapped loaf—with just three men. Railroads keep track of freight cars and route them automatically; many banking activities are completely automated; and new cybernated production devices in the electronics industry can turn out one-inch squares of specialized devices which contain over 1,000,000 components already wired internally. Hand-held electronic calculators (capable of addition, subtraction, multiplication, and division) are produced by automated systems in the United States and Japan and can be purchased for $50. With automation barely started in the automobile manufacturing field (the General Motors Vega plant is an example), the industry turned out the greatest number of cars and trucks in its history in 1972—and Detroit had one of the highest unemployment rates of any major city in the country. Within a decade, engineers estimate, 90 percent of the drafting in this country will be done, accurately and quickly, by computer-controlled devices. In New York City alone, 40,000 elevator operators lost their jobs when automatic elevators were introduced.

Some authorities feel that the service industries will make room for those no longer employed by controlled-production factories. But these too, can be automated. Medicine, for example, is turning more and more to computer-directed equipment—even to semidiagnoses of illnesses. A recent product has the capacity to run twenty-four tests from a single blood sample in ten minutes. Another device will allow a doctor to evaluate the condition of a distant patient's electrocardiogram within minutes.

One automobile manufacturer, at this writing, equips his cars with a multiple connector that will provide the owner with an almost instantaneous printout of engine problems. Computers are being programmed with self-testing devices which immediately designate faulty circuits, and they can be replaced in a matter of seconds. Similar techniques are becoming standard with many of the new color television set models being manufactured. Automation has made the manufacture of pocket transistor radios so inexpensive that it is cheaper to throw away malfunctioning sets than to have them repaired.

In this chapter, Arthur Clarke's "replicator" of the future is breathtaking. "Beam," a "Talk of the Town" article from *The New Yorker* magazine, gives us some idea of the effect of cybernetic production today. Charles Silberman, in a selection from his *Myths of Automation,* is inclined to minimize the impact of cybernetics on employment. Are we all to become a fifteen-digit number in a computer memory bank? The danger is certainly there, and Bob Elliott and Ray Goulding are more than just humorous in "The Day the Computer Got Waldon Ashenfelter."

What are *your* vocational plans?

ALADDIN'S LAMP
Arthur C. Clarke

[1] Today we have devices which can do very much more than this [cameras which can reproduce near-perfect color], though even the names of most of them are not known to the general public. Neutron activation analyzers, infrared and X-ray spectrometers, gas chromatographs can perform, in a matter of seconds, detailed analyses of complex materials over which the chemists of a generation ago could have labored in vain for weeks. The scientists of the future will have far more sophisticated tools, that can lay bare all the secrets of any object presented to them and automatically record all its characteristics. Even a highly complex object could be completely specified on a modest amount of recording medium; you can put the *Ninth Symphony* on a few hundred feet of tape, and this involves much more information or detail than, say, a watch.

[2] It is the "playback," from recording to physical reality, which is rather difficult to visualize, but it may surprise many people to learn that this has already been achieved for certain small-scale operations. In the new technique of microelectronics, solid circuits are built up by controlled sprays of atoms, literally layer by layer. The resulting components are often too tiny to be seen by the naked eye (some are even invisible under high-powered microscopes) and the manufacturing process is of course automatically controlled. I would like to suggest that this represents one of the first primitive breakthroughs toward the type of production we have been trying to imagine. As the punched-tape of the Jacquard loom controls the weaving of the most complex fabrics (and has done so for two hundred years) so we may one day have machines that can lay a three-dimensional warp and woof, organizing solid matter in space

From pp. 158–162 of "Aladdin's Lamp" in *Profiles of the Future*, revised edition, by Arthur C. Clarke. Copyright © 1958 by Arthur C. Clarke. Reprinted by permission of Harper & Row, Publishers, Inc.

from the atoms upward. But for us to attempt the design of those machines now would be rather like the imagined efforts of Leonardo da Vinci . . . to make a TV system.

[3] Leaping lightly across some centuries of intensive development and discovery, let us consider how the replicator would operate. It would consist of three basic parts—which we might call store, memory and organizer. The store would contain, or would have access to, all the necessary raw materials. The memory would contain the recorded instructions specifying the manufacture (a word which would then be even more misleading than it is today!) of all the objects within the size, mass, and complexity limitations of the machine. Within these limits, it could make anything—just as a phonograph can play any conceivable piece of music that is presented to it. The physical size of the memory could be quite small, even if it had a large built-in library of instructions for the most commonly needed artifacts. One can envision a sort of directory, like a Sears Roebuck catalogue, with each item indicated by a code number which could be dialed as required.

[4] The organizer would apply the instructions to the raw material, presenting the finished product to the outside world—or signaling its distress if it had run out of some essential ingredient. Even this might never happen, if the transmutation of matter ever becomes possible as a safe, small-scale operation, for then the replicator might operate on nothing but water or air. Starting with the simple elements, hydrogen, nitrogen, and oxygen, the machine would first synthesize higher ones, then organize these as requested. A rather delicate and fail-safe mass-balancing procedure would be necessary; otherwise the replicator would produce, as a highly unwanted by-product, rather more energy than an H-bomb. This could be absorbed in the production of some easily disposable "ash" such as lead or gold.

[5] Despite what has been said earlier about the appalling difficulty of synthesizing higher organic structures, it is absurd to suppose that machines cannot eventually create any material made by living cells. Any last-ditch vitalists who still doubt this are referred to Chapter 18, where they will discover why inanimate devices can be fundamentally more efficient and more versatile than living ones—though they are very far from being so at the present stage of our technology. There is no reason to suppose, therefore, that the ultimate replicator would not be able to produce any food that men have ever desired or imagined. The creation of an impeccably prepared filet mignon might take a few seconds longer, and require a little more material, than that of a thumbtack, but the principle is the same. If this seems astonishing, no one today is surprised that a hi-fi set can reproduce a Stravinsky climax as easily as the twang of a tuning fork.

[6] The advent of the replicator would mean the end of all factories,

and perhaps all transportation of raw materials and all farming. The entire structure of industry and commerce, as it is now organized, would cease to exist. Every family would produce all that it needed on the spot —as, indeed, it has had to do throughout most of human history. The present machine era of mass production would then be seen as a brief interregnum between two far longer periods of self-sufficiency, and the only valuable items of exchange would be the matrices, or recordings, which had to be inserted in the replicator to control its creations.

[7] No one who has read thus far will, I hope, argue that the replicator would itself be so expensive that nobody could possibly afford it. The prototype, it is true, is hardly likely to cost less than $1,000,000,000,000, spread over a few centuries of time. The second model would cost nothing, because the replicator's first job would be to produce other replicators. It is perhaps relevant to point out that in 1951 the great mathematician John von Neumann established the important principle that a machine could always be designed to build any describable machine— including itself. The human race has squalling proof of this more than a hundred thousand times a day.

[8] A society based on the replicator would be so completely different from ours that the present debate between capitalism and communism would become quite meaningless. All material possessions would be literally as cheap as dirt. Soiled handkerchiefs, diamond tiaras, Mona Lisas totally indistinguishable from the original, once-worn mink stoles, half-consumed bottles of the most superb champagnes—all would go back into the hopper when they were no longer required. Even the furniture in the house of the future might cease to exist when it was not actually in use.

[9] At first sight, it might seem that nothing could be of any real value in this utopia of infinite riches—this world beyond the wildest dreams of Aladdin. This is a superficial reaction, such as might be expected from a tenth century monk if you told him that one day every man could possess all the books he could possibly read. The invention of the printing press has not made books less valuable, or less appreciated, because they are now among the commonest instead of the rarest of objects. Nor has music lost its charms, now that any amount can be obtained at the turn of a switch.

[10] When material objects are all intrinsically worthless, perhaps only then will a real sense of values arise. Works of art would be cherished because they were beautiful, not because they were rare. Nothing—no "things"—would be as priceless as craftsmanship, personal skills, professional services. One of the charges often made against our culture is that it is materialistic. How ironic it will be, therefore, if science gives us such total and absolute control over the material universe that its products no longer tempt us, because they can be too easily obtained.

[11] It is certainly fortunate that the replicator, if it can ever be built at

all, lies far in the future, at the end of many social revolutions. Confronted by it, our own culture would collapse speedily into sybaritic hedonism, followed immediately by the boredom of absolute satiety. Some cynics may doubt if any society of human beings could adjust itself to unlimited abundance and the lifting of the curse of Adam—a curse which may be a blessing in disguise.

[12] Yet in every age, a few men have known such freedom, and not all of them have been corrupted by it. Indeed, I would define a civilized man as one who can be happily occupied for a lifetime even if he has no need to work for a living. This means that the greatest problem of the future is civilizing the human race; but we know that already.

[13] So we may hope, therefore, that one day our age of roaring factories and bulging warehouses will pass away, as the spinning wheel and the home loom and the butter churn passed before them. And then our descendants, no longer cluttered up with possessions, will remember what many of us have forgotten—that the only things in the world that really matter are such imponderables as beauty and wisdom, laughter and love.

from

THE MYTHS OF AUTOMATION
Charles E. Silberman

The Brewmaster's Nose

[1] If there is not now any "cybernetic revolution" in manufacturing, perhaps there will be one soon. How likely is any such event? The answer seems to be—not very. Consider some obstacles that have been encountered in trying to automate continuous-process industries like oil refining, chemicals, and paper.

[2] These industries looked like sitting ducks to manufacturers and designers of computer systems. They are characterized by enormous capital investment in processes in which relatively small increases in efficiency can yield large improvements in profit. By the mid-1950s they had actually gone pretty far toward automation. All that had to be done to achieve complete automation—or so it seemed at the time—was to substitute

Reprinted by permission of the author and *Fortune* Magazine.

computers for the human beings monitoring the instruments and controlling the variables of the production process.

[3] The next step was never taken; there are now about 400 process-control computers in use in the United States, but the essential control of the production process remains in human hands, and minds. Refineries and chemical plants, with their miles of pipes and tubes, and paper mills, with their gigantic machines dwarfing the handful of attendants, may *look* as though they are controlled by machines, but they're not. What is literally meant by "automation" or "cybernation," i.e., a process in which a computer or some other machine controls all aspects of the process from injection of the raw material to the emergence of the final product, determining the proper mix and flow of materials, sensing deviations from the desired operating conditions and correcting these deviations as they occur, or before they occur—we are a long way from all this. In the electric-power industry, for example, which has more than a third of all installations, computers are used mostly as data loggers, recording what happens in the process for the engineers to analyze and study. So far no more than a half dozen or so plants are using computers to control the elaborate sequence of events involved in starting and shutting down a generating station, and only a few plants are using computers to determine the optimum distribution of power throughout the system. In pulp and paper mills, computers serve primarily as data loggers.

[4] Most of these industries have realized large gains in productivity in recent years. But the gains have come less from computers than from better material handling and from installation of larger and more efficient machinery of the conventional sort: for example, bigger electrical turbines and generators, bigger cat crackers in oil refineries, larger-diameter oil and gas pipelines, bigger and faster paper machines. The computers themselves have displaced very few people, if any at all, partly because computers are being used to perform functions that had not existed before; partly because the number of employees involved in controlling the process had already been reduced to the bare minimum needed to take care of emergencies. Computer manufacturers today try to justify their systems by pointing, not to savings in manpower, but to reduction in raw-material costs and increased efficiency in operation.

[5] Full automation is far in the future because, as Peter F. Drucker has observed, "There's no substitute for the brewmaster's nose." The productivity of a paper mill, for example, hinges in large part on such things as a machine operator's ability to establish the proper "freeness," and this he does by watching the water "go along the wire." (The operator watches a mixture of water and fiber going past him; if he feels that the water is traveling too far before draining out, or not far enough, basic operating adjustments have to be made.) There is no *scientific* reason why such operations cannot be automated; in principle, the brewmaster's

nose can be too, and in time it probably will be. But the costs of doing so are inordinately large, and the time inordinately long: no industry understands its production process well enough to automate without huge investments of time and capital.

[6] Consider, for example, the basic oxygen process for making steel. The system designers discovered very rapidly that they didn't have data precise enough to enable them to set up a mathematical model describing what actually goes on in an oxygen converter—the first step in designing a computer-controlled system. The data were too crude because the instruments being used were too crude. And the instruments were crude because steelmen didn't know what quantitative information they needed —not because they were uninterested, but because before computers came along they had no use for more refined data. Hence the computer manufacturer must study the process long enough to determine what information is needed, then find instruments sensitive enough to yield that information in quantitative form, then hook up these instruments to a computer to monitor the process long enough to determine what happens and to identify the critical variables. Only then can it try to develop a mathematical model of what goes on in the process.

[7] And setting up the model can be the most intractable job of all. It turns out, for example, that the mathematics of controlling an oxygen furnace, an oil refinery, or a paper mill are in some ways more complicated than the mathematics of controlling a missile or a satellite. The only mathematical technique now available for handling as many variables as are found in most industrial processes is "linear programing." Unfortunately, as Dr. Thomas M. Stout, a process-control engineer and consultant, says, "practically no relationships in nature are linear." Thus, designers of computer process-control systems have had to develop their own mathematical techniques as they went along.

[8] Each new computer installation, of course, makes the next one easier; in time, computers will be able to control more and more production variables. The point is that the change will be gradual and that it will not lead to peopleless plants. The most fully automated refineries, paper mills, and generating stations now imaginable will still require a work force something like the present one. Even if computers could handle all the operating variables in a paper mill, for example, the number of operators probably would not be reduced below the present seven per machine. As one production man explains it, "at least fourteen hands are needed immediately to re-thread the paper when it breaks"—and the paper breaks an average of twice a day.

The Elephants and the Mahouts

[9] The obstacles are multiplied several times over when firms try to automate the production of more complicated products that have to be

assembled from a large number of parts. Automation, like mechanization in general, proceeds in two ways—either by taking over functions that men perform, e.g., substituting the automobile or the plane for man's feet, substituting the lever, the wheelbarrow, or the power-driven machine for man's arm and shoulder muscles; or by eliminating some of the functions that have to be performed, e.g., eliminating the setting of type through the use of punched tape, eliminating the thousands of operations that are needed to assemble an electronic circuit through the use of printed circuits. Changes that involve the elimination of functions may have great impact when they come—but they come very infrequently.

[10] Most technological change, therefore, involves the mechanization of existing functions—what the brilliant Canadian student of technology, Marshall McLuhan, calls "extensions of man." Three broad kinds of function can be distinguished: muscle power or sheer physical strength; sensory-manipulative operations such as picking things up and moving them elsewhere or guiding a shovel to the right spot with the right amount of force (as distinguished from the exertion of that force); and problem solving, using the brain to analyze a problem, select and process the necessary information, and reach a solution. What distinguishes the computer from most previous technological innovations—what makes it so awesome—is that it can tackle the second and third of these functions, not just the first. This enormous potential of the computer is the kernel of truth—a very large kernel—that the Triple Revolutionists have got hold of, and that gives their arguments so much surface plausibility.

[11] But when we try to apply this newest extension of man to the process of physical production, we start running into difficulty. Many kinds of gross physical activity have already been mechanized out of existence, or soon will be, by simple and relatively inexpensive means, such as conveyer belts, lift trucks, and overhead cranes. The odor of perspiration has largely disappeared from the factory and the construction site. Most of the people left in the production process are involved in sensory-manipulative operations like assembling automobiles or directing a steam shovel. And these tasks—relatively unskilled and uncomplicated as they may appear—are the hardest operations of all to automate.

[12] In addressing a meeting some years ago on the theme "The Corporation: Will It Be Managed by Machines?" Professor Herbert Simon of Carnegie Institute of Technology, one of those working on the furthest frontiers of computer utilization, reflected on a tableau that had been enacted outside his office window the week before, when the foundations for a new building were laid. "After some preliminary skirmishing by men equipped with surveying instruments and sledges for driving pegs," Professor Simon observed, "most of the work [was] done by various species of mechanical elephant and their mahouts. Two kinds of elephants dug out the earth (one with its forelegs, the other with its trunk) and loaded it in trucks (pack elephants, I suppose). Then, after an interlude

during which another group of men carefully fitted some boards into place as forms, a new kind of elephant appeared, its belly full of concrete, which it disgorged back into the forms. It was assisted by two men with wheelbarrows—plain old-fashioned man-handled wheelbarrows—and two or three other men who fussily tamped the poured concrete with metal rods. Twice during this whole period a shovel appeared—on one occasion it was used by a man to remove dirt that had been dropped on a sidewalk; on another occasion it was used to clean a trough down which the concrete slid." Simon concluded, "Here, before me, was a sample of automated, or semi-automated, production."

[13] What the sample suggested was that automation is not, and cannot be, a system of machines operating without men; it can be only a symbiosis of the two. The construction site demonstrated another important fact: we may be further from displacing the eyes, hands, and legs than we are from displacing the brain. The theoretical physicist, the physician, the corporate vice president, the accountant, and the clerk, Simon suggests, may be replaced before the steam-shovel operator or the man on the assembly line.

Our Versatile Children

[14] The reasons are partly technical, partly economic. The technical have to do with man's present superiority over machines in dealing with what Simon calls "rough terrain"—the uneven ground of a construction site, the variations in materials assembled in manufacturing, or the irregularities in the shape of letters, the sound of words, and the syntax of sentences. Man's versatility in handling rough terrain was never really appreciated until engineers and scientists tried to teach computers to read handwriting, recognize colors, translate foreign languages, or respond to vocal commands. The human brain turns out to be, as Herbert Simon puts it, a remarkably "flexible general-purpose problem-solving device." An adult can recognize over a million variations of the color blue. The merest child can recognize an "e" in upper or lower case, in italics or upright, in boldface or regular, in print or handwriting, in manuscript or cursive, and so on almost ad infinitum—and all of these in an almost infinite range of sizes, colors, thicknesses of line, etc. And he can catch the meaning of words spoken by a voice that is masculine or feminine, high-pitched or low, loud or soft, pronounced with an enormous variety of regional and foreign accents. In short, the central nervous system is an incredibly versatile machine.

[15] Its versatility is equally great—perhaps greater—in dealing with activities involving the coordination of eyes, ears, hands, and feet. "Manipulation is a much more complex activity than it appears to be," Ralph S. Mosher of General Electric wrote in the October 1964 *Scientific Amer-*

ican—even the seemingly simple operation of opening a door. "One grasps the doorknob and swings the door in an arc of a circle with the hinge axis at its center," Mosher explained. "The hand pulling the door must follow an arc lying in a plane at the level of the knob parallel to the plane of the floor, and it must conform to the circumference of the circle defined by the distance from the knob to the hinge axis. In doing this the hand, assisted by the human nervous system, is guided by the door's resistance to being pulled along any other path. In other words, the human motor system responds to a feedback of forces that must be interpreted. A strong robot, lacking any means of such interpretation and free to pull in any direction, might easily pull the door off its hinges instead of swinging it open."

[16] The complexity of the economic considerations that determine what to automate, and when, is shown in International Harvester's construction-equipment factory outside Chicago. One of the plant's three engine-block lines is "automated"—i.e., it employs numerically controlled machine tools to machine engine blocks for enormous earth-moving machines, which are produced in relatively small volume. (For any product produced in quantity, conventional tools are cheaper.) But the blocks are moved from one automatic machine station to the next by men, using a simple overhead crane. Right next to this automated line is a conventional machine-tool line turning out vast numbers of engine blocks for tractors and trucks. On this conventional line, first installed in the late Thirties, the engine blocks are moved from station to station by conveyers and other transfer devices. The reason is simple: the volume handled on the "automated" line doesn't justify the cost of installing and operating transfer machinery for a conveyer belt; it's cheaper to move the blocks by hand.

New Jobs, Old Skills

[17] Because it may actually be easier to mechanize or automate clerical, managerial, and professional work than the kinds of blue-collar work that still remain, current discussions of the labor market may be exaggerating the future demand for professional and technical workers and underestimating the future demand for blue-collar workers. . . . The discussions almost certainly overestimate the tendency for automation to upgrade the skill requirements of the labor force. "It is not true," Professor James R. Bright of Harvard Business School, perhaps the most careful academic student of automation in the United States, has written, "that automaticity—automation, advanced mechanization, or whatever we call it —*inevitably* means lack of opportunity for the unskilled worker and/or tremendous retraining problems." In some instances skills are up-graded; in some they are reduced.

[18] Over-all, however, what evidence is available (and there's painfully little) suggests that automation does not radically alter the existing distribution of skills. *Jobs* change, all right, but not the level of skill, particularly as firms gain more experience with automatic equipment. When business computers first came into use, for example, it was generally assumed that computer programers needed at least a college degree. Today most computer users find a high school education adequate, and even this can occasionally be dispensed with. There is an enormous amount of repetitive work, moreover, under automation. The work may involve a different kind of rote, but it is still rote; it's hard to imagine a much more monotonous job than that of key-punch operator.

[19] The crucial point is that we don't have enough experience with automation to make any firm generalizations about how technology will change the structure of occupations. On the one hand, automation may tend to *increase* the proportion of the population working as mahouts and wheelbarrow pushers in Herbert Simon's metaphor and to decrease the proportion working as scientists, engineers, technicians, and managers, because it may prove easier to displace people at these latter jobs than at the former. On the other hand, rising incomes will tend to increase the demand for services, in which jobs typically involve ill-structured problems and "rough terrain"; the demand for teachers, psychiatrists, journalists, and government officials, for example, is likely to expand faster than the demand for ditchdiggers or light-bulb changers. (The large increase in employment of clerical and professional and technical workers that has already occurred has been less the result of technological change per se than of the fact that industries employing relatively large numbers of such workers, e.g., insurance, education, medical care, have increased their output much more rapidly than industries employing relatively few. There has been relatively little change in the proportion of professional and clerical workers *within* individual industries. . . .)

A Question of Costs

[20] Sooner or later, of course, we shall have the technical capability to substitute machines for men in most of the functions men now perform. But the decision to automate would still be an investment decision —not a scientific decision. At any one point in time, businessmen may choose between a wide variety of combinations of capital and labor. Their choice is affected very strongly by the relative costs of capital and labor—illustrated quite clearly, for example, in the fact that International Harvester finds it cheaper to use men than conveyers to move the engine blocks from station to station on that "automated" engine-block line.

[21] In the last analysis, men will not be replaced by machines because widespread substitution of machines for men would tend to reduce

the price of the latter and increase the price of the former, thereby creating a new optimum combination of the two. At any given moment business firms will use capital, i.e., machinery, instead of labor in those operations where machinery's advantage over labor is the greatest, and they will continue to use men in operations where the machine's advantage is the least. For the last 150 years of constant technological change, with only rare exceptions, such as in the 1930s, capital and labor have managed to combine in the United States so as to keep 95 percent or more of the labor force employed. This has been a remarkable record, one that has made the United States economy the envy of the world. It would be premature to conclude that this record cannot continue indefinitely.

BEAM
The New Yorker

[1] One recent morning, we got a phone call from Bill, a public-relations man we've known for a long time. "It's a terrible day in New York, isn't it?" he asked.

[2] "What will your next question be?" we answered, since Bill never calls us to discuss the weather.

[3] "How about going to Fredericksburg, Virginia, with me to see a revolutionary development?" he inquired, unabashed.

[4] Bill suffers from hyperbole, that chronic P.R. malady—he and his colleagues cry revolution a dozen times a month—so we asked him for some details.

[5] Three years ago, he told us, Genesco, Inc., the world's largest apparel company ("A client of yours?" we interrupted. "No," he answered), decided that its cloth-cutting operation was obsolete. "Consider the cutting of a man's suit," Bill said. "A woman in a cutting factory takes a bolt of cloth, unrolls it, stacks it in a pile twenty layers high, puts a cardboard pattern for a specific part of the suit in a specific size—let's say a right sleeve, of a size 44—on top of the pile, outlines the pattern on the top layer of fabric with a piece of chalk, and then cuts through the thick pile with an electric but hand-directed cutting machine. This multiple manual cutting method is slow—a skilled worker can cut only three inches per sec-

ond—and it's inaccurate. One woman may have a sharper piece of chalk or a steadier hand than another, so there are variations in the batches of right sleeves. Furthermore, cutting in batches of twenty may sound economical, but it doesn't work out that way at all. The manufacturer either has to accumulate large numbers of orders for a particular item in his line or has to carry a large inventory on speculation. As for the retailer who wants only three or four green blazers—size 38, short—he has to wait weeks and weeks, until the manufacturer is ready to cut. Reordering becomes impractical, because it's too time-consuming. Are you with me so far?"

[6] "O.K.," we said.

[7] Early in 1968, Bill continued, Genesco went to the Hughes Aircraft Company, which in 1960 achieved the first operating laser ("A client?" we asked. "Yeah," he answered), and asked Hughes to apply space-age technology to its cutting problem. "Three years and one point three million research-and-development dollars later, Hughes came up with a laser fabric cutter," Bill said. "The machine cuts suits far more accurately and faster than has ever been possible before, and it cuts them one at a time, which will give manufacturers and retailers a new flexibility, which will revolutionize the clothing industry. The first public demonstration will be held tomorrow at an L. Greif & Bro. plant in Fredericksburg. Greif, a manufacturer of men's clothing, is one of Genesco's multifarious divisions. Are you coming?"

[8] A few days later, finding ourself in Washington, we decided to travel with Bill to Fredericksburg, where we saw the Lasermatic cutter, as Genesco calls it—a long, sleek gray-and-blue rectangular affair—sitting in lonely splendor in a vast room at the Greif plant. Bill had no sooner told us that it had four principal components—the laser itself, a positioning unit, a conveyor, and a computer (which was off by itself in a nearby room)—than a Hughes technician pushed a button and the Lasermatic cutter went into action. At one end of the machine, a single layer of azure Dacron-and-worsted unrolled from a bolt and moved along the conveyor until it reached the cutting area. Once the cloth had stopped, the computer turned the laser on, and the positioning unit focussed the laser's beam on the cloth, cutting pieces according to programmed instructions. The laser was stationary and its beam was invisible, but we watched the positioning unit going about its business of cutting out the assorted parts of a man's suit—size 40, regular. The positioning unit skittered across the material at a fast clip (thirty inches a second), making Donald Duck-type squawks and causing white sparks (destroyed particles) as the beam vaporized the cloth. Suit fronts, backs, and lapels appeared on the Dacron-and-worsted, and the material soon looked like a page in a child's book of paper-doll clothes. Presently, the Lasermatic cutter came to a stop.

[9] "The laser beam cuts to a tolerance of up to the width of a single thread," Bill said, holding up a trouser leg for us to admire. "Clothes will

fit better—no small advantage in this age of consumer awareness. The computer can store twenty thousand patterns in its memory, and the Lasermatic cutter can cut a man's coat, a woman's blouse, and a child's dress one right after another. With this new flexibility, manufacturers will be able to introduce new styles in midseason. Lasermatic cutters will work twenty-four hours a day, and manufacturers will be able to deliver exactly what retailers want and deliver it in half the usual time. Foreign competitors won't be able to fill orders as fast as domestic producers. The machine isn't patented; Genesco has ordered the first ones that Hughes turns out, but Hughes will also sell them to other apparel manufacturers. They'll cost between four and five hundred thousand dollars each. Genesco's policy is never to fire an employee because of technological advances. Cutters will be given other jobs at the same salaries or higher ones. Would you like to see the cutters at work while you still can?"

[10] We nodded, and Bill opened a door that led from the Lasermatic cutter's rather antiseptic surroundings to a room covering nearly an acre, which was cluttered with long tables, sewing machines, hand cutting machines, and stacks of patterns. Several hundred women, most of them attractive, were busily folding cloth, chalking cloth, sewing cloth, and cutting cloth. Most of the women were wearing slacks, appeared to be in their thirties or forties, and talked to each other as they worked. From a distance, their chatter sounded as Donald Duck-like as the Lasermatic cutter. Each time we approached a cluster of women, they fell silent.

[11] "Why do they clam up when we get near them?" we asked Bill.

[12] "They think we're from Quality Control, and that makes them nervous," Bill said.

THE DAY THE COMPUTERS GOT WALDON ASHENFELTER
Bob Elliott and Ray Goulding

[1] A presidential commission has recommended approval of plans for establishing a computerized data center where all personal information on individual Americans compiled by some twenty scattered

agencies would be assembled in one place and made available to the federal government as a whole.

[2] Backers of the proposal contend that it would lead to greater efficiency, and insist that the cradle-to-grave dossiers on the nation's citizens would be used only in a generalized way to help deal with broad issues. Opponents argue that the ready availability of so much confidential data at the push of a computer button could pose a dangerous threat to the privacy of the individual by enabling the federal bureaucracy to become a monstrous, snooping Big Brother.

[3] Obviously, the plan elicits reactions that are emotional, and cooler heads are needed to envision the aura of quiet, uneventful routine certain to pervade the Central Data Bank once it becomes accepted as just another minor government agency.

[4] Fade in:

[5] *Interior—Basement GHQ of the Central Data Bank—Night. (At stage right, 950 sophisticated third-generation computers may be seen stretching off into the distance. At stage left, the CDB graveyard-shift chargé d'affaires, Nimrod Gippard, is seated behind a desk. He is thirty-five-ish and attired in socks that don't match. At the open, Gippard is efficiently stuffing mimeographed extortion letters to Omaha's 3277 suspected sex deviates into envelopes. He glances up as Waldon Ashenfelter, an indoorsy type of questionable ancestry, enters.)*

[6] GIPPARD Yes, sir?

[7] ASHENFELTER (*flashing ID card*) Ashenfelter. Bureau of Indian Affairs. Like to have you run a check on a key figure named Y. Claude Garfunkel.

[8] GIPPARD (*reaching for pad and pencil*) Sure thing. What's his Social Security number?

[9] ASHENFELTER I dunno.

[10] GIPPARD Hmmm. How about his zip code? Or maybe a cross-reference to some banks where he may have been turned down for a loan. Just any clue at all to his identity.

[11] ASHENFELTER Well, as I say, his name is Y. Claude Garfunkel.

[12] GIPPARD (*after a weary sigh*) It's not much to go on, but I'll see what I can do.

[13] (*Gippard rises and crosses to the master data-recall panel. Ashenfelter strolls to a nearby computer and casually begins checking the confidential reports on his four small children to learn how many are known extremists.*)

[14] ASHENFELTER You're new here, aren't you?

[15] GIPPARD No. Just my first week on the night shift. Everybody got moved around after we lost McElhenny.

[16] ASHENFELTER Wasn't he that heavy-set fellow with beady eyes who drove the Hudson?

[17] GIPPARD Yeah. Terrible thing. Pulled his own dossier one night when things were quiet and found out he was a swish. Kind of made him go all to pieces.

[18] ASHENFELTER That's a shame. And now I suppose he's gone into analysis and gotten himself cross-filed as a loony.

[19] GIPPARD No. He blew his brains out right away. But having a suicide on your record can make things tough, too.

[20] ASHENFELTER Yeah. Shows a strong trend toward instability.

[21] *(The computer informs Ashenfelter that his oldest boy was detained by police in 1963 for roller-skating on municipal property, and that the five-year-old probably founded the Farmer-Labor Party in Minnesota.)*

[22] ASHENFELTER *(cont.)* *(mutters in despair)* Where did I fail them as a father?

[23] GIPPARD Didn't you tell me you're with Indian Affairs?

[24] ASHENFELTER Yeah. Why?

[25] GIPPARD I think I'm onto something hot. Is that like India Indians or whoop-it-up Indians?

[26] ASHENFELTER I guess you'd say whoop-it-up.

[27] GIPPARD Well, either way, no Indian named Garfunkel has ever complied with the Alien Registration Law.

[28] ASHENFELTER I never said he was an Indian. He's Jewish, and I think he's playing around with my wife.

[29] GIPPARD Gee, that's too bad.

[30] ASHENFELTER *(dramatically)* Oh, I blame myself really. I guess I'd started taking LaVerne for granted and—

[31] GIPPARD No. I mean it's too bad he's only Jewish. The computers aren't programmed to feed back home-wreckers by religious affiliation.

[32] ASHENFELTER Oh.

[33] GIPPARD Can you think of anything kinky that's traditional with Jews? You know. Like draft dodging . . . smoking pot . . . something a computer could really hang its hat on.

[34] ASHENFELTER No. They just seem to feed each other a lot of chicken soup. And they do something around Christmastime with candles. But I'm not sure any of it's illegal.

[35] GIPPARD We'll soon see. If the curve on known poultry processors correlates geographically with a year-end upswing in tallow rendering— Well, you can appreciate what that kind of data would mean to the bird dogs at the ICC and the FDA. They'd be able to pinpoint exactly where it was all happening and when.

[36] ASHENFELTER Uh-huh—Where and when what?

[37] GIPPARD That's exactly what I intend to find out.

[38] *(Gippard turns back to the panel and resumes work with a sense of destiny. Ashenfelter, whistling softly to himself, absently begins plunking the basic melody of "Mexicali Rose" on the keyboard of a nearby computer. The machine responds by furnishing him with Howard Hughes's 1965 income tax return and the unlisted phone numbers of eight members of a New Orleans wife-swapping club who may have known Lee Harvey Oswald. As Ashenfelter pockets the information, Major General Courtney ("Old Napalm and Guts") Nimshaw enters. He has a riding crop but no mustache.)*

[39] NIMSHAW Yoohoo! Anybody home?

[40] GIPPARD Back here at the main console.

[41] *(Nimshaw moves to join Gippard, then sees Ashenfelter for the first time and freezes. The two stand eyeing each other suspiciously as Gippard re-enters the scene.)*

[42] GIPPARD Oh, forgive me. General Nimshaw, I'd like for you to meet Ashenfelter from Indian Affairs.

[43] *(Nimshaw and Ashenfelter ad-lib warm greetings as they shake hands. Then each rushes off to pull the dossier of the other. Ashenfelter learns that Nimshaw was a notorious bed wetter during his days at West Point and that his heavy drinking later caused an entire airborne division to be parachuted into Ireland on D-Day. Nimshaw learns that Ashenfelter owns 200 shares of stock in a Canadian steel mill that trades with Communist China and that he has been considered a bad credit risk since 1949, when he refused to pay a Cincinnati dance studio for $5500 worth of tango lessons. Apparently satisfied, both men return to join Gippard, who has been checking out a possible similarity in the patterns of poultry-buying by key Jewish housewives and reported sightings of Soviet fishing trawlers off the Alaskan coast.)*

[44] ASHENFELTER Working late tonight, eh, General?

[45] NIMSHAW *(nervously)* Well, I just stumbled across a little military hardware transport thing. We seem to have mislaid an eighty-six-car trainload of munitions between here and the West Coast. Can't very well write it off as normal pilferage. So I thought maybe Gippard could run a check for me on the engineer and brakeman. You know. Where they hang out in their spare time. Whether they might take a freight train with them. What do you think, Gipp?

[46] GIPPARD Sure. Just have a few more things to run through for Ashenfelter first. He's seeking a final solution to the Jewish problem.

[47] ASHENFELTER *(blanching)* Well, not exactly the whole—

[48] NIMSHAW Oh, has all that come up again?

[49] *(Two janitors carrying lunch pails enter and cross directly to the computer programmed for medical case histories of nymphomaniacs. They pull several dossiers at random and then cross directly to a far corner, unwrapping bacon, lettuce, and tomato sandwiches as they go. They*

spread a picnic cloth on the floor and begin reading the dossiers as they eat. They emit occasional guffaws, but the others pay no attention to them.)

[50] GIPPARD (*as he compares graph curves*) No doubt about it. Whatever those Russian trawlers are up to, it's good for the delicatessen business. This could be the break we've been hoping for.

[51] NIMSHAW Hating Jews been a big thing with you for quite a while, Ashenfelter?

[52] ASHENFELTER (*coldly*) About as long as you've been losing government property by the trainload, I imagine.

[53] *(Nimshaw and Ashenfelter eye each other uneasily for a moment. Then they quickly exchange hush money in the form of drafts drawn against secret Swiss bank accounts as Gippard's assistant, Llewelyn Fordyce, enters. Fordyce is a typical brilliant young career civil servant who has been lost for several hours trying to find his way back from the men's room. He appears haggard, but is in satisfactory condition otherwise.)*

[54] FORDYCE Are you gentlemen being taken care of?

[55] *(Ashenfelter and Nimshaw nod affirmatively. Fordyce hurriedly roots through the desk drawers, pausing only to take a quick, compulsive inventory of paper clips and map pins as he does so.)*

[56] FORDYCE (*cont.*) (*shouts*) Hey, Gipp! I can't find the registry cards for these two idiots out here.

[57] GIPPARD (*faintly, from a distance*) I've been too busy to sign 'em in yet. Take care of it, will you?

[58] *(Fordyce gives a curt, efficient nod, inefficiently failing to realize that Gippard is too far away to see him nodding. Fordyce then brings forth two large pink cards and hands them to Nimshaw and Ashenfelter.)*

[59] FORDYCE If you'd just fill these out please. We're trying to accumulate data on everybody who uses the data bank so we can eventually tie it all in with something or other.

[60] *(Nimshaw studies the section of his card dealing with maximum fines and imprisonment for giving false information, while Ashenfelter skips over the hard part and goes directly to the multiple-choice questions.)*

[61] FORDYCE (*cont.*) And try to be as specific as you can about religious beliefs and your affiliation with subversive groups. We're beginning to think there's more to this business of Quakers denying they belong to the Minutemen than meets the eye.

[62] *(Nimshaw and Ashenfelter squirm uneasily as they sense the implication. Ashenfelter hurriedly changes his answer regarding prayer in public schools from "undecided" to "not necessarily" as Nimshaw perjures himself by listing the principal activity at the Forest Hills Tennis Club as tennis. Meantime, Gippard has rejoined the group, carrying four rolls of computer tape carefully stacked in no particular sequence.)*

[63] GIPPARD I know I'm onto something here, Fordyce, but I'm not

sure what to make of it. Surveillance reports on kosher poultry dealers indicate that most of them don't even show up for work on Saturday. And that timing correlates with an unexplained increase in activity at golf courses near key military installations. But the big thing is that drunken drivers tend to get nabbed most often on Saturday night, and that's exactly when organized groups are endangering national security by deliberately staying up late with their lights turned on to overload public power plants.

[64] FORDYCE (*whistles softly in amazement*) We're really going to catch a covey of them in this net. How'd you happen to stumble across it all?

[65] GIPPARD Well, it seemed pretty innocent at first. This clown from Indian Affairs just asked me to dig up what I could so he'd have some excuse for exterminating the Jews.

[66] (*Ashenfelter emits a burbling throat noise as an apparent prelude to something more coherent, but he is quickly shushed.*)

[67] GIPPARD (*cont.*) But you know how one correlation always leads to another. Now we've got a grizzly by the tail, Fordyce, and I can see "organized conspiracy" written all over it.

[68] FORDYCE Beyond question. And somewhere among those 192 million dossiers is the ID number of the Mister Big we're after. Do the machines compute a cause-and-effect relationship that might help narrow things down?

[69] GIPPARD Well, frankly, the computers have gotten into a pretty nasty argument among themselves over that. Most of them see how golf could lead to drunken driving. But the one that's programmed to chart moral decay and leisure time fun is pretty sure that drunken driving causes golf.

[70] (*Nimshaw glances up from the job of filling out his registry card.*)

[71] NIMSHAW That's the most ridiculous thing I ever heard in my life.

[72] FORDYCE (*with forced restraint*) General, would you please stick to whatever people like you are supposed to know about and leave computer-finding interpretation to analysts who are trained for the job?

[73] (*Nimshaw starts to reply, but then recalls the fate of a fellow officer who was broken to corporal for insubordination. He meekly resumes pondering question No. 153, unable to decide whether admitting or denying the purchase of Girl Scout cookies will weigh most heavily against him in years to come.*)

[74] FORDYCE (*cont.*) Any other cause-and-effect computations that we ought to consider in depth, Gipp?

[75] GIPPARD Not really. Of course, Number 327's been out of step with the others ever since it had that circuitry trouble. It just keeps saying, "Malcolm W. Biggs causes kosher poultry." Types out the same damned thing over and over: "Malcolm W. Biggs causes kosher poultry."

[76] FORDYCE Who's Malcolm W. Biggs?

[77] GIPPARD I think he was a juror at one of the Jimmy Hoffa trials. Number 327 was running a check on him when the circuits blew, and it's had kind of an obsession about him ever since.

[78] FORDYCE Mmmm. Well, personally, I've never paid much attention to the opinions of paranoids. They can get your thinking as screwed up as theirs is.

[79] *(Fordyce notices Ashenfelter making an erasure on his card to change the data regarding his shoe size from 9½ C to something less likely to pinch across the instep.)*

[80] FORDYCE *(cont.)* *(shrieks at Ashenfelter)* What do you think you're doing there? You're trying to hide something from me. I've met your kind before.

[81] *(Ashenfelter wearily goes back to a 9½ C, even though they make his feet hurt, and Fordyce reacts with a look of smug satisfaction.)*

[82] GIPPARD Maybe if I fed this junk back into the machine, it could name some people who fit the pattern.

[83] FORDYCE Why don't you just reprocess the computations in an effort to gain individualized data that correlates?

[84] *(Gippard stares thoughtfully at Fordyce for a long moment and then exits to nail the ringleaders through incriminating association with the key words "drunk," "poultry," "golf," and "kilowatt.")*

[85] NIMSHAW I think maybe I'd better come back sometime when you're not so busy.

[86] *(He slips his registry card into his pocket and starts toward the door, but Fordyce grabs him firmly by the wrist.)*

[87] FORDYCE Just a minute. You can't take that card out of here with you. It may contain classified information you shouldn't even have access to.

[88] NIMSHAW But it's about me. I'm the one who just filled it out.

[89] FORDYCE Don't try to muddy up the issue. Nobody walks out of this department with government property. Let's have it.

[90] *(Nimshaw reluctantly surrenders the card. Fordyce glances at it and reacts with a look of horror.)*

[91] FORDYCE *(cont.)* You've filled this whole thing out in longhand! The instructions clearly state, "Type or print legibly." You'll have to do it over again.

[92] *(Fordyce tears up the card and hands Nimshaw a new one. Nimshaw, suddenly aware that a display of bad conduct could cost him his good conduct medal, goes back to work, sobbing quietly to himself.)*

[93] GIPPARD *(faintly, from a distance)* Eureka! Hot damn!

[94] FORDYCE *(happily)* He's hit paydirt. I know old Gippard, and he hasn't cut loose like that since he linked Ralph Nader with the trouble at Berkeley.

[95] *(Gippard enters on the dead run, unmindful of the computer tape streaming out behind him.)*

[96] GIPPARD   It all correlates beautifully. *(ticks off points on his fingers)* A chicken plucker. Three arrests for common drunk. FBI's observed him playing golf with a known Cuban. Psychiatric report shows he sleeps with all the lights on.

[97] FORDYCE   All wrapped up in one neat bundle. Who is he?

[98] GIPPARD   A virtual unknown. Never been tagged as anything worse than possibly disloyal until I found him. He uses the name Y. Claude Garfunkel.

[99] ASHENFELTER   Y. Claude Garfunkel!

[100] FORDYCE *(menacingly)*   Touch a raw nerve, Ashenfelter?

[101] *(The two janitors, who are really undercover sophomores majoring in forestry at Kansas State on CIA scholarships, rise and slowly converge on Ashenfelter.)*

[102] GIPPARD   Want to tell us about it, Ashenfelter? We have our own methods of computing the truth out of you anyway, you know.

[103] FORDYCE   No point in stalling. What's the connection? The two of you conspired to give false opinions to the Harris Poll, didn't you?

[104] ASHENFELTER *(pitifully)*   No! Nothing like that. I swear.

[105] GIPPARD   Then what, man? What? Have you tried to sabotage the Data Bank by forging each other's Social Security numbers?

[106] ASHENFELTER *(a barely audible whisper)*   No. Please don't build a treason case against me. I'll tell. A neighbor saw him with my wife at a luau in Baltimore.

[107] *(The CIA men posing as college students posing as janitors react intuitively to jab Ashenfelter with a sodiumpentathol injection. Gippard rushes to a computer, where he begins cross-checking Garfunkel and Ashenfelter in the Urban Affairs file on "Polynesian power" advocates in Baltimore's Hawaiian ghetto and Interstate Commerce Commission reports on suspected participants in interstate hanky-panky. Fordyce grabs the red "hot line" telephone on his desk and reacts with annoyance as he gets a busy signal. General Nimshaw, sensing himself caught up in a tide of events which he can neither turn back nor understand, hastily erases the computer tape containing his own dossier and then slashes his wrists under an assumed name.)*

Fade Out.

7

SOURCES OF POWER— SOLUTIONS TO THE ENERGY CRISIS?

The total amount of electric power generated by India would not suffice to light up New York City.—*Robert L. Heilbroner, 1960*[1]

The dimensions of the energy crisis are clear. For example, demand for electricity doubles each decade, but supplies of gas and oil that today furnish 75 per cent of the nation's energy are running out. Estimates are that current domestic supplies of natural gas will be exhausted in the 1990s.—*Frank Carey, 1972*[2]

Johnny had 3 truckloads of plutonium. He used 3 of them to light New York for 1 year. How much plutonium did Johnny have left? *Answer:* 3 truckloads.

—*North American Rockwell advertisement, 1968*[3]

The proposal to harness the winds envisions huge windmills located 10 or more miles off the New England and New York coasts and fixed atop 150-foot size towers rising from stationary floating platforms or anchored directly to the seabed of the continental shelf.—*Frank Carey, 1972*[4]

Reference numbers refer to source notes on page 312.

nless, consciously or unconsciously, we become twentieth-century Luddites (hand weavers who attempted to destroy weaving machines in the early nineteenth century) we need power—enormous quantities of it. Unless we follow Schwartz's warnings in *Overskill* and attempt to stop the onward rush of technology, we must quickly find vast new sources of power. With the exception of coal, our fossil fuels are rapidly running out. Not only has demand for more power in the industrialized world skyrocketed, but the newly-emerging nations are beginning to make their claims for the electricity that will enable them to raise living standards in many impoverished areas.

We can expect little more from hydroelectric sources. More and more frequently we are hearing of the negative effects of the dams used to harness great rivers in terms of the overall ecological picture: huge accumulations of silt, unexpectedly high water evaporation rate in man-made lakes. The Aswan Dam has been termed a disaster by some experts, and others shudder at the hoped-for series of dams suggested for the Mekong in Indochina.

Even if our population were stabilized in the United States, a possibility which is not anticipated until the early part of the twenty-first century despite our drop in birth rate, last year's luxuries have become this year's necessities. Many parts of the country have experienced blackouts and brownouts, almost at the whim of the weather. American industrialization demands power; other highly productive nations are also facing greatly increased energy needs.

Merely building new power generators is not the simple solution it seems to be. New York City is in serious danger of power shortages because plans for atomic fission power plants along the Hudson River have been blocked by aroused citizens who fear radiation poisoning as well as the damage that will result from thermonuclear heating of the river itself. In the four-corners area where Arizona, New Mexico, Colorado and Utah meet, no less than five fossil fuel plants are starting up or being built, to supply power mainly, say the residents bitterly, to residents in southern California. Monstrous machines, capable of gouging 250,000 pounds of rubble out of the earth at a single gulp, are tearing through Black Mesa, a plateau sacred to the Navajos, to strip-mine the low-grade coal which will provide power for the plants.

Nuclear scientists disagree with their colleagues on the safety of nuclear fission plants. Ecologists demand pollution-control devices for fossil fuel utilization that engineers claim are economically impossible to meet. Natural gas sources are diminishing so rapidly that economists anticipate that only huge expenditures for exploration and transportation from outside the United States will enable its continued use.

As a result, great numbers of geologists and other scientists are pressing for new solutions to the power problem. Federal funds for research in the United States have been directed mainly at a nuclear fission-type source called the fast breeder reactor, a miracle source in that it produces more fuel than it consumes. (We could possibly face a future crisis in trying to find a way to dispose of excess plutonium, the reusable product of this method!) A breeder reactor is expected to be in operation before the end of this decade. The U.S.S.R., France, and other nations are attempting to evolve the far more complex technology of fusion reactors, which are presumably safer, and for which there are unlimited supplies of fuel. Other groups are trying to combine the production of atomic power, desalinization of sea water, and production of fertilizers using a single plant. In view of the urgency of the problems, still other researchers are investigating the power potential of earth-core heat, the possible utility of underground steam sources, and a practical method of converting the energy of the sun's rays. Each technology has its positive and negative aspects. Each calls for enormous expenditures for the research alone. Each may present us with entirely new problems which even the most prescient engineers and scientists have not been able to envisage.

Our articles include a report by Richard Post and Scott Kelso on the research being done in this country on nuclear fusion as a source of power. John Lear evaluates the potential for the use of geothermal heat in "Clean Power from Inside the Earth," while Nilo Lindgren describes the work that is being done to take advantage of the unlimited resources of solar power in "Technology Reshapes the Southwest."

Another interesting point of view is formulated by Edmund Faltermayer in the final selection. His article, "Do We Really *Need* All Those Kilowatts?" raises questions which are pointed more at the quality of life than the technology of the laboratory. Must Americans continue to be the electric "gluttons" he describes? Is an electric pencil sharpener or an electric can opener essential to the survival of human beings? How about an electric back scratcher? In essence, to what extent are we willing to waste our natural resources to serve our demands for gadgetry? The home, of course, uses only a small fraction of the power generated. Industry's demands are exponential as the Gross National Product continues to soar. Unless nuclear fusion becomes a reality, we may have to make choices.

Scientists, technologists, and engineers study the problem and come to conclusions that are *economically* sound. Government officials examine the political implications of energy-producing alternatives. Environmentalists are concerned with ecological ramifications. A wide variety of corporations is affected by the conclusions reached. But the rest of us are affected, too. All of us, even as nonexperts, must be a part of the decision-making process by expressing our conclusions to the decision makers.

A PERMANENT AND LIMITLESS ENERGY SOURCE FOR THE WORLD
Richard Post and Scott Kelso

What It Is

[1] Nuclear fusion is not to be confused with the nuclear fission process which is in increasing use by electric utility companies. *Fission* energy is created by the fracturing of the nuclei of *heavy* elements (uranium and plutonium) into lighter elements and releases energy in the form of neutrons, gamma radiation and thermal energy. The *fusion* process fuses together *light* atoms (deuterium, tritium, helium 3, etc.) into other elements or isotopes which are heavier than the elements which entered the reaction. To carry out fusion reactions requires the production of an ultra-high-temperature plasma (ionized gas) composed of these elements, which would then react with the release of energy (in the form of fast-flying reaction products) which can be captured and has the potentiality of being directly converted into electricity. Deuterium, the fusion reactor's main fuel, is found abundantly in water. Each gallon of sea water, for example, can deliver deuterium equal to 300 gallons of gasoline in energy. The cost of separation of deuterium from water is so low that fusion fuel would cost less than one percent of the cost of coal, on a per-unit-of-energy basis.

Why Its Extraordinary Promise

[2] Fusion energy is kind to the ecosystem. The fusion process does not result in radioactive ashes and produces minimal radiation. It burns no fossil fuels and releases no noxious products. In contrast the fission

Reprinted with permission from the October, 1972, issue of *Center Report,* a publication of the Center for the Study of Democratic Institutions, Santa Barbara, California.

process now being used in an ever-growing number of nuclear power plants (nukes) creates a large amount of dangerous radioactive wastes. According to present practice these are shipped by rail or truck and stored in tanks or in underground caverns. There are other dangers inherent in nuclear fission, among them the hazard, wryly called the "China Syndrome," in which a "failure of cooling" accident could occur, allowing the reactor core to melt its way down all the way to China!

[3] According to Post's calculations there is a factor of 100,000 to a million between the biological hazard potential of the fusion reactor and the fission reactor, in favor of fusion. [For more than twenty years, Richard Post, physicist, and colleagues at the Lawrence Livermore Laboratory have been working on achieving fusion power.]

[4] Fusion-derived energy becomes a possibility at a time when the world's conventional energy sources are dwindling. Presently known reserves of fossil fuel will last no more than another 150 years at most at projected rates of usage. High grade sources of uranium and thorium as required by the fission process will have been used up within a relatively few decades, leading to increased costs and sharpening the energy crisis for have-not nations. Fusion fuel reserves, on the other hand, are virtually inexhaustible. The deuterium in a cubic meter of sea water can provide the energy equivalent of 2000 barrels of oil; the total deuterium reserve in the waters of the oceans is good for billions of years at any conceivable rate of energy usage.

[5] A third argument in favor of fusion-derived energy is the problem of material accountability and the possibility of sabotage. Fission reactors utilize substances which can be converted into nuclear weapons. Fusion reactors do not. Fission reactors could be sabotaged with disastrous environmental consequences. Fusion reactors could not.

Where It's At

[6] Controlled fusion research began about twenty years ago, in secrecy and almost simultaneously, in the U.S., the U.K., and the U.S.S.R. Secrecy was ended by international agreement in 1958. Since then an unusually high degree of international cooperation has existed in the field. The present worldwide fusion research effort is about the equivalent of $120,000,000. About 40 per cent of it is taking place in the Soviet Union, 16 per cent of it in the U.S. and the balance in the U.K., Western Europe and Japan. The world political effects of final proof of fusion feasibility are difficult to imagine. It might have a dramatic effect, for example, on the pricing structure of mid-East oil.

When Will It Be Commercially Applicable?

[7] If progress on magnetic confinement of fusion energy continues as expected, fusion experiments proving the scientific feasibility of fusion

reactors could be operational by 1980. Traditionally the time lag between scientific proof and full commercial development ranges between thirty to forty years. For fusion this time lag might be substantially shortened since many of the severe technological problems that must be solved to build a fusion reactor will have already been solved in the course of proving scientific feasibility. Among them: large scale super conducting magnet coils, intense particle beams, good vacuums. These development-type problems have been and are being solved concurrently with the necessary qualitative preparatory research. Today fusion research is centered more on quantitative questions, questions of how to make the various processes sufficiently efficient to achieve net power release.

[8] With high priority governmental support an organized program of concurrent R & D [Research & Development] toward an integrated industrial complex with fusion energy at its core could conceivably lead to early alleviation of the worldwide scarcities caused, in large part, by high energy costs. A bold and far-sighted energy policy should put fusion as the next necessary step *beyond* the fission reactor, supplanting it at the earliest possible date. The cost of exploring the remaining scientific problems of the fusion reactor (primarily confinement physics) is minimal compared to its future value as a permanent and limitless energy source for the world.

How To Put It To Work

[9] (Recent Center resident member, Scott Kelso, who heads a Texas-based fossil fuel and mineral exploration corporation, provided some ideas on how fusion energy plants will be capitalized.) Several alternatives to financing what will probably be a multi-billion dollar effort are available. One model would be the Manhattan Project in which different facets of the project were farmed out under government financing, in large part. Another is the COMSAT model, a corporation which has brought together both private and public funding. A third model is to be found in NASA. One might see certain aerospace and oil companies as prime and sub-contractors. Finally, there could be a consortium.

[10] If this is going to be a multi-billion dollar effort no one company, not even one the size of General Motors, could undertake it. Probably the most efficient method of getting there fast is to tap what private industry can do well and to make ownership available to everybody, COMSAT-style. Because of the magnitude of the venture there is no possibility of fusion energy becoming the domain or province of one or two or three large companies.

[11] There is no real reason not to share the know-how. It is just as much in the U.S. interest for Chile to have inexpensive energy as it is for us to have it. Primary fuel, deuterium, is readily available to everyone. Here is an area which could bring about a new intensity of international

cooperation. There's every chance that fusion energy production will be one of the very few ventures in which we can engage without international competitiveness.

[12] Why? Because if fusion energy were to become feasible our reasons for being competitive might drop by an order of magnitude. It means that everyone would have the means to achieve wealth, namely unlimited energy resources. What would we compete for? Technically it is probably the most promising possibility for dampening destructive competitiveness in the world. *It could be the most revolutionary thing that has happened in a thousand years.*

CLEAN POWER FROM INSIDE THE EARTH
John Lear

CERRO PRIETO, MEXICO

[1] I could see the pillar of water boiling into the sky while our party was still miles away from the spout in the earth from which it spurted.

[2] I could hear the pillar's awesome roaring long before I came to stand beside it and learn that it was moving at the speed of sound.

[3] I felt no trace of dampness in the dry, desert air as I stood there. Though only 20 per cent of the pillar was steam, all but the steam evaporated within 100 feet of the ground—so enormous were the heat and pressure driving the water from below.

[4] What was the source of this fabulous energy?

[5] The spout of it was on the edge of a field of fourteen other blowholes from which trapped steam billowed gently eight miles west of the dormant volcano known hereabouts as "the black hill." The water and the steam together were escaping from a vast underground sponge of porous rock, saturated with brine that had seeped down through the

desert bed of the Colorado River. Trapped within the sponge, the water reached boiling temperature by conduction from the solid rock below it. Under that solid rock lay congealing magma, pushed up from Earth's molten interior by an overturning of the floor of the Pacific Ocean.

[6] In the past fifteen years, geophysicists have come to recognize that this overturning occurs on all the ocean floors and is usually marked by flow of lava through the crests of mid-ocean mountain ridges. The Pacific differs somewhat from the other oceans; instead of a mountain chain it has on its bottom a domed blister that has pushed its way under the North American continent perhaps as far east as the Mississippi River. During the last million or so years, the pressure of this intruding dome has been slowly tearing from the continent the Baja California peninsula of Mexico and the segment of California lying south and west of the San Andreas Fault, a great rift in the planet's surface. As this movement proceeds, the Gulf of California gradually widens. Although the heat thus released is evidenced by hot springs all over the American West, the escaping energy asserts itself especially in the Salton trough, a twenty- to ninety-mile-broad geological feature that extends for 150 miles from the shores of the Gulf to the San Gorgonia Pass in the Santa Rosa Mountains of Southern California.

[7] Photographs taken from Gemini and Apollo spacecraft suggest that at the Mexican border the Salton trough is at least forty miles and maybe sixty miles wide. Gravity anomaly studies indicate that from the border southward the trough is underlaid by sedimentary (spongy) rocks to a depth of 20,000 feet. Geologists have estimated that such an extensive sponge should hold boiling water enough to cover somewhere between three billion and ten billion acres of land to a depth of one foot. Cerro Prieto, "the black hill," is a characteristic symbol of this buried power, and here the Toshiba Company of Japan is installing for the Mexicans a set of specially designed turbines to turn the escaping steam into electric power by the beginning of summer 1972.

[8] The Geothermal Energy Commission, an agency of Mexico's Federal Electricity Commission, has been exploring the potential of underground steam in the Mexicali Valley for the last decade. Up to now, wells have been drilled on less than 1 per cent of the two to four million acres that lie above the subterranean reservoir. The power plant at present under construction has a capacity of 75,000 kilowatts. Plans for quadrupling this output are on the drawing boards. If predictions of qualified experts prove reliable, steam drawn from beneath the valley ultimately may power the equivalent of the metropolis of Los Angeles.

[9] At the moment the Mexicans are concerned only with the steam. But the wells at Cerro Prieto are regularly spaced within a maze of earthen embankments wide enough to carry single-lane motor traffic. Alongside these elevated roadways are ditches running with water, smok-

ing hot. The rectangular basins formed by intersections of the embankments are crusted pebbly white with salts deposited as the escaping water evaporates. These salts and the power together could supply electro chemical plants capable of employing as many as 50,000 primary workers. The usual formulas for servicing such industrial complexes call for five to ten secondary workers in support of each primary job.

[10] It was this dream of a truly golden west for Mexico, about 1,500 air miles away from the national capital and linked economically to the rest of the country by only a railroad line across the Sonora Desert, that brought me here as one of a chartered planeload of guests of the Regents of the University of California. Drinking water is imported in bottles from California to the town of Mexicali, site of the airport at which our plane landed thirty miles from Cerro Prieto. Yet, Mexicali already has a half million residents—more than double the population that was here prior to Yankee industrialists' recent demand for factory space for assembly of various products from toys to trucks in a tariff-free border zone where unskilled workers flock to find jobs. This growth has taken place with the help of a minimum supply of electricity from an oil-fueled generator at Rosarito Beach, which also powers Tijuana and one of the world's biggest sea water desalting plants. A tremendous surge of new growth seems inevitable once Mexicali taps the prodigal source of electricity under its own back yard.

[11] A similar burst of prosperity could be propelled by geothermal steam north of the Mexican border. As was noted earlier, the Salton trough reaches northward from the Mexicali Valley through the rich Imperial Valley of California. The purpose of the visit of the University of California Regents was to applaud Mexican ingenuity and initiative and to suggest their emulation in the United States. In our party was Dr. Robert W. Rex, professor of physics and director of the Institute of Geophysics and Planetary Physics at California's Riverside campus, who is dedicated to a geothermal revolution in the economy of the whole American Southwest.

[12] In addition to the university and the National Science Foundation, financial supporters of Professor Rex's research include the Southern California Edison Company and Standard Oil of California, competitors in the energy market which geothermal steam must enter. For the last half dozen years, Southern California Edison has not been able to find a new fossil- or nuclear-fuel power plant site acceptable to opponents of further pollution of the air and water. And Standard Oil of California, apart from its concern over price competition among oil and gas and nuclear fuel, has been unable to solve the problem of sulfur emissions from oil-burning furnaces. Under these circumstances, geothermal power is attractive because it can be generated much more cheaply than power from

any other source; furthermore, under proper management, it is capable of enhancing rather than deteriorating the environment.

[13] The Bureau of Reclamation of the U.S. Department of the Interior contributes a generous share of Professor Rex's working budget. That share may top $1-million next year. This is appropriate, for the bureau's objective is measurable only in the grand dimensions of promises solemnly made in the name of American democracy. By treaty with Mexico, the U.S. government in 1944 agreed that Mexican farmlands each year should receive from the Colorado River, en route to the Gulf of California, at least 1.5 million acre feet of water suitable for irrigation of crops. Not only has this pledge gone unkept; it has been broken more and more flagrantly with the passing years. Huge flood-controlling dams have conserved the water for use north of the border, the impounded water has lost enormous amounts of its volume by evaporation under the desert sun, the salt content of the water has risen because of the evaporation, and the Yankees have leached the salt out through irrigation ditch drainage and dumped it back into the river, finally leaving the Mexican share of the water not only sadly depleted but so heavily laden with salt that crops irrigated with it are limited both in variety and in yield. Crop failures are commonplace.

[14] There is no greater cause of friction between Mexico and the United States. Two years ago, the Congress moved to demonstrate its good faith by authorizing the Secretary of the Interior to find 2.5 million acre feet of water per year to meet the obligation to Mexico. This amount would provide a safe margin above the 600,000 acre foot loss that occurs by evaporation and otherwise between Lake Mead (created by building of Hoover Dam) and the Mexican border. During the next ten years, the Congressional act decreed, the search for this missing water may not go outside the basin of the Colorado. Interior's Bureau of Reclamation is concentrating the search on three sources: modification of clouds to increase the amount of rain feeding the basin, treatment of sewage in ways that will eventuate in potable water returnable to the basin, and geothermal waters from beneath the basin. Spending for cloud modification now totals $23-million. Arleigh West, who has just been moved up into the Washington, D.C., echelons of the bureau from directorship of the bureau's third region at Boulder City, Nevada, firmly believes that at least as great an expenditure is justified for Professor Rex's scheme to pipe geothermally heated waters to the surface of the Imperial Valley, take off the steam to generate power, use the heat remaining in the brine to evaporate the water (thus slashing the cost of desalination, which consists chiefly of the cost of heat), pipe the distilled water into Lake Mead, and refill the geothermal reservoir underground with salt water from the Pacific Ocean.

[15] The Bureau of Reclamation's hopes are not, of course, built on pure altruism. Yankee farmers and other water consumers north of the border would benefit from dilution of the salinity of Colorado River water as much as would Mexican farmers. Awareness of the potential impact has prompted the largest water distributor in Southern California—the Metropolitan Water District of Los Angeles—and the Imperial Irrigation District to support Rex's work with research grants. Both know that the combined effect of the water and power would be felt all over the Southwest. Furthermore, the power when fed into a national electricity transmission grid could flow across the country to help prevent the brownouts that now plague the East.

[16] The implications of the geothermal initiative of Professor Rex and his team have impressed the Mexican National Electricity Commission, and it has asked him to consider serving Mexico as a scientific consultant. Some such practical expression of the Good Neighbor Policy is long past due. Until today, no Yankee credit can fairly be given for Mexico's geothermal adventure. All praise must go to the Mexicans themselves and to help they obtained from the United Nations.

[17] The roaring pillar of boiling water that awed all of us in the University of California inspection team here at Cerro Prieto is an authentic coda to the Mexican Revolution. It was in 1939, three years after President Lazaro Cardenas expropriated the foreign-owned petroleum properties in Mexico, that he formed the Federal Electricity Commission (CEF) for the purpose of controlling the most powerful means of lifting the peasants from poverty. One of CEF's organizers was Luis F. de Anda, engineer son of a well-to-do Mexican family, who multiplied his inheritance by building hotels.

[18] In those days, the big profit in hotels came from spas where wealthy tourists could soothe their ailing bodies with baths in warm mineral springs. Therefore, de Anda kept his eyes cocked for warm springs while enjoying his favorite pastime of hiking across the hills and valleys of his native countryside. As he clambered over the often volcanic rocks, he came across many bubbling waters in which the Indians cooked potatoes and chickens and boiled off the bark of reeds they then wove into baskets. If the water stayed that hot, de Anda reasoned, Mexico might possess a source of wealth far surpassing the potential of spas. Perhaps the Mexicans could do what the Italians had done since 1904 at Larderello: capture underground steam in pipes and throw it into turbines to generate electricity.

[19] He could think of no reason why he should not drill holes in the earth to test the idea. No reason, that is, except his own lack of technical knowledge of geology. He asked advice of University of Mexico vulcanologist Frederico Mooser and other geologists. The outcome of their consultations was an appeal to the United Nations.

[20] The United Nations turned to Iceland, where geothermal steam had been used to heat homes since 1925. There was Gunnar Bodvarsson, an Icelander with years of experience in exploitation of subterranean water and steam. Bodvarsson went to Mexico in 1954. Now a professor of geophysics at Oregon State University, he recalls that he studied the rocks in the three neighborhoods pointed out to him by de Anda and found them all promising sites of geothermal activity.

[21] In the following years, de Anda started to drill a steam well on one of the sites Bodvarsson had approved—near Pathé, in the state of Hidalgo. Anticipating success in this enterprise, de Anda visited Italy and brought back from Larderello an old electric power turbine. He hitched it up to the steam pipes at Pathé and felt vindicated when it produced usable current.

[22] Luck intervened that same year with the dispatch to far-off Mexicali of a CEF engineer to determine what manner of power scheme might provide a shot in the arm for this forsaken desert region. Outside Mexicali, he saw puddles of ground water bubbling and heard from irrigation ditch diggers how bursts of steam often came up through the ditch bottoms. After confirming these phenomena for himself, he urged de Anda to extend the geothermal search to Baja California.

[23] Five years of deliberation followed in Mexico City. The decision was hard to make. Not only its vast distance from the capital but the almost total isolation of Mexicali had to be weighed. But de Anda's sense of destiny triumphed in the end. By 1960, he was head of the new CEF agency, the Geothermal Energy Commission (CEG). Mooser, who had become chief geologist of CEF, joined him in support of Cerro Prieto's first well. At less than 2,000 feet, the drillers hit boiling water in 1961.

[24] By poetic chance, that happened to be the year in which the United Nations staged a global conference in Rome on unconventional sources of energy. The sun, the wind, the tides of the sea, and the temperature gradients of sea water were considered along with the inner dynamics of Earth itself. When the conference proceedings came to be published, two of the three volumes were occupied entirely with reports of research on geothermal power.

[25] Buoyed by these data and by advice they obtained from New Zealand (where geothermal resources, first put to use in 1925, had demonstrated results worthy of nationalization in 1946), de Anda and his associates applied native Mexican ingenuity to development of an enterprise that is now attracting the investment interests of the World Bank.

[26] Among the earliest Yankees to recognize the significance of the Mexican breakthrough was geologist Robert Rex. In 1961, he was doing research for Standard Oil of California, using heat-flow measurements to determine feasible sites for oil wells in the Imperial Valley. Oil and steam do not mix, because the heat required for the latter dissolves and washes

away the hydrocarbon constituents of the former. In the 1920s, there had been drilling for steam at the southern end of the Salton Sea, which has grown popular as a sportsmen's haunt since it formed in a below-sea-level pocket of the valley between 1905 and 1907 when the Colorado River flooded and shifted course disastrously. Hot water had been recovered from those 1920 steam wells, but the well drillers felt it was too heavily laden with salts to be profitably marketed. So Rex's assignment in the oil well hunt of the 1960s boiled down to deciding where the underground temperatures could be low enough to allow accumulation of oil pools.

[27] In the midst of this heat-flow analysis, Rex heard that the geothermal water brought up at Mexicali held a much lesser burden of minerals than did the Salton Sea steam wells. Deciding to employ his fluency in Spanish to learn more on the spot, he crossed the border and picked up enough information to persuade himself that the geological formations involved would favor the presence of similar lightly salted brine north of the border. He looked again at the heat gradients he had compiled for Standard and concluded that all but one of the proposed oil well sites were too hot to harbor oil. The single exception he considered marginal. He predicted that if a 13,000-foot-deep hole were drilled, the temperature at the bottom would be 500 degrees Fahrenheit. A well was drilled to the proposed depth. The temperature was 500 degrees. The water that came up contained the same percentage of salt as had been recovered at Cerro Prieto.

[28] This well was in the middle of the Imperial Valley. It alone was not enough to convince Standard that drilling for steam would prove as sound an investment as would drilling for oil elsewhere. So Standard abandoned the leases it had obtained for oil exploration. Despite his inability to persuade the company to enter intensive research along his line of thinking, Rex did receive grants of Standard research funds to help support his own studies when he left Standard to join the University of California faculty at Riverside in 1967. Standard made a further concession to Rex in token of its belief in the importance of fundamental research by allowing him to take with him to Riverside the heat-flow statistics he had gathered at Standard's expense and half the staff that had helped him in the gathering.

[29] From that nucleus, in Rex's three years at the university, has grown a laboratory manned by twenty associates and graduate students during the academic year and by thirty persons in the summer months of field work. Key personalities, aside from Rex himself, are Israeli geophysicist Tsvi Meidav, James Combs from the Massachusetts Institute of Technology, Shawn Beihler from the California Institute of Technology, and Tyler Copeland from the University of Chicago.

[30] This crew has determined that heat beneath the valley floor is

two to three times the average for the North American continent, and that spongy rock capable of holding water underground is 15,000 feet thick at the northern end of the valley and 20,000 feet thick at the Mexican border.

[31] In the 1,000-square-mile area covered by this exploratory work, seven especially hot spots have been defined. These suggest the existence of as many pools of buried geothermal energy, bubbling at temperatures above 500 degrees Fahrenheit, with a total potential of twenty million kilowatts of electricity and five to seven million acre feet of distilled water annually for at least three decades and possibly for one to three centuries.

[32] Next spring, Rex and his associates will get down to the serious business of proving out these exploratory findings. Two 1,000-foot-deep wells will be drilled preliminary to a major project set for next fall: a 6,000-foot well from which is expected to be drawn boiling water and steam. Later on, Rex hopes, the National Science Foundation may finance a well that will go all the way down to basement rock and perhaps tap a magma chamber for the first time. Data obtained from study of such a well could lead to a new kind of mining, in which the minerals—instead of being dug from under the earth—would be floated upward to the surface and there separated chemically. Morton International, Inc., which owns some of the geothermal leases on the heavily salted waters under the Salton Sea, has been experimenting with a pilot plant salt separation process and has reported this effort near success.

[33] Rex intends to accept Mexico's invitation to serve it as a geothermal consultant. He considers it profitable to geothermal research in the United States for him to make his sophisticated survey instruments available south of the border. Using the border as a base line, he will define the hot spots simultaneously southward and northward of it in gradual progression and thus arrive at the pattern of heat flow for the entire Salton trough. While exploitation in the north is catching up with that in the south, it will be possible to train young Mexicans and young Yankees together at a Cerro Prieto well that has proved less promising commercially than the rest of the wells in the field. Techniques of power generation and water desalting will be taught as complementary subjects.

[34] In speaking of the future, Rex hedges his public statements with caution. He notes the necessity of refilling the geothermal reservoirs in order to prevent subsidence of the valley floor. He notes that, although geothermal steam is much more cheaply produced than is nuclear steam, geothermal electricity is not always competitive with nuclear electricity because nuclear steam emerges at high pressures and high temperatures suitable for filling large-scale demands, whereas geothermal steam comes out of the earth at relatively low pressures and temperatures better fitted

for smaller markets. As a corollary to this, Rex emphasizes that geothermal steam alone is not a panacea for the current power shortage in the United States.

[35] Privately, however, Rex will admit to a suspicion that the geothermal potential of the United States is considerably greater than anyone now supposes. The Department of Interior's official figure on acreage with demonstrated potential is 1,350,000. But no one really knows because a high percentage of land throughout the West (the area of promising heat-flow measurements) is owned by the federal government and is not now open to geothermal exploration. Since 1962, Senator Alan Bible of Nevada has been sponsoring a bill in Congress to correct this situation, and the two Congressional houses (delayed by one Presidential rebuff) have finally passed slightly varying versions of it after writing in clauses to prevent giveaway of public treasure to private speculators. The differences remain to be resolved in the light of White House insistence that all geothermal leases be subject to competitive bidding.

[36] At the United Nations, there is strong reinforcement for Rex's suspicion. A worldwide conference on geothermal energy held in Pisa, Italy, in the last days of September and first days of October 1970, heard 200 scientific reports, including a significant one from Russia that said the geothermal energy potential of the Soviet Union is greater than all other Soviet energy sources together. Considering Russia's huge reserves of coal, oil, and gas, the Russian declaration has staggering implications. A U.N. official well acquainted with the record of geothermal performance commented after the conference: "We used to think a geothermal field would last only forty years at most before becoming exhausted. We are now beginning to think that a geothermal field, properly managed, may last forever." He cited the experience of Italy, Iceland, and New Zealand in support of this view.

[37] That view may be extreme. But the men who hold it feel justified by the queries they are getting on prospective geothermal land leases from such globally reputed industrial giants as Standard Oil of New Jersey, Shell Oil, Continental Oil, and Union Oil. At worst, these men argue, small and poor nations can use cheap subterranean energy to lift themselves by their bootstraps as Mexico is doing. The U.N. itself is sponsoring geothermal energy exploration in Guatemala, Costa Rica, El Salvador, Nicaragua, Chile, Turkey, Ethiopia, and Kenya. It has been proposed that geothermal resources in the Jordan River valley might be an economic force worthy of being exerted toward a lasting peace pact between the Israelis and the Arabs. Skeptics retort that this idea may be nothing more than a lofty dream. But geothermal energy has contributed to the economic growth of Italy, Iceland, New Zealand, Japan, Hungary, India, Indonesia, and the Philippines.

[38] The United States is planet Earth's backward child in this appli-

cation of science to preservation of the environment. The 1970 U.N. conference just referred to had been suggested by the University of California Riverside campus. No one in Washington cared enough to pursue the honor. But the Italians were enthusiastic; so the conference went to Pisa. And that is only one symptom of the situation that has prevailed in this country for years. As early as 1890, homes and greenhouses in Boise, Idaho, were being heated by steam issuing from the earth. That steam is still flowing today to 200 customers along one avenue of the city. The town of Klamath Falls, Oregon, has used geothermal steam in similar fashion since the 1930s. There the steam comes from 500 wells and is so easily accessible that local plumbers make the connections routinely. Five hundred homes, seven schools, an apartment house, a nursing home, and several factories are supplied with heat in this manner. At a place called The Geysers, ninety miles north of San Francisco, where a bear hunter in 1847 came upon a quarter-mile-long gash in the earth from which steam was pouring through a series of fumaroles, the Pacific Gas and Electric Company now generates 82,000 kilowatts of electricity and has plans for pushing that power up to 220,000 kilowatts by 1972. How many Americans are aware of these circumstances? Do many know that eleven northern California towns with power-generating facilities of their own have contracted for steam they hope two now prospecting companies—Geothermal Resources International and Signal Oil and Gas—will bring up across the canyon from the lands now supplying Pacific Gas and Electric? Or that Standard Oil of California now holds leases on large tracts of potential geothermal steam producing property in the Imperial Valley? Or that Magma Power Company and Union Oil Company are working together at Brady Hot Springs, Nevada, with the intention of pouring geothermal steam power into the nearby electric transmission trunk line of the Sierra Pacific Company?

[39] It took Congress eight years—years characterized by steadily heightening population and power crises—to approach agreement on means of encouraging prospectors to explore promising sites of geothermal energy. The long delay does not indicate much top-level appreciation of regional effects geothermal energy might have in distributing population over the apparent waste lands of the West and thus relieving the burden on our overcrowded cities.

[40] At least we ought to discover how bright the promise of America's geothermal resources really is. In recent weeks, one new geothermal steam strike alone moved the formerly accepted boundary of the country's geothermal province 800 miles eastward. The well was drilled by James (Pat) Dunnigan of Abilene, Texas, in the collapsed volcano cone that now holds the Los Alamos, New Mexico, nuclear explosive research laboratory. Within this caldera, man will epitomize his real attitude toward his environment, his willingness to assign unconventional competi-

tive values to sources of energy that do not pollute the air or the water and do make possible new belts of green in otherwise barren countryside, and finally his determination to apply his imagination as devotedly to the exaltation of life as he has applied it to life's extermination.

[41] What share of the energy supply of the United States could be provided by geothermal steam? That question is impossible to answer at the moment for three reasons. First, a dependable source of geothermal energy must be proved out before it can be committed. It isn't at all like a coal-fueled or oil-fueled boiler, which simply needs to be built soundly to deliver its promised load. Second, geothermal sources cannot be proved until they are discovered, and the discovery process is only now beginning seriously. Third, a need for power must be confirmed before any share in fulfilling the need can be fixed.

[42] Most economists hold that our present living level can be maintained only if more power is made available every year. But the RAND Corporation, the California "think tank" that acquired global fame for the accuracy of its predictions for the U.S. Air Force, is now in the midst of a study, financially supported by the National Science Foundation, to determine whether an ever-upward spiraling energy supply really is necessary or can even be justified. The same question was raised at the 1970 annual meeting of the officers and corporate associates of the American Institute of Physics by Ali Bulent Cambel, Wayne State University's executive vice president for academic affairs and director of a sweeping White House inquiry into energy problems of the nation seven years ago.

[43] Cambel conceded that "there is no doubt whatsoever that the production of power is the main source of the environmental blight that engulfs us everywhere." But he said he "simply cannot conceive of returning to animate power to supply energy consumed by modern industry. Not only would this be impossible technologically; we would also reject it on moral grounds. Were we to naïvely inclined to substitute animate power for electrical power, we would have to increase the world's animal population immensely. In a food-hungry world, this would be going in the wrong direction."

[44] Cambel saw no hope of early improvement in the prevailing power shortage for the following reason: In this country, energy consumption has been rising at an annual rate of 7 to 10 per cent. But new power plant construction planning has been based on an earlier acceleration of 3 to 5 per cent. Furthermore, reliability requirements (e.g., to take care of unexpected loads and generator down-times) call for a 20 per cent excess capacity that "does not exist in several metropolitan areas" and cannot be provided in a hurry.

[45] "Yet," Cambel continued, "several immediate expedients are well known. These are expanding the interconnections among utility systems,

and installing gas turbine and diesel generating units. We could have been on the verge of having still another option, magnetohydrodynamics, had we not drastically curtailed the associated research and development funds."

[46] Fear of thermal pollution from power generation, "although a real one, should be handled with less hysteria," he said. "Instead of rejecting nuclear plants outright, more research should be conducted regarding site levels of thermal pollution; nor have we made exhaustive studies of judicious design and placement of outlets, or of the distribution of plant sites. Generated power could be transmitted and distributed by means of superconducting underground cables. Although still in the research stage, there is indication that such cables are feasible."

[47] Cambel said categorically that "the limitation of energy consumption lies not in any shortage of resources but in environmental limitations." When fossil fuel reserves, uranium and thorium reserves, the nuclear fusion potential of deuterium in sea water, and non-depletable energy sources (hydro, aero, geothermal, tidal, and solar) are all considered together, man need not fear an energy shortage for billions of years. Because some fuels are more abundant than others, however, careful decisions must be made concerning when to switch from one fuel to another. But these are easy in comparison to the effectuation of controls over environmental pollution. The best hope, in Cambel's opinion, is creation of new counter-technologies that will improve upon the natural environment that our present technologies originally sought to modify.

[48] Goverment subsidies and/or tax write-offs should be provided to industry to stimulate creativity through competition, Cambel proposed. As an example, he cited the possibility of developing household hydrocarbon fuel cells that would obtain their supply of gas from coal gasified with heat produced by nuclear-fueled electric power plants. The external electric wiring leading into a house would be abandoned, but the wiring inside the house would continue in use. The power used in this system would compete with the power supplied by public utilities.

[49] Another example: Direct the Antitrust Division of the U.S. Department of Justice, the Internal Revenue Service, and the Department of Transportation to join in encouraging automobile makers to metamorphose into providers of vehicles for all modern modes of transportation.

[50] Cambel also advocated that "every conceivable fiscal encouragement" be given to manufacturers who invent appliances capable of doing accustomed work with less energy. Such devices would include microwave ovens and stoves to replace conventional gas and electric kitchen stoves; ultrasonic dishwashers and laundering machines to replace washers that thresh water about; electric chemiluminescent lighting panels to replace

incandescent and fluorescent lighting fixtures; and thermoelectric refrigeration and air conditioning units to replace conventional compressor-driven coolers.

[51] In short, the Cambel prescription for tomorrow's energy research and development is vigorous orientation toward less dissipation of energy without curtailing human comfort.

TECHNOLOGY RESHAPES THE SOUTHWEST: PLANNING THE ELEMENTS OF A POST-INDUSTRIAL ENVIRONMENT

Nilo Lindgren

[1] Of the triad of genuinely new great industries that may be emerging in the Southwest, possibly the most stupendous in terms of its long-term consequences, the one that could draw many other industries in its train, is that of the conversion of solar energy into electrical power. Solar energy, which has been studied since the 1930s, had gained a tarnished reputation in scientists' eyes in recent years and had been nearly given up for hopeless a bare two years ago. But now the real possibility of practical solar energy—enough to electrify the entire nation—has found its rebirth in the sunny Southwest. The importance of this project, which is already drawing university, industry, utility, and government groups together, can hardly be exaggerated, especially since all objective studies point to the fact of a chronic energy shortage for the remainder of this century.

[2] Most appropriately, one can trace the origin of this development to the establishment of the Kitt Peak National Observatory. It was the first director of Kitt Peak, Aden Meinel, who is now riding the solar energy project.

[3] Dr. Meinel, who had been working in the fields of astrophysics, spectroscopy, optical design, and instrumentation, and his wife, Marjorie,

also a scientist, actually had their attention drawn to the problems of solar energy by a 1970 report of the National Academy of Sciences Committee on Resources and Man. That report, which dismissed solar energy as having little promise for meeting future energy needs, made the Meinels wonder about what had happened to the great predictions for solar energy that had been making newspaper headlines just about the time they arrived in Arizona in 1955.

[4] When they went on sabbatical leave a little more than a year ago, the Meinels decided to trace what had happened in solar energy technology. They knew that crucial problems were besetting the nuclear energy field in which so much hope had also been placed for meeting our long-term energy needs. Work has been going on for twenty years on developing safe breeder reactors, but crucial problems in intensive materials incompatibilities have to be solved, and it is predicted that working on-line safe systems are still ten or fifteen years away. Alternative long-range systems, based on fusion, appear even more remote because of the immense problems in achieving the high temperatures needed in working systems.

[5] And many scientists already are predicting that even if such systems are developed, they will be more hazardous to our environment and to life than our present fossil-based energy-generating systems.

[6] In their search the Meinels reviewed the relevant literature and began to look into what might be available in recent high technology, especially in space and defense technologies that could be applicable to solar power systems. Although solar energy as it comes to us is very dilute, so too, Dr. Meinel argues, is fusion power from uranium.

[7] The Meinels did find a lot of applicable technology, particularly in certain developments in the optical field for utilizing temperatures in absorbing thin-film surfaces. In fact, it looked possible to develop temperatures high enough to generate steam in a system—steam at the same temperature and pressure as used in a modern steam turbine. If a system could be built around this method of converting solar energy to heat, then the electric utilities could look forward to using many of the same technologies that they now use in fossil-fuel steam turbine plants!

[8] Work on optical thin films for thermal conversion had been done at MIT in the 1930s (by Francis Turner), but was abandoned for economic reasons. Since then, however, immense advances in the technology of making evaporated thin films—larger vacuum pumps, components, and so forth—have brought about a change in the *economics* of their production. Today Dr. Turner, having "retired" from Bausch and Lomb, is on the staff of the UA Optical Sciences Center, once again making thin films— coming full circle—for solar energy conversion.

[9] But an important realization had guided this new look at thin films. Almost all solar conversion work has been aimed at low-tempera-

ture conversion, aimed at heating individual houses, hot water, and so on. Once the Meinels began to think in terms of high temperatures—the 1000° F of steam turbines—they found what they needed.

[10] For the Meinels had recognized that the underlying philosophy of most solar work was for individual-house heating systems, and small systems for the so-called undeveloped countries. None of the schemes was audacious enough, the Meinels felt. They said, "Let's look at solar energy for a very advanced nation, using the ultimate of our technical capabilities." It makes no more sense, they felt, to build solar energy systems for individual homes than it does to build single-home nuclear power plants.

[11] Although they had also looked at the solid-state solar cells that had been so superbly developed for spacecraft applications, the Meinels realized, as had many other scientists, that they were impractical and economically noncompetitive for terrestrial bulk power applications. However, once they seized on the optical coating technology, which was being used for controlling radiation in optical instruments, one of the staff members at the Optical Sciences Center also found a way of employing the silicon technology of the semiconductor field in a way that also seemed economically feasible.

[12] The second major ingredient of the system came from work that the Atomic Energy Commission has developed for using liquid metals for extracting heat out of reactors and transferring it to a water-steam loop. In the conceptual system advanced by the Meinels, which now was beginning to look very much like a nuclear system except for the fact that nothing is radioactive, liquid sodium was to act as the transfer medium. It would work in a closed system, taking the heat out of the solar energy collectors and transferring it to the power plant.

[13] The third major ingredient of the system also comes from AEC technology, specifically, its work in certain salts that have low melting points but high heat capacities. Such salts could be used for heat storage so that it could be drawn at will—at night, on cloudy days, etc.—just as hydroelectric power is "stored" in the water behind the dams. Now, in this tripartite technological system, the heat from the salt could be extracted and delivered via a steam line to the power plant as it is needed.

[14] With such a solar energy system, Dr. Meinel states, electrical power would be only about 20% more expensive than power now produced by fossil-fuel or nuclear power plants. Moreover, such a solar energy bulk electrical power system has none of the unacceptable environmental costs of the other systems; it is a closed system, consumes no raw materials, and produces no noxious byproducts such as radioactivity or air pollutants; nor does it require raping the earth as does strip mining of coal.

[15] To provide the electrical needs projected for the year 2000 in the

United States (about 1,000,000 MwE average power) would require a solar collecting area of only seventy by seventy miles or 5,000 square miles. For those who feel this is a lot, Dr. Meinel argues that it is only a thousandth of the area of the continental United States.

[16] In other terms, it represents only 1% of the total agricultural land in the U.S., this total produces 1% of our energy needs in terms of food. One percent of land to produce the other 99% of our energy needs, says Dr. Meinel, seems a good bargain. Moreover, such a solar collecting plant could be built on virtually barren desert.

[17] As if that argument weren't enough, one has only to realize that the Bureau of Land Management in the past year alone leased more than that acreage in the western states for strip mining of coal for power . . . which means the virtual destruction of that area for any human or humane use.

[18] What are the alternatives? People are unhappy about strip mining and are fearful of big nuclear power plants in their vicinity. Natural gas is relatively clean to burn, but the gas wells in Louisiana, Texas, and New Mexico are being depleted. Coal gasification is also being employed, and produces a gas that is clean at the place where it is ultimately burned . . . but the preceding stages produce waste and ash and other environmental detriments. The fact is that the electric utilities are now looking for something else.

• • •

[19] The potential size of a solar electrical industry can be partly measured by the fact that the *new* power equipment business now, whether nuclear or fossil-based, is something like $13 billion a year. (By the end of 1971 total investor owned electrical plant will be $100 billion.) The general public, Dr. Meinel points out, isn't really aware of just how big it is, because utility budgets are not in the public spotlight as are, say, the budgets for DOD or NASA. Says Bradley, who is clearly fascinated with the project, "If it goes, and if it goes right, it can revolutionize the entire power industry in the United States." The *shape* of the industry would also be deeply altered. Power-generating plants would be located in the southern tier of states, where there is more sunshine, and power would be delivered throughout the U.S. over a national power grid.

DO WE REALLY *NEED* ALL THOSE KILOWATTS?

Edmund Faltermayer

[1] The U.S. has become an electricity glutton. We use 1.6 trillion kilowatt-hours a year, ten times as much as in 1940. Only now, amid power shortages and the new ecological worries, are we getting around to wondering how long the feast can go on. Those who took pride a few years ago in the "clean, flameless" heat of their all-electric homes are beginning to realize that most electricity is clean only at the consumer's end of the wire, and that the fuel burned to generate it can run out, just like everything else.

[2] Of course we aren't going all the way back to candles. We all like the living standard that electric lights and motors make possible. Furthermore, we can look forward to the *increased* use of electricity in some very important environmental tasks—grinding up old cars for recycling, powering new rapid transit systems, and lighting dark streets to deter muggers. But if we must consume more electricity for essential purposes, we have a special obligation to make each kilowatt-hour as nonpolluting as we can. And we must stop wasting electricity as if it were free.

[3] Unfortunately, only one electric power company, New York City's Con Edison with its "Save a Watt" buttons, has joined the war on electrical waste. The rest of the utility industry is still encouraging prodigality, at least in the sense of doing little to discourage it. Most utility executives come from an earlier era. "When I joined the industry," says Chairman Charles F. Luce of Con Edison, who has reservations about unlimited growth, "our faith was that the best society used the most electric energy per capita." The industry as a whole seems to keep this faith, and expects that consumption will keep on doubling every ten years or so, reaching a stupefying 8.5 trillion kilowatt-hours by the end of the century.

[4] I find myself doubting the country's very ability to turn out so much electricity. For one thing, the forecasts count a lot of chickens that haven't hatched. They assume that half the power in the year 2000 will come from atomic generators. These now supply only 1% of the country's needs, and the expansion program is behind schedule. They further assume that much of the nuclear power will come from a new type of facility, the fast-breeder reactor, and this may turn out to be too tem-

Edmund Faltermayer, *Life* Magazine; © 1972 Time Inc.

peramental. Even if fast breeders play as big a role as the industry hopes, in order to fill out the projected demand the country will need to burn far more coal and oil than at present—perhaps three times as much coal.

[5] But will we really *need* all that electricity? The forecast assumes that each American alive in the year 2000 will be using more than 20 times as many kilowatt-hours as his counterpart did in 1940. But it's quite possible that the growth curve may soon start to flatten a bit. The manufacturing sector of the industrial economy, which uses a lot of electricity, is growing much more slowly than the services sector, which uses relatively little. And in the home the changeover to major electrical appliances may have already peaked.

[6] The fact remains, however, that we *will* be using more electricity than we do now, and to make sure we have it, we should begin at once to spend more research money on better ways to generate it. Solar and geothermal power, which are nonpolluting, offer some promise. Hydroelectric power, on the other hand, doesn't; the best sites have already been used, and dams are now recognized as possible ecological disasters. Pumped-storage projects, which make power available at periods of peak demand, create no new electricity themselves and have also come under attack from environmentalists. Thermonuclear power is the Holy Grail of both environmentalists and industry: it would be abundant and free of serious radiation hazards. A workable system is not yet in sight.

[7] We must also clean up the existing electric power system. Estimates of the impact of such a clean-up on monthly electric bills vary wildly, since a whole range of things must be done. Strip miners will have to carry out better reclamation than is now required by any state. Air pollution caused by generating plants must be curbed drastically, and cooling towers must be installed where necessary to protect aquatic life from thermal pollution. Electricity's aesthetic damage needs plenty of attention. Those tangled overhead distribution lines that mar commercial arteries and residential neighborhoods belong underground.

8

THE COMMUNICATIONS SPEED-UP

The new satellite will be capable of providing large volumes of information—like 15,000,000 bits of information per second. This is equivalent to an *Encyclopedia Britannica* every few minutes. As a contrast, ERT-A's predecessor, Nimbus, provides about 18,000 bits per second.—*Army Research and Development Magazine, 1972*[1]

A relay satellite in orbit "sees" nearly half the globe's surface at once. With satellite technology we could put our telephone exchanges in orbit for less than the annual cost of new ground installations. Every person could have a portable phone and dial any number on earth. Facsimile mail could be transmitted anywhere in a split second. A single world computer could hold the library of mankind, available to anyone anytime.—*Boeing advertisement, 1971*[2]

Electrocardiogram by telephone. Now a heartbeat can be transmitted instantly to a doctor hundreds of miles away.
—*American Telephone and Telegraph advertisement, 1971*[3]

A "tactile television system," in which the dots on a television screen are converted into a pattern of electrical stimulation in an array of electrodes on the skin, was reported by Carter C. Collins, Ph.D., and Frank A. Saunders, Ph.D., of the Pacific Medical Center at San Francisco.

"With this tactile image converter," they said, "blind and blindfolded subjects have tracked the direction and rate of moving targets and have determined the position, relative size, shape, number and orientation of visible objects."—*Ralph Dighton, 1969*[4]

he computer was the device that led to the cybernetic revolution, but the $3.99 transistor radio, a product of that revolution, in the hands of millions of human beings throughout the world spread the knowledge of "the good life" that could be the result of cybernetics. Man does not revolt against nature but against man, and only when he has discovered that life can be better than it is. The poverty-stricken Indians of northeast Brazil had adjusted to a life expectancy of twenty or thirty years because they had experienced centuries of that condition. They accepted abject poverty because they had become inured to it and knew of no other kind of existence. It was through the squawking little boxes that they learned of a better life, and Brazil has been very aware of their urgent demands ever since.

The transfer of information from person to person has been a major factor in the knowledge explosion. Worldwide, the number of telephones increased from 134.6 million in 1960 to 255.2 million in 1970. With the decreased cost of radio receivers, the number of listeners has reached astronomical figures in the same period. Communications satellites have made it possible to communicate both aurally and visually around the world in fractions of a second. For example, less than half an hour after the assassination of John F. Kennedy, Prime Minister Kenyatta of Kenya led a memorial service for the dead President. Hundreds of millions of people throughout the world watched our first steps on the moon less than two seconds after the actual event. In a period of less than twenty-five years, we went from a few thousand small-picture television sets to millions of color sets in a wide variety of sizes. For normal communication, the telegraph system has been scrapped as too slow, too expensive, and too cumbersome. As a part of this expanding technology, entirely new techniques have been developed to provide communication not only between people but between machines and between computers. Holography (three-dimensional television) is on its way, using the laser beam, an entirely new development which already has shown extraordinary promise as a carrier of meaningful symbols. The superhigh frequencies of pure beams of light have multiplied the wave spectrum available for the transmission of information.

And the new techniques are necessary for the transmission of information resulting from the knowledge explosion. A journal called *Chemical Abstracts,* for example, averages between 400 and 500 pages per issue. Each page carries about a dozen abstracts of papers and books published in all areas of chemistry: the title of the article, the author, the source, and a sentence or two describing the basic theme of the item. And *Chemical Abstracts* is published *weekly*!

A whole new industry called micrographics has arisen from the need to store vast quantities of printed material in miniature form. Beginning with microfilm, a thirty-five-millimeter projectable copy of a book or newspaper page, the industry graduated to microfiche, a sheet of film measuring four by six inches, containing microimages which hold the contents of a 200-page book. Each page can be projected full-size by a small, simple "reader." Ultrafiche, a further advance, makes it possible to incorporate 3,200 pages on the same size card. And several companies have produced projection machines which when used with any of these films will enable the reader to get a Xerox-type print of the page he is reading by pressing a "print" button. The library of the future may contain no volumes at all: the total storage of information may be in microfiche or ultrafiche form.

The storage of information does not stop there. With the huge memory banks used today by large computers, vast quantities of information in those banks may be made available through micrographic projection. Late-model computers can print out 15,000 lines per minute (132 characters per line) on microfilm. What many thinkers in the field of communication have set as a goal is the interconnection of every library (every home?) with such institutions as the Library of Congress, thus making available to the reader, on demand, literally millions of books, periodicals, and documents. In another era of transmission of information, McGraw-Hill suggests that by 1979 it may be possible to get a printout of our daily newspaper by means of a small unit attached to the family television set. And the publishing of the paper will also be primarily electronic, with a computer at the center of the complex.

It will be interesting to watch this area of communication in the next ten years. Every indication points to a gigantic battle among three technologies for control of information processing. The telephone industry, which is expanding in many areas, is a strong contestant in this battle; they make the public aware of their aims through a constant stream of advertisements and press releases pushing their potentials. The newly approved cable TV, the subject of the first selection, is a system that will make as many as eighty channels available to the viewer, thus competing for the multitude of possibilities that may make the home the center of learning, both formal and informal. No matter whether the telephone system or cable TV comes out the victor— either way, the individual will profit. In addition, more and more communications satellites will be floating thousands of miles above the earth, capable of covering the entire globe with almost instantaneous transmission of information, says David Rorvik in his article, "Brave New World."

And we must not forget the RAND Corporation and the year 2030. Howard Fast's "The First Men," a warm, moving story from which the last selection in this chapter is an excerpt, represents the ultimate in human-to-human communication. Perhaps it is the one most to be wished for.

WILL SOCIETY BE RUN BY TV?
Los Angeles Times Service

MENLO PARK, CALIFORNIA

[1] You'll be able to shop, vote, summon police and even let the doctor downtown have a look at your sprained thumb—all while sitting in your living room.

[2] How? By means of two-way cable television. And, according to a report by a Stanford Research Institute research team, you can expect all this within 15 years.

[3] In fact, according to the research group here, it will be possible by 1985 to spend all your life at home, if you're so inclined.

[4] These were some of the conclusions drawn by the SRI after a two-year multination study on the future of community antenna television.

[5] The $300,000 study was sponsored by 41 international industrial organizations, primarily from Japan, Western Europe and the United States. The sponsors included broadcasters, utility companies, motion picture producers and equipment manufacturers.

[6] Robert Peters, a senior industrial economist, who headed the survey, said by the year 2000, CATV will probably have altered American habits in a way that even its most optimistic dreamers could not have imagined when it made its debut about 22 years ago.

[7] As originally conceived, cable television was seen as a method for improving commercial television reception in fringe areas.

[8] In the coming decades it will do much more, Peters said.

[9] The system would involve a two-way television screen and camera in the home, hooked to a central processing center by a cable. The system would permit verbal and visual communication in either direction.

[10] Through the use of this basic system, it would be possible for a

husband to work, his wife shop and his children attend school during the day—all while sitting in the family living room.

[11] At night, the same family could crowd around the screen for entertainment.

[12] Should someone in the family be ill, the television could be used to contact a doctor who could diagnose the problem, if a simple one, and prescribe treatment, all without leaving his home or office.

[13] Through the use of supplemental monitoring screens and sensors throughout the house, a warning could be automatically relayed to the appropriate agency in case of trouble.

[14] Peters said the CATV society is not as Orwellian or remote as many people think.

[15] "Technologically, it can be done today. But economics may be a retardant since it would cost about $20 a month per subscriber," he said.

[16] According to SRI research, it would cost a homeowner about $1,000 initially to install a basic CATV set in his home and connect it with a cable distribution system and a central processor.

[17] Peters said two small model two-way subscription television systems began operating in 1971 in Reston, Va., and Overland Park, Kan. The one in Reston, however, at the moment uses a regular telephone as a "return path" for the information from each subscriber, he said.

[18] Peters said a broad-based sample of 1,200 Californians of all income levels was polled recently on the kinds of cable television they wanted and would be willing to pay for.

[19] He said about half indicated they would pay for such services as a system that can notify police in case of burglary, call firemen in case of fire or provide education programs.

[20] A smaller number said they would be willing to pay for such additional services as shopping via television, listings of what was playing at the local movie house, making reservations or mailing tickets for concerts and movies.

[21] Those in the survey indicated they would be willing to pay $5 a month for each of the services and up to $20 a month for a whole package.

[22] How widespread the utilization of such radical services as working at home by remote control, decentralized home schools, patient diagnosis via the terminal screen and others is likely to depend greatly on society's reaction, Peters said.

[23] He said it would take some time for the people to readjust themselves to the routine of doing everything from their living rooms.

[24] "Institutional changes will also be needed, for example, to retrain teachers so they can accept the idea of unconventional education in the home, where (perhaps) a college-trained housewife would be responsi-

ble for a cluster of neighborhood kids learning via the cable screen," he said.

[25] But despite these uncertainties, Peters predicted widespread use of two-way CATV systems in the United States in the next few decades.

[26] By 1990, he said, capital equipment and program material required to support two-way CATV systems in the home would exceed $30 billion.

[27] He said it is possible that by the early 2000s, CATV will be the dominant communications system in the United States, outstripping the major commercial television networks.

[28] Peters said selectivity in what programs to watch would give CATV an edge over competing commercial television stations which, in turn, would be compelled to upgrade their programming. The overall result could be much better programming all round beginning towards the end of this century.

BRAVE NEW WORLD
David M. Rorvik

[1] An engineer at General Electric has come up with an exciting [less] conventional proposal for long-distance communications. Jared Scott Smith, manager of G.E.'s Data Network Operations, proposes that the mail be delivered, almost instantaneously, via a domestic communications satellite. He declares that this could be done with present technology and at today's postal rates. Letters, initially no more than six hundred words long and costing no more to send than ten cents each, would be transmitted from one teleprinter to another via the orbiting satellite. There are already some 200,000 teleprinters in use in the United States today, and it is estimated there will ultimately be one in nearly every home.

[2] At present, sending messages by teleprinter, though cheaper than by phone, is too expensive for ordinary mail. This is due in large part to the fact that the ground relay network requires a large number of intermediate switching centers. A message going from New York to Los An-

geles, for example (at seventy-five cents per three minutes), goes through at least ten of these centers, with expense mounting at each one. With a data-transmission satellite, most of the centers would become obsolete. Messages would go from home or office teleprinter to one of 175 "earth stations" distributed throughout the country. On the average, each teleprinter would be within six miles of an earth station, from which the message is beamed to the satellite and, from there, back down to the routing center and earth station nearest the target teleprinter.

[3] Smith says it will take an annual revenue of $100,000,000 to sustain the system. If the cost of sending an "airmail" letter is to be held at ten cents, the system must carry at least 2,500,000,000 messages annually. (Four cents from each letter will be used to maintain the satellite and earth stations and six cents for the telephone circuits and to pay for and maintain the teleprinters.) Starting from the fact that the present standard teleprinter-transmission rate is one hundred pulses per second, Smith and his colleagues envision a rate of 300 pulses and have calculated that a digital satellite system could transmit 1,500,000 messages per hour. Thus the 2,500,000,000-message minimum per year would pose no technical problem whatever.

[4] But will the system actually get that much business? Almost certainly, Smith says, estimating that by 1980 there will be nearly 1,000,-000,000 Telex (and other similar machine-to-machine) messages sent annually, even barring the development of a data-transmission satellite. Add to that a large part of the 1,200,000,000 business letters sent by ordinary air mail each year, and even a small percentage of the 37,500,-000,000 other business letters which this system should get, and the business should be booming.

[5] Smith says G.E. has not committed itself to such a system. If it does, it will probably supply the equipment but not run the business, which could fall to government, private concerns, or both. "Whatever the case," he comments, "I think there is no question but that in time such a system will come to pass." At first, he believes, most messages will be transmitted to teleprinters in post offices and then distributed in the conventional way. Later, businesses that don't already have their own teleprinters will acquire them. And, finally, even the average home-owner will install the equipment. "The only people who are likely to complain," Smith concludes, "are lovers. The one thing that I don't think we're going to be able to provide for ten cents a letter is pink, perfumed stationery."

[6] Utopian as the G.E. concept may seem (when compared to our present system of mail delivery), it is far from the last word in communications. The future, if we have one, could bring all sorts of astonishing innovations. Dr. W. Grey Walter of the Burden Neurological Institute in Britain linked the human brain to the computer, via external electrodes,

several years ago. And now Dr. José M. R. Delgado of the Yale University School of Medicine has linked a chimpanzee to a computer with *implanted* brain electrodes, establishing two-way radio communications between corporeal and mechanical grey matter. The success of their experiment has led Dr. Delgado and his associates to assert that it may ultimately be possible for one man to communicate his thoughts directly to another (without any of the confusions of language) by channeling them through a computer.

[7] In light of this, an image of the future conjured up by Dr. Manfred Clynes is perhaps not so whimsical as it might at first seem. Dr. Clynes is director of the Rockland State Hospital Biocybernetics Laboratory, and inventor of the widely used CAT computer. He was an internationally acclaimed concert pianist before he abandoned the concert circuit several years ago to join Dr. Nathan S. Kline, the famed psychiatrist, in applying the computer to mental-health problems.

[8] In the course of his research, Dr. Clynes has made a number of exciting discoveries. Among other things, he has demonstrated that all of our perceptions and emotions have specific, measurable time-space shapes. When two or more people look at the color red, for example, they all produce the same ·sort of brain potentials or signals. These can be detected by delicate sensors and analyzed by a computer. Our emotions, similarly, are related to specific brain potentials so that, as Dr. Clynes has demonstrated, computers can literally read our minds. An understanding of the nature of our thoughts in terms of their precise mathematical, electronic, time-space identities, Dr. Clynes says, will permit us to communicate better than we do at the present time. "We may even find new shapes," he adds, "and discover means of utilizing them to communicate in entirely new ways—ways that cannot even be imagined now."

[9] Like so many other leading computer experts, Dr. Clynes has arrived at the conclusion that intelligence can be packaged in mechanical parts, as well as in DNA. And as the man who coined the word "cyborg," he believes that the man-machine symbiote, the cybernetic organism, will define the next step up on the evolutionary ladder. His conception of the intelligent, conscious computer is really a vision of the ultimate cyborg—humanity in an entirely new organizational package, capable of communicating hates, loves and passions better than ever, electromagnetically. All in all, he foresees quite a pleasant turn of events in the future of communications.

[10] Dr. Clynes believes that "all true progress is progress in love." Thus, he says, "It seems likely that if computers [as defined in the special sense above] can control their condition of awareness and optimize it with greater ease than we can in our present form, they will prefer the state of love. Since one of the characteristics of love is the desire to join

with the object of love, the computers loving each other would want to merge. This will be less a problem for computers than it is for people and will have the advantage that a combined computer could be a little better than each separately. There will arise, then, a succession of merging computers until there will be one enormous computer in a state of bliss, contemplating the order of nature. If this state should become difficult to maintain, in time the computer would have the choice of subdividing itself and reverting to the previous condition of multiple individuals who love each other and would tend to merge again. We actually face, then, a playful state of oscillation in which individuals unite and divide and subdivide in ever new combinations and forms. Strangely, such an image is simply an analogue of nature as we see it today."

THE FIRST MEN
Howard Fast

. . .

[1] For the first time, Eggerton became alive, excited, impatient. He mixed Felton another drink. Then he leaned forward eagerly and waited. Felton took a letter out of his pocket.

[2] "This came from my sister," he said.

[3] "You told me you had no letter from her in almost a year!"

[4] "I've had this almost a year," Felton replied, a note of sadness in his voice. "I haven't opened it. She enclosed this sealed envelope with a short letter, which only said that she was well and quite happy, and that I was to open and read the other letter when it was absolutely necessary to do so. My sister is like that; we think the same way. Now, I suppose it's necessary, don't you?"

[5] The secretary nodded slowly but said nothing. Felton opened the letter and began to read aloud.

June 12, 1964

My dear Harry:

[6] As I write this, it is twenty-two years since I have seen you or

spoken to you. How very long for two people who have such love and regard for each other as we do! And now that you have found it necessary to open this letter and read it, we must face the fact that in all probability we will never see each other again. I hear that you have a wife and three children—all wonderful people. I think it is hardest to know that I will not see them or know them.

[7] Only this saddens me. Otherwise, Mark and I are very happy—and I think you will understand why.

[8] About the barrier—which now exists or you would not have opened the letter—tell them that there is no harm to it and no one will be hurt by it. It cannot be broken into because it is a negative power rather than a positive one, an absence instead of a presence. I will have more to say about it later, but possibly explain it no better. Some of the children could likely put it into intelligible words, but I want this to be my report, not theirs.

[9] Strange that I still call them children and think of them as children—when in all fact we are the children and they are adults. But they still have the quality of children that we know best, the strange innocence and purity that vanishes so quickly in the outside world.

[10] And now I must tell you what came of our experiment—or some of it. Some of it, for how could I ever put down the story of the strangest two decades that men ever lived through? It is all incredible and it is all commonplace. We took a group of wonderful children, and we gave them an abundance of love, security and truth—but I think it was the factor of love that mattered most. During the first year, we weeded out each couple that showed less than a desire to love these children. They were easy to love. And as the years passed, they became our children—in every way. The children who were born to the couples in residence here simply joined the group. No one had *a father* or *a mother;* we were a living functioning group in which all men were the fathers of all children and all women the mothers of all children.

[11] No, this was not easy, Harry—among ourselves, the adults, we had to fight and work and examine and turn ourselves inside out again and again, and tear our guts and hearts out, so that we could present an environment that had never been before, a quality of sanity and truth and security that exists nowhere else in all this world.

[12] How shall I tell you of an American Indian boy, five years old, composing a splendid symphony? Or of the two children, one Bantu, one Italian, one a boy, one a girl, who at the age of six built a machine to measure the speed of light? Will you believe that we, the adults, sat quietly and listened to these six-year-olds explain to us that since the speed of light is a constant everywhere, regardless of the motion of material bodies, the distance between the stars cannot be mentioned in terms of light, since that is not distance on our plane of being? Then

believe also that I put it poorly. In all of these matters, I have the sensa-
tions of an uneducated immigrant whose child is exposed to all the
wonders of school and knowledge. I understand a little, but very little.

[13] If I were to repeat instance after instance, wonder after wonder—
at the age of six and seven and eight and nine, would you think of the
poor, tortured, nervous creatures whose parents boast that they have an
IQ of 160, and in the same breath bemoan the fate that did not give them
normal children? Well, ours were and are *normal* children. Perhaps the
first normal children this world has seen in a long time. If you heard them
laugh or sing only once, you would know that. If you could see how tall
and strong they are, how fine of body and movement. They have a quality
that I have never seen in children before.

[14] Yes, I suppose, dear Harry, that much about them would shock
you. Most of the time, they wear no clothes. Sex has always been a joy
and a good thing to them, and they face it and enjoy it as naturally as we
eat and drink—more naturally, for we have no gluttons in sex or food, no
ulcers of the belly or the soul. They kiss and caress each other and do
many other things that the world has specified as shocking, nasty, etc.—
but whatever they do, they do with grace and joy. Is all this possible?
I tell you that it has been my life for almost twenty years now. I live with
boys and girls who are without evil or sickness, who are like pagans or
gods—however you would look at it.

[15] But the story of the children and of their day-to-day life is one that
will be told properly and in its own time and place. All the indications I
have put down here add up only to great gifts and abilities. Mark and
I never had any doubts about these results; we knew that if we controlled
an environment that was predicated on the future, the children would
learn more than any children do on the outside. In their seventh year of
life they were dealing easily and naturally with scientific problems normally taught on the college level, or higher, outside. This was to be
expected, and we would have been very disappointed if something of
this sort had not developed. But it was the unexpected that we hoped
for and watched for—the flowering of the mind of man that is blocked in
every single human being on the outside.

[16] And it came. Originally, it began with a Chinese child in the
fifth year of our work. The second was an American child, then a Burmese.
Most strangely, it was not thought of as anything very unusual, nor did
we realize what was happening until the seventh year, when there were
already five of them.

[17] Mark and I were taking a walk that day—I remember it so well,
a lovely, cool and clear California day—when we came on a group of
children in a meadow. There were about a dozen children there. Five of
them sat in a little circle, with a sixth in the center of the circle. Their
heads were almost touching. They were full of little giggles, ripples of

mirth and satisfaction. The rest of the children sat in a group about ten feet away—watching intently.

[18] As we came to the scene, the children in the second group put their fingers to their lips, indicating that we should be quiet. So we stood and watched without speaking. After we were there about ten minutes, the little girl in the center of the circle of five, leaped to her feet, crying ecstatically.

[19] "I heard you! I heard you! I heard you!"

[20] There was a kind of achievement and delight in her voice that we had not heard before, not even from our children. Then all of the children there rushed together to kiss her and embrace her, and they did a sort of dance of play and delight around her. All this we watched with no indication of surprise or even very great curiosity. For even though this was the first time anything like this—beyond our guesses or comprehension—had ever happened, we had worked out our own reaction to it.

[21] When the children rushed to us for our congratulations, we nodded and smiled and agreed that it was all very wonderful. "Now, it's my turn, mother," a Senegalese boy told me. "I can almost do it already. Now there are six to help me, and it will be easier."

[22] "Aren't you proud of us?" another cried.

[23] We agreed that we were very proud, and we skirted the rest of the questions. Then, at our staff meeting that evening, Mark described what had happened.

[24] "I noticed that last week," Mary Hengel, our semantics teacher nodded. "I watched them, but they didn't see me."

[25] "How many were there?" Professor Goldbaum asked intently.

[26] "Three. A fourth in the center—their heads together. I thought it was one of their games and I walked away."

[27] "They make no secret of it," someone observed.

[28] "Yes," I said, "they took it for granted that we knew what they were doing."

[29] "No one spoke," Mark said. "I can vouch for that."

[30] "Yet they were listening," I said. "They giggled and laughed as if some great joke was taking place—or the way children laugh about a game that delights them."

[31] It was Dr. Goldbaum who put his finger on it. He said, very gravely, "Do you know, Jean—you always said that we might open that great area of the mind that is closed and blocked in us. I think that they have opened it, I think they are teaching and learning to listen to thoughts."

[32] There was a silence after that, and then Atwater, one of our psychologists, said uneasily, "I don't think I believe it. I've investigated every test and report on telepathy ever published in this country—the Duke stuff and all the rest of it. We know how tiny and feeble brain

waves are—it is fantastic to imagine that they can be a means of communication."

[33] "There is also a statistical factor," Rhoda Lannon, a mathematician, observed. "If this faculty existed even as a potential in mankind, is it conceivable that there would be no recorded instance of it?"

[34] "Maybe it has been recorded," said Fleming, one of our historians. "Can you take all the whippings, burnings and hangings of history and determine which were telepaths?"

[35] "I think I agree with Dr. Goldbaum," Mark said. "The children are becoming telepaths. I am not moved by a historical argument, or by a statistical argument, because our obsession here is environment. There is no record in history of a similar group of unusual children being raised in such an environment. Also, this may be—and probably is—a faculty which must be released in childhood or remain permanently blocked. I believe Dr. Haenigson will bear me out when I say that mental blocks imposed during childhood are not uncommon."

[36] "More than that," Dr. Haenigson, our chief psychiatrist, nodded. "No child in our society escapes the need to erect some mental block in his mind. Whole areas of every human being's mind are blocked in early childhood. This is an absolute of human society."

[37] Dr. Goldbaum was looking at us strangely. I was going to say something—but I stopped. I waited and Dr. Goldbaum said:

[38] "I wonder whether we have begun to realize what we may have done. What is a human being? He is the sum of his memories, which are locked in his brain, and every moment of experience simply builds up the structure of those memories. We don't know as yet what is the extent or power of the gift these children of ours appear to be developing, but suppose they reach a point where they can share the totality of memory? It is not simply that among themselves there can be no lies, no deceit, no rationalization, no secrets, no guilts—it is more than that."

[39] Then he looked from face to face, around the whole circle of our staff. We were beginning to comprehend him. I remember my own reactions at that moment, a sense of wonder and discovery and joy and heartbreak too; a feeling so poignant that it brought tears to my eyes.

[40] "You know, I see," Dr. Goldbaum nodded. "Perhaps it would be best for me to speak about it. I am much older than any of you—and I have been through, lived through the worst years of horror and bestiality that mankind ever knew. When I saw what I saw, I asked myself a thousand times: What is the meaning of mankind—if it has any meaning at all, if it is not simply a haphazard accident, an unusual complexity of molecular structure? I know you have all asked yourselves the same thing. Who are we? What are we destined for? What is our purpose? Where is sanity or reason in these bits of struggling, clawing, sick flesh? We kill, we torture, we hurt and destroy as no other species does. We

ennoble murder and falsehood and hypocrisy and superstition; we destroy our own body with drugs and poisonous food; we deceive ourselves as well as others—and we hate and hate and hate.

[41] "Now something has happened. If these children can go into each other's minds completely—then they will have a single memory, which is the memory of all of them. All experience will be common to all of them, all knowledge, all dreams—and they will be immortal. For as one dies, another child is linked to the whole, and another and another. Death will lose all meaning, all of its dark horror. Mankind will begin, here in this place, to fulfill a part of its intended destiny—to become a single, wonderful unit, a whole—almost in the old words of your poet, John Donne, who sensed what we have all sensed at one time, that no man is an island unto himself. Has any thoughtful man lived without having a sense of that singleness of mankind? I don't think so. We have been living in darkness, in the night, struggling each of us with his own poor brain and then dying with all the memories of a lifetime. It is no wonder that we have achieved so little. The wonder is that we have achieved so much. Yet all that we know, all that we have done will be nothing compared to what these children will know and do and create—"

[42] So the old man spelled it out, Harry—and saw almost all of it from the beginning. That was the beginning. Within the next twelve months, each one of our children was linked to all of the others telepathically. And in the years that followed, every child born in our reservation was shown the way into that linkage by the children. Only we, the adults, were forever barred from joining it. We were of the old, they of the new; their way was closed to us forever—although they could go into our minds, and did. But never could we feel them there or see them there, as they did each other.

[43] I don't know how to tell you of the years that followed, Harry. In our little, guarded reservation, man became what he was always destined to be, but I can explain it only imperfectly. I can hardly comprehend, much less explain, what it means to inhabit forty bodies simultaneously, or what it means to each of the children to have the other personalities within them, a part of them—what it means to live as man and woman always and together. Could the children explain it to us? Hardly, for this is a transformation that must take place, from all we can learn, before puberty—and as it happens, the children accept it as normal and natural—indeed as the most natural thing in the world. We were the unnatural ones—and one thing they never truly comprehended is how we could bear to live in our aloneness, how we could bear to live with the knowledge of death as extinction.

[44] We are happy that this knowledge of us did not come at once. In the beginning, the children could merge their thoughts only when their heads were almost touching. Bit by bit, their command of distance

grew—but not until they were in their fifteenth year did they have the power to reach out and probe with their thoughts anywhere on earth. We thank God for this. By then the children were ready for what they found. Earlier, it might have destroyed them.

[45] I must mention that two of our children met accidental death—in the ninth and the eleventh year. But it made no difference to the others, a little regret, but no grief, no sense of great loss, no tears or weeping. Death is totally different to them than to us; a loss of flesh; the personality itself is immortal and lives consciously in the others. When we spoke of a marked grave or a tombstone, they smiled and said that we could make it if it would give us any comfort. Yet, later, when Dr. Goldbaum died, their grief was deep and terrible, for his was the old kind of death.

[46] Outwardly, they remained individuals—each with his or her own set of characteristics, mannerisms, personality. The boys and the girls make love in a normal sexual manner—though all of them share the experience. Can you comprehend that? I cannot—but for them everything is different. Only the unspoiled devotion of mother for helpless child can approximate the love that binds them together—yet here it is also different, deeper even than that.

[47] Before the transformation took place, there was sufficient of children's petulance and anger and annoyance—but after it took place, we never again heard a voice raised in anger or annoyance. As they themselves put it, when there was trouble among them, they washed it out—when there was sickness, they healed it; and after the ninth year, there was no more sickness—even three or four of them, when they merged their minds, could go into a body and cure it.

[48] I use these words and phrases because I have no others, but they don't describe. Even after all these years of living with the children, day and night, I can only vaguely comprehend the manner of their existence. What they are outwardly, I know, free and healthy and happy as no men were before, but what their inner life is remains beyond me.

[49] I spoke to one of them about it once, Arlene, a tall, lovely child whom we found in an orphanage in Idaho. She was fourteen then. We were discussing personality, and I told her that I could not understand how she could live and work as an individual, when she was also a part of so many others, and they were a part of her.

[50] "But I remain myself, Jean. I could not stop being myself."

[51] "But aren't the others also yourself?"

[52] "Yes. But I am also them."

[53] "But who controls your body?"

[54] "I do. Of course."

[55] "But if they should want to control it instead of you?"

[56] "Why?"

[57] "If you did something they disapproved of," I said lamely.

[58] "How could I?" she asked. "Can you do something you disapprove of?"

[59] "I am afraid I can. And do."

[60] "I don't understand? Then why do you do it?"

[61] So these discussions always ended. We, the adults, had only words for communication. By their tenth year, the children had developed methods of communication as far beyond words as words are beyond the dumb motions of animals. If one of them watched something, there was no necessity for it to be described; the others could see it through his eyes. Even in sleep, they dreamed together.

[62] I could go on for hours attempting to describe something utterly beyond my understanding, but that would not help, would it, Harry? You will have your own problems, and I must try to make you understand what happened, what had to happen. You see, by the tenth year, the children had learned all we knew, all we had among us as material for teaching. In effect, we were teaching a single mind, a mind composed of the unblocked, unfettered talent of forty superb children; a mind so rational and pure and agile that to them we could only be objects of loving pity.

[63] We have among us Axel Cromwell, whose name you will recognize. He is one of the greatest physicists on earth, and it was he who was mainly responsible for the first Atom bomb. After that, he came to us as one would go into a monastery—an act of personal expiation. He and his wife taught the children physics, but by the eighth year, the children were teaching Cromwell. A year later, Cromwell could follow neither their mathematics nor their reasoning; and their symbolism, of course, was out of the structure of their own thoughts.

[64] Let me give you an example. In the far outfield of our baseball diamond, there was a boulder of perhaps ten tons. (I must remark that the athletic skill, the physical reactions of the children, was in its own way almost as extraordinary as their mental powers. They have broken every track and field record in existence—often cutting world records by one third. I have watched them run down our horses. Their movements can be so quick as to make us appear sluggards by comparison. And they love baseball—among other games.)

[65] We had spoken of either blasting the boulder apart or rolling it out of the way with one of our heavy bulldozers, but it was something we had never gotten to. Then, one day, we discovered that the boulder was gone—in its place a pile of thick red dust that the wind was fast leveling. We asked the children what had happened, and they told us that they had reduced the boulder to dust—as if it was no more than kicking a small stone out of one's path. How? Well, they had loosened the molecular structure and it had become dust. They explained, but we

could not understand. They tried to explain to Cromwell how their thoughts could do this, but he could no more comprehend it than the rest of us.

[66] I mention one thing. They built an atomic fusion power plant, out of which we derive an unlimited store of power. They built what they call free fields into all our trucks and cars, so that they rise and travel through the air with the same facility they have on the ground. With the power of thought, they can go into atoms, rearrange electrons, build one element out of another—and all this is elementary to them, as if they were doing tricks to amuse us and amaze us.

[67] So you see something of what the children are, and now I shall tell you what you must know.

[68] In the fifteenth year of the children, our entire staff met with them. There were fifty-two of them now, for all the children born to us were taken into their body of singleness—and flourished in their company, I should add, despite their initially lower IQs. A very formal and serious meeting, for in thirty days the team of observers were scheduled to enter the reservation. Michael, who was born in Italy, spoke for them; they needed only one voice.

[69] He began by telling us how much they loved and cherished us, the adults who were once their teachers. "All that we have, all that we are, you have given us," he said. "You are our fathers and mothers and teachers—and we love you beyond our power to say. For years now, we have wondered at your patience and self-giving, for we have gone into your minds and we know what pain and doubt and fear and confusion you all live with. We have also gone into the minds of the soldiers who guard the reservation. More and more, our power to probe grew—until now there is no mind anywhere on earth that we cannot seek out and read.

[70] "From our seventh year, we knew all the details of this experiment, why we were here and what you were attempting—and from then until now, we have pondered over what our future must be. We have also tried to help you, whom we love so much, and perhaps we have been a little help in easing your discontents, in keeping you as healthy as possible, and in easing your troubled nights in that maze of fear and nightmare that you call sleep.

[71] "We did what we could, but all our efforts to join you with us have failed. Unless that area of the mind is opened before puberty, the tissues change, the brain cells lose all potential of development, and it is closed forever. Of all things, this saddens us most—for you have given us the most precious heritage of mankind, and in return we have given you nothing."

[72] "That isn't so," I said. "You have given us more than we gave you."

[73] "Perhaps," Michael nodded. "You are very good and kind people. But now the fifteen years are over, and the team will be here in thirty days—"

[74] I shook my head. "No. They must be stopped."

[75] "And all of you?" Michael asked, looking from one to another of the adults.

[76] Some of us were weeping. Cromwell said:

[77] "We are your teachers and your fathers and mothers, but you must tell us what to do. You know that."

[78] Michael nodded, and then he told us what they had decided. The reservation must be maintained. I was to go to Washington with Mark and Dr. Goldbaum—and somehow get an extension of time. Then new infants would be brought into the reservation by teams of the children, and educated here.

[79] "But why must they be brought here?" Mark asked. "You can reach them wherever they are—go into their minds, make them a part of you?"

[80] "But they can't reach us," Michael said. "Not for a long time. They would be alone—and their minds would be shattered. What would the people of your world outside do to such children? What happened to people in the past who were possessed of devils, who heard voices? Some became saints, but more were burned at the stake."

[81] "Can't you protect them?" someone asked.

[82] "Some day—yes. Now, no—there are not enough of us. First, we must help move children here, hundreds and hundreds more. Then there must be other places like this one. It will take a long time. The world is a large place and there are a great many children. And we must work carefully. You see, people are so filled with fear—and this would be the worst fear of all. They would go mad with fear and all that they would think of is to kill us."

[83] "And our children could not fight back," Dr. Goldbaum said quietly. "They cannot hurt any human being, much less kill one. Cattle, our old dogs and cats, they are one thing—"

[84] (Here Dr. Goldbaum referred to the fact that we no longer slaughtered our cattle in the old way. We had pet dogs and cats, and when they became very old and sick, the children caused them peacefully to go to sleep—from which they never awakened. Then the children asked us if we might do the same with the cattle we butchered for food.)

[85] "—but not people," Dr. Goldbaum went on. "They cannot hurt people or kill people. We are able to do things that we know are wrong, but that is one power we have that the children lack. They cannot kill and they cannot hurt. Am I right, Michael?"

[86] "Yes,—you are right." Michael nodded. "We must do it slowly

and patiently—and the world must not know what we are doing until we have taken certain measures. We think we need three years more. Can you get us three years, Jean?"

[87] "I will get it," I said.

[88] "And we need all of you to help us. Of course we will not keep any of you here if you wish to go. But we need you—as we have always needed you. We love you and value you, and we beg you to remain with us . . ."

[89] Do you wonder that we all remained, Harry—that no one of us could leave our children—or will ever leave them, except when death takes us away? There is not so much more that I must tell now.

[90] We got the three years we needed, and as for the gray barrier that surrounds us, the children tell me that it is a simple device indeed. As nearly as I can understand, they altered the time sequence of the entire reservation. Not much—by less than one ten thousandth of a second. But the result is that your world outside exists this tiny fraction of a second in the future. The same sun shines on us, the same winds blow, and from inside the barrier, we see your world unaltered. But you cannot see us. When you look at us, the present of our existence has not yet come into being—and instead there is nothing, no space, no heat, no light, only the impenetrable wall of non-existence.

[91] From inside, we can go outside—from the past into the future. I have done this during the moments when we experimented with the barrier. You feel a shudder, a moment of cold—but no more.

[92] There is also a way in which we return, but understandably, I cannot spell it out.

[93] So there is the situation, Harry. We will never see each other again, but I assure you that Mark and I are happier than we have ever been. Man will change, and he will become what he was intended to be, and he will reach out with love and knowledge to all the universes of the firmament. Isn't this what man has always dreamt of, no war or hatred or hunger or sickness or death? We are fortunate to be alive while this is happening, Harry—we should ask no more.

With all my love,
Jean

[94] Felton finished reading, and then there was a long, long silence while the two men looked at each other. Finally, the Secretary spoke:

[95] "You know we shall have to keep knocking at that barrier trying to find a way to break through?"

[96] "I know."

[97] "It will be easier, now that your sister has explained it."

[98] "I don't think it will be easier," Felton said tiredly. "I do not think that she has explained it."

[99] "Not to you and me, perhaps. But we'll put the eggheads to work on it. They'll figure it out. They always do."

[100] "Perhaps not this time."

[101] "Oh, yes," the Secretary nodded. "You see, we've got to stop it. We can't have this kind of thing—immoral, godless, and a threat to every human being on earth. The kids were right. We would have to kill them, you know. It's a disease. The only way to stop a disease is to kill the bugs that cause it. The only way. I wish there was another way, but there isn't."

9

MIND EXPANSION—
OR MIND CONTROL?

The next 5 to 10 years . . . will see a hundredfold increase in the number and type of drugs capable of affecting the mind. . . . And, inevitably, here as in every field of inquiry, *each major addition to our knowledge brings its corollary: power to control.* In brain research, increased knowledge means increased power to control the mind of man. . . .—*Dr. Stanley F. Yolles, 1966*[1]

The researches of Penfield, Olds, and Delgado have demonstrated that the electrical stimulation of the brain through implanted electrodes can induce sheer terror or ecstatic pleasure, and behavior can be controlled, new behavior taught, and memories repetitively elicited.—*Donald N. Michael, 1968*[2]

If you have a rat and your rat is too murderous, the application of methylatropine to its lateral hypothalamus will pacify it. If your rat is not murderous enough, the application of carbachol or neostigmine will render it as savage as you could desire.—Esquire, 1970[3]

I need not spell out for you what . . . understanding of the mind may mean in terms of the control of the mind. And as soon as I utter that embarrassing science fiction phrase, "control of the mind," you immediately know what is on my mind: the problem of ethics and politics and the social good.—*David Krech, 1968*[4]

Reference numbers refer to source notes on page 312.

here is no doubt that today's society is drug addicted. From omnipresent aspirin to dangerous heroin we have become accustomed to pills that ease pain, put us to sleep, wake us up, create euphoria—even to drugs that help us escape from the pressures of everyday living. Few would deny that tragedy stalks the lives of the many young and old who through careless experimentation have sought mind expansion through a wide variety of chemical substances that are harmful, even fatal, in the long run.

The question of addiction and the side effects of untried drugs is one which is of paramount importance in our society today. The law does not quarrel with the pharmaceutical industry with regard to drugs that heal; it is concerned with those that harm. Even these terms are yet to be clearly defined. If marijuana is mind expanding and illicit, why should alcohol be mind expanding and legal? Dr. Thomas Szasz questions the right of society to limit the use of any drug, stating his position clearly in "The Ethics of Drug Addiction."

The pharmaceutical industry, speaking through Dr. Frank Ayd in "Drugs of the Future," sees contributions in the future which will be far greater than in the past as discovery of one new drug leads to a chain of others. Dr. Ayd is not totally enthusiastic about the drugs he sees coming and he is not alone in his condemnation of unlimited drug use. On the other hand, it is obvious that as a result of the drug industry hundreds of thousands of people are alive today who would have perished from physical malfunctions or diseases in generations past.

With the introduction of antibiotics, tranquillizers, and new surgical techniques "the survival of the fittest" is no longer true in the sense it once was. Who would refuse the life extension offered by coronary bypass surgery, a magnificent heart replumbing technique scarcely a half dozen years old? Who would say no to tranquillizing drugs that have enabled psychiatrists to reach mental patients who have been unapproachable for years? Given the chance, would you refuse a drug that would increase longevity? Would society say no to more effective birth-control pills in the face of the dangers of the population explosion?

Although the current literature is still primarily theoretical, it seems expedient to note the great amount of investigation and research concerning one of the least understood areas of the human body—the brain. Because the brain is the most complicated combination of molecules ever devised by nature or man, study of it has been most difficult; there is nothing in nature matching the unique qualities of these few pounds of gray matter which are the focal point of the individual.

183

We can try new drugs on a variety of animals, as we can try new surgical techniques on lower animals, even primates. But when it comes to determining the factors that enable human beings to reason, to remember, to think, we have to work with humans. Our tools at this time are almost primitive when compared with those available for research on other parts of the body. An electroencephalogram with its few electrodes can indicate to the neurologist that a patient is suffering from an epileptic seizure. Venal catheterization can locate hardening of the arteries of the brain, tumors, or hemorrhage, but we have a long way to go before we are sure of what combination of electrochemical action accounts for the psychopath, the melancholiac, the sufferer from schizophrenia. It is comforting to know that hundreds, perhaps thousands of some of our most skilled researchers are probing this critically important area.

Dr. José Delgado at Yale is using implanted electrodes and mild electric shocks to modify the behavior of a variety of animals and has even managed a kind of communication between a chimpanzee and a computer. Dr. Vernon H. Mark, a well-known Boston neurosurgeon, and his colleagues at Massachusetts General Hospital have used electrical stimulation to determine the source of violent behavior in a mental patient. Having found the source, they made a small lesion in the patient's brain at that particular point. The operation has eliminated the violent behavior at least temporarily. Possibilities in this area are endless. Dr. David Krech, a psychologist at the University of California at Berkeley, using the theories developed by Holger Hyden of Sweden, has performed miracles with rats, achieving the transfer of memory by chemical means. His work is described by David Perlman in "The Search for the Memory Molecule."

"Learning" by either of these techniques appears to be a distinct possibility: Calculus, perhaps, by means of a pill! Archeology mastered by a series of shocks. The good life in a pill. . . . But again we have the question—who decides what is to be taught or swallowed? And from what point of view will the teaching be done?

THE ETHICS OF ADDICTION: AN ARGUMENT IN FAVOR OF LETTING AMERICANS TAKE ANY DRUG THEY WANT TO TAKE

Thomas S. Szasz, M.D.

[1] To avoid clichés about "drug abuse," let us analyze its official definition. According to the World Health Organization, "Drug addiction is a state of periodic or chronic intoxication detrimental to the individual and to society, produced by the repeated consumption of a drug (natural or synthetic). Its characteristics include: 1) an overpowering desire or need (compulsion) to continue taking the drug and to obtain it by any means, 2) a tendency to increase the dosage, and 3) a psychic (psychological) and sometimes physical dependence on the effects of the drug."

[2] Since this definition hinges on the harm done to both the individual and society, it is clearly an ethical one. Moreover, by not specifying what is "detrimental," it consigns the problem of addiction to psychiatrists who define the patient's "dangerousness to himself and others."

[3] Next, we come to the effort to obtain the addictive substance "by any means." This suggests that the substance must be prohibited, or is very expensive, and is hence difficult for the ordinary person to obtain (rather than that the person who wants it has an inordinate craving for it). If there were an abundant and inexpensive supply of what the "addict" wants, there would be no reason for him to go to "any means" to obtain it. Thus by the who's definition, one can be addicted only to a substance that is illegal or otherwise difficult to obtain. This surely removes the problem of addiction from the realm of medicine and psychiatry, and puts it squarely into that of morals and law.

[4] In short, drug addiction or drug abuse cannot be defined without specifying the proper and improper uses of certain pharmacologically active agents. The regular administration of morphine by a physician to a patient dying of cancer is the paradigm of the proper use of a narcotic; whereas even its occasional self-administration by a physically healthy person for the purpose of "pharmacological pleasure" is the paradigm of drug abuse.

[5] I submit that these judgments have nothing whatever to do with

medicine, pharmacology, or psychiatry. They are moral judgments. Indeed, our present views on addiction are astonishingly similar to some of our former views on sex. Until recently, masturbation—or self-abuse, as it was called—was professionally declared, and popularly accepted, as both the cause and the symptom of a variety of illnesses. Even today, homosexuality—called a "sexual perversion"—is regarded as a disease by medical and psychiatric experts as well as by "well-informed" laymen.

[6] To be sure, it is now virtually impossible to cite a contemporary medical authority to support the concept of self-abuse. Medical opinion holds that whether a person masturbates or not is medically irrelevant; and that engaging in the practice or refraining from it is a matter of personal morals or life-style. On the other hand, it is virtually impossible to cite a contemporary medical authority to oppose the concept of drug abuse. Medical opinion holds that drug abuse is a major medical, psychiatric, and public health problem; that drug addiction is a disease similar to diabetes, requiring prolonged (or lifelong) and careful, medically supervised treatment; and that taking or not taking drugs is primarily, if not solely, a matter of medical responsibility.

[7] Thus the man on the street can only believe what he hears from all sides—that drug addiction is a disease, "like any other," which has now reached "epidemic proportions," and whose "medical" containment justifies the limitless expenditure of tax monies and the corresponding aggrandizement and enrichment of noble medical warriors against this "plague."

Propaganda To Justify Prohibition

[8] Like any social policy, our drug laws may be examined from two entirely different points of view; technical and moral. Our present inclination is either to ignore the moral perspective or to mistake the technical for the moral.

[9] Since most of the propagandists against drug abuse seek to justify certain repressive policies because of the alleged dangerousness of various drugs, they often falsify the facts about the true pharmacological properties of the drugs they seek to prohibit. They do so for two reasons: first, because many substances in daily use are just as harmful as the substances they want to prohibit; second, because they realize that dangerousness alone is never a sufficiently persuasive argument to justify the prohibition of any drug, substance, or artifact. Accordingly, the more they ignore the moral dimensions of the problem, the more they must escalate their fraudulent claims about the dangers of drugs.

[10] To be sure, some drugs are more dangerous than others. It is easier to kill oneself with heroin than with aspirin. But it is also easier to kill oneself by jumping off a high building than a low one. In the case of

drugs, we regard their potentiality for self-injury as justification for their prohibition; in the case of buildings, we do not.

[11] Furthermore, we systematically blur and confuse the two quite different ways in which narcotics may cause death: by a deliberate act of suicide or by accidental overdosage.

[12] Every individual is capable of injuring or killing himself. This potentiality is a fundamental expression of human freedom. Self-destructive behavior may be regarded as sinful and penalized by means of informal sanctions. But it should not be regarded as a crime or (mental) disease, justifying or warranting the use of the police powers of the state for its control.

[13] Therefore, it is absurd to deprive an adult of a drug (or of anything else) because he might use it to kill himself. To do so is to treat everyone the way institutional psychiatrists treat the so-called suicidal mental patient: they not only imprison such a person but take everything away from him—shoelaces, belts, razor blades, eating utensils, and so forth—until the "patient" lies naked on a mattress in a padded cell—lest he kill himself. The result is degrading tyrannization.

[14] Death by accidental overdose is an altogether different matter. But can anyone doubt that this danger now looms so large precisely because the sale of narcotics and many other drugs is illegal? Those who buy illicit drugs cannot be sure what drug they are getting or how much of it. Free trade in drugs, with governmental action limited to safeguarding the purity of the product and the veracity of the labeling, would reduce the risk of accidental overdose with "dangerous drugs" to the same levels that prevail, and that we find acceptable, with respect to other chemical agents and physical artifacts that abound in our complex technological society.

[15] This essay is not intended as an exposition on the pharmacological properties of narcotics and other mind-affecting drugs. However, I want to make it clear that in my view, *regardless* of their danger, all drugs should be "legalized" (a misleading term I employ reluctantly as a concession to common usage). Although I recognize that some drugs—notably heroin, the amphetamines, and LSD, among those now in vogue—may have undesirable or dangerous consequences, I favor free trade in drugs for the same reason the Founding Fathers favored free trade in ideas. In an open society, it is none of the government's business what idea a man puts into his mind; likewise, it should be none of the government's business what drug he puts into his body.

• • •

The Right of Self-Medication

[16] Clearly, the argument that marijuana—or heroin, methadone, or morphine—is prohibited because it is addictive or dangerous cannot be

supported by facts. For one thing, there are many drugs, from insulin to penicillin, that are neither addictive nor dangerous but are nevertheless also prohibited; they can be obtained only through a physician's prescription. For another, there are many things, from dynamite to guns, that are much more dangerous than narcotics (especially to others) but are not prohibited. As everyone knows, it is still possible in the United States to walk into a store and walk out with a shotgun. We enjoy this right not because we believe that guns are safe but because we believe even more strongly that civil liberties are precious. At the same time, it is not possible in the United States to walk into a store and walk out with a bottle of barbiturates, codeine, or other drugs.

[17] I believe that just as we regard freedom of speech and religion as fundamental rights, so we should also regard freedom of self-medication as a fundamental right. Like most rights, the right of self-medication should apply only to adults; and it should not be an unqualified right. Since these are important qualifications, it is necessary to specify their precise range.

[18] John Stuart Mill said (approximately) that a person's right to swing his arm ends where his neighbor's nose begins. And Oliver Wendell Holmes said that no one has a right to shout "Fire!" in a crowded theater. Similarly, the limiting condition with respect to self-medication should be the inflicting of actual (as against symbolic) harm on others.

[19] Our present practices with respect to alcohol embody and reflect this individualistic ethic. We have the right to buy, possess, and consume alcoholic beverages. Regardless of how offensive drunkenness might be to a person, he cannot interfere with another person's "right" to become inebriated so long as that person drinks in the privacy of his own home or at some other appropriate location, and so long as he conducts himself in an otherwise law-abiding manner. In short, we have a right to be intoxicated—in private. Public intoxication is considered an offense to others and is therefore a violation of the criminal law. It makes sense that what is a "right" in one place may become, by virtue of its disruptive or disturbing effect on others, an offense somewhere else.

[20] The right to self-medication should be hedged in by similar limits. Public intoxication, not only with alcohol but with any drug, should be an offense punishable by the criminal law. Furthermore, acts that may injure others—such as driving a car—should, when carried out in a drug-intoxicated state, be punished especially strictly and severely. The right to self-medication must thus entail unqualified responsibility for the effects of one's drug-intoxicated behavior on others. For unless we are willing to hold ourselves responsible for our own behavior, and hold others responsible for theirs, the liberty to use drugs (or to engage in other acts) degenerates into a license to hurt others.

• • •

Life, Liberty, and the Pursuit of Highs

[21] Sooner or later we shall have to confront the basic moral dilemma underlying this problem: does a person have the right to take a drug, any drug—not because he needs it to cure an illness, but because he wants to take it?

[22] The Declaration of Independence speaks of our inalienable right to "life, liberty, and the pursuit of happiness." How are we to interpret this? By asserting that we ought to be free to pursue happiness by playing golf or watching television, but not by drinking alcohol, or smoking marijuana, or ingesting pep pills?

[23] The Constitution and the Bill of Rights are silent on the subject of drugs. This would seem to imply that the adult citizen has, or ought to have, the right to medicate his own body as he sees fit. Were this not the case, why should there have been a need for a Constitutional Amendment to outlaw drinking? But if ingesting alcohol was, and is now again, a Constitutional right, is ingesting opium, or heroin, or barbiturates, or anything else, not also such a right? If it is, then the Harrison Narcotic Act is not only a bad law but is unconstitutional as well, because it prescribes in a legislative act what ought to be promulgated in a Constitutional Amendment.

[24] The questions remain: as American citizens, should we have the right to take narcotics or other drugs? If we take drugs and conduct ourselves as responsible and law-abiding citizens, should we have a right to remain unmolested by the government? Lastly, if we take drugs and break the law, should we have a right to be treated as persons accused of crime, rather than as patients accused of mental illness?

[25] These are fundamental questions that are conspicuous by their absence from all contemporary discussions of problems of drug addiction and drug abuse. The result is that instead of debating the use of drugs in moral and political terms, we define our task as the ostensibly narrow technical problem of protecting people from poisoning themselves with substances for whose use they cannot possibly assume responsibility. This, I think, best explains the frightening national consensus against personal responsibility for taking drugs and for one's conduct while under their influence. In 1965, for example, when President Johnson sought a bill imposing tight federal controls over pep pills and goof balls, the bill cleared the House by a unanimous vote, 402 to 0.

[26] The failure of such measures to curb the "drug menace" has only served to inflame our legislators' enthusiasm for them. In October 1970 the Senate passed, again by a unanimous vote (54 to 0) "a major narcotics crackdown bill."

[27] To me, unanimity on an issue as basic and complex as this means a complete evasion of the actual problem and an attempt to master it by

attacking and overpowering a scapegoat—"dangerous drugs" and "drug abusers." There is an ominous resemblance between the unanimity with which all "reasonable" men—and especially politicians, physicians, and priests—formerly supported the protective measures of society against witches and Jews, and that with which they now support them against drug addicts and drug abusers.

[28] After all is said and done, the issue comes down to whether we accept or reject the ethical principle John Stuart Mill so clearly enunciated: "The only purpose [he wrote in *On Liberty*] for which power can be rightfully exercised over any member of a civilized community, against his will, is to prevent harm to others. His own good, either physical or moral, is not a sufficient warrant. He cannot rightfully be compelled to do or forbear because it will make him happier, because in the opinions of others, to do so would be wise, or even right . . . In the part [of his conduct] which merely concerns himself, his independence is, of right, absolute. Over himself, over his own body and mind, the individual is sovereign."

[29] By recognizing the problem of drug abuse for what it is—a moral and political question rather than a medical or therapeutic one—we can choose to maximize the sphere of action of the state at the expense of the individual, or of the individual at the expense of the state. In other words, we could commit ourselves to the view that the state, the representative of many, is more important than the individual; that it therefore has the right, indeed the duty, to regulate the life of the individual in the best interests of the group. Or we could commit ourselves to the view that individual dignity and liberty are the supreme values of life, and that the foremost duty of the state is to protect and promote these values.

[30] In short, we must choose between the ethic of collectivism and individualism, and pay the price of either—or of both.

DRUGS AND THE FUTURE
Frank J. Ayd, Jr., M.D.

[1] From the day Eve plucked the forbidden apple from the Tree of Knowledge, man has had an insatiable curiosity about himself—his purpose, his natural and supernatural destinies, his physical and psy-

This article is reprinted from the September, 1969, issue of *Medical Counterpoint*, by permission.

chological composition, and the causes of his behavior. Man also has had an incessant desire to control and to improve man. Consequently, in the perpetual search for knowledge of man, throughout human history each generation of men has studied man with all the means that were available.

[2] Precisely when man first learned that chemicals could affect his mental and physical state favorably or adversely is a secret of history, but ever since, he has sought chemicals to ease pain, to induce pleasure, to preserve and improve health, to enhance his physical and mental powers, to transport himself to mystical heights, to alter and control the behavior of his fellow men, and even to kill his fellow men. Knowing what chemicals can do has impelled man to search continuously for naturally occurring chemicals and, when he became able to do so, to create synthetic ones. The acquisition of the power to produce chemicals which can manipulate man's behavior caused man to strive to learn how these work and where they act in the body so that he could make better and safer subtances to alter human behavior. Man's power to do this has been limited until this twentieth century; but technological, biochemical, and pharmacological developments in the past twenty-five years have made it possible for man to discover, synthesize, and study the direct and indirect effects of drugs on the brain and hence on all human behavior.

[3] Today we have drugs and chemicals which stimulate and counteract fatigue, which are potent pain-easers, which suppress or increase appetite, which induce sleep or cause wakefulness, which enhance or suppress human sexuality, which induce or suppress fertility, which alert or stultify intellectual performance, which can improve mental and emotional illnesses or produce temporary and possible permanent insanity, which can cause synthetic mysticism, which lengthen or shorten motor performance and endurance, which cause or subdue aggressiveness, or which can produce pleasure or pain. In short, we now have drugs and intoxicants that can affect every facet of man and can ennoble, or debase and dehumanize, man. We have chemicals which enable man to change and control individual and group human behavior. Furthermore, modern Western man is not averse to using drugs and intoxicants to alter his own behavior, as statistics on the use of alcohol, narcotic, and psychedelic drugs like LSD demonstrate. Nor is modern man averse to using drugs and intoxicants to alter and to control the behavior of his fellow men, as evidenced by the use of tear gas, mace, and other chemicals on unruly groups and rioters, by the preparations for chemical warfare, and by the advocacy by some individuals of the compulsory uses of antifertility agents to control population size.

[4] Cognizant of what can be done today with drugs, scientists are peering into the future to ascertain what compounds they should concentrate on developing to meet the needs of society and to make possible further manipulation and control of human behavior by chemicals. Be-

fore discussing the drugs on the horizon or in the planning stage, consideration must be given to the philosophical and cultural climate of today, for these influence the types of drugs sought and their application.

[5] Twentieth-century man has become progressively more materialistic and egocentric. A new religion, scientism, has sprung up among some influential scientists and humanists. Many of them have rejected traditional Judeo-Christian morality as obsolete and unworthy of adherence to by man, enlightened and freed as he is by the discoveries of science. They have erected a new hierarchy of values. Ethics, they say, is situational. There is a new morality which holds that every human act—even murder—is good if it is motivated by "love." They champion new sexual mores that permit man to indulge in sexual pleasures in any way he wishes. They advocate new reproduction mores because science has enabled man to be infertile if he wills, and to procreate in new ways. They argue that since man can control the biological makeup of his near and remote descendants, only superior children should be desired and conceived. They tell us that the world no longer needs all the individuals we are capable of bringing into it—especially those who are unable to compete and are an unhappy burden to others. Hence, they advocate contraception and sterilization to prevent the transmission of unwanted life, abortion or fetal euthanasia to destroy the unborn whose lives have been judged unworthy of preservation and protection, and voluntary euthanasia for the chronically ill whose lives have been declared useless.

[6] Many of the high priests of scientism not only endorse an antilife philosophy but also subscribe to the concept that man is the owner of his life and body and therefore can do as he wishes. They have generated a modern foment for man to be totally free and to become the complete master of his destiny and his environment. Paradoxically, they declare that there is no need for self-restraint, unless this is dictated by the "superior" objectives of scientism, such as the attainment, through carefully regulated reproduction, of intellectually and physically superior beings who thoroughly enjoy their sexual activities and their leisure time, immune to disease or illnesses, capable of unlimited longevity, and subject only to accidental death or deliberate self-extinction.

[7] Scientism promises utopia, a synthetic heaven on earth made possible by chemical, biological, and technological developments. To achieve this objective, scientists believe that many drugs must and will be developed.

[8] Among these are:

Drugs Which Will Curb Human Reproduction

[9] Much publicity has been given to the world's population growth. Experts warn that if the growth rate is not soon reduced to zero, the human race will destroy itself by an epidemic of unrestrained breeding.

Experts also agree that the oral contraceptives, the intrauterine devices and all other methods of family planning are not the solution to the population crisis. These methods of fertility control depend for their effectiveness on user motivation and this, to the dismay of birth control advocates, is not sufficiently widespread. Hence, scientists are developing and testing birth control methods which require minimum motivation for their successful use. These include:

[10] *1*. Injectable long-acting preparations capable of rendering a woman infertile for months and possibly for as long as twenty years.

[11] *2*. A contraceptive vaccine which would produce indefinite immunologic infertility.

[12] *3*. Abortifacient pills. Scientists have been synthesizing pills which destroy the fertilized ovum before it implants in the womb, which alter the lining of the uterus making implantation impossible, or which terminate the existence of the embryo after implantation. These chemicals are known as post-passion pills, post-coital pills, morning-after pills, week-after pills, or anti- or contranidation pills.

[13] There is mounting evidence that good and safe abortifacients are on the way and that more will follow. The advantages of these compounds over the oral contraceptives will be manifold. They will have to be taken only after intercourse and probably only once in a cycle instead of daily or every day for twenty days in each cycle. Women are more apt to remember to take an abortifacient drug than to forget, as she may "the pill," since these drugs are used retrospectively. They will allow the same, if not more, sexual freedom and abandonment than the oral contraceptives and yet will be less expensive. They probably will not produce the same endocrine and physiologic changes as "the pill" and probably will not require the same medical supervision as takers of oral contraceptives should and must have. These abortifacients, because of their advantages, will appeal to women at all economic and social levels, especially to the economically disadvantaged, the educationally deprived and wherever medical services are in short supply.

[14] At first some women, because of qualms of conscience, may hesitate to use these drugs. However, since other abortion methods already are used by such vast numbers of women in the world, it would not be long before oral abortifacients would be preferred by most women. This would be true especially if science supplies an oral abortifacient which would have to be taken only once toward the end of a cycle and which would induce menstruation before the woman knew whether she is pregnant or not. It would be easy for her to rationalize her action and not to feel any guilt at all. Thus, abortifacient drugs may become the mainstay of population-control programs, personal and national, throughout the world.

[15] Can you envision procreation being dependent on an antidote for the daily food you eat, or the water you drink?

[16] Sound fantastic, ludicrous, unbelievable?

[17] Maybe, but it isn't inconceivable. In recent years many who are anxious to defuse "The Population Bomb" and who are impatient with the failure of people to be self-motivated to control their fertility, have been advocating that scientists devise chemicals which would make entire populations infertile so that governments could control at will the rate of its population growth. Such drugs have not been developed, but some scientists are predicting that they will be made and used if necessary.

New Chemical Aphrodisiacs

[18] The search for chemical means to increase sexual appetite, potency, and to maximize the sensual pleasures of sexual relationships is as old as the recorded history of man. In this age of "The New Morality," with its emphasis on sexual freedom and on sensory experiences and the separation of reproduction from conjugal relations, many men and women are using what is available to enhance sexual desire, performance, and enjoyment. Hippies testify that making love under the influence of a low dose of LSD is "love at its best." Even the elderly are interested in sexual relations—so much so that recently a compound has been marketed as an aid to sexual appetite for the elderly and the impotent. Scientists have located target areas in the brain which can directly and quickly instigate sexual behavior. They have appropriate testing methods and some knowledge of the types of chemicals to examine. Consequently, they predict that chemical aphrodisiacs soon will be available and widely used.

Drugs To Induce Hibernation and To Ease the Pains of Hunger

[19] Although some agricultural experts have abandoned their pessimism and have become optimistic that the world can feed its growing population during the remainder of this century, there are those who insist that famines are imminent. They warn that, if the quantity of people is not limited, the world's food supply will be insufficient to meet the demands for it, and that sometime between 1970 and 1985, because of vast famines, hundreds of millions of people will be starving. These alleged imminent famines, they assert, can be avoided only by a drastic and immediate reduction of the population and the birthrate. Since this may not be achieved, scientists are being exhorted to make better appetite suppressant drugs and compounds which would ease effectively the pains of hunger during periods of food shortages. Furthermore, since the food requirements of hibernating animals are low, Gordon R. Taylor, in his book, *The Biological Time Bomb*, suggests that in times of food shortage, many people might be placed in hibernation. Drugs to achieve this, at least for

relatively short periods, exist and some scientists believe that compounds can be developed which could be used for mass hibernation for long periods.

Drugs To Combat Boredom

[20] Futurists confidently forecast that in the next twenty-five years man will have more and more time for leisure and idleness. This, they predict, may become a major problem, for it could, as it has in other historical eras, lead to sloth, boredom, melancholy, despair, and an increase in suicide. Hence, they are pressing scientists to make drugs which could counteract the sloth of the future. In response to these promptings, research is underway to discover and perfect antiennui compounds. Marketing analysts visualize high sales for these products. Such financial incentives may make these drugs realities before the twenty-first century.

Drugs To Transport Man to Mystical Heights

[21] Already many individuals are seeking "instant satori" through the use of psychedelic drugs and other intoxicants. It is expected that this trend will continue and that not only hippies and intellectuals but the most cloistered and unadventurous individuals will demand chemicals which will speed up transport to pinnacles of emotion and psychological experiences men otherwise would never have known. Hence, scientists say there is a need for new psychedelics. These can and will be produced so that all present "mind expanders" will be obsolete within the next thirty years.

Drugs To Raise Intelligence to Very High Levels

[22] Drugs now are being used to prevent or delay loss of intelligence, but to cope with the demands generated by scientific and technological developments, increased intellectual capacities are deemed imperative. Currently, scientists are studying drugs to raise or lower IQ, to enhance attention span, to improve memory, to increase capacity to absorb knowledge and to heighten verbal, arithmetical, or artistic abilities or talents at will. Experts in this area, such as California psychology professor David Krech, have declared that within five to ten years science will be able to control intellectual capacities with drugs. Since drugs could create geniuses, Gordon R. Taylor warns that we soon may have "a supernaturally intelligent elite with very little ability to find common ground with normal, unimproved men."

[23] The advent of chemicals which will influence the development of man's intellectual capacities will raise profound social, legal, and ethical questions. This is why Professor Krech has aptly warned that we must prepare controls over these awesome powers, and not permit them to be exercised indiscriminately.

Drugs Which Will Increase Longevity

[24] The quest for the fountain of youth, immortalized by Ponce de Leon, has never ceased. The conquest of communicable diseases has increased life expectancy phenomenally but there has been no significant change in the maximum life span of man because the degenerative diseases, which are largely responsible for death of the elderly, have been affected very little.

[25] Longevity, it seems, is associated both with a stable DNA and with freedom from degenerative diseases which apparently are initiated by mutation in a single cell. If DNA can be stabilized and undesirable mutations controlled, longer life should result. Since a stable DNA could be an ingredient of the legendary elixir of youth, molecular biologists are working to devise chemicals which would stabilize DNA and which would prevent or control cell mutation. These chemicals would alter life expectancy. Futurists are forecasting that these chemicals will be discovered, but at this moment a lengthened life span is only a theoretical possibility.

Drugs To Produce Temporary Incapacitation of a Population

[26] To subdue unruly groups and rioters or the enemy during war, in as humane a way as possible, humanists want scientists to develop chemicals which would temporarily incapacitate a population. They envision, for example, the development of very potent substances which, in very minute quantities, could be placed in an aerosol bomb. This would be exploded and its contents inhaled or absorbed through the skin, rapidly rendering people incapable of normal activity. Then the rioters or the enemy could be disarmed, captured, and imprisoned before the effects of the disabling drug have waned. Efforts to create such substances are going on and, according to some scientists, their development is not only feasible but will be a reality in the immediate future. They acknowledge that such drugs will incapacitate everyone exposed to them—the innocent as well as the offenders.

Comment

[27] These are only a few of the drugs in the offing which can and will be used to manipulate and control human behavior. Society must be aware of these trends and give serious consideration to them and to their implications—good and evil—for the individual and society, before they are realities. No one wants to prevent progress but, at the same time, science should not be allowed to forge ahead unsupervised simply on the justification advanced by many scientists, namely, that what science can do, it must. On the contrary, as Sir Theodore Fox aptly remarked to his

fellow scientists: "We shall have to learn to refrain from doing things merely because we know how to do them."

[28] Desirable as the drugs scientists are contemplating may seem, it is imperative to inquire if this is so. Man is more than a sensate animal. All men have dormant within them capabilities for their physical and spiritual improvement. Should these be germinated by drugs? Can they be? Can man become more virtuous by ingesting chemicals and intoxicants? History testifies that the answer is no. Instead, what has happened when this has been attempted in the past was the achievement of physically sound bodies with morally dulled minds. Whenever individuals or a society concentrated on the betterment of man's physical endowment and on the gratification and enjoyment of the senses, the individual or the society first became debased and then was destroyed.

[29] If we ignore the lessons of history, we are doomed to repeat them. Man may know more today but he certainly is no wiser than the Greeks or the Romans whose demise was preceded by debaucheries and the enslavement of thousands of citizens. We are headed in the same direction, using potent drugs and intoxicants to attain hedonistic goals. We are synthesizing compounds, which, if they ever were controlled by fanatical leaders, could be used to control, subjugate and dehumanize men in ways heretofore impossible. Unless we are alert to the dangers of individual and mass chemical bondage and prepare to face the ethical and moral problems posed by scientific developments, then, to paraphrase Robert Burns, man's inhumanity to man will make countless thousands mourn.

[30] Today the demand for freedom of choice is well established. Many moderns are loathe to discipline themselves. On the contrary, modern man condones and encourages self-indulgence, forgetting that the less demanded of an individual in the way of discipline, observance of rules, and recognition of and respect for authority, the more dispirited and restive he becomes, and paradoxically, the more he wants to control others, since he cannot control himself. Modern man has forgotten also that the fulfillment of one desire is usually the signal for some new wish rather than a cause for contentment.

[31] The Greek philosopher, Epicurus, once remarked: "No pleasure is a bad thing in itself; but the means which produce some pleasures bring with them disturbances many times greater than pleasure." Unmindful of this, many people today, especially the young, in seeking pleasure are using products of science and technology that corrupt the body and the mind. The current frenetic pursuit of carnal pleasures and the ingestion of drugs which alter consciousness are producing a harvest of unhealthy minds and bodies. Psychiatrists are seeing an increasing number of apathetic, academically impaired young people without ambition or social involvement and a history of several years of persistent

abuse of drugs, including marijuana which is not as innocuous as many misguided physicians and educators claim. These victims of drug abuse are living an aimless, utterly hedonic life style. The growth of such a drug-dependent population would not only destroy many potentially productive young people but also face our society with a growing burden of parasitism.

[32] Truly, society must ask itself if the development of more drugs and intoxicants as those I have discussed is desirable and necessary. If they become realities, their use would become fashionable and widespread. Because this could be disastrous, all responsible men must concede that some control over scientific developments is urgently necessary. The issues raised by current scientific trends can only be resolved by true value judgments. These should and must be made by responsible leaders and all citizens. They cannot and should not be made by scientists alone, for they are matters of public welfare, and to delegate to scientists alone social and moral judgments which are the right and duty of every citizen, as history warns, can be very dangerous indeed. If responsible men fail in their duty now, we will have to agree with Homer, who remarked in his *Odyssey:* "What a lamentable thing it is that men should blame the gods and regard them as the source of their troubles, when it is their own wickedness that brings them sufferings worse than any which Destiny allots them."

THE SEARCH FOR THE MEMORY MOLECULE
David Perlman

[1] In the long parade of fish and flatworms, rats, cats and mice that have given their all for science, it is just possible that Rat No. 895—with the help of a bearded psychologist named David Krech—will hold a special significance for the education of our children's children. The rat is one of a group of animals whose life experience may eventually spell out the structural and biochemical nature of memory. He may help point the way to providing education meaningfully enriched—for every child's unique, individual mind.

[2] Rat No. 895 is a gentle, gray-brown creature with the smooth coat and well-fed look of an animal raised in privilege. He lives in the basement of Tolman Hall at the University of California at Berkeley, where Dr. Krech is a professor of psychology.

[3] One recent afternoon, the professor looked on as the rat sat quietly in a white-walled, smooth-floored chamber that was part of a tiny two-room suite in the Tolman Hall laboratories. It was a comfortable room for a rat, perhaps 8 inches square, with a light shining brightly down. In one white wall a small hole opened into the second room of the suite, and for the rat the hole was tempting. It led to an even more attractive room, of equal size, but black-walled and badly lighted. To a rat, darkness is far more inviting than light. Dark rooms are where the action is.

[4] Krech could not know it, because the experiment was being conducted in scientifically "blind" fashion, but Rat No. 895 was carrying inside his body an injection of homogenized liquid from the minced-up brain of a cousin who, just before death, had been trained to fear a black chamber because of an electric shock from a wire-grid floor. Krech had taught No. 895 to fear the shock in the black chamber, too, but that had been four weeks earlier. By now, any normal rat should have largely forgotten the shock and its lesson.

[5] Inside the white chamber, No. 895 now hesitated. He poked his nose through the hole, and withdrew quickly from the black room as his whiskers touched its floor, different, not smooth like the white room's, but a grid of slender metal bars. The rat backed to a corner of its white room, licked a forepaw and stared again at the inviting entrance to the dark room. For 10 minutes the rat considered the matter, then tentatively slipped into the darkness, nose first, then rump, then tail. Nothing happened. The floor did not shock. The rat explored the room carefully, then more actively and, finally, scampered back and forth between the two rooms 30 times within the next 20 minutes.

[6] Now the rat's half-hour of testing was over. A white-coated lab technician, who had sat quietly by, recording every movement, lifted him and replaced him with another one. This rat behaved quite differently: he frisked about the white room for barely two minutes, poked his head into the dark chamber, then scampered through. For 28 minutes, he explored the dark half of his suite happily, just as if he had never received a shock in his life. Krech could not know it in this case either, but this carefree animal also carried an injection of brain extract in his body—an extract from a wholly untrained rat, which had never been taught to fear the darkness that rats love.

[7] These two rats are part of only a single experiment in a hotly debated new research area: interanimal memory transfer. Psychologists in many laboratories are trying to prove that precise mechanisms of memory and learning lie within the chemistry and structure of the brain. In the

most controversial current research, scientists like Krech are hoping to establish that memory itself can be transferred, at least partly in chemical form, from one animal to another.

[8] Did Rat No. 895 really pick up molecules of memory in his injection of trained brain extract? Krech himself believes the suggestion is there, but by no means established. Yet if the transfer phenomenon does in truth exist, it will be the most exciting discovery in the history of psychology. It will prove the molecular basis of learning, and mark the first step toward its control. The day is very near, Krech believes, when the intellectual capacity of human beings will be affected by products of the chemical as well as the teaching laboratory.

[9] Today's activity in molecular memory research was largely started by a slender, soft-spoken Swedish scientist named Holger Hyden at the University of Göteborg. On the basis of his delicate microscopic dissection of single brain cells, Hyden believes that RNA, which carries information for the synthesis of proteins, is a chemical key to memory.

[10] Recently, he trained scores of right-pawed rats to perform unfamiliar left-pawed tasks, like reaching for food down a narrow-necked jar with a left paw. When he dissected their brain cells, Hyden found large increases in the RNA content.

[11] A young, free-swinging psychologist named James V. McConnell at the University of Michigan worked with planarians, the tiny spade-headed flatworms found in ponds and quiet streams. However lowly their intelligence, McConnell trained them to solve simple mazes. Then he minced up a batch of his trained worms, fed them to uneducated planarians—and announced that the uneducated cannibals had apparently eaten an education! Their heady diet enabled them to "remember" the mazes which their newly digested cousins had gotten before being eaten. This was the first of the memory-transfer experiments.

[12] But these models of brave new worlds, Krech feels, hold danger as well as promise. When man can raise or lower IQ and memory and learning at will, when he can strengthen verbal skills, or mathematical reasoning, or artistic talent, "Who is to decide what happens to whom?" Krech asks. "The parent? The huckster? The pediatrician? The school board? And what will be the effects upon our society of either increasing the IQ level of all men, or of increasing the distance between the brighter and the duller? What political changes will they lead to?"

10

CAN WE SURVIVE LEISURE?

[Automation] . . . can reduce the amount of toil required of a given worker, but it cannot make him a whit more capable of the good life. . . . So long as he finds leisure only an occasion for unimaginative indolence, even a four-hour day will drag and vacations with pay will be boredom, as they are now for many wealthier folk.—*Robert Calhoun*, 1935[1]

A Leisure-Oriented "Post-Industrial" Society
(1100 Working Hours Per Year)

7.5-hour working days.
4 working days per week
39 working weeks per year
10 legal holidays
3-day weekends
13 weeks per year vacations
(Or 147 Working Days and 218 Days Off/Year)
—*Herman Kahn and Anthony J. Wiener*, 1967[2]

The real tragedy in America may be that we will satisfy all our material needs and then find leisure time on our hands before the average person is in any way educated to know how to use it.

—*Walter P. Reuther*[3]

"Studies at the University of Wisconsin," Lewis said here this week, "have found that a person's health deteriorates when his use of leisure time is characterized by decreased physical activity, social isolation, sensory deprivation, lack of mental stimulation, and a lack of adequate motivation!"—*Don G. Campbell*, 1969[4]

Reference numbers refer to source notes on page 313.

rom the chapter on automation-cybernation, it appears clear that in the industrialized nations of the world there could be a steady decrease in the number of hours people will have to spend in gainful employment. The four-day work week is rapidly gaining popular approval. Management has found that the results include better employee morale, less absenteeism, and in general, better productivity. The employee is better able to plan for more lengthy weekend trips, fuller contact with his family, and a greater respite from the demands of work. Since further automation seems likely, this chapter attempts to crystallize some of the questions and alternatives that may result.

Sebastian de Grazia thoughtfully analyzes the historical meaning of the word *leisure,* beginning with its use in ancient Greece. In the Greek language, leisure meant doing something desirable for its own sake—playing music, reciting poetry, meditating, even doing nothing. He concludes that "progress" has, in effect, tied people to a clock, and in so doing has distorted the basic meaning of leisure. Says De Grazia: "Leisure is a state of being free from everyday necessity, and the activities of leisure those one would engage in for their own sake. As fact or ideal, it is rarely approached in the industrial world." For most of us, this is all too true of our so-called leisure activities. We are so bound by the work ethic that much of our free time is spent in painting the house, fixing the faucets, washing the car. We look back on a day of such activities with the feeling that our day of leisure was a day of accomplishment. Some individuals are so overwhelmed by the necessity of "doing" that when the work week shortens, they immediately set about finding a second job, regardless of financial need.

Often, leisure is simply nonpaying work. How many thousands of men, retired at age sixty-five by company regulation or family pressure, find themselves incapable of finding activities which provide them with a feeling of worthiness, and therefore, soon fall apart or die. It is interesting to consider the somewhat ironic fact that while sixty-five is the expected age of retirement in our society today, the expected longevity for the American male is 67.4 years . . .

The truth is that many of us do not know how to retire, relax, or engage in activities that are worthwhile as ends in themselves. And meditation, the cultivation of the mind, is considered effete and is disdained by the many. De Grazia discusses these issues in *Of Time, Work and Leisure.*

There seems to be little question that free time will increase; there seems to be a big question as to what we will do with it. In order to keep ourselves from being bored to death will we have to quadruple the number of football games available on television and expand the output of beer?

The problem is not only a matter of the number of hours spent at work each week. A clause which drew little attention in the 1970 contract between the Automobile Workers Union and General Motors allows a worker who has completed thirty years with the company to retire at age fifty-six with a $500 per month pension for life. Current negotiators want this age lowered. A U. S. Senate committee passed a bill in late 1972 that made possible Social Security retirement at age sixty, although the bill never reached the floor of the Senate. One of America's largest electronics giants strongly urges executives over fifty to retire, with pension rights, and the firm offers up to two years' salary as a retirement bonus. The trend, then, is toward a shorter work week (even one of three days has been experimented with) and earlier retirement. And because of that trend we need, and yet strenuously avoid, education for the creative use of leisure time. That very idea is anathema to the Puritan work ethic.

Stuart Chase asks "Is Man a Working Animal?" in a chapter from *The Most Probable World.* His answer has several variables, and we should try to fit ourselves into the framework he offers, and make our own judgments. Columnist Robert S. Rosefsky describes a program intended "to integrate the real world of work into the actual classroom curriculum," part of a U. S. Office of Education venture aimed at exposing elementary school children to the careers open to them upon graduation. But who can guarantee what jobs will be available? And shouldn't the program suggest worthwhile goals for leisure time? E. B. White's "The Decline of Sport" satirizes what leisure might become. Beneath his comedy, it is only too easy to see a Roman Circus.

The word "leisure" needs redefining. Should we be granted more free time without being prepared for it? For some, those much-desired free hours might be catastrophic. To change from the work ethic to the growth ethic will be difficult for most of us. We shall have to learn how to use leisure time creatively. And that course has not even been designed yet.

from

OF TIME, WORK AND LEISURE
Sebastian de Grazia

[1] The Reformation's ideas of work have been examined by many scholars. It was, in fact, one of the most intense areas of historical study in the first half of the twentieth century. Many points of controversy sprang up—whether religious ideas or industrial necessity first created the new idea of work, whether its first flowering was in Catholicism or in Protestantism, whether work is less prominent for the reformers than other doctrines were, and so on. With or without saying so explicitly, however, most students agreed that out of the Reformation came a new atmosphere. Labor commanded a new tone. Once, man worked for a livelihood, to be able to live. Now he worked for something beyond his daily bread. He worked because somehow it was the right or moral thing to do.

[2] It is outside our limits to trace the spread of this work ethic or gospel of work, as it much later came to be called, over Germany, England, Scandinavia and elsewhere in Europe. We are chiefly interested in the fact that it eventually reached the United States, there to obtain the fullest expression. Perhaps the linking of work to God is no longer so clear as it once was, yet we can certainly see that the shadows of the great reformers fell over the idea of work in America. Here, all who can must work, and idleness is bad; too many holidays means nothing gets done, and by steady methodical work alone can we build a great and prosperous nation. Here, too, work is good for you, a remedy for pain, loneliness, the death of a dear one, a disappointment in love, or doubts about the purpose of life.

[3] Today the American without a job is a misfit. To hold a job means to have status, to belong in the way of life. Between the ages of twenty-five and fifty-five, that is, after school age and before retirement age, nearly 95 per cent of all males work, and about 35 per cent of all females. Being without a job in prosperous times is bad enough, but being without one in a depression is worse yet. Then the American without work—or the German or Englishman—is a damned soul. Various studies have portrayed the unemployed man as confused, panicky, prone to suicide, mayhem, and revolt. Totalitarian regimes seem to know what unemployment can mean: they never permit it.

Sebastian de Grazia, *Of Time, Work and Leisure;* © 1962 by The Twentieth Century Fund, New York.

[4] The modern doctrine of work affects all countries that try to solve their problems by industrialization. It has migrated to Russia, to China, India, and will make inroads on every modernizing nation, for work cannot be made methodical, rational or impersonal without the addition of some incentive besides the schoolbook triumvirate of food, clothing, and shelter.

. . .

[5] When Americans are asked why they would like a few hours, a half day, a day more of free time, they answer typically that they could then get the shopping done, or take the children to the dentist, or replace that worn-out weather stripping on the back door. They mention such unfree things because they assume "free" means "off-the-job." The word leisure has turned into the phrase free time, and the two are now almost interchangeable. We have slipped backward to the level of ancient Greece before Plato, when *scholē* [from which "school" comes] meant either leisure time or free time. It was through the efforts of the philosophers that leisure found its identity. Today the benefit of their thinking is largely lost to us.

[6] Why should this confusion in terminology continue to exist? Does anyone benefit from it? In a way everyone benefits from it. The confusion helps us to think of our life as the best of existing or possible worlds. Industrialization gives us not only work and many other good things; it gives us the gift of leisure, that is, free time, more free time than ever this hitherto backward old world has seen. It is the signal for a new era, a new way of life, a tribute to freedom and democracy and the fruits they have borne us. Only industrialism and democracy could ever have produced such a marvel. If people somehow feel that this leisure is not passing their way, it is easy to show them how wrong they are. Cite the facts, in leisure hours gained; compare today's leisure with 1850 or 1900. They can go on thinking they have lots of free time and wondering why they do not. Perhaps this makes each person feel petulantly virtuous; he believes all his fellow Americans are having a gay old snap of it while he works like a dog and never has a moment's free time.

[7] Large numbers of persons, it seems, earnestly desire or need more free time, although we may not be able to say whether they would not, if given a choice, prefer something else. Most interview studies tell us about the present moment, and while it interests us, we are also interested in other things. The man whose family is starving will not be much preoccupied with leisure. Lack of food or money is his worry. Restored by food and drink, he begins to think of other things in life. Similarly labor-union leaders may on one day say that the shorter work week will be labor's major battle over the next five years, but six months later, with the onset of a business recession or an inflation, the subject is dropped from the program. Still, if we leave to one side short-run fluctuations like re-

cessions, or the ups and downs of bargaining about the work week, there is the longer-run change that is spanned by at least a generation. Since the turn of the century Americans have pursued time.

• • •

[8] To calculate how much free time you have, take the job's official hours and subtract them from 24; or, to be more exact, take 8 out for sleeping, and subtract the job hours from 16; or another way is to take the work week ten or twenty years ago and from it subtract today's. That also should give a clear gain. In the meantime other processes began insinuating themselves into the worker's life so that he was bearing the cost of added hours without knowing it. If he lived first in one of those concentric circles of the big city characteristic of the early part of the century, his house was fairly near the factory. If the factory moved out to the periphery because of cheaper land or labor, he had to follow it or another factory, or, if not he, his sidekick had to move out there. The factory did not assume the cost of the longer time it might now take him to get to work. And, to make the point, no one counted the loss of time anywhere as part of work time. This is one example of how the American finds himself with fewer on-the-job hours and less free time.

• • •

[9] But is this all? Is the American's chase after time due to this, that he sought to cut down work in only one of its guises, and as it appeared with other faces he did not recognize it? Is free time valued so highly today only because no one has it?

[10] The desire for time we have just considered seems really to be a need for time in which to rest or to get done the many tasks or duties that fall to one's lot after 4:30 or 5:00 or 5:30 P.M. There is more than this alone, it would seem. How else would we explain the important change in our vocabulary over the last fifty or one hundred years, a change in which the "idleness problem" has been supplanted by the "leisure problem," and though idleness was excoriated and leisure is lauded, the problem is still the same—the problem of free time. We have seen there is not so much free time as has been believed and this ought to lessen the fears of those remaining in the anti-idleness class. It is something like saying that, really, workers don't have as much time as we think to get drunk; they are hard at work at numerous chores involving shopping, transportation, housework, repairs and children. The anti-idleness people might reply that the workers have always had enough free time and have more than enough today. If they didn't waste so much of it in frivolous or inane things like TV, they would have time to spare for children and housework. But many people will be disappointed to hear that there is less free time than they had thought. Even were there enough to get all the chores done, they would not be satisfied.

[11] Just as, for some, idleness and leisure like an hourglass have been

turned upside down, but remain the same problem of time, so for others, work and leisure have been turned topsy-turvy. For us of the twentieth century the hymns to work are dim memories of infancy. To look for one today is like looking for the dodo. Not even corporation presidents go all out in favor of work. A paean to leisure, though, can be found in almost any magazine one picks up nowadays. Leisure is in the air.

• • •

[12] All this I would call no more than a change in vocabulary. But a change in vocabulary, though subtle, is an event in human history. This change is an important one, for, by turning things upside down, it reveals itself as a revolution. The linguistic evidence is the strongest we have that a change in attitude has taken place, stronger certainly than the data we brought to bear in the beginning of this chapter. Linguistically it is also important that the word leisure has now become a full adjective. It indicates that the word is getting extraordinarily heavy usage. We now have leisure time, leisure rooms, leisure trips to leisure lakes, leisure clothes, leisure equipment, leisure spending on leisure items. This is too great a change, I think, to be explained simply by the fact that the amount of free time the American is supposed to have is more fiction than fact. As in the very phrase free time, there seems lurking here some hostility to the idea of work. Since in American life, work stands high, and since leisure is thought to be the opposite of work, just the pursuit of leisure implies slowing down on the race track of work.

[13] Since *free time* as a substitute term for *leisure* has its own difficulties, perhaps the moment is right to redefine the terms we have dealt with thus far in this study. Earlier we found leisure as an idea fully explored by the Greeks. Though it had many meanings in common speech, the one that gave it its long life was this: *leisure* is the state of being free of everyday necessity. The man in that state is at leisure and whatever he does is done leisurely. *Play* is what children do, frolic and sport, the lively spraying of wind with water. Adults play too, though their games are less muscular and more intricate. Play has a special relation to leisure. Men may play games in recreation, indeed except for men who work, play is a form of recreation. As far as leisure is concerned, Aristotle had said that we neither work nor play at it. Though this does not describe the exact state of things, play and leisure do have a special relation which we shall want to examine in greater detail later. *Recreation* is activity that rests men from work, often by giving them a change (distraction, diversion), and restores (re-creates) them for work. When adults play— as they do, of course, with persons, things, and symbols—they play for recreation. Like the Romans', our own conception of leisure is mainly recreative. *Work* can be taken in its modern sense as effort or exertion done typically to make a living or keep a house. The activities engaged in while at work all must fall within moral and legal limits, however

broadly defined. A man, though a traitor and a spy, may exert himself to earn a living, but he does not work except perhaps in his own eyes or those of his hirer (note that *employer* is not the right word here).

[14] [Earlier, I] distinguished *work time,* that spent in work or on the job, from *work-related time,* that spent in order to appear at work presentably (time spent in journeying to work or in grooming oneself for work) or in doing things that one would not ordinarily do were it not for work, like the husband's doing a share of his working wife's housework. *Free time* we accepted as time off the job that was neither work-related nor *subsistence time.* The last we named after activities like eating, sleeping, keeping out of the cold and rain, going to the doctor when ill, all presumably performed to maintain the state of a healthy organism, regardless of whether that organism is put to work or leisure.

[15] We did not use any name to designate those activities of free time engaged in because of the influence of the kind of work done, the busman's holiday kind of activity. Obviously activities in recreation may resemble or contrast with work. And recreation may react in the same fashion to family life or religious devotion. Likewise work may be affected by recreative pursuits, drunkenness being the historic example, along with gambling, romance, and adventure. (Were we interested in coining words, the constant and complex flux of relationships, the lack of pertinent physiological knowledge, and the shifting positions of work, free time, subsistence, the family, recreation, and play would enable us to fill a treasury.) The central idea is easy to grasp and accept, however: work and recreation can be affected by each other as well as by other activities, such as taking care of a brood of children. And for this idea a phrase like work-affected recreation or recreation-affected work is not much of a help, being only one syllable shorter than "work affected by recreation."

[16] Leisure, it should be clear, remains unaffected by either work or recreation. It is outside their everyday world. We further would not call work those lifelong pursuits whose scope is not clearly or primarily earning a living. For the clergy, the career ranks of the military and government, the artist and man of letters, the physician, the professor—for all of these we prefer the word *calling.* They don't work, they have a vocation, something they are called to by nature, inclination, God, taste, or the Muses. One will find such persons among the upper ranks of business, also, where the end often is (and often denied to be) not making money but doing good works in the religious or community spirit.

[17] Free time relies on the negative sense of freedom, freedom from something, in this case freedom from the job. I pointed out earlier how it differed from spare time and pastime. Free time, as defined, while reflecting a poor opinion of work, did help in making it seem that the modern world was progressing toward more free time. It left us, however, with serious difficulties. One was deciding whether free time was free

from anything else but work. Taking the negative sense in which the idea originated, can it be said that the meaning now has got to the point, or ought to get to the point, where freedom from other things is sought? For instance, every now and then we have had to ask ourselves, what about family pleasures and responsibilities—does free time mean freedom from them too? If so, the man watching TV at home in the midst of his family is not enjoying free time until he picks up his hat and goes out the door. And then, if he wants to be on free time, he should go neither to local party headquarters to lick envelopes for the coming campaign, nor to the church for evening services, nor to the committee meeting on charity. Does free time mean freedom from all these, too? If not, then it is obvious that the pleasures of free time are laced with duties and responsibilities, thereby clouding the whole idea in paradox. Thus even the negative conception of free time is by no means clear.

[18] To conclude this enigmatic subject: Technology, it seems, is no friend of leisure. The machine, the hero of a dream, the bestower of free time to men, brings a neutralized idea of time that makes it seem free, and then chains it to another machine. . . .

IS MAN A WORKING ANIMAL?
Stuart Chase

[1] Computers and automatic mechanisms have already taken over a great deal of routine work, such as bank bookkeeping, and they are expected to take over a great deal more. Not only large plants and offices will be computerized, but also small organizations, as the hardware becomes less costly.

[2] What then will happen to *people?* Uncounted thousands have already lost their employment to automation; other thousands are postponing the event through crippling strikes on the railroads, the docks, and in newspapers and printing plants. Gerard Piel estimates that if hours had *not* come down below 60 a week, there would now be 27 million unemployed in the United States.

[3] If people have no jobs, how can they buy the products made by

"Is Man a Working Animal?" (pp. 136–148) from *The Most Probable World* by Stuart Chase. Copyright © 1968 by Stuart Chase. Reprinted by permission of Harper & Row, Publishers, Inc.

the workers who remain? If, on the other hand, it is possible to subsidize the jobless as consumers, what happens to their nervous systems, self-confidence, and character? Most of us would rather be occupied than not, as I shall try to demonstrate, but in what form? There are three main possibilities:

[4] *1.* By "having fun," by sight-seeing, tropical cruises, and consuming *furioso.* The "jet set" provides a model.

[5] *2.* By finding new varieties of economic work on a regular payroll, such as rebuilding Megalopolis.

[6] *3.* By expanding noneconomic occupations, such as serious hobbies, amateur arts, community activities on unpaid town boards, and the like.

[7] We will examine these alternatives later in the chapter. Meanwhile let us see what happens to some people who have money but no work, and to others who have work which they dislike extremely. There are a number of reliable studies which throw light on man and his occupations.

Some Cases

[8] A few years ago I acted as consultant in a survey of male employees, both blue-collar and white-, who had been retired at age 65 from one of America's largest corporations. From chairman of the board down to janitor they had to quit. How were they getting on? They had few financial problems, thanks to the company's generous pension system. They were primarily in the money-but-no-work class.

[9] Some got into the family car on retirement and headed for Florida or California, glad to be rid of the daily grind—or so they thought. In six months most of them were back in New York. Those with well-developed hobbies, or part-time business interests, were usually all right; those with nothing to involve them deeply were often in trouble. Some had mental breakdowns; one committed suicide. Another—perhaps the saddest case on the record—set his alarm clock at the habitual hour and went every morning to the old shop to watch the other men do what he once did.

[10] As a result of the survey, the company set up a panel of psychiatric counsellors to help employees who were approaching retirement to find activities which could hold their interest when the regular job expired. Leisure with an adequate income, but without involvement, had been found a disintegrating experience for all too many, despite their age. If this happened to older men at 65, what would happen to more vigorous men at 35 or 40? In the light of this study, man seemed indeed to be a working animal.

[11] The Secretary of Health, Education and Welfare, John W. Gardner, has called for "mid-career clinics" to prepare middle-aged workers for their retirement—"one of life's toughest adjustments." He points out

that the typical man retiring at 65 can expect 25,000 hours of extra time for the rest of his life, "a vast amount either for constructive use or aimless boredom." Secretary Gardner wants management, unions, and universities to cooperate in setting up clinics to keep life meaningful after retirement.

[12] John Wilkinson, of the Center for the Study of Democratic Institutions at Santa Barbara, has reported on what took place when automation invaded the great oil refineries in the Middle East. Tribesmen who had jobs in the refineries lost their work but not their comforts and amenities; income continued. King Ibn Saud complained to the oil companies that the men were sitting around doing nothing and growing dangerously restless. They had schools, hospitals, and air-conditioned homes; but their idleness, said Saud, was making for a "potentially violent revolutionary situation." He urged the engineers to put the men back on the floor and find something for them to do. The company, however, feared that men on the floor might interfere with the automated process, and then the refinery itself might have a nervous breakdown.

[13] In the 1960's workers in American steel mills won a 13-week paid vacation for veteran employees, in their union contract. This was hailed as a great victory, but did not prove very successful. While some of the workers pursued interesting hobbies which they had developed earlier, "many others complained that they just didn't know what to do with all that time."

[14] The Council on Aging corroborates this complaint. It finds three difficulties with uninterrupted leisure, especially for the less educated:

[15] *1.* Most American workers are simply not prepared to shift from an established routine to "uncharted hours of retirement." Many low-income workers regard the learning of hobbies with contempt. They have not developed outside interests during their working life, and boredom, suffered in the past only on weekends, comes to spread a blight over the months and years of retirement.

[16] *2.* In a work-oriented culture, the Council continues, the loss of identity with the job can devastate a worker's self-respect. He comes to think of retirement as akin to the shame of unemployment.

[17] *3.* Retirement can also disrupt a comfortable lifetime relationship between man and wife. When the husband sits around the house all day with little to do, deeply grooved habits are disturbed and family quarrels develop.

[18] The Council on Aging pointedly asks if a rule for arbitrary retirement at 60 or 65 is worth these three risks.

[19] Arthur M. Schlesinger, Jr., the historian, is even more emphatic. "The most dangerous threat hanging over American society," he says, "is the threat of leisure . . . and those who have the least preparation for it will have the most of it." One may question his priority—there are other

serious threats in American society—but he is quite right in identifying the group which will suffer most if and when automation creates a serious vacuum in the job market. It will be those citizens who have developed only limited interests outside the job, or no interests at all.

[20] Novelists and storytellers since time out of mind have a stock character in the profligate son, who lives on the family inheritance and has nothing to do but gamble, drink, and seduce the innocent. The plain moral, that money without work is corrupting, may derive more from the Puritan ethic than from sound sociology, but great novelists, such as Tolstoy, have used it. Most of us can recall such cases in our personal acquaintance.

[21] Kipling in *Barrack Room Ballads* draws a sharp picture of soldiers in peacetime, bored to death and getting into all kinds of trouble. "Drill, ye Terriers, drill!" They long for a war to give them some purpose in life. Even in wartime the interminable waiting around has been found disintegrating.

Opinion Survey

[22] Dr. Robert L. Kahn of the University of Michigan asked a nationwide sample of American workers "whether or not they would continue to work even if, by some chance, they had enough money to satisfy all their needs." No less than 80 percent replied they would go right on working. Among the reasons: they wanted to keep occupied, to keep interested, to avoid being bored. "This finding," said Dr. Kahn, "is pretty general for most occupations and ages of the respondents, and argues a nearly universal need for work."

[23] When the same respondents, however, were asked if they *liked* their present jobs, two-thirds of them said they did not. They wanted to go on working, yes, but at something else—preferably a little business of their own. "While work certainly seems necessary for a balanced emotional life," Dr. Kahn concludes, "many people are doing kinds of work which they don't want to do." In another opinion survey, in a large modern well-appointed plant, one apathetic worker told the interviewer: "The only satisfaction around here, Doc, is the old buck."

[24] A study of 1,800 men on an automobile assembly line in Connecticut found only one man in 10 liking, or at least not disliking, his job.[1] The belt was heartily resented by 90 percent. The resentment arose primarily because the whole process was preplanned, giving the worker no responsibility for the pace of his labor or its content. Nor was there a chance for the age-old motivation of teamwork. The man worked alone

---

[1] Charles Walker and Robert H. Guest, *The Man on the Assembly Line,* Harvard University Press, 1952.

with almost no contact with his fellows. "We suggest," the report noted, "that the sense of becoming depersonalized is, for those who feel it, a psychologically more disturbing result than the boredom." When the line occasionally broke down, a great spontaneous "Hurrah!" filled the plant. Many said that they were bored to the limit of endurance. "The job is so sickening, day in and day out plugging in ignition wires. I get through one motor, turn around, and there's another one staring me in the face."

[25] Norbert Wiener, the father of cybernetics, feels for the man on the assembly line. It is a humiliation, he says, for a human being to be chained to a galley and used as a source of power; but it is equally humiliating to ask a worker in a factory to repeat over and over again an action which requires only one-millionth of the capacity of his brain for its fulfillment.[2]

What Do They Want To Do?

[26] That men want to work seems pretty clear in the light of the above evidence, but not always at what they are doing. There is work and work. We remember Art Young's famous cartoon of a laborer stumbling into his kitchen after a hot summer day. He says to his wife, "By gorry, I'm tired." She replies, "There you go! You're tired! Here I be a-standin' over a hot stove all day, and you're workin' in a nice cool sewer!"

[27] Asked to define "work," about half the respondents in the Kahn survey just cited said that work was something one has to do, or something one doesn't like to do. We have here, of course, prime evidence of the strong Puritan ethic in our culture. Painful things are good for one, pleasurable things are bad, and Satan always finds employment for idle hands.

[28] The chief definition of "work" in American history has been a condition where one is earning a living in field, factory, office, or bringing up a family. It is dubious, under this canon, whether I am working or not as I write these words; artists and writers have been suspect as useful producers since pioneer days. American males over age 50 have been reared on this ethic. Even if we were rich enough to be spared earning a living, we were careful to present substitute credentials. I used to visit in a wealthy community where very few males had to work beyond galloping after foxes. To a man, however, they were at the station every workday morning to take the 8:15 for Boston. What they did in Boston would make an interesting study for a sociologist. After the ceremonial appearance at "the office" most of them came home early.

[29] A farmer works in the fields all day and then returns to his house,

---

[2] *The Human Use of Human Beings: Cybernetics and Society*, Houghton Mifflin, 1950.

turns on the light, and reads *True Stories*. The editor of *True Stories* works to a frantic deadline all day, then drives home for an hour's pleasant exercise in his flower garden. One man's work can be another man's leisure.

There Is Work and Work

[30] The Census lists hundreds of occupations on a spectrum between the exciting and pleasurable, on one hand, and the deadly dull, if not hateful, on the other. . . . "I turn around and there is another motor staring me in the face." Most human beings prefer some variety in their activities; minds and bodies have been shaped by evolution more for change than repetitive monotony. The factory system has taken a biological species, evolved in a free outdoor life, and forced it into a rigid environment controlled by clocks, bells, and whistles. No tribe from the North Cape to Patagonia ever tolerated anything like this. The machine age has built a cage of concrete and steel and put man in it, like an animal in a zoo. Some animals survive in zoos. Some die.

[31] The real distinction, I believe, is between an activity which involves one's whole personality and a vacuum. If automation is to condemn more and more of us to existing in a vacuum, Dr. Schlesinger's prediction may well be justified. Dr. Joshua Lederberg, Nobel Prize winner in medicine, goes a step further. He says that the lack of useful occupation for many older women today "is a preview of the leisure society where work may become the prerogative of a chosen elite." Only the top brass will be lucky enough to have something useful to do! The boredom resulting from nonwork, he fears, may develop into a pernicious nervous disorder. "Perhaps the scientist, who works for the joy of it, will be the most nearly pre-adapted for that topsy-turvy world."[3]

[32] We are not in that topsy-turvy world yet, but high-energy societies are making considerable progress in that direction. There is, of course, no question about the decline in the hours of payroll work, which have fallen from 84 hours a week—seven 12-hour days—at the beginning of the industrial revolution, to around 40. Clerical work is down from 48 to 35 hours, while American labor unions are demanding a 30-hour standard work week. Meanwhile Dr. Richard Bellman of the Rand Corporation makes the startling prediction that by the end of the century 2 percent of the United States labor force will be able to produce everything the country can consume. The Technocrats in their most romantic prophecies never equaled that figure.

[33] Professor William Gombey delves a little deeper, and makes the sound point that we live in a whirling-dervish economy, keyed to compulsive consumption. Planned obsolescence and annual models, he says,

[3] *Bulletin of the Atomic Scientists,* October, 1966.

tend to mask the problem for a time, but how long before unemployment due to automation becomes chronic and accelerating? It cannot be masked indefinitely.

[34] Now let us return to the three possible occupations for those displaced by automation listed at the beginning of the chapter: fun, new fields for paid work, unpaid work.

Having Fun

[35] Some observers predict that the growth of leisure will result in a flowering of art, culture, and philosophy. Others, including your author, are more dubious—at least without a lot of training for the candidates. How do many of us spend our leisure now? Russell Baker takes a look at "having fun" in Florida. The tourist season is in full swing, he says, and the motels are crowded. There are various places to which one can drive from the motels. Some fun-seekers drive into the swamps to see the alligators. The alligators have a stabilizing influence. They have been around for a long time, and help to offset the feeling that the whole state was built last week. Or one can drive to the beach and watch planes drag streamers above the breaking waves advertising cocktail lounges. He can also watch the surf toss the garbage back on the beach. Baker goes on:

> Florida tourism is built on the theory that what we want to do with our leisure time is to invest it entirely in relishing the present moment. Its goal is total fun in total comfort . . . but they wind up by being total bores, and in the process pleasure is lost.[4]

[36] It is not inconceivable that the total-fun contingent might have more fun running a straight furrow, or even an old-fashioned spinning wheel. If man is a working animal, total fun may turn out to be a total bore. It is ironic to note that while fun-makers watch the melon rinds and the pop bottles being tossed back on the beach, a few miles away, at Cape Kennedy, mankind is making its most concentrated and adventurous advance, preparing to land on the moon.

New Fields of Work

[37] There seem to be two chief prospects for new fields of activity to keep us from the vacuum of total comfort and total fun. The first is the very considerable amount of work needed to make living space livable again—especially the reconstruction of Megalopolis and the control of pollutants.

[38] Consider the task of transforming New York City into a livable environment. Consider building the 350 "new towns" Victor Gruen calls

[4] *New York Times,* August 9, 1964.

for. Consider all the proposals for high-speed mass transportation which are gathering on the agenda, with San Francisco and Tokyo leading the way. Consider the work involved in exchanging gasoline motors for vehicles powered by electric batteries or fuel cells.

Noneconomic Work

[39] This field is wide, but not any too well explored. It includes any activity which can seriously involve a human being and which is not primarily concerned with earning a living.

[40] Art forms are expanding in the United States at an exponential rate—painting, music, the dance, the theater. Much of the product is pretty bad, some of it is done for publicity, but as Gifford Phillips has pointed out, there is no question about its dynamism, and the extent of involvement by budding young artists. In our small rural town in Connecticut we have painters and sculptors exhibiting in the local bank, the barbershop, and the dry cleaners. We have string quartets, the Choral Society, the Redding Players, and rehearsals for the symphony concert series given in the next town. Nobody, unless it be the supply trade, is making real money out of this activity. There is a direct correlation between the growth of these local arts and the growth of leisure time.

[41] Is it possible for a whole community to become involved? I have visited villages in Mexico where nearly every family was producing fine craftsmanship—pottery, glass, silverwork, serapes, furniture. If this means anything—will anthropologists please check me?—it means that every normal human being is a potential craftsman, if not an artist. Ishi from the Stone Age was a master craftsman. The tendency must be in the pool of genes, ready for encouragement by the culture.

[42] Again, take hobbies. Sports are expanding rapidly with leisure, and in many of them the player must participate, and not just sit before a TV screen watching someone else perform. The list is long and includes skiing, bowling, snorkling, surf-boarding, bird-watching, rock-climbing. Any one of these can be fun, and some present the bright face of danger. Collecting can also involve one—ship models, Sandwich glass, Mexican *santos,* stamps, coins, lusterwork.

[43] Coming back to useful work, there is the vast field, discussed in an earlier chapter, of helping the Hungry World to its feet, of which the Peace Corps is a pioneer example. This work may pay a living wage, but is certainly not a profit-making enterprise. Its power will come from a combination of idealism and intelligence, especially in young men and women. Indeed, the idea may extend to a kind of universal Job Corps, where every youngster gives a disciplined year or more to going down into that nice cool sewer and doing some of the dirty work of the world, work which no machine can be designed to do. On this agenda, too,

would be much hospital work, care of the aged, supervision of young children, first aid in emergencies, and a wide variety of conservation work, like the CCC camps of the 1930's. It was William James, in his historic essay, "The Moral Equivalent of War," who inaugurated the idea. Already a Job Corps is being experimented with in America for unemployed youngsters.

[44] Education in America is still directed primarily to getting a job. "The more specifically education is directed to jobs," says Gerard Piel, "the more ineffective it is bound to be." The cure, he says, is deliberate training for "no-jobs," for the useful employment of leisure, training to make people more human. It will not be impossible, he thinks, to engineer the transition from a "working society" to a "learning society." A prime function of education should be to supply the intellectual tools and disciplines for an understanding of the problems which the world now faces. We have been brought up, Piel says, in the Horatio Alger ethic of working hard for a living, and it is as far out of date as *The Arabian Nights*.

In Conclusion

[45] I think that we are safe in concluding that automation and the computer will go on making it possible to produce more stuff with less human work. Unless the new occupations and activities just described follow a similar upward trend, we are in for chronic unemployment on an ever grander scale—"structural unemployment" is the technical term used by the economists.

[46] We are reasonably safe in concluding that man is a working animal, in the sense of requiring some activity to interest and involve him, if not in the sense of the Puritan ethic. Without such involvement he is at a loss—if not, indeed, a mental case. What he does, however, hardly needs to follow the ethic of income-producing labor on farm or industrial payroll. A normal life can be seriously distorted by repetitive, monotonous labor.

[47] We are reasonably safe in concluding that there will be enough new fields of work of the payroll variety to keep unemployment in bounds for years to come, especially the reconstruction of Megalopolis. Beyond that is the possibility of Peace Corps work, involvement in the arts and crafts, amateur science, and hobbies which can be more rewarding than watching the alligators in the swamps of Florida. These activities will take some special training, however. Indeed, as automation gains, it promises to shake traditional education to its foundation.

[48] Also, as automation gains, one can readily understand the very human reason for featherbedding in certain traditional occupations. There is no solution, however, in "making work" that makes no sense; no solu-

tion in riding a locomotive cab when there is no coal to be shoveled; no solution in resetting type by hand for advertisements already printed by offset. Such "work" may be even more destructive to the personality than doing nothing at all. Dostoevsky made this point when he said: "If it were desired to crush a man completely, to punish him so severely that even the most hardened murderer would quail, it would only be needed to make his work pointless and absurd."

[49] It will not solve the problem of work to subsidize every family which does not earn enough to meet the health and decency standards —now about $3,000 a year in the United States. Such subsidy, under the label of "negative income tax," is being widely debated, and even blessed by such a conservative economist as Dr. Milton Friedman. It is certainly more than justified for the children of the poor, but it can demoralize their parents—if the parents continue idle and uninvolved. Along with the negative income tax should go carefully planned opportunities for useful work in reducing public squalor.

[50] When all is said and done, however, it is less serious to face the challenge of abundance than to face the prospect of a stripped planet, and a downward spiral into scarcity.

CAREER PROGRAM IS STEP FORWARD
Robert S. Rosefsky

[1] How familiar are the patterns?

[2] At the age of 4, a child expresses an interest in a career in medicine, or space flight, or driving a fire engine. We smile and nod with amusement.

[3] At the age of 14, the child is consumed by a world of dating and pop music and sports. We smile and nod understandingly, more than half wishing we were back at that age again.

[4] At the age of 24, the child is bewildered, at sea, barely coping with the world around him. The cocoon of youth was placid and secure. The new world is a tumult. The child flounders. What will he or she do with the years ahead? We frown, and nod sympathetically, for we recall our

By Robert S. Rosefsky; © 1972 Los Angeles Times Syndicate.

own aimless floundering, our struggles—perhaps still continuing—to cope with a world we weren't prepared for.

[5] When did we, as children, acquire a meaningful understanding of the real world of work—in terms that we could relate to? I don't mean an awareness that "Daddy and/or Mommy go to work everyday so that we can eat." I mean an awareness that "There's a real world out there, and some day I'm going to be a part of it. I want to do more than just function in it. I want to enjoy it, and contribute to it, and learn from it—the good and the rough both."

[6] Our parents may have tried to have given us this awareness, but they were only two people singularly engaged in their own individual life careers. What about the broader view? What about that whole world of alternatives?

[7] The State of Arizona has embarked on an imaginative, forward-looking program designed to come to grips with this problem. As far as is known, it's the first state in the union to make such a move, and it's backed by substantial funding from the public coffers.

[8] Designated "Career Education," the intent is to integrate the real world of work into the actual classroom curriculum. (There are many state and federal programs geared to on-the-job training, but this one is unique in that the classroom itself is the learning arena, and awareness is geared towards the elementary grades and up, not just the high school level.)

[9] On a national level, the U.S. Office of Education has funded six experimental programs in school districts spotted around the country. Each of the six experiments has been granted $1 million in U.S. funds. By comparison, Arizona's program, now in its second year, has been granted $5.7 million in state funds.

[10] The funds are allocated to 18 separate school-based programs, each of which will develop its own structure, working towards the same broad goals. In addition, there are two public information grants, which will supplement the in-school program via radio and television.

[11] While the program is still in its infant stages, one of the major aspects of it is clearly stated: the program is not intended to exclude or replace parental influence and guidance. To the contrary, parents are urged to involve themselves in working with the children, at home and in the classroom, towards the ultimate goal of awareness.

[12] How does the program work? Space permits only a few small examples: In the pre-high school grades, a blank, meaningless page of multiplication problems is replaced by children working on sample offerings from an employment agency.

[13] How much would you earn in a 40 hour week if you made $3.25 per hour, then deducted 80 cents per hour for withholding, and a bit more for fringe benefits? It's still multiplication, but it gains meaning.

[14] Language skills might jump from the rote recitation of verbs and pronouns, to the preparation of a job résumé. One seventh grade program will split the class into teams, each of which will be a mini-industry, developing a raw material into a product, then selling it, etc. This is on the order of the popular extracurricular Junior Achievement program found in many major cities, but it's classroom based, and ties into the math, social studies and language skills curricula.

[15] In many respects, the program is revolutionary. Teacher reception, according to the program's coordinator, has been "beautiful."

[16] Interested parents and educators can get more information on the program by writing to Gene Dorr, associate superintendent of career education, Arizona State Department of Education, 1535 W. Jefferson, Phoenix 85007.

THE DECLINE OF SPORT
E. B. White

[1] In the third decade of the supersonic age, sport gripped the nation in an ever-tightening grip. The horse tracks, the ballparks, the fight rings, the gridirons, all drew crowds in steadily increasing numbers. Every time a game was played, an attendance record was broken. Usually some other sort of record was broken, too—such as the record for the number of consecutive doubles hit by left-handed batters in a Series game, or some such thing as that. Records fell like ripe apples on a windy day. Customs and manners changed, and the five-day business week was reduced to four days, then to three, to give everyone a better chance to memorize the scores.

[2] Not only did sport proliferate but the demands it made on the spectator became greater. Nobody was content to take in one event at a time, and thanks to the magic of radio and television nobody had to. A Yale alumnus, class of 1962, returning to the Bowl with 197,000 others to see the Yale-Cornell football game would take along his pocket radio and pick up the Yankee Stadium, so that while his eye might be following a fumble on the Cornell twenty-two-yard line, his ear would be following

"The Decline of Sport" (pp. 41–45) from *The Second Tree from the Corner* by E. B. White. Copyright 1947 by E. B. White. Originally appeared in *The New Yorker* and reprinted by permission of Harper & Row, Publishers, Inc.

a man going down to second in the top of the fifth, seventy miles away. High in the blue sky above the Bowl, skywriters would be at work writing the scores of other major and minor sporting contests, weaving an interminable record of victory and defeat, and using the new high-visibility pink news-smoke perfected by Pepsi-Cola engineers. And in the frames of the giant video sets, just behind the goal-posts, this same alumnus could watch Dejected win the Futurity before a record-breaking crowd of 349,872 at Belmont, each of whom was tuned to the Yale Bowl and following the World Series game in the video and searching the sky for further news of events either under way or just completed. The effect of this vast cyclorama of sport was to divide the spectator's attention, over-subtilize his appreciation, and deaden his passion. As the fourth supersonic decade was ushered in, the picture changed and sport began to wane.

[3] A good many factors contributed to the decline of sport. Substitutions in football had increased to such an extent that there were very few fans in the United States capable of holding the players in mind during play. Each play that was called saw two entirely new elevens lined up, and the players whose names and faces you had familiarized yourself with in the first period were seldom seen or heard of again. The spectacle became as diffuse as the main concourse in Grand Central at the commuting hour.

[4] Express motor highways leading to the parks and stadia had become so wide, so unobstructed, so devoid of all life except automobiles and trees that sport fans had got into the habit of traveling enormous distances to attend events. The normal driving speed had been stepped up to ninety-five miles an hour, and the distance between cars had been decreased to fifteen feet. This put an extraordinary strain on the sport lover's nervous system, and he arrived home from a Saturday game, after a road trip of three hundred and fifty miles, glassy-eyed, dazed, and spent. He hadn't really had any relaxation and he had failed to see Czlika (who had gone in for Trusky) take the pass from Bkeeo (who had gone in for Bjallo) in the third period, because at that moment a youngster named Lavagetto had been put in to pinch-hit for Art Gurlack in the bottom of the ninth with the tying run on second, and the skywriter who was attempting to write "Princeton 0–Lafayette 43" had banked the wrong way, muffed the "3," and distracted everyone's attention from the fact that Lavagetto had been whiffed.

[5] Cheering, of course, lost its stimulating effect on players, because cheers were no longer associated necessarily with the immediate scene but might as easily apply to something that was happening somewhere else. This was enough to infuriate even the steadiest performer. A football star, hearing the stands break into a roar before the ball was snapped, would realize that their minds were not on him, and would become dispir-

ited and grumpy. Two or three of the big coaches worried so about this that they considered equipping all players with tiny ear sets, so that they, too, could keep abreast of other sporting events while playing, but the idea was abandoned as impractical, and the coaches put it aside in tickler files, to bring up again later.

[6] I think the event that marked the turning point in sport and started it downhill was the Midwest's classic Dust Bowl game of 1975, when Eastern Reserve's great right end, Ed Pistachio, was shot by a spectator. This man, the one who did the shooting, was seated well down in the stands near the forty-yard line on a bleak October afternoon and was so saturated with sport and with the disappointments of sport that he had clearly become deranged. With a minute and fifteen seconds to play and the score tied, the Eastern Reserve quarterback had whipped a long pass over Army's heads into Pistachio's waiting arms. There was no other player anywhere near him, and all Pistachio had to do was catch the ball and run it across the line. He dropped it. At exactly this moment, the spectator—a man named Homer T. Parkinson, of 35 Edgemere Drive, Toledo, O. —suffered at least three other major disappointments in the realm of sport. His horse, Hiccough, on which he had a five-hundred-dollar bet, fell while getting away from the starting gate at Pimlico and broke its leg (clearly visible in the video); his favorite shortstop, Lucky Frimstitch, struck out and let three men die on base in the final game of the Series (to which Parkinson was tuned); and the Governor Dummer soccer team, on which Parkinson's youngest son played goalie, lost in Kent, 4–3, as recorded in the sky overhead. Before anyone could stop him, he drew a gun and drilled Pistachio, before 954,000 persons, the largest crowd that had ever attended a football game and the *second*-largest crowd that had ever assembled for any sporting event in any month except July.

[7] This tragedy, by itself, wouldn't have caused sport to decline, I suppose, but it set in motion a chain of other tragedies, the cumulative effect of which was terrific. Almost as soon as the shot was fired, the news flash was picked up by one of the skywriters directly above the field. He glanced down to see whether he could spot the trouble below, and in doing so failed to see another skywriter approaching. The two planes collided and fell, wings locked, leaving a confusing trail of smoke, which some observers tried to interpret as a late sports score. The planes struck in the middle of the nearby eastbound coast-to-coast Sunlight Parkway, and a motorist driving a convertible coupé stopped so short, to avoid hitting them, that he was bumped from behind. The pileup of cars that ensued involved 1,482 vehicles, a record for eastbound parkways. A total of more than three thousand persons lost their lives in the highway accident, including the two pilots, and when panic broke out in the stadium, it cost another 872 in dead and injured. News of the disaster spread quickly to other sports arenas, and started other panics among the crowds

trying to get to the exits, where they could buy a paper and study a list of the dead. All in all, the afternoon of sport cost 20,003 lives, a record. And nobody had much to show for it except one small Midwestern boy who hung around the smoking wrecks of the planes, captured some aero news-smoke in a milk bottle, and took it home as a souvenir.

[8] From that day on, sport waned. Through long, noncompetitive Saturday afternoons, the stadia slumbered. Even the parkways fell into disuse as motorists rediscovered the charms of old, twisty roads that led through main streets and past barnyards, with their mild congestions and pleasant smells.

11

ECONOMICS AND GOVERNMENT IN A DYNAMIC SOCIETY

The truth, the central stupendous truth, about developed countries today is that they can have—in anything but the shortest run—the kind and scale of resources they decide to have. . . . It is no longer resources that limit decisions. It is the decision that makes the resources.—*U Thant, 1969*[1]

The sociologist Edward Shils has said that the cultural battle in our time is between the new sense of individuality and the personal expressiveness that flows from a wide experience of affluence and the more traditional sense that life is lived in scarcity.
                                        —*Joseph Featherstone, 1971*[2]

What we need is world government to start with and a national government whose constitution makes clear its relationship to the world government. Then, next, we need decentraliaztion and local participation. But today when you have a world technology, a world military problem, and a world health problem, when all problems are world problems, to emphasize local political boundaries and local political power is anachronistic.—*Robert M. Hutchins, 1971*[3]

Quoting an Asian friend, "Even if you Americans end racism and religious intolerance; even if, like us backward Indians, you elect a woman President; even if you turn over your colleges and universities to those who have never attended either so they can decide what is to be taught and then teach it, . . . even if you guarantee an annual wage, even if you do all these things, do you propose to do anything about the real scourges of mankind—war, famine, and pestilence— these scourges that aggravate each other?"—*Stringfellow Barr, 1971*[4]

Reference numbers refer to source notes on page 313.

e now approach the question that, in view of current rampant nationalism, is the trickiest, most delicate one of all. Who will be in control in this age of affluence, this period in history when the industrial nations of the world can produce more than can be consumed? How will goods be distributed? And, as in all of the issues we have so far discussed, we are dealing with the total matrix of what makes up mankind.

As mentioned earlier, futurists agree that despite cultural differences, if we are to survive, it will only be as "one world." For instance, considering ecology, what use would there be in the United States taking strong measures against air pollution if these were ignored by Canada? Even if Zero Population Growth succeeds in Europe, how could we handle unlimited growth in Asia? International agencies, far more powerful than our existing United Nations, must be developed to cope with such dilemmas.

No nation, not even among the great powers, will be able to erect barricades adequately protecting it from the rest of the world, and we must face this issue as squarely and quickly as possible. Communications satellite transmissions know no national boundary lines. Without international trade, all nations are in trouble, and without a sound international currency, there can be no world trade. Like it or not, the nations of the world must work in greater harmony for economic survival. Hopefully, paths toward this goal will develop and expand.

It would be foolish not to recognize the magnitude of the problems to be created if we try to unify a world that contains superindustrial countries such as the United States, Japan, the European nations, and the U.S.S.R., as well as the emerging nations of Asia, Africa, and Central and South America. We must find a mediating balance between the American user of the electric toothbrush and the impoverished Ugandan who not only has never used a toothbrush but is unaware of the dentistry profession.

We will certainly have to devote grave consideration to changes in governmental institutions and economic distribution, unless cowardice and apathy dominate the next few decades. There will be risks; of that there is no question. But, as Oscar Wilde put it, "An idea that isn't dangerous is hardly worth calling an idea at all."

Could Herman Kahn be right when he says that the multinational corporations will inherit the earth for the good of all mankind, that war will simply not be good for business? But nonbusiness planners can find flaws even when the systems analysis of the megacorporations considers the good of all mankind. Let us assume a hypothetical situation, again with a touch of ecology. It cost the automobile manufacturers one-and-a-half billion dollars to convert from the 1971 to the 1972 models. Vast quantities of iron, steel, aluminum, copper, chrome, and now precious platinum went into the gleaming new models; hundreds of thousands of tons of metal went down the drain as older cars were junked. Suppose the powers that be decided that there were to be no model changes in any automobile for five years. Concurrently, all car manufacturers must guarantee *all* parts, except items such as tires and batteries, for the full five-year period. (Let's exempt safety improvement in this wild dream.) Increased cost of quality control might possibly be balanced by the elimination of model changeover costs during the first year. Assuming a production of ten million cars, the savings of the second year would approach $150 per car, with probable savings increases over the balance of the period. But what would happen to our obsolescence-oriented economy? Unemployment figures would soar, the corner garage would no longer replace shock absorbers designed to disintegrate after ten thousand miles, advertising agencies would go wild trying to find new names for old cosmetics to make up for the loss of revenue from the car manufacturers. In short, our forced consumption economy would collapse.

Perhaps it already has, without knowing it. Gerard Piel, in "Consumers of Abundance," seriously questions the basis of current economics. Lord Snow, in an excerpt from *The Two Cultures,* tersely outlines the responsibilities of the "have" nations to the "have-nots." In a devastating social science fiction story, William Tenn spells out what *could* happen if we allow the "average" to become the accepted. As a final article, Technocracy, Inc., presents its version of a method of distribution in a totally "rational" society.

Some of these ideas may shock, even offend, you. But they are alternatives and deserve your critical evaluation. Perhaps "no-new-models-for-five-years" is not the way to do it, but there must be other, more efficient ways for human beings to live, grow, and enjoy their lives.

"You see things and say 'Why?' " said Bernard Shaw. "But I dream things that never were and I say 'Why not?' "

CONSUMERS OF ABUNDANCE
Gerard Piel

[1] The advance of science has for many years been undermining the two pillars of our economy—property and work. Each at length has fallen from its place. Property is no longer the primary source of economic power, and ownership no longer establishes the significant, functioning connection between people and the things they consume. Work occupies fewer hours and years in the lives of everyone; what work there is grows less like work every year, and the less the people work, the more their product grows. In the place of work and property, illusions and old habits and compulsions now support the social edifice. Public understanding must eventually overtake this transformation in the relationship of modern man to his physical environment. Fundamental changes in· the social order—in man's relationship to man—are therefore in prospect and are already in process.

[2] It is difficult and perhaps dangerous to forecast where these changes may lead. Full employment, for example, now seems to be not only an unattainable but an out-moded objective of economic policy. What takes the place of wages in a workless society? If such a question must be asked, then others follow. Does profit remain a useful standard of accounting in a propertyless society? But these questions are not only too big; they are premature. Before they can even be asked, the scientific revoluton that occasions them must be more closely examined.

[3] As the withering of these institutions from the life of society suggests, property and work are artifacts of civilization. In the kinship economies of pre-agricultural societies they have no place whatever or appear only in the faintest analogues. The wampum hoard that confers prestige in one culture becomes the potlatch of another. Hunting and food-gathering are not work, but adventure, assertion of manhood, magic, and craft.

[4] Property and work make their appearance with the agricultural revolution. They are devices for gathering and impounding the surplus that four families at work upon the land can now produce to support a fifth family off the land. Property is the institution by which the church, the state, and their individual agents assert their control over the land as one of the two primary factors of production. Work is the institution by which they assert their control over the other primary factor of production—the energy of human muscle. The word "work" signifies toil and at the same time the product of toil; it is the measure ("according to his

With permission of the author from *Science in the Cause of Man*. Gerard Piel. Alfred A. Knopf, New York, 1962.

works") of the portion of the product that may be allocated to the un-propertied worker. The two institutions together furnished the rationale for the compulsions necessary to assure the removal of the surplus from the land. Thanks to these arrangements, even fairly primitive agricultural technologies were capable of supporting substantial urban civilizations, as in Mexico.

[5] In the feudal societies identified with agricultural technology, land was the only economically significant property. It was typically inalienable, except by order of the suzerain; it was cherished and maintained from generation to generation, physically occupied by its possessors, who enjoyed all the rights of usufruct as well as the power to exploit. In medieval Europe the land so completely dominated economic life that the taking of interest was synonymous with usury, a crime as well as a sin. It took a religious revolution to establish the practice of selling things for more than they cost and to secure propriety for profit in the worldly virtue of thrift.

[6] Profit, thrift, and the accumulation of capital brought an entirely new kind of property into ascendance in economic affairs. This was the machine. At first the machine had the same immemorial look of permanence as the land. It embodied a high ratio of brute material to design and was built for depreciation over at least one generation of ownership. Through such time periods, ownership of the machine carried the same stability of power and place as ownership of the mine or plantation.

[7] It was not long, however, before the ratio of design to material in the machine began to rise and then reverse. As the machine became ever less substantial, its lifetime grew shorter. Today the economically significant industrial property is not the machine, but the design, and not so much the design as the capacity to innovate design in process and product. This is scarcely property at all, but is rather a capacity inhering in an organization. To have that capacity encumbered by a gigantic plant can be hazardous. This is what the steel industry has found in the present technological free-for-all that has brought steel into competition with materials—glass, ceramics, reconstructed wood, plastics, and exotic new metals—that no self-respecting steelmaker ever heard of fifteen years ago. The most profitable manufacturing enterprises are those that show a shrinking ratio of plant to output and a rising ratio of instrumentation to plant. Not only the plant but the product and the very industry in which the company is engaged may be subject to obsolescence. The decisive factor of production is research and development.

[8] As the nature of property, in the sense of the thing that is owned, has changed, so has the nature of the social institution of property. Property was subverted by another social institution, the corporation. With ownership represented by stock certificates, the proprietor ceased to occupy the premises. The right of property vested in the stockholder, as

A. A. Berle, Jr., and Gardiner C. Means made clear more than a generation ago in *The Modern Corporation and Private Property,* was reduced
to the right to vote for the directors of the corporation (if the stockholder bothers to return the proxy statement) and to a claim on earnings
(if the directors declare them out in dividends on his class of stock).
Even these vestiges of power are delegated today to a third party for the
increasing percentage of the voting equities in American industrial enterprise that is held by insurance companies, pension funds, and mutual
investment companies.

• • •

[9] The same transformation of the nature of property is to be seen
again in the relationship of the owner to property as usufruct. There are
more home-owners today in the United States than ever before in this
century, more than 60 per cent of the occupiers of dwelling places compared with less than 50 per cent in 1900. But whereas 30 per cent of the
homes were mortgaged to 40 per cent of their aggregate value in 1900,
more than 60 per cent are mortgaged to more than half their aggregate
value today. The builders and bankers of the new suburbs will tell you
that the ownership of one out of six homes there turns over every year.
Plainly, the so-called home-owner is buying not a home but a housing
service, much as he buys transportation, not a car, from the auto industry.
His equity in these two utilities rarely controls before he turns in the old
house or car for the new model. By the same token, the total installment
debt represents, from one year to the next, by far the major property interest in all of the other consumer durable goods in use in the country.
The householder is correct in regarding these transactions as the purchase of a service rather than property. For the objects themselves are
self-consuming, designed for depreciation to desuetude in 1,000 hours of
service.

[10] In sum, the typical American consumer owns no property in the
classical meaning of the term. Out of current income he pays for services
currently rendered. Through income set aside in social security taxes and
in pension and insurance funds, he reserves a claim on services to be
rendered in the future.

[11] Mention of the social security now provided for the overwhelming number of United States citizens brings this discussion to the topic
of work. Social security is one of the devices evolved in the recent history
of our industrial economy to help solve the problem of "distribution."
This, as is well known, is the last frontier of economics. Viewed from the
vantage of the economy as a whole, it is the problem of finding people
qualified to consume the increasing abundance of goods produced by a
declining number of workers. From the point of view of the individual
citizen, it is the problem of finding work in a shrinking labor market in

order to qualify as a consumer of that abundance. Thus, as we shall see, the primary function of work is the distribution of goods. This is clearly a different situation from that which prevailed in the valleys of the Tigris and Euphrates 7,000 years ago, when the surplus had to be extracted from scarcity by coercion.

[12] Modern industrial technology produces a vast material surplus of goods, many times greater than the need of the workers engaged in producing it. That surplus goes begging for consumers because technology has subverted the social institution of work. The subversion of work began, of course, with the displacement of the biologically generated energy of human muscle by the mechanically generated energy of steam engines. The reciprocal steam engine gave way after little more than half a century to the steam turbine, the generator of electrical energy in the huge quantities that are measured in kilowatts. Studies conducted many years ago, when muscles were yielding a day's work to steam, showed that one man can put out about 48 kilowatt-hours in useful work in a year. On that basis, the 750 billion kilowatt-hours of electricity generated in the United States puts the equivalent of eighty-five slaves at the disposal of each man, woman, and child in the population.

[13] But this is an old story. The new story is the disemployment of the human nervous system. In industrial production the function of the human worker has been to set the tool, start up the machine, supervise its performance, correct its error, and keep its parts in working order. The machine has been doing all the work, including work that exceeds human physical capacity. But, for lack of a nervous system, it has had to depend upon human beings to regulate its operations.

[14] The robot, or artificial nervous system, is the steam engine of the present phase of the industrial revolution. Unlike the steam engine, it does not announce its presence by huffing and puffing, and it has no easily recognized anatomical structure. But it does have a single underlying principle, which is as clear-cut and universal as the idea of converting heat into mechanical energy. This essential idea is known to engineers as feedback.

[15] Feedback is the principle that underlies all self-regulating systems, including living organisms. The nearest and simplest example of feedback in action is the household thermostat: A mechanical sense organ absorbs a little of the heat generated by the household heating plant and thereby makes a measurement of its output. This small fraction of the output is fed back in the form of a signal to correct the input of fuel to the heating unit. By this feeding-back of output to input, the household heating plant is made to regulate itself.

[16] Now, the principle of converting heat to mechanical energy is embodied in about half a dozen economically important heat engines—including the steam turbine, the internal combustion engine, the gas tur-

bine, and the rocket engine. The feedback control systems in our economy, on the other hand, appear in a host of species and varieties—electrical, electronic, pneumatic, hydraulic, mechanical—and in such diversity of design and appearance that they have only the essential feedback principle in common.

[17] An accurate census of these robots has not been made. But the evidence is strong that they now out-number the human workers employed in industry. Our entire energy economy—from the steam plant out across the high-tension lines to the rotating machinery of industry—is now subject to automatic control. The new technology of atomic energy is critically dependent upon automatic control; dozens of feedback circuits in the depths of a nuclear reactor control the dreadful flux of atomic particles in which no living things could survive. Our petroleum refineries and almost all of our chemical process plants are today so highly robotized that their entire operations are controlled by one or two human operators stationed at the central push-button control panel.

[18] It is only a few steps from here to the fully automatic factory. In the petroleum industry, such a factory would make use of an instrument —such as the nuclear resonance spectrometer, which has only recently graduated from the laboratory—to analyze the output stream of a refinery. The spectrometer would feed back its reading to a mechanical computer, one of the "giant brain" variety. These machines are already equal to doing the work of the human operator at the control panel; they need merely to be equipped with instructions covering all possible contingencies in the operation of the plant. Comparing the spectrometer report on the output of the refinery with the instructions stored in its memory, the computer would check and correct the performance of the robot valves at all points on the process stream. In fact, the first full-scale refineries incorporating the principal elements of the self-regulating robot factory are now "on stream."

[19] Obviously, the purpose in designing the automatic petroleum refinery is not to replace the one or two human operators who still remain on the payroll. This was the naïve idea of a Middle Eastern petroleum prince for whom an American oil company was building a refinery not long ago. Out of consideration for the underemployed *fellaheen* who were to squat in the sand outside the refinery fence, he asked whether jobs might not be created by disengaging the robots from the valves. The engineers took him seriously enough to re-examine the entire control system. They had to conclude that no team of human beings could be trained and coordinated to do its work.

• • •

[20] The evidence that full employment is no longer an attainable objective seems to be growing. Of course, the arms budget can be arbitrarily increased, and the size of the armed forces along with it, to offset tech-

nological disemployment in the armament industries. But no one really wants to contemplate an indefinite continuation of the arms race. Alternatively, or concurrently, some of the slack can be taken up by a thirty-hour work week, a measure advocated by both presidential candidates as long ago as 1956. After that, the work week could be reduced to twenty-five, then twenty hours—and the inefficiencies inherent in such a short work week would help to create more jobs. At that point the nation will have come really close to being a workless society.

from

THE TWO CULTURES: AND A SECOND LOOK
C. P. Snow

[1] There is no getting away from it. It is technically possible to carry out the scientific revolution in India, Africa, South-east Asia, Latin America, the Middle East, within fifty years. There is no excuse for western man not to know this. And not to know that this is the one way out through the three menaces which stand in our way—H-bomb war, over-population, the gap between the rich and the poor. This is one of the situations where the worst crime is innocence.

[2] Since the gap between the rich countries and the poor can be removed, it will be. If we are shortsighted, inept, incapable either of good-will or enlightened self-interest, then it may be removed to the accompaniment of war and starvation: but removed it will be. The questions are, how, and by whom. To those questions, one can only give partial answers: but that may be enough to set us thinking. The scientific revolution on the world-scale needs, first and foremost, capital: capital in all forms, including capital machinery. The poor countries, until they have got beyond a certain point on the industrial curve cannot accumulate that capital. That is why the gap between rich and poor is widening. The capital must come from outside.

[3] There are only two possible sources. One is the West, which means mainly the U.S., the other is the U.S.S.R. Even the United States hasn't

From *The Two Cultures: And a Second Look* by C. P. Snow. Reprinted by permission of Cambridge University Press, New York.

infinite resources of such capital. If they or Russia tried to do it alone, it would mean an effort greater than either had to make industrially in the war. If they both took part, it wouldn't mean that order of sacrifice—though in my view it's optimistic to think, as some wise men do, that it would mean no sacrifice at all. The scale of the operation requires that it would have to be a national one. Private industry, even the biggest private industry, can't touch it, and in no sense is it a fair business risk. It's a bit like asking Duponts or I.C.I. back in 1940 to finance the entire development of the atomic bomb.

[4] The second requirement, after capital, as important as capital, is men. That is, trained scientists and engineers adaptable enough to devote themselves to a foreign country's industrialisation for at least ten years out of their lives. Here, unless and until the Americans and we educate ourselves both sensibly and imaginatively, the Russians have a clear edge. This is where their educational policy has already paid big dividends. They have such men to spare if they are needed. We just haven't, and the Americans aren't much better off. Imagine, for example, that the U.S. government and ours had agreed to help the Indians to carry out a major industrialisation, similar in scale to the Chinese. Imagine that the capital could be found. It would then require something like ten thousand to twenty thousand engineers from the U.S. and here [U.K.] to help get the thing going. At present, we couldn't find them.

[5] These men, whom we don't yet possess, need to be trained not only in scientific but in human terms. They could not do their job if they did not shrug off every trace of paternalism. Plenty of Europeans, from St. Francis Xavier to Schweitzer, have devoted their lives to Asians and Africans, nobly but paternally. These are not the Europeans whom Asians and Africans are going to welcome now. They want men who will muck in as colleagues, who will pass on what they know, do an honest technical job, and get out. Fortunately, this is an attitude which comes easily to scientists. They are freer than most people from racial feeling; their own culture is in its human relations a democratic one. In their own internal climate, the breeze of the equality of man hits you in the face, sometimes rather roughly, just as it does in Norway.

[6] That is why scientists would do us good all over Asia and Africa. And they would do their part too in the third essential of the scientific revolution—which, in a country like India, would have to run in parallel with the capital investment and the initial foreign help. That is, an educational programme as complete as the Chinese, who appear in ten years to have transformed their universities and built so many new ones that they are now nearly independent of scientists and engineers from outside. Ten years. With scientific teachers from this country and the U.S., and what is also necessary, with teachers of English, other poor countries could do the same in twenty.

[7] That is the size of the problem. An immense capital outlay, an immense investment in men, both scientists and linguists, most of whom the West does not yet possess. With rewards negligible in the short term, apart from doing the job: and in the long term most uncertain.

[8] People will ask me, in fact in private they have already asked me —'This is all very fine and large. But you are supposed to be a realistic man. You are interested in the fine structure of politics; you have spent some time studying how men behave in the pursuit of their own ends. Can you possibly believe that men will behave as you say they ought to? Can you imagine a political technique, in parliamentary societies like the U.S. or our own, by which any such plan could become real? Do you really believe that there is one chance in ten that any of this will happen?'

[9] That is fair comment. I can only reply that I don't know. On the one hand, it is a mistake, and it is a mistake, of course, which anyone who is called realistic is specially liable to fall into, to think that when we have said something about the egotisms, the weaknesses, the vanities, the power-seekings of men, that we have said everything. Yes, they are like that. They are the bricks with which we have got to build, and one can judge them through the extent of one's own selfishness. But they are sometimes capable of more, and any 'realism' which doesn't admit of that isn't serious.

[10] On the other hand, I confess, and I should be less than honest if I didn't, that I can't see the political techniques through which the good human capabilities of the West can get into action. The best one can do, and it is a poor best, is to nag away. That is perhaps too easy a palliative for one's disquiet. For, though I don't know how we can do what we need to do, or whether we shall do anything at all, I do know this: that, if we don't do it, the Communist countries will in time. They will do it at great cost to themselves and others, but they will do it. If that is how it turns out, we shall have failed, both practically and morally. At best, the West will have become an *enclave* in a different world—and this country will be the *enclave* of an *enclave*. Are we resigning ourselves to that? History is merciless to failure. In any case, if that happens, we shall not be writing the history.

[11] Meanwhile, there are steps to be taken which aren't outside the powers of reflective people. Education isn't the total solution to this problem: but without education the West can't even begin to cope. All the arrows point the same way. Closing the gap between our cultures is a necessity in the most abstract intellectual sense, as well as in the most practical. When those two senses have grown apart, then no society is going to be able to think with wisdom. For the sake of the intellectual life, for the sake of this country's special danger, for the sake of the western society living precariously rich among the poor, for the sake of the poor who needn't be poor if there is intelligence in the world, it is ob-

ligatory for us and the Americans and the whole West to look at our education with fresh eyes. This is one of the cases where we and the Americans have the most to learn from each other. We have each a good deal to learn from the Russians, if we are not too proud. Incidentally, the Russians have a good deal to learn from us, too.

[12] Isn't it time we began? The danger is, we have been brought up to think as though we had all the time in the world. We have very little time. So little that I dare not guess at it.

NULL-P
William Tenn

[1] Several months after the Second Atomic War, when radioactivity still held one-third of the planet in desolation, Dr. Daniel Glurt of Fillmore Township, Wisc., stumbled upon a discovery which was to generate humanity's ultimate sociological advance.

[2] Like Columbus, smug over his voyage to India; like Nobel, proud of the synthesis of dynamite which made combat between nations impossible, the doctor misinterpreted his discovery. Years later, he cackled to a visiting historian:

[3] "Had no idea it would lead to this, no idea at all. You remember, the war had just ended: we were feeling mighty subdued what with the eastern and western coasts of the United States practically sizzled away. Well, word came down from the new capitol at Topeka in Kansas for us doctors to give all our patients a complete physical check. Sort of be on the lookout, you know, for radioactive burns and them fancy new diseases the armies had been tossing back and forth. Well, sir, that's absolutely all I set out to do. I'd known George Abnego for over thirty years—treated him for chicken-pox and pneumonia and ptomaine poisoning. I'd *never* suspected!"

[4] Having reported to Dr. Glurt's office immediately after work in accordance with the proclamation shouted through the streets by the county clerk, and having waited patiently in line for an hour and a half, George Abnego was at last received into the small consulting room. Here he was thoroughly chest-thumped, X-rayed, blood-sampled and urine-

analyzed. His skin was examined carefully, and he was made to answer the five hundred questions prepared by the Department of Health in a pathetic attempt to cover the symptoms of the new ailments.

[5] George Abnego then dressed and went home to the cereal supper permitted for that day by the ration board. Dr. Glurt placed his folder in a drawer and called for the next patient. He had noticed nothing up to this point; yet already he had unwittingly begun the Abnegite Revolution.

[6] Four days later, the health survey of Fillmore, Wisc., being complete, the doctor forwarded the examination reports to Topeka. Just before signing George Abnego's sheet, he glanced at it cursorily, raised his eyebrows and entered the following note: "Despite the tendency to dental caries and athlete's foot, I would consider this man to be of average health. Physically, he is the Fillmore Township norm."

[7] It was this last sentence which caused the government medical official to chuckle and glance at the sheet once more. His smile was puzzled after this; it was even more puzzled after he had checked the figures and statements on the form against standard medical references.

[8] He wrote a phrase in red ink in the right-hand corner and sent it along to Research.

[9] His name is lost to history.

[10] Research wondered why the report on George Abnego had been sent up—he had no unusual symptoms portending exotic innovations like cerebral measles or arterial trilhinosis. Then it observed the phrase in red ink and Dr. Glurt's remark. Research shrugged its anonymous shoulders and assigned a crew of statisticians to go further into the matter.

[11] A week later, as a result of their findings, another crew—nine medical specialists—left for Fillmore. They examined George Abnego with coordinated precision. Afterwards, they called on Dr. Glurt briefly, leaving a copy of their examination report with him when he expressed interest.

[12] Ironically, the government copies were destroyed in the Topeka Hard-Shelled Baptist Riots a month later, the same riots which stimulated Dr. Glurt to launch the Abnegite Revolution.

[13] This Baptist denomination, because of population shrinkage due to atomic and bacteriological warfare, was now the largest single religious body in the nation. It was then controlled by a group pledged to the establishment of a Hard-Shelled Baptist theocracy in what was left of the United States. The rioters were quelled after much destruction and bloodshed; their leader, the Reverend Hemingway T. Gaunt—who had vowed that he would remove neither the pistol from his left hand nor the Bible from his right until the Rule of God had been established and the Third Temple built—was sentenced to death by a jury composed of stern-faced fellow Baptists.

[14] Commenting on the riots, the Fillmore, Wisc., *Bugle-Herald* drew a mournful parallel between the Topeka street battles and the destruction wreaked upon the world by atomic conflict.

[15] "International communication and transportation having broken down," the editorial went on broodingly, "we now know little of the smashed world in which we live beyond such meager facts as the complete disappearance of Australia beneath the waves, and the contraction of Europe to the Pyrenees and Ural Mountains. We know that our planet's physical appearance has changed as much from what it was ten years ago, as the infant monstrosities and mutants being born everywhere as a result of radioactivity are unpleasantly different from their parents.

[16] "Truly, in these days of mounting catastrophe and change, our faltering spirits beg the heavens for a sign, a portent, that all will be well again, that all will yet be as it once was, that the waters of disaster will subside and we shall once more walk upon the solid ground of normalcy."

[17] It was this last word which attracted Dr. Glurt's attention. That night, he slid the report of the special government medical crew into the newspaper's mail slot. He had penciled a laconic note in the margin of the first page:

[18] "Noticed your interest in the subject."

[19] Next week's edition of the Fillmore *Bugle-Herald* flaunted a page one five-column headline.

FILLMORE CITIZEN THE SIGN?

Normal Man of Fillmore May Be Answer From Above
Local Doctor Reveals Government Medical Secret

[20] The story that followed was liberally sprinkled with quotations taken equally from the government report and the Psalms of David. The startled residents of Fillmore learned that one George Abnego, a citizen unnoticed in their midst for almost forty years, was a living abstraction. Through a combination of circumstances no more remarkable than those producing a royal flush in stud poker, Abnego's physique, psyche, and other miscellaneous attributes had resulted in that legendary creature—the statistical average.

[21] According to the last census taken before the war, George Abnego's height and weight were identical with the mean of the American adult male. He had married at the exact age—year, month, day—when statisticians had estimated the marriage of the average man took place; he had married a woman the *average* number of years younger than himself; his income as declared on his last tax statement was the *average* income for that year. The very teeth in his mouth tallied in quantity and condition with those predicted by the American Dental Association to be found on a man extracted at random from the population. Abnego's me-

tabolism and blood pressure, his bodily proportions and private neuroses, were all cross-sections of the latest available records. Subjected to every psychological and personality test available, his final, overall grade corrected out to show that he was both average and normal.

[22] Finally, Mrs. Abnego had been recently delivered of their third child, a boy. This development had not only occurred at exactly the right time according to the population indices, but it had resulted in an entirely normal sample of humanity—unlike most babies being born throughout the land.

[23] The *Bugle-Herald* blared its hymn to the new celebrity around a greasy photograph of the family in which the assembled Abnegos stared glassily out at the reader, looking, as many put it, "Average—average as hell!"

[24] Newspapers in other states were invited to copy.

[25] They did, slowly at first, then with an accelerating, contagious enthusiasm. Indeed, as the intense public interest in this symbol of stability, this refugee from the extremes, became manifest, newspaper columns gushed fountains of purple prose about the "Normal Man of Fillmore."

[26] At Nebraska State University, Professor Roderick Klingmeister noticed that many members of his biology class were wearing extra-large buttons decorated with pictures of George Abnego. "Before beginning my lecture," he chuckled, "I would like to tell you that this 'normal man' of yours is no Messiah. All he is, I am afraid, is a bell-shaped curve with ambitions, the median made flesh—"

[27] He got no further. He was brained with his own demonstration microscope.

[28] Even that early, a few watchful politicians noticed that no one was punished for this hasty act.

[29] The incident could be related to many others which followed: the unfortunate and unknown citizen of Duluth, for example, who—at the high point of that city's *Welcome Average Old Abnego* parade—was heard to remark in good-natured amazement, "Why, he's just an ordinary jerk like you and me," and was immediately torn into celebratory confetti by horrified neighbors in the crowd.

[30] Developments such as these received careful consideration from men whose power was derived from the just, if well-directed, consent of the governed.

[31] George Abnego, these gentry concluded, represented the maturation of a great national myth which, implicit in the culture for over a century, had been brought to garish fulfillment by the mass communication and entertainment media.

[32] This was the myth that began with the juvenile appeal to be "A Normal Red-Blooded American Boy" and ended, on the highest political

levels, with a shirtsleeved, suspendered seeker after political office boasting, "Shucks, everybody knows who I am. I'm folks—just plain folks."

[33] This was the myth from which were derived such superficially disparate practices as the rite of political baby-kissing, the cult of "keeping up with the Joneses," the foppish, foolish, forever-changing fads which went through the population with the monotonous regularity and sweep of a windshield wiper. The myth of styles and fraternal organizations. The myth of the "regular fellow."

[34] There was a presidential election that year.

[35] Since all that remained of the United States was the Middle West, the Democratic Party had disappeared. Its remnants had been absorbed by a group calling itself the Old Guard Republicans, the closest thing to an American Left. The party in power—the Conservative Republicans—so far right as to verge upon royalism, had acquired enough pledged theocratic votes to make them smug about the election.

[36] Desperately, the Old Guard Republicans searched for a candidate. Having regretfully passed over the adolescent epileptic recently elected to the governorship of South Dakota in violation of the state constitution —and deciding against the psalm-singing grandmother from Oklahoma who punctuated her senatorial speeches with religious music upon the banjo—the party strategists arrived, one summer afternoon, in Fillmore, Wisconsin.

[37] From the moment that Abnego was persuaded to accept the nomination and his last well-intentioned but flimsy objection was overcome (the fact that he was a registered member of the opposition party), it was obvious that the tide of battle had turned, that the fabled grass roots had caught fire.

[38] Abnego ran for President on the slogan "Back to Normal with the Normal Man!"

[39] By the time the Conservative Republicans met in conference assembled, the danger of loss by landslide was already apparent. They changed their tactics, tried to meet the attack head-on and imaginatively.

[40] They nominated a hunchback for the presidency. This man suffered from the additional disability of being a distinguished professor of law in a leading university; he had married with no issue and divorced with much publicity; and finally, he had once admitted to a congressional investigating committee that he had written and published surrealist poetry. Posters depicting him leering horribly, his hump twice life-size, were smeared across the country over the slogan: "An Abnormal Man for an Abnormal World!"

[41] Despite this brilliant political stroke, the issue was never in doubt. On Election Day, the nostalgic slogan defeated its medicative adversary by three to one. Four years later, with the same opponents, it had risen

to five and a half to one. And there was no organized opposition when Abnego ran for a third term. . . .

[42] Not that he had crushed it. There was more casual liberty of political thought allowed during Abnego's administration than in many previous ones. But less political thinking was done.

[43] Whenever possible, Abnego avoided decision. When a decision was unavoidable, he made it entirely on the basis of precedent. He rarely spoke on a topic of current interest and never committed himself. He was garrulous and an exhibitionist only about his family.

[44] "How can you lampoon a vacuum?" This had been the wail of many opposition newspaper writers and cartoonists during the early years of the Abnegite Revolution, when men still ran against Abnego at election time. They tried to draw him into ridiculous statements or admissions time and again without success. Abnego was simply incapable of saying anything that any major cross-section of the population would consider ridiculous.

[45] Emergencies? "Well," Abnego had said, in the story every schoolchild knew, "I've noticed even the biggest forest fire will burn itself out. Main thing is not to get excited."

[46] He made them e down in low blood-pressure areas. And, after years of building and d truction, of stimulation and conflict, of accelerating anxieties and torments, they rested and were humbly grateful.

[47] It seemed to many, from the day Abnego was sworn in, that chaos began to waver and everywhere a glorious welcome stability flowered. In some respects, such as the decrease in the number of monstrous births, processes were under way which had nothing at all to do with the Normal Man of Fillmore; in others—the astonished announcement by lexicographers, for example, that slang expressions peculiar to teen agers in Abnego's first term were used by their children in exactly the same contexts eighteen years later in his fifth administration—the historical leveling-out and patting-down effects of the Abnegite trowel were obvious.

[48] The verbal expression of this great calm was the Abnegism.

[49] History's earliest record of these deftly phrased inadequacies relates to the administration in which Abnego, at last feeling secure enough to do so, appointed a cabinet without any regard to the wishes of his party hierarchy. A journalist, attempting to point up the absolute lack of color in the new official family, asked if any one of them—from Secretary of State to Postmaster-General—had ever committed himself publicly on any issue or, in previous positions, had been responsible for a single constructive step in any direction.

[50] To which the President supposedly replied with a bland, unhesitating smile, "I always say there's no hard feelings if no one's defeated.

Well, sir, no one's defeated in a fight where the referee can't make a decision."

[51] Apocryphal though it may have been, this remark expressed the mood of Abnegite America perfectly. "As pleasant as a no-decision bout" became part of everyday language.

[52] Certainly as apocryphal as the George Washington cherry-tree legend, but the most definite Abnegism of them all was the one attributed to the President after a performance of *Romeo and Juliet*. "It is better not to have loved at all, than to have loved and lost," he is reported to have remarked at the morbid end of the play.

[53] At the inception of Abnego's sixth term—the first in which his oldest son served with him as Vice-President—a group of Europeans reopened trade with the United States by arriving in a cargo ship assembled from the salvaged parts of three sunken destroyers and one capsized aircraft carrier.

[54] Received everywhere with undemonstrative cordiality, they traveled the country, amazed at the placidity—the almost total absence of political and military excitement on the one hand, and the rapid technological retrogression on the other. One of the emissaries sufficiently mislaid his diplomatic caution to comment before he left:

[55] "We came to America, to these cathedrals of industrialism, in the hope that we would find solutions to many vexing problems of applied science. These problems—the development of atomic power for factory use, the application of nuclear fission to such small arms as pistols and hand grenades—stand in the way of our postwar recovery. But you, in what remains of the United States of America, don't even see what we, in what remains of Europe, consider so complex and pressing. Excuse me, but what you have here is a national trance!"

[56] His American hosts were not offended: they received his expostulations with polite smiles and shrugs. The delegate returned to tell his countrymen that the Americans, always notorious for their madness, had finally specialized in cretinism.

[57] But another delegate who had observed widely and asked many searching questions went back to his native Toulouse (French culture had once more coagulated in Provence) to define the philosophical foundations of the Abnegite Revolution.

[58] In a book which was read by the world with enormous interest, Michel Gaston Fouffnique, sometime Professor of History at the Sorbonne, pointed out that while twentieth-century man had escaped from the narrow Greek formulations sufficiently to visualize a non-Aristotelian logic and a non-Euclidean geometry, he had not yet had the intellectual temerity to create a non-Platonic system of politics. Not until Abnego.

[59] "Since the time of Socrates," wrote Monsieur Fouffnique, "Man's political viewpoints have been in thrall to the conception that the best

should govern. How to determine that 'best,' the scale of values to be used in order that the 'best' and not mere undifferentiated 'betters' should rule —these have been the basic issues around which have raged the fires of political controversy for almost three millennia. Whether an aristocracy of birth or intellect should prevail is an argument over values; whether rulers should be determined by the will of a god as determined by the entrails of a hog, or selected by the whole people on the basis of a ballot tally—these are alternatives in method. But hitherto no political system has ventured away from the implicit and unexamined assumption first embodied in the philosopher-state of Plato's *Republic*.

[60] "Now, at last, America has turned and questioned the pragmatic validity of the axiom. The young democracy to the west, which introduced the concept of the Rights of Man to jurisprudence, now gives a feverish world the Doctrine of the Lowest Common Denominator in government. According to this doctrine as I have come to understand it through prolonged observation, it is *not* the worst who should govern— as many of my prejudiced fellow-delegates insist—but the mean: what might be termed the 'unbest' or the 'non-élite.' "

[61] Situated amid the still-radioactive rubbish of modern war, the people of Europe listened devoutly to readings from Fouffnique's monograph. They were enthralled by the peaceful monotonies said to exist in the United States and bored by the academician's reasons thereto: that a governing group who knew to begin with that they were "unbest" would be free of the myriad jealousies and conflicts arising from the need to prove individual superiority, and that such a group would tend to smooth any major quarrel very rapidly because of the dangerous opportunities created for imaginative and resourceful people by conditions of struggle and strain.

[62] There were oligarchs here and bosses there; in one nation an ancient religious order still held sway, in another, calculating and brilliant men continued to lead the people. But the word was preached. Shamans appeared in the population, ordinary-looking folk who were called "abnegos." Tyrants found it impossible to destroy these shamans, since they were not chosen for any special abilities but simply because they represented the median of a given group: the middle of any population grouping, it was found, lasts as long as the group itself. Therefore, through bloodshed and much time, the abnegos spread their philosophy and flourished.

[63] Oliver Abnego, who became the first President of the World, was President Abnego VI of the United States of America. His son presided —as Vice President—over a Senate composed mostly of his uncles and his cousins in an economy which had deteriorated very, very slightly from the conditions experienced by the founder of their line.

[64] As world president, Oliver Abnego approved only one measure— that granting preferential university scholarships to students whose grades

were closest to their age-group median all over the planet. The President could hardly have been accused of originality and innovation unbecoming to his high office, however, since for some time now all reward systems—scholastic, athletic, and even industrial—had been adjusted to recognition of the most average achievement while castigating equally the highest and lowest scores.

[65] When the usable oil gave out shortly afterwards, men turned with perfect calmness to coal. The last turbines were placed in museums while still in operating condition: the people they served felt their isolated and individual use of electricity was too ostentatious for good abnegism.

[66] Outstanding cultural phenomena of this period were carefully rhymed and exactly metered poems addressed to the nondescript beauties and vague charms of a wife or sweetheart. Had not anthropology disappeared long ago, it would have become a matter of common knowledge that there was a startling tendency to uniformity everywhere in such qualities as bone structure, features and pigmentation, not to mention intelligence, musculature, and personality. Humanity was breeding rapidly and unconsciously in towards its center.

[67] Nonetheless, just before the exhaustion of coal, there was a brief sputter of intellect among a group who established themselves on a site northwest of Cairo. These Nilotics, as they were known, consisted mostly of unreconstructed dissidents expelled by their communities, with a leavening of the mentally ill and the physically handicapped; they had at their peak an immense number of technical gadgets and yellowing books culled from crumbling museums and libraries the world over.

[68] Intensely ignored by their fellow-men, the Nilotics carried on shrill and interminable debates while plowing their muddy fields just enough to keep alive. They concluded that they were the only surviving heirs of *homo sapiens,* the bulk of the world's population now being composed of what they termed *homo abnegus.*

[69] Man's evolutionary success, they concluded, had been due chiefly to his lack of specialization. While other creatures had been forced to standardize to a particular and limited environment, mankind had been free for a tremendous spurt, until ultimately it had struck an environmental factor which demanded the price all viable forms had to pay eventually—specialization.

[70] Having come this far in discussion, the Nilotics determined to use the ancient weapons at their disposal to save *homo abnegus* from himself. However, violent disagreements over the methods of re-education to be employed, led them to a bloody internecine conflict with those same weapons in the course of which the entire colony was destroyed and its site made untenable for life. About this time, his coal used up, Man re-entered the broad, self-replenishing forests.

[71] The reign of *homo abnegus* endured for a quarter of a million years. It was disputed finally—and successfully—by a group of Newfound-

land retrievers who had been marooned on an island in Hudson Bay when the cargo vessel transporting them to new owners had sunk back in the twentieth century.

[72] These sturdy and highly intelligent dogs, limited perforce to each other's growling society for several hundred millennia, learned to talk in much the same manner that mankind's simian ancestors had learned to walk when a sudden shift in botany destroyed their ancient arboreal homes—out of boredom. Their wits sharpened further by the hardships of their bleak island, their imaginations stimulated by the cold, the articulate retrievers built a most remarkable canine civilization in the Arctic before sweeping southward to enslave and eventually domesticate humanity.

[73] Domestication took the form of breeding men solely for their ability to throw sticks and other objects, the retrieving of which was a sport still popular among the new masters of the planet, however sedentary certain erudite individuals might have become.

[74] Highly prized as pets were a group of men with incredibly thin and long arms; another school of retrievers, however, favored a stocky breed whose arms were short, but extremely sinewy; while, occasionally, interesting results were obtained by inducing rickets for a few generations to produce a pet whose arms were sufficiently limber as to appear almost boneless. This last type, while intriguing both esthetically and scientifically, was generally decried as a sign of decadence in the owner as well as a functional insult to the animal.

[75] Eventually, of course, the retriever civilization developed machines which could throw sticks farther, faster, and with more frequency. Thereupon, except in the most backward canine communities, Man disappeared.

DISTRIBUTION OF ABUNDANCE: EQUAL INCOMES FOR ALL
Technocracy, Inc.

Obsolete System

[1] The Price System grew out of the days of scarcity, when trading his crude materials or stealing them, was the only way in which

By permission of Technocracy Inc., Savannah, Ohio 44874.

man could acquire the articles which he required. Through complex ramifications the trading system has grown until it is now the overwhelming structure of finance, business, commerce, and politics, in short, the Price System in toto—a gigantic structure, but still just a method of exchanging goods, springing from the ancient custom and necessity of barter. No intention or pretense is made of accurate measurement or control; no physical accounting is involved; no accurate predictions can be made; and no stabilization can be assured. The Price System is simply a method of erratic exchange. In scarcity it sufficed well enough as an exchange method; in abundance it cannot even do that.

[2] The dislocation of the commodity exchange method of distributing goods and services became apparent after World War I. The disrupted conditions at that time led to a scientific investigation which in turn proved that the only common denominator of all goods and services was *energy*.

[3] The scientists who pointed this out simply proposed to measure the total amount of energy used by the North American Continent in a given period; measure the energy cost of physical production and services; and use these measurements as the basis for regulation of all Continental production and distribution.

Technocracy Is the Tool

[4] Technocracy's basic postulate is, "The phenomena involved in the functional operation of a social mechanism are metrical." In other words, anything that materially affects us or changes our environment is measurable. The scientists and technologists know this and have applied it directly to the task of equipping North America with the most intricate and efficient productive mechanism ever to exist on earth. When they are given their chance they will see that the abundant goods and services produced are adequately distributed to everyone on the Continent. Technocracy is the tool by which North Americans may gain abundance and security.

[5] Technocracy would put into operation a Continental control of all flow lines of production and distribution—a Continental statistical system which would record the desires of every citizen in his choice of consumable goods and available services. This system would do the following things in a physical area where abundance is certain:

[6] *(1)* Register on a continuous 24-hour-per-day basis the total net conversion of energy, which would determine (a) the availability of energy for Continental plant construction and maintenance, (b) the amount of physical wealth available in the form of consumable goods and services for consumption by the total population during the balance-load period.

[7] *(2)* By means of the registration of energy converted and consumed, make possible a balanced load.

[8] *(3)* Provide a continuous inventory of all production and consumption.

[9] *(4)* Provide a specific registration of the type, kind, etc., of all goods and services, where produced, and where used.

[10] *(5)* Provide a specific registration of the consumption of each individual, plus a record and description of the individual.

[11] *(6)* Allow the citizen the widest latitude of choice in consuming his individual share of Continental physical wealth.

[12] *(7)* Distribute goods and services abundantly to every member of the population.

Why Not Money?

[13] On the basis of these requirements, it is interesting to consider money as a possible medium of distribution. But before doing this, let us bear in mind what the properties of money are. In the first place, money relationships are all based upon "value," which in turn is a function of scarcity. Hence money is not a "measure" of anything. Secondly, money is a debt claim against society and is valid in the hands of any bearer. In other words, it is negotiable; it can be traded, stolen, given or gambled away. Thirdly, money can be saved. Fourthly, money circulates, and is not destroyed or cancelled out upon being spent. On each of these counts money fails to meet our requirements as our medium of distribution.

Money Is Inadequate

[14] Suppose, for instance, that we attempted to distribute by means of money the goods and services produced. Suppose that it were decided that 200 billion dollars' worth of goods and services were to be produced in a given year, and suppose further that 200 billion dollars were distributed to the population during that time with which to purchase these goods and services. Immediately the foregoing properties of money would create trouble. Due to the fact that money is not a *physical* measure of goods and services, there is no assurance that prices would not change during the year, and that 200 billion dollars issued for use in a given year would be used in that year. If it were not used this would immediately begin to curtail production and start oscillations. Due to the fact that money is negotiable, and that certain human beings, by hook or crook, have a facility for getting it away from other human beings, this would defeat the requirement that distribution must reach all human beings. A further consequence of the negotiability of money is that it can be used very effectively for purposes of bribery. Hence the most success-

THE TECHNATE ☯ OF AMERICA

DISTRIBUTION CERTIFICATE 180

William Smith 1972-73

9038·L 16794	8141	8 33·16 3	22-11
13090-23	205 21·05	H 76302	Z 97321
34·46-11 E·7·8			

The Distribution Certificate

IT IS   a Medium of Distribution
A Continental Accounting System
24 Hour Inventory
Identification and Record of Holder
Guarantee of Security

IT IS NOT   a Medium of Exchange
Subject to Fluctuation of 'Value'
Subject to Theft or Loss
Subject to Hoarding or Gambling
A Means to Wealth or Prestige
A Means of Creating Debt

ful accumulators of money would be able eventually not only to disrupt the flow line, but also to buy a controlling interest in the social mechanism itself, which brings us right back to where we started from.

[15] Due to the fact that money is a species of debt, and hence cumulative, the amount would have to be continuously increased, which, in conjunction with its property of being negotiable, would lead inevitably to concentration of control in a few hands, and to general disruption of the distribution system which was supposed to be maintained.

[16] Thus, money in any form whatsoever is completely inadequate as a medium of distribution in an economy of abundance with a Price System control. Any social system employing commodity evaluation (commodity valuations are the basis of all money) is a Price System. Hence it is not possible to maintain an economy of abundance by means of a Price System.

The Scientific Answer

[17] Technocracy's Energy Certificate is the only instrument of distribution which can be used in this Continent's emerging era of abundance —the progress of which is being speeded up by automation. This Energy Certificate provides the accounting means whereby each individual North American can express his individual preference as to what he wants of the products North America is capable of producing. That is its function— to record the demand for goods and services and, thereby, to determine the amount to be produced.

[18] By applying one specific technological measuring device, produc-

tion and consumption can be balanced and the first specification for social harmony is immediately achievable.

Vote with Meaning

[19] The only real vote is purchasing power. What we buy we vote for. With an abundance of purchasing power we can vote as often as we like, every day of the year, and always win our vote. In a Technate each adult American citizen would have a standard of living equivalent to an annual income of $40,000 or more.

[20] The Energy Certificate eliminates both the basis and the need of all social work and charity. It would reduce crime to but a small fraction of what exists today.

[21] If you don't like the war, the poverty, the misery, the worry, the crime, the disease, and the corruption which the Price System spawns, why do you stick with it? If you have the courage to prepare for social change, you will join TECHNOCRACY—the only Organization which has offered a design for the distribution of abundance to all the people of this Continental Area.

12

UTOPIA-DYSTOPIA:
HAVE WE A CHOICE?

The world of today is as different from the world I was born in as that world was from Julius Caesar's. . . . Almost as much has happened since I was born as happened before.—*Kenneth Boulding, 1964*[1]

Individual freedom and human dignity have outlived their usefulness and should be replaced by a designed culture with controls, says psychologist B. F. Skinner.—The Arizona Republic, 1971[2]

If the temptation of the traditional Utopia was to slip away into totalitarianism, the temptation of the new is to dream one's life away.
—Edwin Warner[3]

Without the Utopians of other times, men would still live in caves, miserable and naked. Utopia is the principle of all progress, and the essay into a better world.—*Anatole France*[4]

Reference numbers refer to source notes on page 313.

history of Utopias would begin with the Garden of Eden and would certainly include Plato's Republic as a notable early example. The selections in this chapter, however, have been excerpted from works of this century, primarily the latter half.

Science fiction, the richest source of novels of this genre, has been evaluated in some depth by Lyman Sargent.* He classifies novels which have concentrated on the cultures of the future as "social science fiction." Among the generalizations and conclusions found in his article are several that are particularly striking:

1. Dystopias (cultures dominated by evil forces) far outnumber Utopias. Sargent partially accounts for this depressing fact by pointing out that the dystopian novel provides a climate for a protagonist to rebel against; the Utopian hero, almost by definition, lives in a world with minimum conflict.

2. Sex has entered the world of science fiction and assumes a major function in many novels, particularly in conjunction with those dystopias threatened by overpopulation. Homosexuality is often accepted and occasionally encouraged as one of the many measures taken to control population. On the other hand, in Robert Heinlein's *Stranger in a Strange Land,* communally shared sex is an accepted aspect of community activities.

3. A frequently recurring theme is the return to barbarism, which sometimes is caused by a nuclear holocaust, occasionally by the invasion of extraterrestrial beings, often because of the famine, disease, and psychological trauma resulting from overpopulation.

4. Dystopias emphasize conformity and dictatorship in one form or another; Utopias stress individualism and political systems that are "vague, none or run by an intellectual elite."

Our selections are from writers whose works are included in a wide diversity of fields. The reader may wonder why the emphasis in this chapter has been on the dystopic, rather than on the more optimistic. For instance, Edward Bellamy's *Looking Backward,* though published in 1888, is still in print today and available in almost any bookstore. Its hopes, based on a belief in the fundamental goodness of man, would certainly have presented a brighter prediction of the future. Again, four centuries ago Sir Thomas More's *Utopia* described an ideal state, and a century later philosopher-statesman-scientist Sir Francis Bacon de-

---

* Lyman Sargent, "Utopia and Dystopia in Contemporary Science Fiction," *The Futurist,* June, 1972.

scribed in *New Atlantis* a civilization that would move many of us to overpowering nostalgia. But euphoria was not the purpose of this chapter, nor of this volume. Unbridled change tends to bring out the worst, not the best, in people. We tend to seek only those paths which feed our own interests and to avoid the responsibilities of decision-making.

Is it not a Utopian dream that keeps all of us going—a better life, a freer world? But we must realize we have no time to dream; in actuality, we may have too little time to act. We can no longer afford material luxury if its delights are accompanied by apathy.

Famed psychologist B. F. Skinner's *Walden Two* describes a society which his followers label Utopic, but which his opponents call a super-symbol of the denial of freedom. Certainly control in the book is "elitist"; without question, efficiency is the order of the day. The nonconformist is nonexistent. But before you damn Walden, thoughtful inquiry may reveal a number of intriguing advantages, and Skinner's followers are many.

Kurt Vonnegut's biting "Harrison Bergeron" from *Welcome to the Monkey House* is the second selection. In a few pages, this master critic of society creates an unforgettable example of a controlled world. Dystopia in a nutshell!

In the epilogue to *Utopia or Oblivion,* Buckminster Fuller describes one concept of future human living quarters with all the gusto that he brings to his soaring images of the future. This contemporary Renaissance Man is one of our truly great futurists in every sense.

Most readers think of Aldous Huxley's contribution to the future in connection with his widely-read *Brave New World,* a middle-thirties best-seller which has been reprinted dozens of times and in many languages. Far less familiar and much later (1962) is his Utopian novel *Island,* in which appears a series of paragraphs describing a civilization differing radically from the rigid culture of the earlier book. Huxley's ideas of what people *could* be show clearly in *Island.*

Despite the many people who decry the powerful surges of technology and the waves of knowledge seemingly too great to assimilate, we can endure. Forewarned and aware, we have the capacity to capitalize on the advances made in our understanding of nature and humankind. We can create the kind of world that is most desirable—our own, planned Utopia. Is it not reasonable to believe that a technology which sent men to the moon is capable of solving the technical problems of mass transportation, of smog-free air and unpolluted waters? Is it any more "unnatural" for us to raise the intelligence level of *Homo sapiens* than it was to eliminate pain from surgery? Utopia or dystopia should not be a matter of chance; it should be the result of choice.

from

WALDEN TWO
B. F. Skinner

[1] We found space near the windows of a small lounge and drew up chairs so that we could look out over the slowly darkening landscape. Frazier seemed to have no particular discussion prepared and he had begun to look a little tired. Castle must have been full of things to say, but he apparently felt that I should open the conversation.

[2] "We are grateful for your kindness," I said to Frazier, "not only in asking us to visit Walden Two but in giving us so much of your time. I'm afraid it's something of an imposition."

[3] "On the contrary," said Frazier. "I'm fully paid for talking with you. Two labor-credits are allowed each day for taking charge of guests of Walden Two. I can use only one of them, but it's a bargain even so, because I'm more than fairly paid by your company."

[4] "Labor-credits?" I said.

[5] "I'm sorry. I had forgotten. Labor-credits are a sort of money. But they're not coins or bills—just entries in a ledger. All goods and services are free, as you saw in the dining room this evening. Each of us pays for what he uses with twelve hundred labor-credits each year—say, four credits for each workday. We change the value according to the needs of the community. At two hours of work per credit—an eight-hour day—we could operate at a handsome profit. We're satisfied to keep just a shade beyond breaking even. The profit system is bad even when the worker gets the profits, because the strain of overwork isn't relieved by even a large reward. All we ask is to make expenses, with a slight margin of safety; we adjust the value of the labor-credit accordingly. At present it's about one hour of work per credit."

[6] "Your members work only four hours a day?" I said. There was an overtone of outraged virtue in my voice, as if I had asked if they were all adulterous.

[7] "On the average," Frazier replied casually. In spite of our obvious interest he went on at once to another point. "A credit system also makes it possible to evaluate a job in terms of the willingness of the members to undertake it. After all, a man isn't doing more or less than his share because of the time he puts in; it's what he's doing that counts. So we simply assign different credit values to different kinds of work, and ad-

just them from time to time on the basis of demand. Bellamy suggested the principle in *Looking Backward.*"

[8] "An unpleasant job like cleaning sewers has a high value, I suppose," I said.

[9] "Exactly. Somewhere around one and a half credits per hour. The sewer man works a little over two hours a day. Pleasanter jobs have lower values—say point seven or point eight. That means five hours a day, or even more. Working in the flower gardens has a very low value—point one. No one makes a living at it, but many people like to spend a little time that way, and we give them credit. In the long run, when the values have been adjusted, all kinds of work are equally desirable. If they weren't, there would be a demand for the more desirable, and the credit value would be changed. Once in a while we manipulate a preference, if some job seems to be avoided without cause."

[10] "I suppose you put phonographs in your dormitories which repeat 'I like to work in sewers. Sewers are lots of fun,'" said Castle.

[11] "No, Walden Two isn't that kind of brave new world," said Frazier. "We don't *propagandize.* That's a basic principle. I don't deny that it would be possible. We could make the heaviest work appear most honorable and desirable. Something of the sort has always been done by well-organized governments—to facilitate the recruiting of armies, for example. But not here. You may say that we propagandize *all* labor, if you like, but I see no objection to that. If we can make work pleasanter by proper training, why shouldn't we? But I digress."

[12] "What about the knowledge and skill required in many jobs?" said Castle. "Doesn't that interfere with free bidding? Certainly you can't allow just anyone to work as a doctor."

[13] "No, of course not. The principle has to be modified where long training is needed. Still, the preferences of the community as a whole determine the final value. If our doctors were conspicuously overworked *according to our standards,* it would be hard to get young people to choose that profession. We must see to it that there are enough doctors to bring the average schedule within range of the Walden Two standard."

[14] "What if nobody wanted to be a doctor?" I said.

[15] "Our trouble is the other way round."

[16] "I thought as much," said Castle. "Too many of your young members will want to go into interesting lines in spite of the work load. What do you do, then?"

[17] "Let them know how many places will be available, and let them decide. We're glad to have more than enough doctors, of course, and could always find some sort of work for them, but we can't offer more of a strictly medical practice than our disgustingly good health affords."

[18] "Then you don't offer complete personal freedom, do you?" said Castle, with ill-concealed excitement.

[19] "You haven't really resolved the conflict between a *laissez-faire* and a planned society."

[20] "I think we have. Yes. But you must know more about our educational system before I can show you how. The fact is, it's very unlikely that anyone at Walden Two will set his heart on a course of action so firmly that he'll be unhappy if it isn't open to him. That's as true of the choice of a girl as of a profession. Personal jealousy is almost unknown among us, and for a simple reason: we provide a broad experience and many attractive alternatives. The tender sentiment of the 'one and only' has less to do with constancy of heart than with singleness of opportunity. The chances are that our superfluous young premedic will find other courses open to him which will very soon prove equally attractive."

[21] "There's another case, too," I said. "You must have some sort of government. I don't see how you can permit a free choice of jobs there."

[22] "Our only government is a Board of Planners," said Frazier, with a change of tone which suggested that I had set off another standard harangue. "The name goes back to the days when Walden Two existed only on paper. There are six Planners, usually three men and three women. The sexes are on such equal terms here that no one guards equality very jealously. They may serve for ten years, but no longer. Three of us who've been on the Board since the beginning retire this year.

[23] "The Planners are charged with the success of the community. They make policies, review the work of the Managers, keep an eye on the state of the nation in general. They also have certain judicial functions. They're allowed six hundred credits a year for their services, which leaves two credits still due each day. At least one must be worked out in straight physical labor. That's why I can claim only one credit for acting as your Virgil through *il paradiso*."

[24] "It was Beatrice," I corrected.

[25] "How do you choose your Planners?" said Rodge.

[26] "The Board selects a replacement from a pair of names supplied by the Managers."

[27] "The members don't vote for them?" said Castle.

[28] "*No,*" said Frazier emphatically.

[29] "What are Managers?" I said hastily.

[30] "What the name implies: specialists in charge of the divisions and services of Walden Two. There are Managers of Food, Health, Play, Arts, Dentistry, Dairy, various industries, Supply, Labor, Nursery School, Advanced Education, and dozens of others. They requisition labor according to their needs, and their job is the managerial function which survives after they've assigned as much as possible to others. They're the hardest workers among us. It's an exceptional person who seeks and finds a place as Manager. He must have ability and a real concern for the welfare of the community."

[31] "*They* are elected by the members, I suppose?" said Castle, but it was obvious that he hoped for nothing of the sort.

[32] "The Managers aren't honorific personages, but carefully trained and tested specialists. How could the members gauge their ability? No, these are very much like Civil Service jobs. You work up to be a Manager —through intermediate positions which carry a good deal of responsibility and provide the necessary apprenticeship."

[33] "Then the members have no voice whatsoever," said Castle in a carefully controlled voice, as if he were filing the point away for future use.

[34] "Nor do they wish to have," said Frazier flatly.

[35] "Do you count your professional people as Managers?" I said, again hastily.

[36] "Some of them. The Manager of Health is one of our doctors— Mr. Meyerson. But the word 'profession' has little meaning here. All professional training is paid for by the community and is looked upon as part of our common capital, exactly like any other tool."

[37] "*Mr.* Meyerson?" I said. "Your doctor is not an M.D.? Not a real physician?"

[38] "As real as they come, with a degree from a top-ranking medical school. But we don't use honorific titles. Why call him *Doctor* Meyerson? We don't call our Dairy Manager *Dairyman* Larson. The medical profession has been slow to give up the chicanery of prescientific medicine. It's abandoning the hocus-pocus of the ciphered prescription, but the honorific title is still too dear. In Walden Two—"

[39] "Then you distinguish only Planners, Managers, and Workers," I said to prevent what threatened to be a major distraction.

[40] "And Scientists. The community supports a certain amount of research. Experiments are in progress in plant and animal breeding, the control of infant behavior, educational processes of several sorts, and the use of some of our raw materials. Scientists receive the same labor-credits as Managers—two or three per day depending upon the work."

[41] "No pure science?" exclaimed Castle with mock surprise.

[42] "Only in our spare time," said Frazier. "And I shan't be much disturbed by your elevated eyebrows until you show me where any other condition prevails. Our policy is better than that of your educational institutions, where the would-be scientist pays his way by teaching."

[43] "Have you forgotten our centers of pure research?" I said.

[44] "Pure? If you mean completely unshackled with respect to means and ends, I challenge you to name five. It's otherwise pay-as-you-go. Do you know of any 'pure' scientist in our universities who wouldn't settle for two hours of physical labor each day instead of the soul-searching work he's now compelled to do in the name of education?"

[45] I had no ready answer, for I had to consider the cultural engi-

neering needed to equate the two possibilities. My silence began to seem significant, and I cast about for a question along a different line.

[46] "Why should everyone engage in menial work?" I asked. "Isn't that really a misuse of manpower if a man has special talents or abilities?"

[47] "There's no misuse. Some of us would be smart enough to get along without doing physical work, but we're also smart enough to know that in the long run it would mean trouble. A leisure class would grow like a cancer until the strain upon the rest of the community became intolerable. We might escape the consequences in our own lifetime, but we couldn't visualize a permanent society on such a plan. The really intelligent man doesn't want to feel that his work is being done by anyone else. He's sensitive enough to be disturbed by slight resentments which, multiplied a millionfold, mean his downfall. Perhaps he remembers his own reactions when others have imposed on him; perhaps he has had a more severe ethical training. Call it conscience, if you like." He threw his head back and studied the ceiling. When he resumed, his tone was dramatically far-away.

[48] "That's the virtue of Walden Two which pleases me most. I was never happy in being waited on. I could never enjoy the fleshpots for thinking of what might be going on below stairs." It was obviously a borrowed expression, for Frazier's early life had not been affluent. But he suddenly continued in a loud, clear voice which could leave no doubt of his sincerity, "Here a man can hold up his head and say, 'I've done my share!'"

[49] He seemed ashamed of his excitement, of his show of sentiment, and I felt a strange affection for him. Castle missed the overtones and broke in abruptly.

[50] "But can't superior ability be held in check so it won't lead to tyranny? And isn't it possible to convince the menial laborer that he's only doing the kind of work for which he's best suited and that the smart fellow is really working, too?"

[51] "Provided the smart fellow is really working," Frazier answered, rallying himself with an effort. "Nobody resents the fact that our Planners and Managers could wear white collars if they wished. But you're quite right: with adequate cultural design a society might run smoothly, even though the physical work were not evenly distributed. It might even be possible, through such engineering, to sustain a small leisure class without serious danger. A well-organized society is so efficient and productive that a small area of waste is unimportant. A caste system of brains and brawn could be made to work because it's in the interest of brains to make it fair to brawn."

[52] "Then why insist upon universal brawn?" said Castle impatiently.

[53] "Simply because brains and brawn are never exclusive. No one of us is all brains or all brawn, and our lives must be adjusted accord-

ingly. It's fatal to forget the minority element—fatal to treat brawn as if there were no brains, and perhaps more speedily fatal to treat brains as if there were no brawn. One or two hours of physical work each day is a health measure. Men have always lived by their muscles—you can tell that from their physiques. We mustn't let our big muscles atrophy just because we've devised superior ways of using the little ones. We haven't yet evolved a pure Man Thinking. Ask any doctor about the occupational diseases of the unoccupied. Because of certain cultural prejudices which Veblen might have noted, the doctor can prescribe nothing more than golf, or a mechanical horse, or chopping wood, provided the patient has no real need for wood. But what the doctor would like to say is 'Go to work!'

[54] "But there's a better reason why brains must not neglect brawn," Frazier continued. "Nowadays it's the smart fellow, the small-muscle user, who finds himself in the position of governor. In Walden Two he makes plans, obtains materials, devises codes, evaluates trends, conducts experiments. In work of this sort the manager must keep an eye on the managed, must understand his needs, must experience his lot. That's why our Planners, Managers, and Scientists are required to work out some of their labor-credits in menial tasks. It's our constitutional guarantee that the problems of the big-muscle user won't be forgotten."

[55] We fell silent. Our reflections in the windows mingled confusingly with the last traces of daylight in the southern sky. Finally Castle roused himself.

[56] "But four hours a day!" he said. "I can't take that seriously. Think of the struggle to get a forty-hour week! What would our industrialists not give for your secret. Or our politicians! Mr. Frazier, we're all compelled to admire the life you are showing us, but I feel somehow as if you were exhibiting a lovely lady floating in mid-air. You've even passed a hoop about her to emphasize your wizardry. Now, when you pretend to tell us how the trick is done, we're told that the lady is supported by a slender thread. The explanation is as hard to accept as the illusion. Where's your proof?"

[57] "The proof of an accomplished fact? Don't be absurd! But perhaps I can satisfy you by telling you how we knew it could be done before we tried."

[58] "That would be something," said Castle dryly.

[59] "Very well, then," said Frazier. "Let's take a standard seven-day week of eight hours a day. (The forty-hour week hasn't reached into every walk of life. Many a farmer would call it a vacation.) That's nearly 3000 hours per year. Our plan was to reduce it to 1500. Actually we did better than that, but how were we sure we could cut it in half? Will an answer to that satisfy you?"

[60] "It will astonish me," said Castle.

[61] "Very well, then," said Frazier quickly, as if he had actually been spurred on by Castle's remark. "First of all we have the obvious fact that four is more than half of eight. We work more skillfully and faster during the first four hours of the day. The eventual effect of a four-hour day is enormous, provided the rest of a man's time isn't spent too strenuously. Let's take a conservative estimate, to allow for tasks which can't be speeded up, and say that our four hours are the equivalent of five out of the usual eight. Do you agree?"

[62] "I should be contentious if I didn't," said Castle. "But you're a long way from eight."

[63] "Secondly," said Frazier, with a satisfied smile which promised that eight would be reached in due time, "we have the extra motivation that comes when a man is working for himself instead of for a profit-taking boss. That's a true 'incentive wage' and the effect is prodigious. Waste is avoided, workmanship is better, deliberate slowdowns unheard of. Shall we say that four hours for oneself are worth six out of eight for the other fellow?"

[64] "And I hope you will point out," I said, "that the four are no harder than the six. Loafing doesn't really make a job easier. Boredom's more exhausting than heavy work. But what about the other two?"

[65] "Let me remind you that not all Americans capable of working are now employed," said Frazier. "We're really comparing eight hours a day on the part of *some* with four hours on the part of practically *all*. In Walden Two we have no leisure class, no prematurely aged or occupationally disabled, no drunkenness, no criminals, far fewer sick. We have no unemployment due to bad planning. No one is paid to sit idle for the sake of maintaining labor standards. Our children work at an early age —moderately, but happily. What will you settle for, Mr. Castle? May I add another hour to my six?"

[66] "I'm afraid I should let you add more than that," said Castle, laughing with surprising good nature.

[67] "But let's be conservative," said Frazier, obviously pleased, "and say that when every potential worker puts in four hours for himself we have the equivalent of perhaps two-thirds of all available workers putting in seven out of eight hours for somebody else. Now, what about those who are actually at work? Are they working to the best advantage? Have they been carefully selected for the work they are doing? Are they making the best use of labor-saving machines and methods? What percentage of the farms in America are mechanized as we are here? Do the workers welcome and improve upon labor-saving devices and methods? How many good workers are free to move on to more productive levels? How much education do workers receive to make them as efficient as possible?"

[68] "I can't let you claim much credit for a better use of manpower," said Castle, "if you give your members a free choice of jobs."

[69] "It's an extravagance, you're right," said Frazier. "In another generation we shall do better; our educational system will see to that. I agree. Add nothing for the waste due to misplaced talents." He was silent a moment, as if calculating whether he could afford to make this concession.

[70] "You still have an hour to account for," I reminded him.

[71] "I know, I know," he said. "Well, how much of the machinery of distribution have we eliminated—with the release of how many men? How many jobs have we simply eliminated? Walk down any city street. How often will you find people really usefully engaged? There's a bank. And beyond it a loan company. And an advertising agency. And over there an insurance office. And another." It was not effective showmanship, but Frazier seemed content to make his point at the cost of some personal dignity. "We have a hard time explaining insurance to our children. Insurance against what? And there's a funeral home—a crematory disposes of our ashes as it sees fit." He threw off this subject with a shake of the head. "And there and there the ubiquitous bars and taverns, equally useless. Drinking isn't prohibited in Walden Two, but we all give it up as soon as we gratify the needs which are responsible for the habit in the world at large."

HARRISON BERGERON
Kurt Vonnegut, Jr.

[1] The year was 2081, and everybody was finally equal. They weren't only equal before God and the law. They were equal every which way. Nobody was smarter than anybody else. Nobody was better looking than anybody else. Nobody was stronger or quicker than anybody else. All this equality was due to the 211th, 212th, and 213th Amendments to the Constitution, and to the unceasing vigilance of agents of the United States Handicapper General.

[2] Some things about living still weren't quite right, though. April, for instance, still drove people crazy by not being springtime. And it was in that clammy month that the H-G men took George and Hazel Bergeron's fourteen-year-old son, Harrison, away.

[3] It was tragic, all right, but George and Hazel couldn't think about it very hard. Hazel had a perfectly average intelligence, which meant she couldn't think about anything except in short bursts. And George, while his intelligence was way above normal, had a little mental handicap radio in his ear. He was required by law to wear it at all times. It was tuned to a government transmitter. Every twenty seconds or so, the transmitter would send out some sharp noise to keep people like George from taking unfair advantage of their brains.

[4] George and Hazel were watching television. There were tears on Hazel's cheeks, but she'd forgotten for the moment what they were about.

[5] On the television screen were ballerinas.

[6] A buzzer sounded in George's head. His thoughts fled in panic, like bandits from a burglar alarm.

[7] "That was a real pretty dance, that dance they just did," said Hazel.

[8] "Huh?" said George.

[9] "That dance—it was nice," said Hazel.

[10] "Yup," said George. He tried to think a little about the ballerinas. They weren't really very good—no better than anybody else would have been, anyway. They were burdened with sash-weights and bags of bird-shot, and their faces were masked, so that no one, seeing a free and graceful gesture or a pretty face, would feel like something the cat drug in. George was toying with the vague notion that maybe dancers shouldn't be handicapped. But he didn't get very far with it before another noise in his ear radio scattered his thoughts.

[11] George winced. So did two out of the eight ballerinas.

[12] Hazel saw him wince. Having no mental handicap herself, she had to ask George what the latest sound had been.

[13] "Sounded like somebody hitting a milk bottle with a ball peen hammer," said George.

[14] "I'd think it would be real interesting, hearing all the different sounds," said Hazel, a little envious. "All the things they think up."

[15] "Um," said George.

[16] "Only, if I was Handicapper General, you know what I would do?" said Hazel. Hazel, as a matter of fact, bore a strong resemblance to the Handicapper General, a woman named Diana Moon Glampers. "If I was Diana Moon Glampers," said Hazel, "I'd have chimes on Sunday—just chimes. Kind of in honor of religion."

[17] "I could think, if it was just chimes," said George.

[18] "Well—maybe make 'em real loud," said Hazel, "I think I'd make a good Handicapper General."

[19] "Good as anybody else," said George.

[20] "Who knows better'n I do what normal is?" said Hazel.

[21] "Right," said George. He began to think glimmeringly about his abnormal son who was now in jail, about Harrison, but a twenty-one-gun salute in his head stopped that.

[22] "Boy!" said Hazel, "that was a doozy, wasn't it?"

[23] It was such a doozy that George was white and trembling, and tears stood on the rims of his red eyes. Two of the eight ballerinas had collapsed to the studio floor, were holding their temples.

[24] "All of a sudden you look so tired," said Hazel. "Why don't you stretch out on the sofa, so's you can rest your handicap bag on the pillows, honeybunch." She was referring to the forty-seven pounds of birdshot in a canvas bag, which was padlocked around George's neck. "Go on and rest the bag for a little while," she said. "I don't care if you're not equal to me for a while."

[25] George weighed the bag with his hands. "I don't mind it," he said. "I don't notice it any more. It's just a part of me."

[26] "You been so tired lately—kind of wore out," said Hazel. "If there was just some way we could make a little hole in the bottom of the bag, and just take out a few of them lead balls. Just a few."

[27] "Two years in prison and two thousand dollars fine for every ball I took out," said George. "I don't call that a bargain."

[28] "If you could just take a few out when you came home from work," said Hazel. "I mean—you don't compete with anybody around here. You just set around."

[29] "If I tried to get away with it," said George, "then other people'd get away with it—and pretty soon we'd be right back to the dark ages again, with everybody competing against everybody else. You wouldn't like that, would you?"

[30] "I'd hate it," said Hazel.

[31] "There you are," said George. "The minute people start cheating on laws, what do you think happens to society?"

[32] If Hazel hadn't been able to come up with an answer to this question, George couldn't have supplied one. A siren was going off in his head.

[33] "Reckon it'd fall all apart," said Hazel.

[34] "What would?" said George blankly.

[35] "Society," said Hazel uncertainly. "Wasn't that what you just said?"

[36] "Who knows?" said George.

[37] The television program was suddenly interrupted for a news bulletin. It wasn't clear at first as to what the bulletin was about, since the announcer, like all announcers, had a serious speech impediment. For about half a minute, and in a state of high excitement, the announcer tried to say, "Ladies and gentlemen—"

[38] He finally gave up, handed the bulletin to a ballerina to read.

[39] "That's all right—" Hazel said of the announcer, "he tried. That's the big thing. He tried to do the best he could with what God gave him. He should get a nice raise for trying so hard."

[40] "Ladies and gentlemen—" said the ballerina, reading the bulletin.

She must have been extraordinarily beautiful, because the mask she wore was hideous. And it was easy to see that she was the strongest and most graceful of all the dancers, for her handicap bags were as big as those worn by two-hundred-pound men.

[41] And she had to apologize at once for her voice, which was a very unfair voice for a woman to use. Her voice was a warm, luminous, timeless melody. "Excuse me—" she said, and she began again, making her voice absolutely uncompetitive.

[42] "Harrison Bergeron, age fourteen," she said in a grackle squawk, "has just escaped from jail, where he was held on suspicion of plotting to overthrow the government. He is a genius and an athlete, is under-handicapped, and should be regarded as extremely dangerous."

[43] A police photograph of Harrison Bergeron was flashed on the screen—upside down, then sideways, upside down again, then right side up. The picture showed the full length of Harrison against a background calibrated in feet and inches. He was exactly seven feet tall.

[44] The rest of Harrison's appearance was Halloween and hardware. Nobody had ever borne heavier handicaps. He had outgrown hindrances faster than the H-G men could think them up. Instead of a little ear radio for a mental handicap, he wore a tremendous pair of earphones, and spectacles with thick wavy lenses. The spectacles were intended to make him not only half blind, but to give him whanging headaches besides.

[45] Scrap metal was hung all over him. Ordinarily, there was a certain symmetry, a military neatness to the handicaps issued to strong people, but Harrison looked like a walking junkyard. In the race of life, Harrison carried three hundred pounds.

[46] And to offset his good looks, the H-G men required that he wear at all times a red rubber ball for a nose, keep his eyebrows shaved off, and cover his even white teeth with black caps at snaggle-tooth random.

[47] "If you see this boy," said the ballerina, "do not—I repeat, do not —try to reason with him."

[48] There was the shriek of a door being torn from its hinges.

[49] Screams and barking cries of consternation came from the television set. The photograph of Harrison Bergeron on the screen jumped again and again, as though dancing to the tune of an earthquake.

[50] George Bergeron correctly identified the earthquake, and well he might have—for many was the time his own home had danced to the same crashing tune. "My God—" said George, "that must be Harrison!"

[51] The realization was blasted from his mind instantly by the sound of an automobile collision in his head.

[52] When George could open his eyes again, the photograph of Harrison was gone. A living, breathing Harrison filled the screen.

[53] Clanking, clownish, and huge, Harrison stood in the center of the

studio. The knob of the uprooted studio door was still in his hand. Ballerinas, technicians, musicians, and announcers cowered on their knees before him, expecting to die.

[54] "I am the Emperor!" cried Harrison. "Do you hear? I am the Emperor! Everybody must do what I say at once!" He stamped his foot and the studio shook.

[55] "Even as I stand here—" he bellowed, "crippled, hobbled, sickened —I am a greater ruler than any man who ever lived! Now watch me become what I *can* become!"

[56] Harrison tore the straps of his handicap harness like wet tissue paper, tore straps guaranteed to support five thousand pounds.

[57] Harrison's scrap-iron handicaps crashed to the floor.

[58] Harrison thrust his thumbs under the bar of the padlock that secured his head harness. The bar snapped like celery. Harrison smashed his headphones and spectacles against the wall.

[59] He flung away his rubber-ball nose, revealed a man that would have awed Thor, the god of thunder.

[60] "I shall now select my Empress!" he said, looking down on the cowering people. "Let the first woman who dares rise to her feet claim her mate and her throne!"

[61] A moment passed, and then a ballerina arose, swaying like a willow.

[62] Harrison plucked the mental handicap from her ear, snapped off her physical handicaps with marvellous delicacy. Last of all, he removed her mask.

[63] She was blindingly beautiful.

[64] "Now—" said Harrison, taking her hand, "shall we show the people the meaning of the word dance? Music!" he commanded.

[65] The musicians scrambled back into their chairs, and Harrison stripped them of their handicaps, too. "Play your best," he told them, "and I'll make you barons and dukes and earls."

[66] The music began. It was normal at first—cheap, silly, false. But Harrison snatched two musicians from their chairs, waved them like batons as he sang the music as he wanted it played. He slammed them back into their chairs.

[67] The music began again and was much improved.

[68] Harrison and his Empress merely listened to the music for a while —listened gravely, as though synchronizing their heartbeats with it.

[69] They shifted their weights to their toes.

[70] Harrison placed his big hands on the girl's tiny waist, letting her sense the weightlessness that would soon be hers.

[71] And then, in an explosion of joy and grace, into the air they sprang!

[72] Not only were the laws of the land abandoned, but the law of gravity and the laws of motion as well.

[73] They reeled, whirled, swiveled, flounced, capered, gamboled, and spun.

[74] They leaped like deer on the moon.

[75] The studio ceiling was thirty feet high, but each leap brought the dancers nearer to it.

[76] It became their obvious intention to kiss the ceiling.

[77] They kissed it.

[78] And then, neutralizing gravity with love and pure will, they remained suspended in air inches below the ceiling, and they kissed each other for a long, long time.

[79] It was then that Diana Moon Glampers, the Handicapper General, came into the studio with a double-barreled ten-gauge shotgun. She fired twice, and the Emperor and the Empress were dead before they hit the floor.

[80] Diana Moon Glampers loaded the gun again. She aimed it at the musicians and told them they had ten seconds to get their handicaps back on.

[81] It was then that the Bergerons' television tube burned out.

[82] Hazel turned to comment about the blackout to George. But George had gone out into the kitchen for a can of beer.

[83] George came back in with the beer, paused while a handicap signal shook him up. And then he sat down again. "You been crying?" he said to Hazel.

[84] "Yup," she said.

[85] "What about?" he said.

[86] "I forget," she said. "Something real sad on television."

[87] "What was it?" he said.

[88] "It's all kind of mixed up in my mind," said Hazel.

[89] "Forget sad things," said George.

[90] "I always do," said Hazel.

[91] "That's my girl," said George. He winced. There was the sound of a riveting gun in his head.

[92] "Gee—I could tell that one was a doozy," said Hazel.

[93] "You can say that again," said George.

[94] "Gee—" said Hazel, "I could tell that one was a doozy."

from

EPILOGUE TO

UTOPIA OR OBLIVION
R. Buckminster Fuller

[1] My task as inventor is to employ the earth's resources and energy income in such a way as to support all humanity while also enabling all people to enjoy the whole earth, all its historical artifacts and its beautiful places without one man interfering with the other, and without any man enjoying life around earth at the cost of another. Always the cost must be prepaid by design-science competence in modifying the environment.

[2] Man now sprawls horizontally upon the land—uncheckable by planners who enjoy only the right to "suggest." Visionless realtors, backed by government funds, operate indiscriminately in acquiring low-cost options on farmland upon which they install speculator houses. This continually reduces the productive land per capita and unbalances the ecological regeneration of life on earth. Despite the fact that the average American family now moves out of town every four years man is forced by the government-backed realtors to buy his home on 30-year mortgages which never get amortized. Man was designed with legs—not roots. He is destined to ever-increasing freedom of individually selected motions, articulated in preferred directions, as his spaceship, *Earth,* spinning its equator at 1000 miles per hour, orbits the sun at one million miles per day, as all the while the quadrillions of atomic components of which man is composed intergyrate and transform at seven million miles per hour. Both man and universe are indeed complex aggregates of motion.

[3] Over ten million humans have now traveled more than three million miles around their spinning orbiting spaceship *Earth's* surface in contrast to the 30,000 miles per lifetime averaged by all humanity prior to the year 1900. So ignorantly, myopically, and staticly conceived and so obsolete is the whole housing art that its death led the Crash of 1929, since when its ghost script has been kept in rehearsal by U.S. government subsidy at a total underwriting cost to date of $200 billion.

[4] If we take inventor heed of all the foregoing conditions and trends and if we build vertically, both outwardly and inwardly of the earth's

From *Utopia or Oblivion: The Prospects for Humanity* by R. Buckminster Fuller. Copyright © 1969 by Buckminster Fuller. Published by Bantam Books, Inc., and Overlook Press.

surface, we may use less land and return good soil lands to metabolic productivity. We can also install vertical habitations upon and within the three-quarters of the earth covered by water.

[5] The *Queen Elizabeth* is a luxuriously comfortable abode either at sea or in port. She is a mobile city. She is shaped to get passengers across oceans in a hurry. If such floating cities didn't have to speed and were designed only to be towed to an anchorage, having their occupants boated or flown to them, they might have an efficiently symmetrical shape. It is eminently feasible and economical to develop floatable organic cities of immense size.

[6] It has been discovered also that it costs no more to go into the ground and remove earth than it does to go skyward. The great atom-war-anticipating government cave building of the last 20 years cost the same per cubic foot as building fireproof skyscrapers.

[7] Frank Lloyd Wright designed a proposed one-mile-high tower building. His magnificent drawings excited people. But there was no engineering analysis to show whether his structure would stand under adverse conditions such as earthquakes and tornadoes. A one-mile tower is four times the height of the Empire State Building which is, as yet, in 1966, the tallest occupied building man has erected. However, in recent months calculations, only feasible by computers, have been made on a 2¼-mile-high tower habitation which will be approximately ten times the height of the Empire State. It is as high as Mount Fuji. The calculations show such a tower is physically feasible—assuming winds up to 600 m.p.h. and the tower members all encased in ice one foot thick in all directions as it is shaken by earthquakes. Though the project is feasible, the amount of steel required is formidable.

[8] To visualize the various design-controlling conditions under which such a high building can be constructed pinch a camera tripod's legs together in parallel. Take hold of the very bottom of the tripod in one hand and try to hold it vertically on the top of an automobile going at 70 miles an hour over rough terrain. But as we open the legs of the tripod, each time we spread them, the tripod gets steadier and steadier. This is the stabilizing effect obtained when tension stays are rigged from top to bottom on three sides of a mast, as with radio towers. It is equally effective to have the legs spread outwardly as in the Eiffel Tower. When the three legs are spread apart so that the length of the edges of their base triangle equals the length of each of the legs the tripod attains its maximum stability. This conformation of the tripod and its base triangle is that of the regular or equilateral tetrahedron. As the tripod's legs go further apart than the regular tetrahedron, its top can support less and less load. Thus we learn that the most stable structure is the regular tetrahedron.

[9] Following that design-science clue we find that a tetrahedronal city to house a million people is both technologically and economically

feasible. Such a vertical-tetrahedronal city can be constructed with all of its 300,000 families each having balconied "outside" apartments of 2000 square feet, i.e., 200 square meters, of floor space each. All of the organic machinery necessary to its operation will be housed inside the tetrahedron. It is found that such a one-million-passenger tetrahedronal city is so structurally efficient, and therefore so relatively light, that together with its hollow box-sectioned reinforced-concrete foundations it can float.

[10] Such tetrahedronal floating cities would measure two miles to an edge. That is, each of the three base legs will be two miles long. This means that their reinforced-concrete, box-sectioned, and frequently partitioned bottom foundations will be 200 feet in depth and several hundreds of feet wide. Such a tetrahedronal floating city can be floated in a triangularly patterned canal. The structure can be assembled on the floating foundations. This will make the whole structure earthquake-proof. The whole city can be floated out into the ocean to any point and anchored. The depth of its foundation will go below the turbulence level of the seas so that the floating tetrahedronal island will be, in effect, a floating triangular atoll. Its two-mile-long "boat" foundation, on each of the three bottom edges, will constitute landing strips for jet airplanes. Its interior two-mile harbor will provide refuge for the largest and smallest ocean vessels. The total structural and mechanical materials involved in production of a number of such one-million-inhabitant tetrahedronal cities are within feasibility magnitude of the already operating steel and other metals manufacturing capabilities of any one company of the several major industrial nations around the earth.

[11] Tetrahedra are geometrically unique in that they can be added to on any one of their four surfaces while increasing symmetrically in size. The tetrahedron city can grow symmetrically by adding to any one of its faces. Tetrahedronal cities will be symmetrically growable as are biological systems. They may start with a thousand occupants and grow to hold millions without changing overall shape though always providing each family with 2000 square feet of floor space.

[12] Withdrawal of materials from obsolete buildings on the land will permit the production of enough of these floating cities to support frequently spaced floating cities of various sizes around the oceans of the earth at distances negotiable by relatively small boats such as operate safely between Miami, Florida, and Nassau on the Bahama Islands.

[13] At the present time, ocean cargoes must go from one country to another, e.g., from Buenos Aires to London because ships cannot dock beside one another on the ever-heaving ocean to transfer cargo. Because the depth of their "foundations" goes below wave turbulence, permitting dropped thresholds over which the deepest draft ships may pass, such floating tetrahedron cities will permit midocean cargo transferring within their harbors and therewith extraordinary increase of efficiency of the

interdistribution of the world's raw and finished products as well as of the passenger traffic. Such tetrahedronal cities floated upon the oceans will generate their own energy with atomic reactors whose by-product heat will be used to desalinate the city's water supply. All major ships of the sea already desalinate their water.

[14] Such ocean-passage-shortening habitats of ever-transient humanity will permit his individual flying, sailing, economic steppingstone travel around the whole earth in many directions. Three-quarters of the earth is covered by water. Man is clearly intent on penetrating those world-around ocean waters in every way to work both their ocean bottoms and their marine-life and chemistry resources.

[15] When we double the length of an airplane fuselage, we increase its surface area by four and increase its volume by eight. This means that every time we double the length of a ship we eightfold its useful cargo and passenger space while only fourfolding its surface. The amount of surface of a ship governs its friction and drag. The larger the ship, the more economically its cargo may be carried. Yesterday's limitation in relation to the bigness of airplanes was occasioned by their horizontal speeds requiring longer and longer landing strips. The new generation of large airplanes emerging, which will carry 700 to 1000 passengers and "up," are all equipped for vertical takeoff and landing, which does away altogether with the necessity for prepared landing strips. With the long landing-strip limitation removed, the size of the airplanes will multiply very rapidly.

[16] To take advantage of the progressive economy gains of increasing size, leading airplane manufacturers already have airplanes on their engineering boards of a size adequate to carry 10,000 passengers or their equivalent in cargo. The 10,000-passenger ship has a length equivalent to that of the Empire State Building. The leading aircraft manufacturers realize that it will be possible to produce Empire State Building-size skyscrapers in horizontal position under factory-controlled conditions in mass-production jigs with mass-production tools.

[17] Working on scaffolds, the Empire State Building was erected under approximately noncontrolled conditions of wind, rain, heat, and cold in the heart of New York City's traffic. One man was killed for every floor of the Empire State Building's 102 stories. No men should be killed in the production of the horizontal skyscraper in the airplane factory. Such skyscraper-size airplanes may then be taken from their factory and with vertical takeoffs and temporarily applied wings will be flown horizontally, with minimum effort, to any position around the world and horizontally landed. Using their vertical takeoff equipment they will be upended to serve as skyscrapers, anchored, and braced. Thus we see that whole cities can be flown to any location around the world and also removed in one day to another part of the world just as fleets of ships can

come in to port and anchor in one day, or be off for other parts of the world.

[18] In 1954, the United States Marine Corps helicopter-lifted, at 60 miles per hour, a geodesic dome large enough to house an American family. This dome had a floor area of 1000 square feet. In 1955, the Marines air-delivered geodesic domes twice that size, from aircraft carriers to the land, fully skinned and ready to occupy, also at 60 miles per hour. In 1962, the Ford Motor Company helicopter lift delivered a geodesic dome covering a five-times-larger-again floor area of 10,000 square feet. The latest helicopters being built for Vietnam can air-deliver geodesic domes, at 60 miles per hour, large enough to cover an American football field including the end zones, the quarter-mile running track and side bleachers. By 1970, it will be possible to air-deliver geodesic domes large enough to cover complete baseball stadiums. By 1975, it would be possible to air-deliver geodesic domes able to cover small cities. It is now possible with a number of separate helicopter lifts to deliver large subassemblies to complete a geodesic dome large enough to cover a large city and do so within three months' time.

[19] Domed-over cities have extraordinary economic advantage. A two-mile diameter dome has been calculated to cover mid-Manhattan Island, spanning west to east at 42nd Street from the Hudson River to the East River, and spanning south to north from 22nd Street to 62nd Street.

[20] When we wish to make a good air-cooled engine, we design it with many thin fins and spicules to carry away the heat by providing the greatest possible external surface area. The dome calculated for mid-Manhattan has a surface which is only $\frac{1}{85}$ the total area of the buildings which it would cover. It would reduce the energy losses either in winter heating or summer cooling to $\frac{1}{85}$ the present energy cost obviating snow removals. The cost saving in ten years would pay for the dome.

[21] Domed cities are going to be essential to the occupation of the Arctic and the Antarctic. The Russians are already experimenting with them in the Arctic. The Canadians are also studying them. Mining of the great resources of the Antarctic will require domed-over cities. Domed-over cities will be used in desert areas to shield new growth from the sun while preventing wasteful evaporation of piped in, desalinized water. Gradually the success of new domed cities in remote places will bring about their use in covering old cities, particularly where antiquities are to be protected.

[22] The domed-over cities will be so high and their structural members so delicate that their structural members will be approximately invisible. They will operate like a controlled cloud to bring shadow when shadow is desirable and bring sun when sun is desirable, always keeping out rain, snow, and storms as well as exterior industrial fumes, while collecting all the rainwater in reservoirs. The temperature inside the dome

will be so stabilized that a semitropical atmosphere will exist. Inasmuch as there will be no rain or snow in the area, people will live in gardens, or upon garden-terrace skyscrapers needing only local screening for privacy.

[23] There are already 5000 geodesic domes in 50 countries around the world, many so light and strong as to have been air-delivered.

from

ISLAND

Aldous Huxley

[1] "Did you come to Pala by the airplane?"

[2] "I came out of the sea."

[3] "Out of the sea? Do you have a boat?"

[4] "I did have one." With his mind's eye Will saw the waves breaking over the stranded hulk, heard with his inner ear the crash of their impact. Under her questioning he told her what had happened. The storm, the beaching of the boat, the long nightmare of the climb, the snakes, the horror of falling . . . He began to tremble again, more violently than ever.

• • •

[5] There was a final click of the scissors, and the trouser leg fell away, exposing the knee. "Messy," was Dr. MacPhail's verdict after a first intent scrutiny. "But I don't think there's anything too serious." He turned to his granddaughter. "I'd like you to run back to the station and ask Vijaya to come here with one of the other men. Tell them to pick up a stretcher at the infirmary."

[6] Mary Sarojini nodded and, without a word, rose to her feet and hurried away across the glade.

• • •

[7] "Ready," Vijaya called.

[8] Will turned his head and saw the stretcher lying on the ground beside him.

[9] "Good!" said Dr. MacPhail. "Let's lift him onto it. Carefully. Carefully . . ."

[10] A minute later the little procession was winding its way up the narrow path between the trees. Mary Sarojini was in the van, her grandfather brought up the rear and, between them, came Murugan and Vijaya at either end of the stretcher.

[11] From his moving bed Will Farnaby looked up through the green darkness as though from the floor of a living sea. Far overhead, near the surface, there was a rustling among the leaves, a noise of monkeys. And now it was a dozen hornbills hopping, like the figments of a disordered imagination, through a cloud of orchids.

[12] "Are you comfortable?" Vijaya asked, bending solicitously to look into his face.

[13] Will smiled back at him.

[14] "Luxuriously comfortable," he said.

●   ●   ●

[15] An hour later Dr. Robert was back in his bungalow.

[16] "You're going to be all alone this morning," he announced, after changing the dressing on Will Farnaby's knee. "I have to drive down to Shivapuram for a meeting of the Privy Council. One of our student nurses will come in around twelve to give you your injection and get you something to eat. And in the afternoon, as soon as she's finished her work at the school, Susila will be dropping in again. And now I must be going." Dr. Robert rose and laid his hand for a moment on Will's arm. "Till this evening." Halfway to the door he halted and turned back. "I almost forgot to give you this." From one of the side pockets of his sagging jacket he pulled out a small green booklet. "It's the Old Raja's *Notes on What's What, and on What It Might be Reasonable to Do about What's What.*"

[17] "What an admirable title!" said Will as he took the proffered book.

[18] "And you'll like the contents, too," Dr. Robert assured him. "Just a few pages, that's all. But if you want to know what Pala is all about, there's no better introduction."

[19] "Incidentally," Will asked, "who *is* the Old Raja?"

[20] "Who *was* he, I'm afraid. The Old Raja died in 'thirty-eight—after a reign three years longer than Queen Victoria's. His eldest son died before he did, and he was succeeded by his grandson, who was an ass—but made up for it by being short-lived. The present Raja is his great-grandson."

[21] "And, if I may ask a personal question, how does anybody called MacPhail come into the picture?"

[22] "The first MacPhail of Pala came into it under the Old Raja's grandfather—the Raja of the Reform, we call him. Between them, he and my great-grandfather invented modern Pala. The Old Raja consolidated their work and carried it further. And today we're doing our best to follow in his footsteps."

[23] Will held up the *Notes on What's What.*

[24] "Does this give the history of the reforms?"

[25] Dr. Robert shook his head. "It merely states the underlying principles. Read about those first.

• • •

[26] The Ambassador nodded. "In those days Pala was still completely off the map. The idea of turning it into an oasis of freedom and happiness made sense. So long as it remains out of touch with the rest of the world, an ideal society can be a viable society. Pala was completely viable, I'd say, until about 1905. Then, in less than a single generation, the world completely changed. Movies, cars, airplanes, radio. Mass production, mass slaughter, mass communication and, above all, plain mass—more and more people in bigger and bigger slums or suburbs. By 1930 any clear-sighted observer could have seen that, for three quarters of the human race, freedom and happiness were almost out of the question. Today, thirty years later, they're completely out of the question. And meanwhile the outside world has been closing in on this little island of freedom and happiness. Closing in steadily and inexorably, coming nearer and nearer. What was once a viable ideal is now no longer viable."

[27] "So Pala will have to be changed—is that your conclusion?"

[28] Mr. Bahu nodded. "Radically."

• • •

[29] "Apart from the Rani and Murugan and us two here," he asked after swallowing the first mouthful, "how many people from the outside have you ever met?"

[30] "Well, there was that group of American doctors," she answered. "They came to Shivapuram last year, while I was working at the Central Hospital."

[31] "What were they doing here?"

[32] "They wanted to find out why we have such a low rate of neurosis and cardiovascular trouble. Those doctors!" She shook her head. "I tell you, Mr. Farnaby, they really made my hair stand on end—made everybody's hair stand on end in the whole hospital."

[33] "So you think our medicine's pretty primitive?"

[34] "That's the wrong word. It isn't primitive. It's fifty per cent terrific and fifty per cent nonexistent. Marvelous antibiotics—but absolutely no methods for increasing resistance, so that antibiotics won't be necessary. Fantastic operations—but when it comes to teaching people the way of going through life without having to be chopped up, absolutely nothing. And it's the same all along the line. Alpha Plus for patching you up when you've started to fall apart; but Delta Minus for keeping you healthy. Apart from sewerage systems and synthetic vitamins, you don't seem to do anything at all about prevention. And yet you've got a proverb: prevention is better than cure."

[35] "But cure," said Will, "is so much more dramatic than prevention. And for the doctors it's also a lot more profitable."

[36] "Maybe for your doctors," said the little nurse. "Not for ours. Ours get paid for keeping people well."

[37] "How is it to be done?"

[38] "We've been asking that question for a hundred years, and we've found a lot of answers. Chemical answers, psychological answers, answers in terms of what you eat, how you make love, what you see and hear, how you feel about being who you are in this kind of world."

[39] "And which are the best answers?"

[40] "None of them is best without the others."

[41] "So there's no panacea."

[42] "How can there be?" And she quoted the little rhyme that every student nurse had to learn by heart on the first day of her training.

> " 'I' am a crowd, obeying as many laws
> As it has members. Chemically impure
> Are all 'my' beings. There's no single cure
> For what can never have a single cause.

"So whether it's prevention or whether it's cure, we attack on all the fronts at once. *All* the fronts," she insisted, "from diet to autosuggestion, from negative ions to meditation."

[43] "Very sensible," was Will's comment.

• • •

[44] Smiling at his own little joke, "Were you taught *maithuna* at school?" he asked ironically.

[45] "At school," Radha answered with a simple matter-of-factness that took all the Rabelaisian wind out of his sails.

[46] "Everybody's taught it," Ranga added.

[47] "And when does the teaching begin?"

[48] "About the same time as trigonometry and advanced biology. That's between fifteen and fifteen and a half."

[49] "And after they've learned *maithuna,* after they've gone out into the world and got married—that is, if you ever do get married?"

[50] "Oh, we do, we do," Radha assured him.

[51] "Do they still practice it?"

[52] "Not all of them, of course. But a good many do."

[53] "All the time?"

[54] "Except when they want to have a baby."

[55] "And those who don't want to have babies, but who might like to have a little change from *maithuna*—what do *they* do?"

[56] "Contraceptives," said Ranga laconically.

[57] "And are the contraceptives available?"

[58] "Available! They're distributed by the government. Free, gratis,

and for nothing—except of course that they have to be paid for out of taxes."

[59] "The postman," Radha added, "delivers a thirty-night supply at the beginning of each month."

[60] "And the babies don't arrive?"

[61] "Only those we want. Nobody has more than three, and most people stop at two."

. . .

[62] "*My* sympathies were always with my father. Physically and temperamentally I'm very close to him, not in the least like my mother. I remember, even as a tiny child, how I used to shrink away from her exuberance. She was like a permanent invasion of one's privacy. She still is."

[63] "Do you have to see a lot of her?"

[64] "Very little. She has her own job and her own friends. In our part of the world 'Mother' is strictly the name of a function. When the function has been duly fulfilled, the title lapses; the ex-child and the woman who used to be called 'Mother' establish a new kind of relationship. If they get on well together, they continue to see a lot of one another. If they don't, they drift apart. Nobody expects them to cling, and clinging isn't equated with loving—isn't regarded as anything particularly creditable."

[65] "So all's well *now*. But what about *then?* What happened when you were a child, growing up between two people who couldn't bridge the gulf that separated them? I know what *that* means—the fairy-story ending in reverse, 'And so they lived unhappily ever after.'"

[66] "And I've no doubt," said Susila, "that if we hadn't been born in Pala, we would have lived unhappily ever after. As it was, we got on, all things considered, remarkably well."

[67] "How did you manage to do that?"

[68] "We didn't; it was all managed for us. Have you read what the Old Raja says about getting rid of the two thirds of sorrow that's homemade and gratuitous?"

[69] Will nodded. "I was just reading it when you came in."

[70] "Well, in the bad old days," she went on, "Palanese families could be just as victimizing, tyrant-producing and liar-creating as yours can be today. In fact they were so awful that Dr. Andrew and the Raja of the Reform decided that something had to be done about it. Buddhist ethics and primitive village communism were skillfully made to serve the purposes of reason, and in a single generation the whole family system was radically changed." She hesitated for a moment. "Let me explain," she went on, "in terms of my own particular case—the case of an only child of two people who couldn't understand one another and were always at cross-purposes or actually quarreling. In the old days, a little girl brought

up in those surroundings would have emerged as either a wreck, a rebel, or a resigned hypocritical conformist. Under the new dispensation I didn't have to undergo unnecessary suffering, I wasn't wrecked or forced into rebellion or resignation. Why? Because from the moment I could toddle, I was free to escape."

[71] "To escape?" he repeated. "To escape?" It seemed too good to be true.

[72] "Escape," she explained, "is built into the new system. Whenever the parental Home Sweet Home becomes too unbearable, the child is allowed, is actively encouraged—and the whole weight of public opinion is behind the encouragement—to migrate to one of its other homes."

[73] "How many homes does a Palanese child have?"

[74] "About twenty on the average."

[75] "Twenty? My God!"

• • •

[76] " 'Patriotism is not enough.' But neither is anything else. Science is not enough, religion is not enough, art is not enough, politics and economics are not enough, nor is love, nor is duty, nor is action however disinterested, nor, however sublime, is contemplation. Nothing short of everything will really do."

• • •

[77] Do you know what goes on inside your skull, when you've taken a dose of the mushroom?"

[78] "We know a little."

[79] "And we're trying all the time to find out more," Vijaya added.

[80] "For example," said Dr. Robert, "we've found that the people whose EEG doesn't show any alpha-wave activity when they're relaxed aren't likely to respond significantly to the *moksha*-medicine. That means that, for about fifteen per cent of the population, we have to find other approaches to liberation."

[81] "Another thing we're just beginning to understand," said Vijaya, "is the neurological correlate of these experiences. What's happening in the brain when you're having a vision? And what's happening when you pass from a premystical to a genuinely mystical state of mind?"

[82] "Do you know?" Will asked.

[83] " 'Know' is a big word. Let's say we're in a position to make some plausible guesses. Angels and New Jerusalems and Madonnas and Future Buddhas—they're all related to some kind of unusual stimulation of the brain areas of primary projection—the visual cortex, for example. Just how the *moksha*-medicine produces those unusual stimuli we haven't yet found out. The important fact is that, somehow or other, it does produce them. And somehow or other, it also does something unusual to the silent areas

of the brain, the areas not specifically concerned with perceiving, or moving, or feeling."

[84] "And how do the silent areas respond?" Will enquired.

[85] "Let's start with what they *don't* respond with. They don't respond with visions or auditions, they don't respond with telepathy or clairvoyance or any other kind of parapsychological performance. None of that amusing premystical stuff. Their response is the full-blown mystical experience. You know—One in all and All in one. The basic experience with its corollaries—boundless compassion, fathomless mystery and meaning."

[86] "Not to mention joy," said Dr. Robert, "inexpressible joy."

[87] "And the whole caboodle is inside your skull," said Will. "Strictly private. No reference to any external fact except a toadstool."

• • •

[88] The car climbed on and now they were on a ridge between two headlong descents, with a tree-fringed lake down at the bottom of a gorge to their left and to the right a broader valley where, between two tree-shaded villages, like an incongruous piece of pure geometry, sprawled a huge factory.

[89] "Cement?" Will questioned.

[90] Dr. Robert nodded. "One of the indispensable industries. We produce all we need and a surplus for export."

[91] "And those villages supply the manpower?"

[92] "In the intervals of agriculture and work in the forest and the sawmills."

[93] "Does that kind of part-time system work well?"

[94] "It depends what you mean by 'well.' It doesn't result in maximum efficiency. But then in Pala maximum efficiency isn't the categorical imperative that it is with you. You think first of getting the biggest possible output in the shortest possible time. We think first of human beings and their satisfactions. Changing jobs doesn't make for the biggest output in the fewest days. But most people like it better than doing one kind of job all their lives. If it's a choice between mechanical efficiency and human satisfaction, we choose satisfaction."

• • •

[95] "What kinds of people are moved by the lust for power, the passion to bully and domineer? And the ruthless ones, the men and women who know what they want and have no qualms about hurting and killing in order to get it, the monsters who hurt and kill, not for profit, but gratuitously, because hurting and killing are such fun—who *are* they? I used to discuss these questions with the experts—doctors, phychologists, social scientists, teachers. Mantegazza and Galton had gone out of fashion, and most of my experts assured me that the only valid answers to these questions were answers in terms of culture, economics, and the family. It was

all a matter of mothers and toilet training, of early conditioning and traumatic environments. I was only half convinced. Mothers and toilet training and the circumambient nonsense—these were obviously important. But were they *all*-important? In the course of my prison visiting I'd begun to see evidence of some kind of a built-in pattern—or rather of two kinds of built-in patterns; for dangerous delinquents and power-loving troublemakers don't belong to a single species. Most of them, as I was beginning to realize even then, belong to one or other of two distinct and dissimilar species—the Muscle People and the Peter Pans. I've specialized in the treatment of Peter Pans."

[96] "The boys who never grow up?" Will queried.

[97] " 'Never' is the wrong word. In real life Peter Pan always ends by growing up. He merely grows up too late—grows up physiologically more slowly than he grows up in terms of birthdays."

• • •

[98] Meanwhile, from a low building at the foot of the cliff—the tropical version, evidently, of an Alpine hut—a group of young people had come out to see what was happening. They belonged, Will was told, to three other parties of climbers who had taken their Postelementary Test earlier in the day.

[99] "Does the best team win a prize?" Will asked.

[100] "Nobody wins anything," Vijaya answered. "This isn't a competition. It's more like an ordeal."

[101] "An ordeal," Dr. Robert explained, "which is the first stage of their initiation out of childhood into adolescence. An ordeal that helps them to understand the world they'll have to live in, helps them to realize the omnipresence of death, the essential precariousness of all existence. But after the ordeal comes the revelation. In a few minutes these boys and girls will be given their first experience of the *moksha*-medicine. They'll all take it together, and there'll be a religious ceremony in the temple."

[102] "Something like the Confirmation Service?"

[103] "Except that this is more than just a piece of theological rigmarole. Thanks to the *moksha*-medicine, it includes an actual experience of the real thing."

[104] "The real thing?" Will shook his head. "Is there such a thing? I wish I could believe it."

[105] "You're not being asked to believe it," said Dr. Robert. "The real thing isn't a proposition; it's a state of being. We don't teach our children creeds or get them worked up over emotionally charged symbols. When it's time for them to learn the deepest truths of religion, we set them to climb a precipice and then give them four hundred milligrams of revelation. Two firsthand experiences of reality, from which any reasonably intelligent boy or girl can derive a very good idea of what's what."

[106] "And don't forget the dear old power problem," said Vijaya. "Rock climbing's a branch of applied ethics; it's another preventive substitute for bullying."

· · ·

[107] The expressive symbols created by Palanese artists are no better than the expressive symbols created by artists elsewhere. Being the products of happiness and a sense of fulfillment, they are probably less moving, perhaps less satisfying aesthetically, than the tragic or compensatory symbols created by victims of frustration and ignorance, of tyranny, war and guilt-fostering, crime-inciting superstitions. Palanese superiority does not lie in symbolic expression but in an art which, though higher and far more valuable than all the rest, can yet be practiced by everyone—the art of adequately experiencing, the art of becoming more intimately acquainted with all the worlds that, as human beings, we find ourselves inhabiting. Palanese culture is not to be judged as (for lack of any better criterion) we judge other cultures. It is not to be judged by the accomplishments of a few gifted manipulators of artistic or philosophical symbols. No, it is to be judged by what all the members of the community, the ordinary as well as the extraordinary, can and do experience in every contingency and at each successive intersection of time and eternity.

· · ·

[108] "Well, you certainly ask plenty of searching questions about your little pupils," Will concluded after a brief silence. "What do you do when you've found the answers?"

[109] "We start educating accordingly," said Mr. Menon. "For example, we ask questions about every child's physique and temperament. When we have the answers, we sort out all the shyest, tensest, most overresponsive and introverted children, and assemble them in a single group. Then, little by little, the group is enlarged. First a few children with tendencies towards indiscriminate sociability are introduced. Then one or two little muscle men and muscle women—children with tendencies towards aggressiveness and love of power. It's the best method, we've found, for getting little boys and girls at the three polar extremes to understand and tolerate one another. After a few months of carefully controlled mixing, they're ready to admit that people with a different kind of hereditary makeup have just as good a right to exist as they have."

· · ·

[110] "What about formal education?" Will now asked. "What about indispensable information and the necessary intellectual skills? Do you teach the way we do?"

[111] "We teach the way you're probably going to teach in another ten or fifteen years. Take mathematics, for example. Historically mathematics began with the elaboration of useful tricks, soared up into meta-

physics and finally explained itself in terms of structure and logical transformations. In our schools we reverse the historical process. We begin with structure and logic; then, skipping the metaphysics, we go on from general principles to particular applications."

[112] "And the children understand?"

[113] "Far better than they understand when one starts with utilitarian tricks. From about five onwards practically any intelligent child can learn practically anything, provided always that you present it to him in the right way. Logic and structure in the form of games and puzzles. The children play and, incredibly quickly, they catch the point. After which you can go on to practical applications. Taught in this way, most children can learn at least three times as much, four times as thoroughly, in half the time. Or consider another field where one can use games to implant an understanding of basic principles. All scientific thinking is in terms of probability. The old eternal verities are merely a high degree of likeliness; the immutable laws of nature are just statistical averages. How does one get these profoundly unobvious notions into children's heads? By playing roulette with them, by spinning coins and drawing lots. By teaching them all kinds of games with cards and boards and dice."

13
EDUCATION— FOR POWER AND PLEASURE

Knowledge, rather than agriculture and mining, has become the primary industry supplying the essential and central resources of production.—*Peter F. Drucker, 1969*[1]

The past no longer has enough of the answers. In the years ahead, problems will arise for which there are no precedents. To keep the future open we must teach our children not only what to learn, but *how* to learn, *how* to see, *how* to analyze.

—Atlantic Richfield advertisement, 1972[2]

The pathetic superstition prevails that by knowing more and more facts one arrives at knowledge of reality. Hundreds of scattered and unrelated facts are dumped into the heads of students; their time and energy are taken up by learning more and more facts so that there is little left for thinking. To be sure, thinking without a knowledge of facts remains empty and fictitious; but "information" alone can be just as much an obstacle to thinking as the lack of it.—*Erich Fromm, 1941*[3]

[The child of today] is being educated for professions that can't yet be described, for occupations that don't exist. And during the next ten years, say the experts, school children will move even further away from desks and blackboards into the realms of cybernetics and mind chemistry.—*Judith Regan, 1971*[4]

With regard to the education of the feelings, the self, the emotions: we must educate for empathy, compassion, trust, non-exhibitiveness, for self-growth, and self-esteem, for tolerance of ambiguity, for acknowledgement of error, for patience, for suffering.

—Donald N. Michael, 1968[5]

Reference numbers refer to source notes on page 313.

e now arrive at the heart of these comments on the future—the crucial tool that will enable us to make those vital decisions affecting the future of man: education. And again, we face questions. Education for whom? By whom? For what purpose and to what extent? And by what methods?

In his introduction to *Dialogue on Education,* Robert Theobald gives us a succinct answer to the first question: education for whom? "The development of the technological society makes it essential that impartial information become available to every individual in such a form that he can understand the critical issues in his society and the nature of his cultural heritage."* *Every individual.* And *in such a form that he can understand.* If participatory democracy is to survive, issues must be decided by an informed public, aware of the importance of the conclusions to be reached. Theobald does not demand that we all be either philosophers or scientists; he asks only that we be informed impartially, to the extent that each of us can understand.

Implicit in the Theobald statement is a sharp criticism of today's education: Are we not taught to be historians, or electronic technicians, or physicists, or draftsmen? How many curricula call for an understanding of the critical issues that our society faces, for an overall grasp of the broad questions? It is no longer enough to be an expert systems analyst or a crack plumber. We cannot leave social, cultural decisions to an anonymous few. In a dynamic society, we simply cannot afford ignorance.

No public institution in the United States is being attacked as fiercely as formal education is today. The embattled taxpayer, his raises erased by the increased cost of living, has become enraged at the schools' attempts to bring the classroom into the twentieth century. School boards are being pummeled by aroused parents who rebel at experimental techniques and yet are totally dissatisfied with the results of old methods.

Perhaps the travail of education symbolizes the problems of our supercharged society. Cybernation threatens the work ethic; abundance threatens an economic system based on poverty. New genetic techniques and a new awareness of self challenge long-established concepts of the role of woman. The knowledge-technology explosion solves thousands of problems but raises thousands of new questions.

Educators, specifically the educators of educators, are desperately searching for answers, better techniques, and goals. If, as many indus-

* Robert Theobald, ed., *Dialogue on Education,* New York, Bobbs-Merrill, 1967.

trial economists predict, the average citizen will have to be retrained three times before an early retirement, then education for a single vocation is clearly inadequate. And if the number of hours per work week is to diminish, does not education have the responsibility of pointing out to students the roads that lead to the creative use of leisure? More important, must not education assume the responsibility for teaching people how to live full lives, to better understand themselves and the other human beings with whom they interact? And this kind of education is not for a fixed period of time. It covers the whole span of life. It is education for the sake of human growth.

Are teachers and textbooks anachronisms? The University of Illinois at Urbana is attempting total computerization in many areas during this decade. Stanford University has a highly regarded department teaching several mathematics courses with a minimum of human instruction. Textbooks in many physical and life science courses are approaching obsolescence (technical, if not economic) by the time they reach the students' universities. But once beyond the realm of facts, how do we decide which philosophies and whose mores should be taught?

And as computerization increases, what of the interaction between student and teacher? More important, perhaps, the give-and-take between student and student? There are no easy answers here, but only too obviously an urgent need for experimentation and research.

In "Visiting Day 2001 A.D." from his *Education and Ecstasy,* George Leonard has perfected the educational ideal—the naturally curious, totally stimulated mind of the child seeking, searching, asking again. Education and computer expert Anthony Oettinger brings us sharply back to reality in *Run, Computer, Run.* Columnist and philosopher Sydney Harris states the issue in blunt words: "Learning how to learn is the most important part of education." And he reinforces his conclusion with examples from the world of business. John Goodlad in "The Future of Learning: Into the 21st Century" outlines the weaknesses and problems in today's education and describes "the massive task ahead," pointing out that "most of today's teachers are prepared for yesterday's schools. . . ." Few forward-looking teachers would disagree with his conclusions.

VISITING DAY 2001 A.D.

George Leonard

[1] My wife and I find our pace quickening as we approach the most active and spectacular learning environment at Kennedy. We go in through one of three tunnel-like entrances and emerge near the center of a great dome lit only by the glow of laser learning displays that completely surround us on the dome's periphery. Sitting or sprawled on cushions scattered on the floor are other parents and older children who have come just for the experience, in addition to the little children waiting their turns at the learning consoles. We settle down and open our senses.

[2] No matter how many times you visit the Basics Dome, its initial effect is literally stunning. It takes a while for the nervous system to begin processing; first, you have to surrender to the overwhelming sensory bombardment that comes from every side. There are, around us, forty learning consoles, at each of which is seated a child between the ages of three and seven, facing outward toward the learning displays. Each child sits at a keyboard, essentially less complex than that of an old-fashioned typewriter, but fitted with a number of shifts so that almost every symbol known to human cultures can be produced. The child's learning display, about ten feet square, is reflected from the hologram-conversion screen that runs all the way around the inner surface of the dome. The image appears to stand out from the screen in sometimes startling colors and dimensions. The screen is slightly elevated above the child's horizontal eye level so that everyone in the dome, by turning all the way around, can view all of the learning displays. Each display joins the one on either side of it, so that the total effect is panoramic. And each has its own set of stereo speakers, joining in a panorama of sound.

• • •

[3] When a child takes the chair to begin learning, another radio receiver senses his presence through his EID [Electronic Identification Device] and signals the central learning computer to plug in that particular child's learning history. The child puts on his combination earphones and brain-wave sensors, so that OBA [Ongoing Brain-wave Analysis] can become an element in the dialogue. (Some schools use the brain-wave pattern, much in the manner of a fingerprint, to identify the learner.) Once the computer picks up the child's ongoing brain-waves, it imme-

diately begins reiterating (in drastically foreshortened form) his last learning session. The child watches his most recent lesson reeling by on his display. If he wants to continue where he left off last time, he holds down his "yes" key until the reiteration is finished. If not, he presses "no," and the computer begins searching for other material appropriate to the child's level of learning, material which is flashed onto the display until the child presses "yes." The "select" process generally takes less than two minutes. The dialogue then begins.

[4] At any given time during the dialogue, five variables are at hand:

[5] *1.* A full bank of the basic, commonly agreed-upon cultural knowledge, arranged in dialogue form. Most children go through the entire basics bank in the four years from age three through age six.

[6] *2.* Basic material arranged in Cross-Matrix Stimulus and Response form. This material appears at random intervals along with the dialogued material, to provide novelty and surprise and to help the child learn to make those unexpected leaps which are so much a part of discovery.

[7] *3.* The child's brain-wave pattern, analyzed in terms of general consciousness state and short-term memory strength.

[8] *4.* The child's overt motor responses as typed on the keyboard or spoken into a directional microphone mounted on the console.

[9] *5.* Communal Interconnect (CI). This is one of the very latest educational developments. Only a few of the nation's schools have it. Through CI, the material on one learning display sometimes influences and is influenced by the material on nearby displays. This makes the learning process far more communal. It also helps tie together all forty displays into a single learning-art object, enhancing learning and appreciation, not only for the children at the consoles, but for the many spectators in the dome as well.

[10] As soon as our senses become accustomed to the sounds and sights and smells in the dome, we look around for Sally. We are pleased to find her at one of the consoles. We move over to the side of the circle of spectators nearest her.

[11] Sally, we notice on the electronic tablet on her chair, is only five minutes into her learning session. There is a Negro boy, probably six, on her left who is deep into a simple calculus session. On Sally's right, a girl of four or five is dialoguing about primitive cultures. Sally herself, as in her last several sessions, is concerned with simple language skills. It quickly becomes apparent that she has launched into a session on breaking her linguistic set. Standard spelling and syntax are generally learned during the first half of a child's third year of age. During the second half (where Sally is now) an equal or greater amount of time is spent trying out alternate forms. This leads eventually, after the basics are finished,

to a key project; almost every child, working with friends, creates an entire new language before leaving Kennedy School.

[12] We watch Sally's display, which now seems to be billowing with pink and lavender clouds. Gradually, the clouds take the shape of some kind of animal's face. Before I can make out what it is, I hear Sally saying "Cat" into her microphone. Almost instantly, a huge, grinning cat's face gathers form and the word "cat" appears at the bottom of the display. Then a written conversation begins between Sally and the Computer-Assisted Dialogue, with the words of each appearing on the display:

[13] CAD   Can you think of an alternate spelling?
[14] SALLY (*typing*)   kat.

[15] On the display, the giant cat face recedes and is transformed into a white Angora cat, surrounded by vibrating, jagged radial lines of many colors. A purring sound comes from the display.

[16] CAD   How about another?
[17] SALLY (*pausing a moment*)   katte.

[18] The purring becomes louder.

[19] CAD   A cat is a kat is a katte.
[20] SALLY (*quickly*)   A katte is a kat is a cat.
[21] CAD   Copy cat.
[22] SALLY Koppy kat.

[23] There is a pause as the cat image gradually fades and the purring mingles with sweeping electronic music coming from the display on the left. As the dialogue goes on there between boy and CAD in the lovely visual symbols of calculus, a spinning wheel fills most of the display. Through its spokes, slender and glistening like the spokes of a bicycle wheel, may be viewed the rush of its motion—across grassy fields, deserts, down winding mountain roads. A ghostly image of the wheel appears on Sally's display, too, along with multicolored, dancing wave forms, related somehow to her brain waves. On the display at the right, an African pygmy with a blowgun stalks an unseen prey through dense jungle as the girl at the console carries on a voice-only dialogue with CAD. Suddenly Sally begins to type again:

[24] SALLY A cat hiss a kat hiss a katte.
[25] CAD   WILD!!!

[26] Sally's display explodes for a moment with dazzling bursts of color, then becomes the jungle of the girl at the right, in which may be seen the prey of the hunter, a leopard. A tentative, suspenseful drumming

echoes back and forth between the two displays. The two girls turn to each other smiling, then Sally quickly starts typing:

[27] SALLY   A tiger is a tigger./ A gunne has a trigger.

[28] A moment after the last letter of Sally's couplet appears on her display, the jungle remains the same, but the leopard becomes a tiger and the pygmy becomes a white hunter of the early twentieth century, carrying a gun. The girl at the right snaps her head around at Sally, smiling, and Sally laughs delightedly.

[29] CAD   Why not "leopard"?
[30] SALLY   "Leopard" doesn't rime with "trigger."
[31] CAD   Okay. How about some alternate spellings for "leopard"?
[32] SALLY   That's easy. Leppurd.

[33] Meanwhile, the girl at the right keeps talking to CAD and suddenly the tiger becomes a leopard, the white hunter, a pygmy again. The pygmy lifts his blowgun and with a sharp, explosive exhalation that echoes through the dome, sends a dart into the air. The display becomes a closeup of the dart coursing in slow motion across the girl's display, across Sally's and into the boy's at the left, disappearing in the hub of the spinning wheel. Another dart arches across the three displays, then another and another, sailing, soaring, starting always from different angles but ending invariably in the center of the boy's spinning wheel.

[34] "Beautiful CI!" I hear my wife exclaim, and I notice that several people are watching the sequence and listening to the rise and fall of the accompanying electronic music. I also see that the flight of the darts is beginning to influence displays even farther along the line. But the boy continues his calculus dialogue and Sally goes on, too:

[35] CAD   "Leppurd" is good, but you don't have to stay with sound correspondence. Would you like to try something farther out?

[36] Sally presses her "yes" key, then pauses before beginning to type:

[37] SALLY   Leap-heart.
[38] CAD   Nice. Do you want to do another?
[39] SALLY   No.

[40] The flying darts begin to fade. Gradually, Sally's display takes on the deep, rich, undulating plum purple that often characterizes the brain's alpha-wave pattern. Some of the gorgeous richness spills over onto the displays at either side. We know her eyes are closed. She is serene. It is one of education's more valuable moments. We, too, are serene. It is easy, in this setting, to share Sally's feelings. We also share the sheer delight of the educators who set up and constantly modify this learning environment. It is a kind of delight that was unknown to lecturers.

[41] When Sally's session is finished, we walk with her out of the Basics Dome. We talk for a while, but soon she sees some of her friends and leaves us. They run off toward the thickest grove of trees to continue an animal game that may take them the rest of the day.

[42] So we stroll from one place to another, looking (but not too strenuously) for Johnny, our nine-year-old. If we were in a hurry to find him, it would be easy enough. We would merely go to the Central Dome and present one of our electronic identification devices to the ongoing scan, then read out Johnny's approximate present location. Every child wears an EID whenever he is on the school grounds, and the central computer continually tabulates how much time he spends in each educational environment. In addition, whenever the child is in dialogue with a CAD, his learning experience is stored in the computer. This allows Kennedy's educators, not only to keep track of each child's educational development with a minimum of effort, but also to evaluate the drawing power and effectiveness of each environment. The first principle of free learning is that if an environment fails to draw or to educate, it is the environment's, not the learner's, fault.

[43] Visiting educators from educationally underdeveloped nations sometimes find it hard to understand that EID tracking serves not to enforce conformity, but just the opposite. In fact, "asymmetry" is highly valued. Will Hawthorne becomes quite excited when a young child resists the enticements of the Basics Dome for a year or two. Such a child may turn out to be so unique that much can be learned from him. And individual uniqueness is itself one of the main goals of the educational process.

[44] Anyway, learning the basics, the commonly agreed-upon cultural stuff, is so sure and easy that there's never any worry about delay in starting it. It seems incredible to today's children that there ever was.

[45] "I still find it hard to believe," Johnny sometimes says, "that people of Grandpa's generation spent *most* of their time in school learning just what the little kids learn in Basics."

[46] "It's really true," my wife tells him. "They learned *much less.* And they did spend almost all their school time working at it."

[47] "*Working?*" Sally asks in amazement.

[48] "Yes. *Really.* And there were all sorts of discussions and arguments about how to do it and every kind of agony you can imagine."

THE COMPUTER IN EDUCATION
Anthony G. Oettinger
with Sema Marks

The Computer's Muted Trumpet

[1] If books are old-fashioned, tape recorders of limited scope, and well-trained people stubborn, militant, and scarce, where shall we turn? The answer seems simple when one listens to the trumpets of praise for computers.

[2] Patrick Suppes leads off an article in the *Scientific American* as follows: "One can predict that in a few more years millions of school children will have access to what Philip of Macedon's son Alexander enjoyed as a royal prerogative: the personal services of a tutor as well-informed and responsive as Aristotle."[1] The individual tutor evidently stands for the epitome of tailoring the application of an educational process, however produced. As we have seen, he may serve either universal or particular goals. Individual tutors offer learners many options between lone learning and group effort. Suppes claims the same for computers.

[3] Computers can serve any goal. They are indifferent to how the processes they apply are created. The man-made programs that control computers can embody universal or particular goals; they can be mass-produced or hand-tailored on the spot. Computers can perform for either groups or lone individuals.

[4] Stored-program technology endows any one computer with great flexibility. It can accept and execute any properly prepared program. It is at least as general as a blackboard. Almost anything may be written into the computer once we have figured out what to write. Multiple access and communications techniques promise parallelism and easy physical accessibility. A computer is potentially an excellent tool for scheduling anything, including itself, provided we tell it how. Like good tutors who can marshall resources beyond their own, computers can marshal most other educational devices and make them perform at their command, provided we have told them what to command.

[5] Learning to exploit such grand clerks takes time. Hence Suppes quickly admits, "The basis for this seemingly extravagant prediction is

[1] Patrick Suppes, "The Uses of Computers in Education," *Scientific American*, 215 (September 1966), 207.

not apparent in many examinations of the computer's role in education today."[2] Later in the same article, the introductory trumpet is muted still further: "The instruction of large numbers of students at computer terminals will soon (if academic and industrial soothsayers are right) be one of the most important fields of application for computers . . . although all these efforts, including ours at Stanford, are still in the developmental stage."[3]

[6] Troubles, as we shall see, arise from cost, amount, reliability, maintenance, complexity, comfort, standardization, integration, and content. In short, much longitudinal lead time is still between us and the realization even of glorified clerical functions. Hence, when the trumpet's sound reached the halls of Congress through the testimony of Donald Hornig, Director of the Office of Science and Technology in the Executive Office of the President of the United States, it was yet more muted: "I would add the promising field of computer-assisted instruction, which conceivably may make it possible some day for us to provide to each student some of the high quality individual attention that young Alexander received from Aristotle."[4]

[7] Others, less circumspect, show traces of the familiar semantic perversion. Speaking in fund-oriented tones they forecast that computer technology's "greatest benefits may come from its effect on culturally deprived children—the student population often of most concern to the central city school district."[5] The same report, prepared by Technomics, Inc., for the Philadelphia school system, flatly states that: "*Computer Centered Learning* offers the first real opportunity for individualizing the educational experience of millions of children . . . As a direct teaching and learning tool, the computer offers the likelihood—over the next decade or two—of making learning an exciting and welcome experience for *every child* in the school system!"[6] The only stated qualification is revealing: "These revolutionary changes in the capability of educational systems will not come about without a great deal of effort, planning, and leadership."[7]

[2] Ibid.

[3] Ibid., pp. 212–213.

[4] Donald F. Hornig, testimony delivered before a subcommittee of the Committee on Government Operations, House of Representatives, *Data Processing Management in the Federal Government* (Washington, D.C.: Government Printing Office, 1967), p. 146.

[5] Technomics, Inc., *Computer System Support for Comprehensive Educational Advancement,* a study authorized by the School Board of the City of Philadelphia, in conjunction with the Brooks Foundation (Santa Monica, Calif.: Technomics, Inc., 1966), p. 3.

[6] Ibid., p. 5.

[7] Ibid., p. 3.

Computers and Individualization

[8] Have experiments with computer-aided systems indeed yielded important additions to current educational practice? There is no denying that computers are becoming as valuable to the administration of education as they have become to the conduct of the routine clerical business of any other enterprise. But instruction and learning, not administration, are the primary purposes of school.

[9] A computer is a serviceable tool for marshaling the stimulus-response-reinforcement contingencies which advocates of programmed instruction see as the essence of learning. Computers, serving as expensive page turners, have therefore been used to mimic programmed instruction texts. Deprived of the ability to skim, however, the learner may find himself more restricted than with the cheaper, conventional printed programmed material. Some claim that the advantage of a computer over simpler "teaching machines" lies in its capability for practically infinite branching. But the real bottleneck is our inability to foresee more than a very few of the most common possible learner responses.

[10] Another advantage is seen in a computer's ability to handle responses constructed ad lib by the learner, rather than selected from preordained alternatives. Some capability to recognize misspelled words and to pick out preselected key words does exist, but has not been used to the fullness of its limited advantages. Responses to requests like "describe a relationship," "define a concept," or "explain how something works," are well beyond the realm of current computer capability. Recognizing arbitrary English sentences by computer is still beyond the frontier of either linguistic or computer science. Scoring some of the Individually Prescribed Instruction (IPI) material is thus beyond foreseeable computer abilities.

[11] These facts have been disguised somewhat by spending much time, effort, and money on so-called "author languages" meant to allow the designers of drill-and-practice or tutorial systems to encode their material conveniently in palatable forms. Most of these languages elicit a question and the correct responses from the author. They then enable him to specify one or more wrong answers which trigger a return to the question, some cute response, or other branching action. The following is a sample of one author's "dialogue" with a computer:

[12] 2. SPECIFY QUESTION.
   WHO INVENTED THE ELECTRIC LIGHT?

   3. SA.
   A + THOMAS EDISON
   B ALEXANDER BELL

4. SAT.
A F: THATS VERY GOOD B:3
B R: HE INVENTED THE TELEPHONE, TRY
AGAIN . . .[8]

[13] Suppes has reported on extensive experiments with drill-and-practice in mathematics offered to pupils at individual teletypewriter terminals. As in IPI, the emphasis is on rate tailoring. Learning is not altogether by rote, but, since responses to exercises must lend themselves to evaluation by a computer, the replies as of now are restricted to multiple choice among very specific preordained answers. The learner is constrained to answer on the author's terms.

[14] The student's response *is* evaluated immediately. His rate of progress through review exercises or problems of increasing difficulty is determined by the machine on the basis of evaluated responses. The harassing human bookkeeping of IPI in its current state is therefore avoided, but some of its limited flexibility of response is also lost.

[15] Suppes recognizes that "we do not yet have substantial evidence of the efficacy and efficiency of computer-assisted instruction of the sort that is often claimed."[9] In fact, the very techniques of evaluation are still being developed: "The problems of internal comparative evaluation have not yet received intensive consideration in our drill-and-practice program nor as far as I know, in other areas of computer assisted instruction."[10]

[16] Intuition and anecdotal evidence do support the optimism necessary to continue experiments. Like myself and many others, Suppes has found that students rise to impressive levels of intensity and concentration while working at computer consoles. No one can say as yet how much of this is merely a consequence of the unusual attention students receive in experimental situations, a consequence well-known as "the Hawthorne effect." Moreover, the reliability and response-time of current computer systems still create problems. . . .

[17] As with the other rate-tailored processes I have examined, scheduling is a serious problem with computer systems. This problem is manageable with ten minutes a day of drill-and-practice experiments, but becomes more severe in more ambitious undertakings. The careful organization of Suppes' Stanford University–Brentwood School experiment illustrates this point. The experiment is intended to develop *tutorial* programs

[8] Samuel Feingold, "PLANIT—A Language for CAI," *Datamation,* 14 (September 1968), 45.
[9] Patrick Suppes, "Another Look at the Problems of Computer-Assisted Instruction" (unpub. critique presented at the conference on the draft version of *Run, Computer, Run* held in Cambridge, Mass., May 1–2, 1968), p. 13.
[10] Suppes, "Another Look," p. 19.

enabling a computer system to carry the main load of instruction in elementary mathematics.

[18] The computerized classroom at Brentwood is in a separate, windowless building on the grounds of the Brentwood School. This building was financed with federal funds and is dedicated entirely to the experiment. The building includes a set of offices, a conventional machine room where the principal components of the computer are housed, and a classroom with carrels holding the individual computer-teaching terminals. There is also, immediately adjacent to the computerized classroom, a conventional classroom with low tables and chairs and a blackboard.

[19] The description of the project issued to the public misleads in stating that "the Stanford-Brentwood Computer-Aided Instruction Laboratory is the first to be an *integral part* [emphasis added] of a public school," unless one appreciates the full significance of the qualification that it "is housed in a specially-built classroom/laboratory."[11] The significance becomes clear when one interprets the public explanation, which is couched as a catechism:

[20] Q: How does the laboratory fit in the organization of the school?

[21] A: The school sends children to the laboratory at regular periods each day. The children stay for a half-hour to study either reading or mathematics and at the close of the period return to their own classroom. For the first year, there will be eight half-hour periods per day.

[22] Q: Will the classroom teachers go with their children to the CAI laboratory?

[23] A: The laboratory can handle only 16 children at one time, so the classroom teacher ordinarily stays in her room, to work with the children who come to the laboratory during another period. The laboratory is always open to the teachers, and they frequently come to observe.

Being "an integral part of a public school" therefore means only that the facility is on the same plot of ground as the school and serves the same children. The laboratory essentially guarantees that the children who are delivered to it will be kept there for a full half-hour, come what may. This arrangement insulates the remainder of the school from possible schedule disruptions. The insulation is provided, among other things, by the conventional classroom adjacent to the computer-aided classroom: when the machine won't work, the children are taken into that room and taught or amused in conventional ways, until the guaranteed time period is up. It is therefore risky to generalize from this experimental set-up to arbitrary school environments.

[11] Stanford University, Institute for Mathematical Studies in the Social Sciences, "The Stanford-Brentwood CAI Laboratory Project" (n.d., circa 1966).

[24] How very sheltered this situation is in still other ways is revealed by additional questions and answers:

[25] Q: Who operates the làboratory?

[26] A: The laboratory is operated by the Institute. There are specially trained teachers and computer technicians on duty at all times during the school hours.

[27] Q: Who supervises the children while they are in the laboratory?

[28] A: The Institute's staff includes experienced, certified[12] elementary school teachers whose main job is to supervise the children and help them use the system.

[29] Q: Do the teachers who will be in the laboratory need special training?

[30] A: The laboratory teachers must know the curriculum material thoroughly and must also be trained to operate the CAI system.

[31] Q: How long have you been developing curriculum materials for this project?

[32] A: The Brentwood CAI Project began in June, 1964. However, personnel of the Institute have been involved in developing learning materials for younger children for over 10 years.

[33] The *promise* of "revolutionary changes in the capability of educational systems"[13] is still just that. The required "effort, planning and leadership"[14] is nothing short of revolutionary.

MAN MUST LEARN HOW TO LEARN
Sydney J. Harris

[1] If, this June, your son received a Ph.D. degree in aerospace engineering, half of what he knows when he graduates will be obsolete in 10 years. For fully half of what he needs to know for the next 10 years is completely unknown today.

Reprinted by permission of Sydney J. Harris and Publishers-Hall Syndicate.

---

[12] This is partly a consequence of state licensing laws that impose the equivalent of the presence of a fireman in every Diesel locomotive.

[13] Technomics, *Computer System,* p. 3.

[14] Ibid.

[2] This "obsolescence of knowledge," especially in scientific fields, is changing the whole idea of what constitutes a "good" college education. And it reaffirms those of us who have been saying for a long time that learning how to learn is the most important part of education.

[3] The real reason that vocational and "specialist" training is largely pointless today lies in the rapid outdating of so much technical knowledge and skills. Even our newest profession—that of programming computers —will soon be obsolete, when the computers are built that will program themselves.

[4] What the new society of the future calls for are versatility and flexibility and creativity. These cannot be learned in a technical sense; they are part of a liberal education, which teaches men and women how to think, not just how to put things together and make them work.

[5] The new machines will be able to put things together much better than people can.

[6] It is no accident that, for the first time, the prestigious Massachusetts Institute of Technology has appointed a president who is neither a scientist nor a technician.

[7] Or that business schools, such as those at Harvard and Columbia, have shifted their emphasis from the technical aspects of business administration to a broader program of liberal arts.

[8] In a recent talk. Dr. Arnold Ducoffe, director of Georgia Tech's School of Aerospace Engineering, remarked that this obsolescence of knowledge is the big reason that today's engineering schools no longer stress the "mechanical," but rather the "philosophical" elements in science —not how to do something, but why something is true.

[9] If we learn the reasons behind phenomena, then we can cope with changing conditions.

[10] Our pressing need is for men and women who can adapt to needs and acquire skills that are barely on the horizon today.

[11] More and more, the function of the specialist is being taken over by the machines: it is the "generalist," who can make decisions based on an imaginative projection of the future, we so desperately require to keep the wheels turning.

[12] In the past, the average man would change his job three times during his lifetime. In the future, we are told, the average man may have to change his vocation three times during his lifetime.

[13] Unless he learns how to learn, in a philosophical sense, the specialist may become a dropout from the economic community.

THE FUTURE OF LEARNING:
INTO THE 21st CENTURY
John I. Goodlad

[1] In a nation that speaks of inalienable rights, the right to learn must be paramount. Yet that right, in its full meaning, has been denied to many in this nation. It has been denied because of color, religion, poverty, infirmity, and residence. And it has been denied because of our often mindless adherence to many unproductive teaching concepts and practices.

[2] The right to learn is the goal we seek for the twenty-first century. We want for our children a range of learning opportunities as broad as the unknown range of their talents. We want a learning environment that nurtures those talents. We want our children to know themselves and, secure in that knowledge, to open themselves to others. We want them to have freedom, and the order, justice, and peace that the preservation of their freedom demands.

What and How To Learn

[3] Achieving our goals must bring us to profound questions of what and how to learn.

[4] The first step—a difficult step for some of us—is acceptance of what should be obvious: school is but a part of the learning environment.

[5] Schools and teachers have been with us for so long that they have often been equated with education, and, worse, with learning. Yet the infant learns to walk and to talk, to trust and to distrust; he learns fear and love and hate—all without benefit of school. By the age of five, the child has sat before a television set for at least the number of hours he will spend in the first three grades of school. Yet still, we equate learning with school.

[6] Although we believed, until recently, that school was the most powerful part of the learning environment, we know now that it is not. . . .

[7] . . . Much of the subject matter of today's learning is unrealistically narrow and antiseptic. Those who have selected and prescribed it have done so through the biases of their Western culture, looking more to the past than to the future. . . .

[8] What is to be learned is refined by our filtering system until, too

From *AACTE Bulletin*, March, 1971. Reprinted by permission of American Association of Colleges for Teacher Education.

often, it has little power to grip the learner and thus defrauds or cheats him. From the truly exciting possibilities of a culture—or conscience—embracing mankind, we slide to the homogenized "adventures" of Dick and Jane and a field trip to the supermarket.

[9] With regard to the "how" of learning, we have only begun to question the outworn notion that certain subjects or concepts are to be learned by all individuals at successive stages of growth at stipulated times in sterile places. Reading is for the first grade, long division for the fourth, and fractions for the fifth and sixth. All of this takes place between the hours of nine and three in a big box divided into cells. . . .

[10] In this lockstep, as in so many other ways, we teach that each phase of life is instrumental to the next rather than of ultimate value in itself. We see the man we want the child to become rather than the child seeking to become himself. In the words of Hannah Arendt, "Man sees wood in every tree."

"Winter of Discontent"

[11] This is the winter of our educational discontent. Until recently, we believed that we had only to provide some new subject matter here, inject a heavier dose of phonics there, or tighten the discipline a little, to improve both the system and society. Better schools (defined in largely quantitative terms) would mean more jobs, a brisker economy, safer cities, and more aware, dedicated citizens. Or so we thought. Dwindling confidence in these relationships reflects both declining public confidence in the schools and the tenacity with which we cling to the "learning equals school" equation. Painfully, we are coming to realize that grades predict grades, that success in school begets success in more school but is no guarantee of good workers, committed citizens, happy mothers and fathers, or compassionate human beings. . . .

[12] For a brief span of years, we believed that serious problems existed only in the schools of our great cities. Increasingly we have come to understand that suburban and, to an even greater degree, rural schools do not assure the diet or provide the vitality our children deserve. Even the middle-class school around the corner reveals ragged edges surrounding a soft center. The failures of our schools are apparent in dropout rates, in barely minimal learning on the part of many who do remain in school, and in growing alienation among the young of all colors and classes.

[13] At the root of the problem is an implicit denial of diversity. The schools have become great sorting machines, labeling and certifying those who presumably will be winners and losers as adults. The winners are disproportionately white and affluent. The losers, too often, are poor, and brown, or black, or red.

[14] But many of the winners are losers, too. For they are shaped, directed, and judged according to a narrow conception of what is right and proper. This process begins very early; the environment of expectations, rewards and punishments is established before mother and child leave the hospital. And in the home, infants are encouraged in their efforts to walk and talk, but their responses to sound, color, and smell are ignored or stifled. This process of channeling energy and talent is refined and perfected in the schools through a network of expectations, rules, grades, required subjects, and rewards for what is wanted and the subtle extinction of the great range of talents and achievements which are not wanted. . . .

Call for Change

[15] A massive task of change lies ahead. . . . We cannot point pridefully at those who have "made it" while half of us believe that life has passed us by. . . .

[16] . . . Among many of our people there is a sense of outrage induced by the discrepancy between what is and what could be. . . . We have more than a little hope that a new era can be both described and created. At the core of this hope is a fresh awareness of children: of their intrinsic rather than instrumental value, of their ability to learn, and of the kind of learning they could and should have as we look to the twenty-first century. . . .

[17] To speak, as we have in the past, of giving our young the "tools" with which to survive, to speak of techniques and "subjects" as the essential components of education, is to speak of trivialities. And, it is to send our children unequipped into the unknowable.

[18] All that we can predict with certainty is that the central issue of the twenty-first century, as it is of this one, will be the struggle to assert truly human values and to achieve their ascendancy in a mass, technological society. It will be the struggle to place man in a healthy relationship with his natural environment; to place him in command of, rather than subservient to, the wondrous technology he is creating; and to give him the breadth and depth of understanding which can result in the formation of a world culture, embracing and nurturing within its transcending characteristics the diverse cultures of today's world.

21st Century Man

[19] We ask first, then, not what kind of education we want to provide but what kind of human being we want to emerge. What would we have twenty-first century man be?

[20] We would have him be a man with a strong sense of himself and his own humanness, with awareness of his thoughts and feelings, with the capacity to feel and express love and joy and to recognize tragedy

and feel grief. We would have him be a man who, with a strong and realistic sense of his own worth, is able to relate openly with others, to cooperate effectively with them toward common ends, and to view mankind as one while respecting diversity and difference. We would want him to be a being who, even while very young, somehow senses that he has it within himself to become more than he now is, that he has the capacity for lifelong spiritual and intellectual growth. We would want him to cherish that vision of the man he is capable of becoming and to cherish the development of the same potentiality in others.

[21] The education of this kind of human being is necessarily an enabling process rather than an instructional process. It requires opening the whole of the world to the learner and giving him easy access to that world. This implies enormous respect for the child's capacity to learn, and with the granting of respect goes, by implication, the granting of freedom.

[22] When we look to education in the new century to come, we see learning not as a means to some end but as an end in itself. Education will not be an imitation of life but life examined and enjoyed. . . .

In the Year 2000

[23] Compulsory education—or compulsory attendance, as it might better be called—will be a thing of the past. School as we now know it will have been replaced by a diffused learning environment involving homes, parks, public buildings, museums, business offices, guidance centers. Many such resources that are now unendorsed, unofficial, unrecognized, unstructured, or unsupervised—and unused—will be endorsed and made fully available for learning. There will be successors to our present schools—places designed for people to gather for purposes of learning things together.

[24] The mere availability of a broad range of options will signify what we believe will be an important, and essential, change in our national value system. The word "success" will have been redefined, and a far wider range of choices—of study, of taste, of career, of "life style"—will be legitimized and seen as praiseworthy. Little boys will not be made to feel that they must grow up to be aggressive—or even affluent—men. Little girls will not need to feel that domesticity is the necessary end-all and be-all of existence. A career in science will not have higher status than a career in the creative arts. We will, in short, give substance to our longstanding but never fulfilled commitment to honor and develop the entire range of human talent. . . .

[25] It is possible that advanced technology will return the family to the center of the stage as the basic learning unit. Each home could become a school, in effect, via an electronic console connected to a central

computer system in a learning hub, a videotape and microfilm library regulated by a computer, and a national educational television network. Whether at home or elsewhere, each student, of whatever age, will have at the touch of a button access to a comprehensive "learning package," including printed lessons, experiments to be performed, recorded information, videotaped lectures, and films . . .

Role of Teachers

[26] In such an educational world, everyone will be from time to time both teacher and learner, but there will still be great need for teachers who, for the first time, will be free to engage in truly human tasks. No longer will they need to function as ineffective machines imparting "facts" by rote, since real machines will have taken over that function.

[27] Some will spend many hours preparing a single lesson, to be viewed by thousands or even millions of individuals of every age. Others will be engaging with groups of all ages in dialogue designed to enhance human communication and understanding. The freedom and sense of potency we want for our children will be experienced, at long last, by their teachers. The entire enterprise will be directed toward increasing the freedom and the power of each individual to shape himself, to live at ease in his community, and in doing both to experience self-fulfillment.

[28] We have sketched a kind of learning Utopia. Achieving it will not be easy. In fact, without massive, thoughtful, social reconstruction, we will not get there at all. To stand aside—unconcerned, uncommitted, and unresolved—may very well be to assure no twenty-first century, least of all our Utopia. . . .

• • •

"Unshackling" the Schools

[29] The top agenda item, then, in seeking to enhance learning in the seventies is unshackling the schools. The process must begin by decentralizing authority and responsibility for instructional decision making to individual schools. Simply dividing large school districts into smaller districts is not the answer. Schools, like individuals, are different: in size, problems, clientele, types of communities served, and the like. They must create programs appropriate to their local circumstances, encouraged and supported in the diversity such a process necessarily entails.

[30] Many schools are not ready to take quick advantage of sudden freedoms. Too long fettered by the larger system, their staffs will be timid and uncertain. *We recommend, therefore, that substantial government funds be allocated for the deliberate development of schools, accountable to the public, whose sole reason for being is experimental.* Designed for purposes of providing alternatives, such schools could provide options in

the community and thus would attract more supportive parent groups. In time, such schools would provide models for replication in networks of cooperating schools seeking to learn from each other.

[31] Such schools need not arise solely within "the system." We are at a time in history when the need to break out of established patterns is critical. We need alternatives wherever we can find them. Some of the "free" schools springing up around the country offer diversity and should be encouraged to the point where their practices truly reflect their underlying philosophies.

[32] *We urge that support be given to schools endeavoring to abolish grade levels, develop new evaluation procedures, use the full range of community resources for learning, automate certain kinds of learning, explore instructional techniques for developing self-awareness and creative thinking, reschedule the school year, and more. Most of all, we urge that substantial financial support be given to schools seeking to redesign the entire learning environment, from the curriculum through the structure of the school to completely new instructional procedures.*

Early Childhood Learning

[33] Especially needed are well-developed models of early learning. We know now that the first five years of life largely determine the characteristics of the young adult. And yet, we fail these years shamefully either through neglect, or through narrow, thoughtless shaping, or through erratic shifts from too little to too much concern. . . .

[34] Two successive governments have promised and failed to deliver on a vast effort for expansion and improvement in the education of young children. A National Laboratory in Early Childhood Education suffered a crippled birth under one administration and is now starving to death under another. *We need research on the developmental processes of the young: educational programs based on what we now know; thousands of adequately prepared teachers to staff nursery and play schools; and exemplary models of programs stressing cognitive, aesthetic, motor, and affective development.*

Overhaul of Teacher Education

[35] High on our list of "old business" is the overhaul of teacher education from top to bottom. The continuing debate over the value of "methods" courses, whether to have more or fewer of them, and how to regulate teacher education by legislative fiat only reveals the poverty of our approaches to the problem. Shuffling courses about is not the answer. Required are change strategies which take account of the fact that pre-service teacher education, in-service teacher education, and the schools

themselves are dependent, interrelated, and interacting components of one social system, albeit a malfunctioning one.

[36] *It becomes apparent, therefore, that financial resources must be directed toward those strategies that link schools seeking to change with teacher education institutions seeking to shake out of established patterns.* In brief, the teacher for tomorrow's learning must be prepared in school settings endeavoring to create a new kind of tomorrow. Most of today's teachers are prepared for yesterday's schools. . . .

[37] *We must stop talking about the possibilities of electronic educational aids and engage in experimentation on a much broader scale.* . . .

[38] . . . We must recognize the fact that electronic devices constitute a new kind of instructional energy—indefatigable, relatively immune to changes in the weather, and contemptuous of time of day or day of week. The human teacher, on the other hand, is sharply limited in energy pattern, highly susceptible to chills, immobile in times of flood and snow, and sensitive to time of day. Clearly, the tasks for human and machine teachers should be both different and complementary. . . .

Freedom To Learn

[39] . . . Something resembling a school—and this something might take many forms—is needed for those important human activities of interaction, exploration, finding one's self through others and others through one's self. . . .

[40] One way for us to begin to grow accustomed to this non-school freedom is to use much more vigorously the learning resources lying outside of school. Children should be excused from school for blocks of time in order to gain access to a non-school teacher, to serve as apprentice to an artisan, or to practice a hobby in depth. The biggest block to the kind of learning future we are endeavoring to describe is not its availability. It is our individual difficulty in seeking to shake ourselves loose from the vice-like grip of our present stereotyped thinking. . . .

[41] We had better begin now because we will need all of our imagination and our wisdom to cope with some of the critical moral questions soon to be thrust upon us. . . .

[42] The question of who is to make what decisions for whom probably is the most pressing educational question both today and tomorrow. It is at the core of current discussions of accountability, voucher systems, and the like, in schooling. It is at the core of any minority group demand for self-determination and equality. Ultimately, it brings us into the matter of who owns the child and who is to determine his freedom. To come back to where we began, the right to learn means the freedom of each individual to learn what he needs in his own way and at his own rate, in his own place and time. . . .

EPILOGUE

mong the few—hopefully to become the many—who are conscious of the changes in our dynamic society, the often-heard complaints are: What can *we* do? What power can *we* exert? They (that ubiquitous "they" again) control. They have the power.

We can surrender, of course, and allow ourselves to be washed along in the surging currents of an unfettered technology. And we will drown.

Or, if I might borrow a phrase from futurist Bert Nanus, who has established a Futures Studies division for graduate students at the University of Southern California, we can become active members of a "participatory, anticipatory democracy."

There are some portents of hope. An aroused citizenry delayed, perhaps stopped, the supersonic transport. Pushed by Senator Edward Kennedy, Congress passed the Technology Assessment Act of 1972, which set up a commission designed to provide the Congress with "competent, unbiased information concerning the physical, biological, economic, social, and political effects of technological proposals." Though the funding has been minuscule, the commission membership political, at least it represents a start.

From now on, it's up to us.

SOURCES OF CHAPTER-OPENING QUOTATIONS

Chapter 1

1. Gerald Feinberg, *The Prometheus Project: Mankind's Search for Long-Range Goals,* Garden City, N.Y., Doubleday & Company, 1968.
2. John McHale, *The Future of the Future,* New York, Braziller, 1969.
3. Bertrand de Jouvenal, "Utopia for Practical Purposes," *Daedalus,* Spring, 1965 (as quoted in John McHale, *The Future of the Future,* New York, Braziller, 1969).
4. *Time,* February 15, 1971.

Chapter 2

1. Gerald Feinberg, *The Prometheus Project: Mankind's Search for Long-Range Goals,* Garden City, N.Y., Doubleday & Company, 1968.
2. Franklin Russel, review of Konrad Lorenz, *On Aggression,* in *Life,* June 3, 1966.
3. Los Angeles Times Service, January 6, 1971.
4. Wayne Oates, *Confessions of a Workaholic: The Facts About Work Addiction,* New York, World Publishing Company, 1971.

Chapter 3

1. John Davy, London Observer Service, November 20, 1966.
2. New York Times Service, October 12, 1972.
3. Carl T. Rowan, columnist, *The Arizona Republic,* February 6, 1973.
4. Jane E. Brody and Edward B. Fiske, New York Times Service, April 5, 1971.

Chapter 4

1. Vera Glaser, Women's News Service, March 14, 1969.
2. Alison Lurie, *Life,* March 3, 1972.

3. Betty Rollin, *Look,* September 22, 1970.
4. Gloria Steinem, *Ms.,* July, 1972.

Chapter 5

1. Arthur C. Clarke, *Profiles of the Future: A Daring Look at Tomorrow's Fantastic World,* New York, Harper & Row, 1963.
2. Robert Kirsch, Los Angeles Times Service, *The Arizona Republic,* March 12, 1967.
3. B. F. Skinner, *Beyond Freedom and Dignity,* New York, Alfred A. Knopf, 1971.
4. Joseph Featherstone, *Schools Where Children Learn,* New York, Liveright Publishing Corporation, 1971.

Chapter 6

1. Robert Theobald, ed., *Social Policies for America in the Seventies,* Garden City, N.Y., Doubleday & Company, 1968.
2. Henry J. Taylor, *The Phoenix Gazette,* February 1, 1973.
3. Sylvia Porter, financial columnist, *The Arizona Republic,* October 23, 1971.
4. Nekoosa-Edwards Paper Company, "What's It Going To Be Like Tomorrow, Daddy?" advertising pamphlet, 1971.
5. Sir Julian Huxley, introduction to Pierre Teilhard de Chardin, *The Phenomenon of Man,* New York, Harper & Row, 1959.

Chapter 7

1. Robert L. Heilbroner, *The Future as History,* New York, Harper & Row, 1960.
2. Frank Carey, AP science writer, *The Phoenix Gazette,* October 9, 1972.
3. North American Rockwell advertisement, *Saturday Review,* September 7, 1968.
4. Frank Carey, AP science writer, *The Phoenix Gazette,* October 12, 1972.

Chapter 8

1. *Army Research and Development Magazine,* August, 1972.
2. Boeing Company advertisement, *Harper's Magazine,* May, 1971.
3. American Telephone and Telegraph Company advertisement, 1971.
4. Ralph Dighton, AP science writer, *The Arizona Republic,* August 7, 1969.

Chapter 9

1. Dr. Stanley F. Yolles, Director of the National Institute of Mental Health, to a U. S. Senate subcommittee, May 24, 1966 (as quoted in Herman Kahn and Anthony J. Wiener, *The Year 2000: A Framework for Speculation on the Next Thirty-Three Years,* New York, The Macmillan Company, 1967).

2. Donald N. Michael, *The Unprepared Society*, New York, Basic Books, Inc., 1968.
3. *Esquire*, July, 1970.
4. David Krech, psychologist (as quoted in Donald N. Michael, *The Unprepared Society*, New York, Basic Books, Inc., 1968).

Chapter 10

1. Robert Calhoun, *God and the Common Life*, New York, Charles Scribner's Sons, 1935.
2. Herman Kahn and Anthony J. Wiener, *The Year 2000: A Framework for Speculation on the Next Thirty-Three Years*, New York, The Macmillan Company, 1967.
3. Walter P. Reuther, "First Things First" (as quoted in Donald Fabun, *The Dynamics of Change*, Englewood Cliffs, N.J., Prentice-Hall, 1967).
4. Don G. Campbell, columnist, *The Arizona Republic*, February 2, 1969.

Chapter 11

1. U Thant, Secretary-General, The United Nations, address before conference on "The Second United Nations Development Decade: A Challenge to Rich and Poor Countries," United Nations Headquarters, May 9, 1969.
2. Joseph Featherstone, *Schools Where Children Learn*, New York, Liveright Publishing Corporation, 1971.
3. Robert M. Hutchins, *The Center Report*, April, 1971.
4. Stringfellow Barr, "The Young May Do It," *The Center Magazine*, November–December, 1971.

Chapter 12

1. Kenneth Boulding, *The Meaning of the Twentieth Century*, New York, Harper & Row, 1964.
2. *The Arizona Republic*, October 14, 1971.
3. Edwin Warner.
4. Anatole France (1844–1924); awarded Nobel Prize for literature, 1921.

Chapter 13

1. Peter F. Drucker, *The Age of Discontinuity: Guidelines to Our Changing Society*, New York, Harper & Row, 1969.
2. Atlantic Richfield Company advertisement, *Time*, July 17, 1972.
3. Erich Fromm, *Escape from Freedom*, New York, Holt, Rinehart and Winston, 1941.
4. Judith Regan, "Making Better Use of Brainpower," Woman's News Service, *The Arizona Republic*, October 27, 1971.
5. Donald N. Michael, *The Unprepared Society*, New York, Basic Books, Inc., 1968.

APPENDIX: QUESTIONS FOR DISCUSSION AND WRITING

This appendix gives information about authors and poses questions for discussion and writing. The focus is on the meaning of the selections and their implications for the lives of readers. Cross references facilitate comparison of the ideas of different authors on the same subjects.

1 THE FUTURISTS VIEW HEAVEN—OR HELL

Introduction to Future Shock—Alvin Toffler Alvin Toffler (b. 1928) is author of *The Culture Consumers* and editor of *Schoolhouse in the City.*

1. Toffler argues that man must learn to control the rate of change in his world or suffer massive breakdown. Does Toffler suggest that man cannot learn to adapt to the rapid flux? To anticipate the next chapter of this book, what is the nature of man? Is he capable of adapting? What about this facet of man: "Some geneticists believe that 85 percent of our genetic heritage is constantly in reserve to make it possible for us to adapt to new environments."[1]

2. The Delphi technique of forecasting by consulting experts through questionnaires produces results quite similar to those obtained by extrapolations or simulations from hard data. What forecasting techniques and kinds of data does Toffler use in turning the rear-view mirror forward to study history? Are they valid?

3. What courses or teachers do you know which are preparing students for a world of change and instability?

The Predicament of Mankind—Dennis L. Meadows Dennis L. Meadows is the author of *Dynamics of Commodity Production Cycles.*

Extrapolating from current trends, the Meadows group analyzed interactions among population, pollution, natural resources, food, and economic development. They offer six conclusions, which generate many questions.

1. Is the goodness of life measurable by material well-being? Is the "higher standard of material wealth" doomed? Why? In what ways do you think the standard of living might decline?

2. What may we have to trade off in personal freedom?

3. If there is no way of bringing the developing nations up to the material level of the developed nations, is a "class war" inevitable?

4. What planning time horizons are currently being used? Are the Soviet and Chinese five-year plans the longest looks ahead? What do we consider in central planning besides cost and technical feasibility?

5. The report stresses "global interaction." What avenues are open for international planning?

The New Reality—Robert Theobald Robert Theobald, British socio-economist, is the author of *The Rich and the Poor* and *The Challenge of Abundance.*

1. Theobald's optimism is high. Do you agree that man can do what he wants to, or do you think man is limited?

---

[1] E. Jantsch, "For a Science of Man," in *Can We Survive Our Future*, G. R. Urban, ed., 1971, p. 117.

315

2. What would happen if we could produce gold? Have you any suggestions for changing the basis of the world's money supply? Could we do without money? "Distribution of Abundance" in Chapter 11 discusses a moneyless society.

3. How can we change education so that people learn to ask questions and not just give back ready-made answers? See Chapter 13 for some proposals.

4. What "inefficient" human activities might man want to preserve? Compare Huxley's ideas on efficiency in "Island," Chapter 12.

5. What beliefs have you been taught, or seen others taught, that you think are no longer relevant?

6. Do you think international violence can be abolished? See the articles by Morris and Montagu, and Chapter 3 for varying views.

Universalizing Technology—F. M. Esfandiary   F. M. Esfandiary (b. 1930), an Iranian, teaches at the New School for Social Research in New York City.

As Esfandiary's book and selection titles show, he believes that we are at the beginning of a brighter future because of the internationalizing, universalizing results of technology.

1. What Old World attitudes does Esfandiary contrast with newly developing attitudes?

2. What examples does he give to support his belief that nationalism and the concept of nation are disappearing?

3. What are the differences in outlook among Toffler, Meadows, and Esfandiary?

Chapter 1 presents four authors. Compare and contrast their points of view. Are there indeed prospects for heaven or hell? Are the cases for pessimism and optimism convincingly presented? Which do you favor? Why?

2   ARGUMENTS ON THE NATURE OF MAN

Fighting—Desmond Morris   Desmond Morris (b. 1928) lives in Malta and is the author of *Apes and Monkeys, Big Cats,* and *Intimate Behavior.*

1. Man's aggressiveness may spring from his animal nature. What "human refinements" has he added?

2. What has been the result of long-distance weapons?

3. Give examples from your own experience of group territorial defense and group exclusiveness.

4. Morris dismisses four proposed solutions to aggression. Does he consider combining them all? Can you suggest any other solutions?

5. How might the argument in the last paragraph be affected if we understood the irrational part of man? What in your education has helped you understand the emotional nature of man? Have you personally concentrated more on knowing, or on feeling?

6. Try an experiment in which you test some of Morris' ideas about aggression. For example, an experiment was done a few years ago in which some people played the role of prisoners and others played the role of guards. What kinds of feelings and actions do you think might develop?

Nature and the Myth of War—Ashley Montagu   Ashley Montagu (b. 1905), anthropologist, has taught anatomy and anthropology and written such books as *Man's Most Dangerous Myth: Race, The Natural Superiority of Women,* and *Touching.*

Montagu's statement about what man thinks is "natural" reveals much about why we are unthinkingly the way we are.

1. Conditioned by error and prejudice, we do not question what is "natural." Can we train people to examine the obvious, to question tradition? How?

2. Does Montagu satisfactorily refute Morris' argument about man's basic aggressiveness? Do you favor the theory of cultural influence or of biological nature? Why?

3. Montagu introduces a subject that will recur throughout this book: the idea of control. Sometimes the authors will be concerned with control of the human mind, sometimes with the control of nature. Some people decry both kinds of control; some see salvation in control. Schwartz, for example, thinks the idea of controlling nature, introduced by such scientists as Bacon, Descartes, and Galileo, led to the present environmental problems. Some people fear mind control as the worst imaginable tyranny. What are Montagu's ideas about control, and what do you think of them?

The Person of Tomorrow—Carl R. Rogers   Carl R. Rogers (b. 1902), psychologist at the Center for Studies of the Person, is the author of many books, including *On Becoming a Person* and *Freedom to Learn.*

1. How much are you the person whom Rogers describes? Are there any orthodoxies which have influenced you whose traces you can detect? Compare Montagu's statement about the traditions which have influenced men.

2. What Puritan beliefs and controls have shaped our country?

3. Are you ambitious and productive? Do you see these as bad qualities?

4. Why does the new man have a better chance for survival? Compare Toffler's remarks on the need for adaptability.

5. What has been your experience with bureaucracies, such as schools and state agencies? Do you want the same thing the new man does from institutions?

6. Why is traditional education "the most rigid, outdated, incompetent institution in our culture?"

7. What effect does establishing and leaving close relationships quickly have on you?

Summarize the attitudes of the three authors in this section toward man.

3   GENETICS: CAN WE PERFECT US?

Man into Superman: The Promise and Peril of the New Genetics—*Time*

1. Comment on Pasternak's definition of life as self-renewing and everchanging. Is this statement a fair definition of evolution? How does it fit Toffler's and Rogers' concepts of the kind of person who can survive?

2. Would you want a child cloned from your own cells?

3. Several writers have suggested that the basic nature of man must be drastically altered before certain social changes can occur. Desmond Morris, for instance, said, "The natural tendency to form social in-groups could never be eradicated without a major genetic change in our make-up. . . ." G. R. Urban said that to plan effectively (to forestall a global class war for scarce resources), we would need a "cultural transformation so radical that only a genetic remodelling of man himself could do justice to the problem."[2] It might be pos-

[2] Introduction, *Can We Survive Our Future,* p. 16.

sible some day to cut out some of the rapacious, greedy, fearful drives of man through genetic surgery. On the other hand, some people fear that genetic engineering may lead to an inconceivable totalitarianism. And Lord Ritchie-Calder, in the next essay, objects that we do not know the genetic code for will, judgment, and kindness. Might these get burned out in genetic surgery? Where should we start, and where should we stop, taking risks?

4. What physical changes would you like to suggest for man? Consider Don in "Day Million" in Chapter 4. Answer the question posed at the end of this article: Is he a man?

The Doctor's Dilemma—Lord Ritchie-Calder Baron Peter Ritchie-Calder (b. 1906) is the author of many books, including *The Birth of the Future, Men Against the Desert,* and *Commonsense About a Starving World.*

1. Ritchie-Calder actually deals with several dilemmas. What ties them together?

2. Does Ritchie-Calder convince you that bio-engineering should stop? Did "Man into Superman" persuade you that it should go on?

3. A number of scientists are quoted in support of the stand against genetic manipulation. Do you think that scientists should decide what science should do? Are they doing that, or are they looking for a broader consultation?

4. Is the fact that we have not done enough for the cultural improvement of the species, according to Beadle, sufficient reason not to manipulate genes and to devote ourselves to working with "well-confirmed methods"?

5. What kinds of fashions in babies can you imagine developing?

6. Find some of the statements made within the last few years concerning a patient's right to die. Consult indexes to periodicals and newspapers for sources. Draft your own version of a statement which "involves a basic human right—the right to live or die with dignity."

Invit: The View from the Glass Oviduct—*Saturday Review/Science*

1. What is the "misleading Scandinavian echo" of *Invit?* What does a reference like this do for the tone of the article?

2. Compare the remarks of the Nobel laureates referred to here with Ritchie-Calder's version of the laureates' ideas.

3. Do you agree that "the whole nation should decide whether or not these experiments should continue"? What kind of mechanism could be used for getting the whole nation's decision?

4. Edwards is taking an egg from the wife and a sperm from the husband; do you agree with the criticisms that he is "committing an abominable act"?

5. What benefits would accrue from shielding Invit, maybe not even telling it of its origins?

The No-Child Family: Going Against 100,000 Years of Biology—Rita Kramer

1. Do some of the questions posed about genetic engineering become more or less important if fewer people have children?

2. What social pressures do you observe which "push people into parenthood"?

3. What countervailing forces do you observe?

4. One writer suggests that parenthood is at least as serious a matter as driving a car. We license drivers. Should we license people to be parents? On what criteria, if so?

5. What criticism could happy parents make of the statements by non-parents?

6. Summarize the ideas about why not as many people are having children as formerly. Which reasons do you think are the most valid?

7. Analyze your own "deeply held feelings" and see where you stand on this issue of parenthood. Do you see any possible future influences which may change you?

4 WOMAN AND MARRIAGE: NOW WHAT?

Sexual Equality Is Not the Issue—Gene Hoffman Gene Hoffman is a columnist for the Los Angeles *Times.*

1. Why isn't equality a proper goal? What does Hoffman want that is different from equality?

2. What goals are no longer valid? Why? Should there be new goals?

3. How do we prepare for "relationships with others"?

4. What kind of environment sustains, nurtures, cherishes? Skinner's in *Walden Two* (Chapter 12)? Fast's in "The First Men" (Chapter 8)?

5. Is the pairing of a religious group like the Quakers with a drug experimentation group odd? Is there anything to be learned from the way each group brings about fulfillment of its members?

6. Is a guaranteed annual income guaranteed to free us for a life of self-discovery and awareness? See Section 10 on man as a working animal for some comments on this.

The Future of Marriage—Morton Hunt Morton Hunt has won an award for science journalism for his article "Man and Beast." He is the author of *The World of the Formerly Married* and *The Natural History of Love.*

1. Why are we going to have greater need for intimacy, warmth, companionship, and reliability?

2. Examine the marriages you know—perhaps including your own or your parents'—to see if they have "patriarchalism."

3. Read some of the recently published contracts drawn up between couples to see how closely they resemble Hunt's predictions of redefining roles and sharing rights.

4. What do you think about marriage that will last less than a lifetime? Do you, in love, envision yourself as spending the rest of your life with one person?

From *Proposition 31*—Robert H. Rimmer Robert H. Rimmer is a Boston businessman and novelist. He has written *That Girl from Boston, The Rebellion of Yale Marratt,* and *The Harrad Experiment.*

The title of the selection comes from the place of Nancy's petition on the California ballot.

1. Why does Nancy not tell Horace the proposition before they leave for the studio?

2. Why does Rimmer have Nancy do nearly all the talking?

3. Are the ideas of "greater family identity," "greater economic strength" and "sexual variety" developed?

4. Why should a group marriage be limited to three couples? (Compare Hunt's remarks on numbers in group marriages.) Why should they be past age 30? What are the advantages of incorporating?

5. Do you think you could be happy in a group marriage? What kinds of partners do you think would be necessary?

6. What drop-out or divorce provisions should a group marriage have?

See Rimmer's *The Harrard Experiment* for the college experiment Horace refers to, where the men and women live together.

Day Million—Frederik Pohl　Frederik Pohl (b. 1919) is an editor of science fiction magazines and paperback books and author of *The Case Against Tomorrow, Drunkard's Walk,* and *Practical Politics.*

1. Many of the predictions in *Dimensions of the Future* have some grounding in either current behavior or current scientific practice. What do you see in human nature or sexual relations which substantiates Pohl's predictions?

2. Many people believe that science fiction is much closer to what will really happen in the future than scientific or data-based extrapolations are. As you read this story and other science fiction, try to decide if you disagree. You might compare the predictions of science fiction writers in the past with what actually came to pass.

3. How widespread do you think the narrator's attitude towards genetic manipulation will become? To him, it's like filling a tooth or wearing a hearing aid.

4. See "Man into Superman" for some suggested modifications of the human body. In what ways do Don and Dora differ from current anatomy? Are there any desirable improvements?

5. See Rorvik's "Brave New World" (Chapter 8) for details on how communication can be improved through computers: it is the brain, not the skin, that feels; thus computer communication is plausible. Do you want it?

5　THE KNOWLEDGE-TECHNOLOGY EXPLOSION

The Frontiers of Science—*Comment!* Edwin Newman (b. 1919) is a news commentator who has narrated such television specials as "Who Shall Live?", "Justice for All," and "Politics: The Outer Fringe."

1. Gell-Mann finds the problems of disease, hard labor, and narrow horizons solvable by technology. What are the other scientists concerned with?

2. Give examples of technological innovation based chiefly on economics. Why can we no longer afford this? Wht kinds of modification of our economic system will protect us from unwanted technology? How do we keep the poor from paying the burden of reforms?

3. What steps can be taken toward technology control argeements? What kind of world institutions can be utilized or invented?

4. Heisenberg speaks of progress. Look through some of the many books about progress. Has the idea of progress had a history of steady development and acceptance?

5. Give other examples of the "ambivalence of science."

6. Many futurists see a slowing of economic growth as a good thing. Why?

7. Heisenberg says it may be necessary to return to a "more natural life." Which of your artificial comforts would you be willing to give up? See Faltermayer's "Do We Really *Need* All Those Kilowatts?" (Chapter 7) for similar suggestions.

8. Zuckerman says the nature and significance of new or still unmade discoveries cannot be defined in advance. Do you agree with him or with "Kahn

and Co.?" Lord Ritchie-Calder says that Kahn's predictions about massive re-
taliation and limited wars had this result: "By planning for his predictions, the
military reinforced his predictions."[3] Might our threatening predictions be
self-fulfilling?

9. Give examples to support (or refute) Zuckerman's contention that human
institutions do not adapt in a predictable way.

10. Do you agree with Wald's definition of science and technology? What
does he imply about the "moral" nature of science?

11. The question of human limits is very old. Adam, Prometheus, Oedipus,
and Faust—all strove against limits. What has been, and what is now mankind's
attitude toward the exploration of limits?

12. How can one get decisions by the people who live with products rather
than by makers of the product? Is this desirable? Might the majority turn down
potentially good things because of fear of change?

Some Roads That Will Be Opened—Gerald Feinberg Gerald Feinberg (b.
1933), educator and physicist, "followed a habit of technologists, who like to
refer their actions back to the ancients, and . . . called this attempt to find new
goals *The Prometheus Project*."[4] Why do you think technologists like ancient
names, such as Apollo and Saturn?

1. What new world conditions does Feinberg say will help us to estimate
future effects and to choose goals?

2. What kinds of homogeneity do you see developing in the human race?
What fosters them?

3. Why should neither government agencies nor scientists make decisions
about technology? Whom would you recommend for the "various groups, with
as wide a composition as possible" to discuss these problems?

4. What fundamental principles do you think ought to be the basis for the
decisions which will "radically transform human life"?

From Introduction to *Overskill*—Eugene S. Schwartz Eugene S. Schwartz has
been senior science specialist in computer and information services at the
Illinois Institute of Technological Research and has published articles in *The
Nation* and *The New Leader*.

Schwartz objects to the basic premise that man is to master nature, which
he believes was introduced by Bacon, who called on man to extend his power
and dominion over the universe; by Galileo, who thought there was no connection between the moral and physical worlds; and by Descartes, who under-
mined the belief in providence by saying that reason was supreme and the
laws of nature invariable.[5]

1. Compare Schwartz's views of science and technology with those of Gell-
Mann and Wald in "The Frontiers of Science." Do you think more technology
will help solve our problems?

2. Have "science and technology excluded all morality and ethics from their
practices"?

3. Do you agree with Brooks that once we have formulated our needs in the

[3] "Our Problems Are Here on Earth," *The Center Magazine*, March/April, 1971,
p. 5.

[4] *The Futurist*, June, 1969, p. 62.

[5] *Overskill*, pp. 24–26.

right way, the technological solutions will be forthcoming? Do we need more or less technology? The issue of more or less technology is a recurring motif in this book.

Don't Ask the Barber Whether You Need a Haircut—Daniel S. Greenberg

1. Greenberg presents his case against asking the experts with a good deal of humor. Is he just as convincing as a more serious writer, such as Schwartz?
2. What specific examples does he give to support his argument? Compare his comments on why scientists should not be decision makers with Feinberg's more general comments on the same issue.
3. What recommendations does he make for improving our present system of consultation and technology assessment?
4. Select one controversial issue that may be confronting your city (such as a new highway, billboard blight, or a power plant). Imagine a town meeting devoted to discussion of the issue. Whom would you expect to present their views? What would they say? Where would you find experts who had "least to gain from the proposition at hand"?

6   AUTOMATION-CYBERNATION: THE THIRD REVOLUTION

Aladdin's Lamp—Arthur C. Clarke   Arthur C. Clarke (b. 1917) has been chairman of the British Interplanetary Society and has written such books as *Interplanetary Flight, The Treasure of the Great Reef,* and *A Space Odyssey*—from which the movie *2001: A Space Odyssey* was made.

1. How would a replicator make the "present debate between capitalism and communism . . . quite useless"? Would it solve the problems of distribution and production? Clarke earlier in his book said that politics and economics will not be important in the future: we will have outgrown them, like the theological debates in the Middle Ages. Do you agree?
2. Do you agree that real values will arise? What changes may occur which will make a future society less susceptible to sybaritic hedonism than ours?
3. Compare Clarke's reference to the curse-blessing of Adam with the attitudes toward work in Chapter 10, especially Chase's essay. Do you know any of Clarke's civilized men?

From *The Myths of Automation*—Charles E. Silberman   Charles E. Silberman (b. 1925), an editor of *Fortune,* has written *Crisis in Black and White* and *Crisis in the Classroom.*

1. What is the chief myth of automation which Silberman is refuting?
2. Why won't automation lead to peopleless planets?
3. In what way is technology an "extension of man"?
4. What are the implications of Silberman's belief that automation can only be a symbiosis of men and machines?
5. He argues that people with low skill levels may not necessarily lack opportunity. Such people probably have generally low IQ levels. See Chapter 3 on genetics for discussion of the possibilities of creating people with much higher IQs than presently exist. If we can create such people, should we?
6. What is "rough terrain"?
7. Has there been an increased demand for teachers, psychiatrists, journalists, and government officials?

Beam—*The New Yorker*

1. "Would you like to see the cutters at work while you still can?" How does this fit with Silberman's comment that jobs change, though not necessarily levels of skills?
2. Do you think it likely that women will have more satisfying jobs?
3. Who benefits most from the lasermatic cutter?
4. Is it a gadget that should not have been made?
5. What are the similarities and differences in outlook among "Aladdin's Lamp," "The Myths of Automation," and "Beam"?

The Day the Computers Got Waldon Ashenfelter—Bob Elliott and Ray Goulding
Bob Elliott and Ray Goulding, radio and television performers, have created such characters as Mary Backstage, Noble Wife, and Steve Bosco the sportscaster.

1. This grimly humorous account of a national data center gives us some idea of the kinds of information one might find there. What details are stored in the memory banks?
2. Fear of federal snooping, damaging errors in information reported, misuse of information—these and other dangers argue against central data banks. Are there any reasons why we should have such collections of information? Why have the proposals been made?
3. If we can agree that centralized information is useful, can we agree on what kinds? On who will have access to it? How much privacy can or should we give up?

7 SOURCES OF POWER—SOLUTIONS TO THE ENERGY CRISIS?

A Permanent and Limitless Energy Source for the World—Richard Post and Scott Kelso
Richard Post is a nuclear physicist at The Lawrence Livermore Laboratory in Livermore, California. Scott Kelso, a former member of the Center for the Study of Democratic Institutions, Santa Barbara, heads a fossil fuel and mineral exploration corporation.

1. What are the benefits of fusion over fission as a power source?
2. In his essay, "Don't Ask the Barber," Greenberg talks of the one-in-a-million argument concerning dangers in new technologies: "What isn't mentioned is that one in a million can occur anywhere en route from the first to the millionth chance. . . ." What do you think of Post's odds of 1 to 10, 100,000 to a million, in favor of fusion over fission in relation to biological hazard?
3. What explanation can you give for the different percentages in national expenditures for fusion research—40 percent U.S.S.R., 16 percent U.S., 44 percent for the rest of the world?
4. Discuss some of the political and economic ramifications of replacing fuel oil with fusion.
5. What are the advantages and disadvantages of the financing suggested?
6. Several writers in this book speak of the drop in competition if energy were readily available. Discuss. What else besides energy has to be available?

Clean Power from Inside the Earth—John Lear
John Lear (b. 1909) is a writer (*Forgotten Front*) and former science editor of *Saturday Review*. He directed atomic and automation studies for the Research Institute of America.

1. Trace the steps in the Mexican decision to support geothermal energy research. Can you generalize from this on how economic support develops? Compare the recommendations in the preceding essay on financing fusion energy.

2. The U. S. Congress took eight years to agree to encourage geothermal exploration. Is that a reasonable time? Is it necessary to move slowly to prevent mistakes? If not, what can be done to shorten the time of political action?

3. Does Rex's concern for refilling the reservoirs to prevent subsidence provide any kind of pattern for developing technological innovations?

4. Contrast Cambel's advocacy of new, saving counter-technologies with Schwartz's rejection of them in "Introduction to *Overskill*". Who is more convincing?

Technology Reshapes the Southwest: Planning the Elements of a Post-Industrial Society—Nilo Lindgren

1. What are the advantages and disadvantages of solar energy over other sources?

2. Has the hunt for power been the main source of environmental blight? Give examples from your own experience and from other selections in the text.

3. Lindgren is more pessimistic than Cambel, cited in Lear's essay as believing that a combination of the various sources of energy would produce enough for our needs. Lindgren sees a "chronic energy shortage for the remainder of the century." Which point of view do you think is right?

4. What made the difference between thinking small and thinking big in solar energy? Why did the Meinels make the leap? Can this kind of thinking be patterned and taught?

Do We Really *Need* All Those Kilowatts?—Edmund Faltermayer

1. It has been customary to measure the standard of living by the number of kilowatts consumed. What would you use to measure the standard of living? Quantitative material standards? Additional standards of quality?

2. Why are dams ecological disasters?

3. What esthetic damage is caused by electricity?

4. What uses of electricity are you willing to give up? Would you consider your standard of living lower if you gave up any of your uses?

8 THE COMMUNICATIONS SPEED-UP

Will Society Be Run By TV?—Los Angeles Times Service

1. What are the benefits to individuals who use the services of CATV? Would you like to spend as much time at home as it promises?

2. Why might the CATV society be called "Orwellian"? How much surveillance would there be?

3. Protection and education are highly sought services of CATV. Is your ranking of services the same as those indicated by the Californians?

4. Peters predicts that CATV will bring about an improvement in commercial TV. The same thing might have been predicted for the Public Broadcasting Service. Has that result come about?

Brave New World—David M. Rorvik David M. Rorvik is a frequent contributor to *Esquire*. Some of his columns are called "Present Shock."

1. What would you gain from satellite mail service?
2. Would privacy of mail be affected?
3. Compare the prediction of communication without language, directly between people (probably linked by machines) with the story of direct intellectual communication in the next selection, "The First Men." Does the factual description of perceptions in this essay help explain the kind of communication the children have?
4. Would you like to have electromagnetic communication in place of or in addition to what you now have?
5. What does Clynes mean by "all true progress is progress in love"?
6. Is Rorvik optimistic? Why?

The First Men—Howard Fast   Howard Fast (b. 1914) is the author of *Strange Yesterday, Spartacus, The Children,* and *The Passion of Sacco and Vanzetti.*

1. Why does Jean say "in all fact we are the children and they are the adults"? Does the statement help explain the title?
2. Compare the upbringing of children in this story with that in *Walden Two.* Is there "an abundance of love, security and truth" in both? Does the mere statement that there is an environment of sanity and truth and security unlike anything ever before make it clear to you why a five-year-old could compose a symphony, or two children measure light? Is the environment and education in Jean's world (predicated on the future) different from education in the outside world? Is our education predicated on the past—on looking backward?
3. What kinds of mental blocks are imposed on children in our society?
4. Compare the roles of the parent and family in this story with those in "Proposition 31" and *Island* (Chapter 12).
5. Dr. Goldbaum describes a great unity attainable by the children. Can you think of any other examples of a similar kind of unity between men? Is there anything in Goldbaum's statement which implies unity of man and his environment, or is he talking only about the community of mankind? What concept of immortality is involved?
6. How effective is the conclusion?
7. How many of the stories and essays in this book are based on the idea of the perfectibility of man?

Worldwide communications present promises and threats. Esfandiary's "Universalizing Technology" suggests how we might be influenced toward greater unity, toward shared feelings. Control of such communications in the hands of able propagandists could be devastating. Do you think the advantages outweigh the disadvantages?

9   MIND EXPANSION—OR MIND CONTROL?

The Ethics of Addiction—Thomas S. Szasz, M.D.   Thomas Szasz was born in Hungary in 1920 and came to the U.S. in 1938. He is a psychiatrist and author of *Pain and Pleasure, The Myth of Mental Illness, The Ethics of Psychoanalysis,* and *The Manufacture of Madness.* In "The Ethics of Suicide," Szasz claims a person has a right to control himself, including the right to take his own life.

1. What does human freedom mean to Szasz? What does it include?
2. Is the taking of drugs comparable to the taking of ideas? ". . . it is none

of the government's business what ideas a man puts into his mind; likewise, it should be none of the government's business what drug he puts into his body."

3. Why do many people believe we should be protected from ourselves, that morals should be legislated? Consider the 1973 Supreme Court decisions on pornography and the much earlier constitutional amendment prohibiting alcohol.

4. Why should most rights apply only to adults? At what age does adulthood begin?

5. How does Mill's quotation support Szasz's theme?

6. Can you resolve the issue of the state versus the individual in this case? In all cases (for example, gun control)?

Drugs and the Future—Frank J. Ayd, Jr., M.D.

1. Do you agree with Ayd's assessment of the moral climate of today?

2. Can you find examples of scientists who practice "scientism"?

3. Contrast Szasz's view and Ayd's complaint that some people believe man is the owner of his life and body, free to do as he wishes.

4. Is it a "modern foment" for man to become the master of his environment? Schwartz, in *Overskill*, traced that idea back to Bacon, Galileo, and Descartes. Arnold Toynbee took it as far back as the development of monotheism, which destroyed the idea of "Mother Nature."

5. Which of the types of drugs seem most useful to you? Would you like to hibernate for a while? Why not have instant pinnacles of emotion?

6. Is Ayd's report biased? Give evidence.

The Search for the Memory Molecule—David Perlman David Perlman is science editor of the San Francisco *Chronicle*.

1. Do you agree that the transfer of memory would be the most exciting discovery in psychology?

2. What would you choose to have transferred from someone else's memory to your mind?

3. Perlman talks of memory being biochemical; Rorvik's earlier essay described our perceptions in physical terms. Does it disturb you, or make you more optimistic, that more and more parts of man are being explained on the basis of chemistry or physics?

4. Can you answer the final questions Krech poses? Add any questions?

5. Anticipate the possibilities of increased and improved memory implied in this story, and compare them with the kind of unifying memory (almost an oversoul) which the children have in "The First Men."

After reading the selections in this chapter, what do you think is the proper title for it—mind expansion or mind control? Can the two be separated?

10 CAN WE SURVIVE LEISURE?

From *Of Time, Work and Leisure*—Sebastian de Grazia Sebastian de Grazia (b. 1917) is a professor of politics and author of *The Political Community* and *Errors of Psychotherapy*.

1. What were the Reformation ideas of work? What are the connections between capitalism and Protestantism? The writings of Max Weber and R. H. Tawney are particularly relevant.

2. Why did the work ethic reach its fullest expression in the U.S.?

3. Why do totalitarian regimes not permit unemployment, while democracies do?

4. What is involved in the change of wording from "idleness problem" to "leisure problem"? Why does de Grazia say that a change in vocabulary is an event in human history? Can you cite other significant vocabulary changes? What about "biosphere," which used to be "nature"? Or "human engineering," which used to be called "education"?

5. How much leisure time do you have? What do you do with it? Would you like to change your use of it?

Is Man a Working Animal?—Stuart Chase   Stuart Chase (b. 1888) is the author of many books, including *The Tragedy of Waste, Men and Machines, Goals for America,* and *Live and Let Live.*

1. According to one famous definition, "Man is a rational animal." What are the implications of Chase's description of man as a working animal?

2. What factors make nonworking a terrifying or boring state?

3. Are you pursuing a specific education, the kind aimed at getting a job? Do you agree with Piel that it is an ineffective education?

4. What steps could be taken to start employing people in the reconstruction of the megalopolis? Would a consensus of goals have to be reached?

5. Comment on Chase's definition of the Puritan ethic. Why is the ethic so widely held? Is it a religious goal formulated in a time when the relationship between man and his world was different?

Career Program Is Step Forward—Robert S. Rosefsky

1. Is the educational career program really a step forward? or a step backward? Contrast the aims described here with the ideas discussed by de Grazia and Chase. Consider Piel's comments on career education (quoted in Chase).

2. Comment on the effectiveness of increasing student motivation with the techniques described—using salary calculations to teach math, writing job résumés to teach language, and so on. How important is it to tie together various fields, such as mathematics, social studies, and language?

The Decline of Sport—E. B. White   E. B. White (b. 1899) is the author of many books, including *Is Sex Necessary?, Charlotte's Web,* and *The Elements of Style.*

1. Satire depends on a basis in reality. What do you see around you that became absurd practices in White's story?

2. Are we close to the supersaturation point White describes in his spectators? If so, are we deadened?

3. Why are the people preoccupied with broken records? Are we?

4. The introduction to Chapter 10 raises the question of whether we will increase beer production and put more football on TV to fill our coming vacant hours. What can be done to keep the pleasure of sports without creating the situation White satirizes?

11   ECONOMICS AND GOVERNMENT IN A DYNAMIC SOCIETY

Consumers of Abundance—Gerard Piel   Gerard Piel (b. 1915) was science editor of *Life* and is the publisher of *Scientific American.*

1. What are Piel's definitions of work and property?

2. Are property and work still the pillars of our society to many people? What illusions, old habits, and compulsions support the social edifice?

3. Note Piel's linking of the Reformation with the approval of profit. Compare de Grazia's essay (and question 1 for it).

4. Can you see any consequences of the change to property ownership by corporations? What attitude do shareholders have?

5. Compare Piel's view that work exists to make people consumers with Chase's comments about consumers and our "whirling-dervish economy, keyed to compulsive consumption." How can changes be made?

From *The Two Cultures: And a Second Look*—C. P. Snow   Lord Snow (b. 1905) is the author of many books, including *Strangers and Brothers, Corridors of Power,* and *Science and Government.*

1. Snow says that it is possible to carry out the scientific revolution throughout the world. Other writers have said it is impossible to bring the Third World up to the level of the U.S. and Europe. (See Dennis Meadows' second conclusion in "The Predicament of Mankind.") Which point of view do you accept?

2. Are there now any more sources of capital beside the U.S. and Russia? What about prosperous industrial states such as Germany and Japan, or the oil-rich Arab states? How could such sources be drawn together?

3. Why does Russia have engineers and scientists to spare, while the U.S. and England do not?

4. Has the gap between science and humanism changed since Snow first wrote about it?

5. What changes in education do you think Snow would recommend? Compare these with the suggestions made in Section 12.

Null-P—William Tenn   William Tenn is the pseudonym of Philip Klass (b. 1920); the author of *Men and Monsters,* he teaches English and writing at Pennsylvania State University.

The title may mean "null-probability"—thus that nothing is likely to happen or change.

1. What conditions of life made people want to choose an average man as their leader? Why did they not want an above-average President? What conditions do you see around you that foster a cult of the average? Do you think of yourself as average?

2. What point about language and society is illustrated by the fact that slang does not change in this placid country?

3. What problems do the Europeans want help with? Why? Are the Americans "better off" than the Europeans?

4. Why do stories often depict animals as masters of men?

Distribution of Abundance: Equal Incomes for All—Technocracy, Inc.   Technocracy, Inc., publishes a quarterly bulletin at Long Beach, California. Started in 1918, Technocracy says it is "the only North American social movement with a North American program." One of the organization's main goals is the elimination of money as a medium of exchange, thus eliminating debt and taxes and crimes involving money and property.[6]

[6] Monty Mountford, "America's Future," *The Technocrat,* June, 1973, p. 6.

1. Why is the price system, *the* enemy according to Technocracy, obsolete?
2. Do the technocrats give too much importance to money as the medium which makes flaws in society?
3. In "A Permanent and Limitless Energy Source for the World," Chapter 7, Post and Kelso say that if fusion energy were readily available, everyone would have the means to achieve unlimited wealth. Compare that point of view with Technocracy's.

12 UTOPIA-DYSTOPIA: HAVE WE A CHOICE?

From *Walden Two*—B. F. Skinner B. F. Skinner (b. 1904), psychologist, author, and educator, has roused much controversy by his theories of conditioning human behavior, perhaps most by his *Beyond Freedom and Dignity*, in which he suggests that those concepts are outmoded.

See an article by a member of the Twin Oaks community in *The Futurist*, December, 1967, pp. 86–89. Life in that commune is based on *Walden Two*. Varying credits are given for labor. There is no punishment for rule breaking, just the reward of harmonious feelings when rules are not broken.

1. Do labor credits resemble Technocracy's distribution certificates?
2. Objections to Skinner center on his method of conditioning people through stimulus-response-reinforcement, which critics say takes away free choice. Do people in Walden have freedom of choice? Of vocational choice?
3. Compare Frazier's work week with Herman Kahn's prediction of a 7.5-hour workday, 4 days a week, with 13 weeks vacation. Why don't the Walden people suffer the ills of not having work to fill their days?
4. How would Carl Rogers' "new man" fit into Walden Two?

Harrison Bergeron—Kurt Vonnegut, Jr. Kurt Vonnegut, Jr. (b. 1922) is the author of *Player Piano, God Bless You Mr. Rosewater, Happy Birthday, Wanda June,* and other books.

1. Compare the premise of "Null-P" with that of "Harrison Bergeron."
2. George thinks the world would regress to the dark ages if everybody were not equalized, and everybody would compete against everybody else. What is our present view of competition? Are we trying to eliminate it? In schools?
3. Compare the ending of this story with that of "The First Men." Is the Secretary like the Handicapper General?

From Epilogue to *Utopia or Oblivion*—R. Buckminster Fuller R. Buckminster Fuller (b. 1895) is an architectural engineer, educator, and inventor. Famous for the geodesic dome, he also evolved a three-wheeled car that he proposed for general use. He has written *Operating Manual for Spaceship Earth* and *New Worlds in Engineering*.

1. How can cost be prepaid by design-science competence?
2. What is real estate development like in your city? Is it unchecked and visionless, eating up farmland?
3. Why is housing construction such an important economic indicator?
4. Would you like to live in Fuller's floating city? Would there be any advantages over your present environment?
5. Compare Fuller's city with Paolo Soleri's city plans, arcologies. At the Cosanti Foundation in Arizona, Soleri is trying to redesign urban civilization.

From *Island*—Aldous Huxley Aldous Huxley (1894–1963), British novelist and critic, is probably most famous for *Brave New World*.

1. *Island* is in many mays a reverse image of *Brave New World*. What is bad in one is countered by utopian goodness in the other. Both cultures use drugs, but *World's* inhabitants do so to lose themselves, the Palanese to reach a higher reality: "When it's time for them to learn the deepest truths of religion, we . . . give them four hundred milligrams of revelation." Is instant ecstasy valid? Or must one discipline himself for a long time to achieve unity with God or Being?

2. *Maithuna* is defined as the yoga of love, in which one learns who he is and experiences a great sense of unity. Compare sex in "Day Million," "Proposition 31," and *Island*.

3. What are family relationships like in *Island*? Why does the Palanese child move so often? Is the family structure like that in "The First Men"?

4. What are Palanese ideas of efficiency? What are ours?

5. What does the educational process in Pala teach? What do you think of it?

13 EDUCATION—FOR POWER AND PLEASURE

Visiting Day 2001 A.D.—George Leonard George Leonard (b. 1923), journalist and educational consultant, is vice president of Esalen and was editor of *Look*.

1. What advantages do the children gain from sharing one another's screens?

2. Do we presently stress individual and competitive performance in education? Is cooperative learning gaining?

3. Why does each child create a new language? What good does it do?

4. How imaginative are the responses of the computer? A basic complaint about CAI is that the student must follow the programmer's path. (See Oettinger and Marks' essay.) Is the CAD beyond that?

5. How often in school have you come across the idea that if the environment fails to draw out or to educate, it is the environment's, not the learner's, fault?

6. How is conformity avoided?

7. How much are emotions and esthetic response developed in Leonard's school? How much is self-fulfillment a part of the program?

The Computer in Education—Anthony G. Oettinger with Sema Marks Anthony G. Oettinger (b. Germany 1919) is a professor of mathematics and linguistics. He has written *A Study for the Design of an Automatic Dictionary* and *Automatic Language Translation*.

1. According to the quotation from Professor Suppes, why does the computer offer "the first real opportunity for individualizing the educational experience"?

2. What features of computer instruction seem most appealing to you? Immediate evaluation? Do any features of computerized learning seem less satisfactory than traditional and current methods?

3. What is the significance of Oettinger's heading, "The Computer's Muted Trumpet"?

4. What are the problems in utilizing the computer for educational purposes at this time?

5. How much do you really learn about CAI from this essay?

6. Have you any suggestions for accomplishing the effort, planning, and leadership required to bring the promises of CAI into real existence?

Man Must Learn How To Learn—Sydney J. Harris   Sydney J. Harris (b. 1917) is a syndicated newspaper columnist in Chicago. He is the author of *Strictly Personal, A Majority of One,* and *Leaving the Surface.*

1. The Department of Labor 1960 census showed that people had four different careers on the average; in 1970, the census reported that people averaged ten different careers. What are the implications of that for education? Is "learning how to learn" the most important part of education? How much learning how to learn are you doing presently?

2. What elements of a liberal education produce versatility, flexibility, and creativity? Compare these qualities with those listed in the chapter-opening quotation by Donald N. Michael: empathy, compassion, trust, non-exhibitiveness, self-growth, self-esteem, tolerance of ambiguity, and so on. What will nurture these qualities?

The Future of Learning: Into the 21st Century—John I. Goodlad   John I. Goodlad (b. 1920) is the author of *The Elementary School, Computers and Information Systems in Education,* and *The Changing American High School.*

1. Goodlad speaks of "the subtle extinction of the great range of talents and achievements which are not wanted." How is this done? What in our schools closes people in?

2. What will education in the 21st century develop in man?

3. How will education "open the whole of the world to the learner" and give him access to it?

4. What biases of Western culture have made our curriculum unrealistically narrow and antiseptic? What changes would you make to overcome these biases?

5. What are the dangers and benefits of decentralizing decision-making to individual schools?

6. What should we study? Many people think that we need generalists, people with an interdisciplinary approach, rather than specialists. Stuart Chase recommends that to prepare for the future, we should study behavioral science, communications theory, biology, history, economics, and international law. How would these help us? Would you add other disciplines? What about studying the future itself? Should academic chairs of future studies be as common as chairs of history?

Index of Authors and Titles

333